TRELAWNY

THE MACMILLAN COMPANY
NEW YORK · BOSTON · CHICAGO
DALLAS · ATLANTA · SAN FRANCISCO

MACMILLAN AND CO., LIMITED
LONDON · BOMBAY · CALCUTTA
MADRAS · MELBOURNE

THE MACMILLAN COMPANY
OF CANADA, LIMITED
TORONTO

TRELAWNY

From the Portrait by Benjamin West. Now in the possession of
Trelawny's great-niece, Mrs. Rigby.

TRELAWNY

A Man's Life

———•—•———

By Margaret Armstrong

———•—•———

Worldwide Liberty's lifelong lover,
Lover no less of the strength of song,
Sea-king, swordsman, hater of wrong.
—SWINBURNE, "Trelawny"

THE MACMILLAN COMPANY

NEW YORK

1940

There are no imaginary characters, events, or conversations in this book. It is fact, not fiction. The narrative is based on Trelawny's writings, corrected and amplified from reliable sources.

TRELAWNY

CHAPTER I

"We have a saying in our country that a Trelawny never lacked courage, nor a Godolphin wit, nor a Grenville loyalty."
—LORD LANSDOWNE.

Now and then a man is born with a surname that fits him so well it might have been chosen for him by a poet or a painter. Edward Trelawny was one of these fortunate persons. There is a wild flavor in *Trelawny* that would lend a touch of romance to the most commonplace family; and that the Trelawnys never were. They were courageous, adventurous, full of vitality, eccentric, unreliable, prone to extremes; never, to judge from the family records, commonplace.

And the records go a long way back, back to the reign of Edward the Confessor when Eduni de Treloen, the first ancestor, selected a certain green river valley on the east coast of Cornwall as a favorable place to plant a family tree; selected so well—with such an eye for shelter, fertile soil, and a charming landscape—that his descendants have been content to live there ever since, on one or other of the estates along the Looe with their pleasantly rhyming names:

"Trelawne, Trelask, Trelay,
Ashleighcross, little Bell Hay
And Trendaway."

Of these Trelawne became the chief manor. Uncles and cousins of our Edward Trelawny were living there in his time. Trelawne's wooded combe, its fuchsias and myrtles and green grassplots are still in the possession of the family today.

That means a stretch of some nine hundred years—Eduni came to Trelawne five hundred years before a Byron came to Newstead: a long stretch even for Cornwall, strewn from end to end with the dolmens and stone circles of prehistoric men and where an older race than man—"that small sort of airy people called fairies"—found shelter until Wesley frightened them away. Add King Arthur and the Spanish Armada, and you have the most romantic county in England.

But a hard country as well as a romantic; windswept, sea-threatened, breeding hard people: smugglers, pirates, fisher-men, miners. A country of "huge stones, mighty rocks, strong stout men and handsome women." So the Trelawny back-ground was both romantic and hard—a combination likely to foster courage; and courage became the conspicuous family characteristic. It was a flamboyant kind of courage: hearty, heady, self-assured, untinged by modesty. As a family, the Trelawnys seem to have excelled in the art of blowing their own horns and blowing them loud and long. Take a look at them all down the line.

An early Sir John of Trelawne made himself so con-spicuous at Agincourt that Henry V gave him three oak leaves to brighten up the British wolf in his coat-of-arms, and ordered a tribute to be carved over the royal statue at Launceston:

> "He that will do ought for me
> Let him love well Sir John Tirlawnee."

Equally conspicuous was a later Sir John, who led his Cornish tens of thousands into battle during the Perkin Warbeck rebellion—not, however, to victory. Having chosen the wrong side, he soon found himself in the Tower. But the news of his imprisonment threw "all the west into an agony of rage" and his countrymen came hurrying to London, shouting:

"And have they fixed the where and when,
　　And shall Trelawny die?
Then thirty thousand Cornishmen
　　Will know the reason why!"

They must have come in great numbers and shouted very convincingly, for they saved their lord's head; the rebel got off with a heavy fine.

Sir John of the Civil Wars, on the other hand, stuck to his king and, in the end, was obliged by Cromwell to do what no Trelawny ever did with equanimity: become inconspicuous. "He retired to his stronghold at Trelawne and brought up his family as well as the impoverished times would permit."

Did retrenchment make for modesty? Certainly not. The son of this impoverished gentleman, Sir Jonathan, lost his temper during a debate in Parliament, "dealt his opponent, Mr. Ashe, a thundering box on the ear," and then "flashed his sword"; which brought the usual family punishment. He was sent to the Tower—Mr. Ashe being merely "consigned to the Black Rod"—and got off with a fine.

But of all the hotheaded Trelawnys, the next one, another Sir Jonathan, was the most conspicuous; for he was a bishop —of Bristol, Exeter, and Winchester—and surely a hotheaded bishop is more conspicuous than any hotheaded layman can possibly be. He seems to have been a typical Trelawny, possessing all the family virtues and all the family vices. Described by Agnes Strickland, the historian, as "blending in his person the duties of the temporal and ecclesiastical noble," yet with a happy faculty for keeping these duties in separate compartments. Reproved for profane swearing by a brother cleric, he answered—Miss Strickland again—"with shameless facetiousness: 'When I swear I do not swear as a bishop. I swear as Sir Jonathan Trelawny, a country gentleman and a baronet.' " No doubt he deserved the epithets, "spiritual dragon, Christian Turk," given him by a contemporary satirist; on the other hand, Wykehamists should revere his memory, for he ordered that "the children were to be relieved of the foul office of making their own beds," and need not rise before six between Michaelmas and Lady Day.

But this Trelawny is best remembered as one of the "Seven Bishops of the Tower," who went to prison for refusing to allow James II's "declaration for liberty of conscience" to be read in the churches, believing that "the king did not possess this dispensing power."

The affair made a great stir. "When the bishops were led out as prisoners and embarked at Whitehall Stairs, the populace exhibited the most passionate demonstrations of sympathy and affection, and they were received at Traitors' Gate with more than royal honors; all the garrison, officers as well as privates, knelt and begged their blessing. . . . When the verdict of 'Not guilty' was finally returned, the Marquis of Halifax waved his hat and cried 'Huzzah!', the lords and ladies took up the shout, and from thence it was carried as fast as it could fly over the whole kingdom."

During the trial, the old Cornish protest, "And shall Trelawny die?" was revived in Sir Jonathan's favor (later on, Hawker of Morwenstowe made it the refrain of his well known "Song of the Western Men") and may have influenced the verdict. But he was by no means the worthiest of the "Seven." He goes strutting on through history, the insignia of the Order of the Garter blazing on his bosom; crowning William and Mary, entertaining at Chelsea Palace, enjoying agreeable interludes at Trelawne, "a family seat which many centuries of cultivation had made truly delicious," and finally, and no doubt unwillingly, subsiding into a grave in his ancestral church at Pelynt.

In a family so soldierly as the Trelawnys it is strange that the top notch of conspicuousness should have been reached by an ecclesiastic. But from then on, flamboyance suffered a slight decline. By 1792, when the story of our Edward Trelawny begins, no very distinguished new names were showing on the family tree. Our Edward's grandfather became a general, to be sure, and governor of Languard Fort; but his fighting was under Howe in America, and that was not a glorious campaign. Our Edward's father, Charles Brereton Trelawny, ended his career in the Army as a mere lieutenant colonel, and although tall, handsome, and arrogant enough, his chief characteristic seems to have been a love of money.

The trait showed itself early in life. Charles married for money; threw over the girl he loved and was engaged to, in order to marry a Cornish heiress, Maria Hawkins, who had taken a fancy to him when they met at a county ball. She was not attractive—too dark and hard-featured; but Charles could overlook this disadvantage, for she was the sister of Christopher Hawkins of Trewithen, a great person in his part of Cornwall, and had money of her own.

The marriage turned out badly; it brought Charles less money than he had expected and much unhappiness. But it had one advantage that Charles himself was never to realize. The Hawkins blood came to refresh his branch of the family tree at an opportune time, just as it was beginning to weaken with the dry rot of old age. For the Hawkins family was of fairly recent origin, famous for its spirit of high adventure rather than for its antiquity.

The first ancestor, William Hawkins, sea captain and shipowner of Plymouth, emerges from obscurity in the reign of Henry VIII, voyaging to Brazil in his own ship, the *Paul,* bringing glory and wealth to his home town. His son, John Hawkins, widened the scope of the family business. "Being assured that good store of negroes might easily be had upon the coast of Guinea," he lost no time in acting on the information and thus acquired the doubtful honor of being the first Englishman to engage in the slave trade. Not a doubtful honor in his day, however. When John returned with rich cargoes of gold, pearls, precious stones, ginger, and hides no one minded that negroes had been the medium of exchange, or considered John a hypocrite for being able to combine piety with blackbirding. John was a very religious man. His crews were commanded to "serve God daily; love one another; preserve your provisions; beware of fire, and keep good company." Not even the strain of a long hot calm, with slaves dying in the hold like flies, could destroy John's faith; for he knew, as he said himself, "that God would not suffer His Elect to perish." Before long, success brought him a handsome coat of arms from Elizabeth, topped by an appropriate crest, "a demi-Moor in his proper color, bound and captive, with annulets on his arms and ears, or," and his son Richard was encouraged to endear himself to Elizabeth by "preying upon the overseas possessions of the King of Spain."

Sir John and Sir Richard both distinguished themselves during the invasion of the Armada, both voyaged with Drake; they are the greatest names on the Hawkins family tree. Succeeding generations, though prosperous enough, were conspicuous in much smaller ways. Theirs was the first coach to be seen in West Cornwall; wherever the roads were good enough for speeding, they went rattling along at the rate of three miles an hour, and "riding thus," an old chronicler remarks, "with their cavalcade of belles and beaux, they doubtless thought themselves as grand as Solomon and the Queen of Sheba—till they stuck fast in some hole."

But even this trifling kind of distinction was on the wane. When the marriage that united Hawkins to Trelawny—the marriage of our Edward's parents—took place, there was little to choose between the families of Maria and Charles as far as nobility of spirit was concerned.

Indeed, the head of Maria's family at that time, her brother Christopher Hawkins of Trewithen, seems to have been singularly lacking in even the more commonplace virtues of his class. He suffered from the same failing that was to ruin Charles Trelawny's character; Christopher was a miser. That he began at an early age to note how money was spent is suggested by another anecdote illustrating the badness of Cornish roads in his time: "Young Mr. Christopher Hawkins, returning by post-chaise to Eton after a Christmas holiday in Cornwall, occupied five whole days on the journey and spent fifteen pounds."

Economy grew on him. By middle age his meanness had become proverbial. His tenants hated and despised "Sir Kit." One morning a paper was found affixed to the gates of Trewithen. It read:

"A large house, and no cheer,
A large park, and no deer,
A large cellar, and no beer,
Sir Christopher Hawkins lives here."

Such a house, in spite of its size and imposing situation "on high ground commanding an extensive panorama of wild hills," could not have been a happy place for a girl to grow up in, nor would miserly Sir Kit have been likely to enliven a wedding by providing a handsome breakfast. So Maria Hawkins was probably glad enough to see the last of Trewithen when she bade it goodbye after her marriage to Charles Trelawny in the family church; the ancient church dedicated to Saint Probus and Saint Grace, where her ancestors lay buried in the family vault. Over the rood screen was carved a prayer: "Jesus hear us, and send us Grace and Good forever." But neither ancestors nor patron saints could bring a blessing to that marriage.

It seems to have been as unhappy as a marriage well could be. Charles and Maria soon developed a hearty and mutual dislike—although, after the peculiar fashion of their time, dislike was not allowed to interfere with the production of a large family of children. Both of them were bad-tempered and dictatorial. Charles soon discovered that Maria was extravagant as well as quarrelsome, and after a few London years of spending more than they could afford, he found himself almost as badly off as before marriage, and was obliged to sell his commission and retire to vegetate and practice economy in the country. They did not, however, settle in their native Cornwall but in Cheshire; and for a very good reason. Charles was heir presumptive to an estate in the Wirral, the peninsula that thrusts itself out towards the sea between Mersey and Dee, belonging to his first cousin, Owen Salusbury Brereton of Shotwick.

The landscape—meadow and orchard, marsh and river—must have seemed flat and sleepy to Cornish folk, and the Sands of Dee a tame substitute for Penare Head and Tregeagle Cove. But Charles and Maria probably liked the Wirral well enough and were as contented as it was in their natures to be. There was good duck shooting for Charles and good society for Maria—Cheshire had long been known as "the seed-plot of gentilitie," and the Brereton estate was worth waiting for. It comprised not only the seven hundred acres of Shotwick Park, an "extra-parochial liberty," but also the manors of Great and Little Saughall which still retained their manorial privileges of holding "court-leet" and "court-baron"; although the family had long since relinquished the right, exercised in 1368, to hold a fair at Brereton-cum-Smethwick on the festival of Saint Peter.

Several fine houses were scattered about the estate. The Trelawnys may have gone straight from London to the chief manor house at Great Saughall where Owen Brereton himself lived, or, temporarily, to some less important one. But it must have been a fairly large house, for there were some five or six children to be disposed of now, and as Charles and Maria disliked their children as heartily as they disliked each other, they would have required space in order to escape from their offspring.

In any case, they were soon in possession of as large a house as the most uncongenial family could require. In 1798 Owen Salusbury Brereton died and Charles Trelawny inherited the Shotwick estate, on condition that he add the name and arms of Brereton to his own. Charles would have done a good deal more than that in return for such a handsome property, but, as a matter of fact, he felt no reluctance. Brereton of Brinton was almost as old a family as Trelawny of Trelawne, having "come over" with William the Conqueror in the train of Hugh d'Avranche, the Conqueror's nephew.

But the Brereton money came too late for Charles in more ways than one. Economy had by then become so sweet that he could not let it go, and—fostered, perhaps, by association with his miserly brother-in-law Sir Kit—it soon grew from a failing to a vice, responsible for much of the misery of that unhappy household. In the end, it was to ruin Charles's character and cramp and scar the lives of all his children, including the life of our Edward, his younger son.

There were only two boys in the family. The older one received his grandfather's name, Harry; the second son was christened Edward John, thus combining the most ancient Trelawny name, Eduni, with that of the most celebrated Hawkins ancestor—a combination more prophetic of the baby's future character than his parents suspected. Born in London, November 13, 1792, our Edward was brought away from town so young that Cheshire provided his first memories. But his babyhood must have been as commonplace as that of most children; when he wrote his autobiography in after life, he found nothing worth setting down until he came to a certain summer's day when he had reached the age of five.

His life history begins with the events of that day and, like the story of our first parents, it begins in a garden; a garden, moreover, whose chief attraction was its wealth of forbidden fruit. So, although the garden was in Cheshire and the central figure a child of five, the story of that day is a modern version of the old story of temptation, and just as echoes of the "fall" may be heard ringing on all through the Bible from Genesis to Revelation, so echoes of that day may be heard ringing on and on all through the life of Edward Trelawny—for neither old age nor experience could quite destroy his hankering for forbidden fruit!

"Among other petty restrictions," Trelawny wrote, thirty-two years later,* "we were not allowed to stray off the gravelled paths of the garden. My brother, mild and uncomplaining, submitted to this; but, with me, opposition only sharpened desire. My father had a fancy for a raven that, with ragged wings and a grave, antique aspect, used to wander solitarily about the garden. As he abhorred children and used to chase us out of his way, we had all, from the time we could walk, considered him and my father the two most powerful, awful and tyrannical persons on earth.

"The raven was getting into years. He had a gray and grizzly look; he halted on one leg; his joints were stiff, his legs rough as the bark of a cork tree, and he was covered with large warts; his eyes had a bleared and sinister expression and he passed most of his time idling in the sun under a south wall against which grew the delicious plums of the garden. Many were the stratagems we used to lure him from this spot; even the garbage on which he gloated was offered in vain. His moroseness and ferocity, and our difficulty in getting fruit, were insupportable. We tried to intimidate him with sticks, but were too weak to make the least impression on his weather-beaten carcass and got the worst of it. I used, when I could do so slyly, to throw stones at him; but this had no effect. I in vain sought for redress from the gardener and servants; they laughed at us and jeered us. Thus things continued.

"One day I had a little girl for my companion, a favorite sister whom I had enticed from the nursery to endeavor to get some fruit clandestinely. We slunk out, and entered the garden unobserved. Just as we were congratulating ourselves under a cherry tree, up comes the accursed monster of a raven. He seized hold of the little girl's frock; she was too frightened to scream. I threw myself upon him. He let her go

---

* *Adventures of a Younger Son.* Here, and elsewhere in extracts from Trelawny's books, the writing has been condensed and simplified, but the sense remains unchanged in any smallest particular.

and attacked me with bill and talon. I got hold of him by the neck, lifted him heavily, and struck his body against the tree and the ground. Nothing seemed to hurt him. He was as hard as a rock. Thus we struggled, I evidently the weaker party. The little girl wanted to call the gardener. But I forbade her, knowing he would tell my father.

"'Give me your sash!' I cried, 'and I will hang the old fellow.'

"She did so and, though dreadfully mauled, I succeeded with great exertion in fastening one end of the ribbon around the old tyrant's neck; then I climbed the cherry tree, suspended my foe from a branch and jumped to the ground.

"My brother came running up, shouting for joy when he saw our old enemy swinging in the air, and we commenced stoning him to death. When we tired of this sport, and he was to all appearances dead, we let him down. He fell on his side; I laid hold of a raspberry stake to make sure of him, by belaboring his head. To our utter amazement and consternation, he sprung up with a hoarse scream and caught hold of me. So I again fell upon him and calling my brother to keep fast hold of the ribbon, I climbed the tree. The raven's look was now most terrifying; one eye was hanging out of his head, the blood coming from his mouth, his wings flapping in disorder, and with a ragged tail which I had half plucked by pulling at him during his first execution. He made a horrible struggle for existence, and I was bleeding all over. At last we succeeded in gibbeting him again and then with sticks we cudgelled him to death, beating his head to pieces. Afterwards we tied a stone to him, and sunk him in a duck pond."

A terrible story, and infinitely sad for it shows how a young, soft, pliable twig can be given a first twist so cruel that the tree will never quite recover and will grow up distorted in trunk and branch. But it has a certain grandeur that seems to lift it out of everyday life. This must be more than a scrap between a little boy and a bird. It is a struggle in the world of demigods; the child is an infant Hercules and the raven a fabulous monster—a harpy, or a roc.

But taken merely as an anecdote its importance cannot be exaggerated, for it provides a key to many of the strangest contradictions in Trelawny's character and accounts for some of the least understandable actions of his life—as he himself must have realized, for he added:

"This was the first and most awful duel I ever had. I mention it, childish though it be, not only because it lives vividly in my memory, but as an event that, as I review my life, seems evidently to be the first ring on which the links of a long chain have been formed. It shows that I could long endure annoyance and oppression, but when, at last, excited I never tried half-measures, but proceeded to extremities without stop or pause. This has always been my most grievous fault, and grievously have I repented it."

CHAPTER II

"Irregular noble scapegrace . . .
Faulty—and peradventure ours the fault
Who still misteach, mislead, throw hook and line,
Thinking to lead Leviathan forsooth,
Tame the scaled neck, play with him as a bird."
—ROBERT BROWNING.

Children were not expected to enjoy themselves in the early part of the nineteenth century, even those belonging to liberal households ruled by kind parents. It was the "seen and not heard" period at its very worst. Children were regarded as potential sinners: the boys as prone to vices of gluttony and sloth, the girls to vanity. Children's stories warned of these besetting sins: if girls wore their best bonnets to picnics they got drowned; if boys ate too much plum cake they were gored by bulls. All parents believed in the "hardening" derived from starvation, cold, and early rising. So little girls rose at five in order to get in a couple of hours practicing before breakfast in icy drawing rooms, until their fingers were numb and they dropped off the piano stools fainting from hunger. Children's food was not only plain—bread, pudding, and mutton; mutton, pudding, and bread—they were allowed so little of it that the boys stole jam from cupboards and fruit from orchards and got birched so vigorously and incessantly that their fathers and tutors can have needed no other athletic exercise.

"Speak when you're spoken to,
    Do as you're bid,
Shut the door after you,
    Never be chid!"

13

was a counsel of perfection approved by even the fondest parents. Exhibitionism was taboo unless it took the form of "infant piety," so admired in evangelical families of the day that a child of three could quote texts, admonish parents for light conduct and playmates for profaning the Sabbath, and "get away with it." But it is unlikely that any of the little Trelawnys were allowed this method of self-expression. One may be sure that Charles never quoted the motto carved in the dining room of one of the old Brereton houses: "Though thou be for thy pedigre accompted as ancient as Saturn, riche as Croesus, or for thy beautie as Flora, yet if thou be carles of religion, thou arte a caytife most vyle and miserable." As for Maria, Sir John Hawkins's piety must have died out as completely as his spirit of adventure; for no sermons, family prayers, catechisms, or Sunday restrictions were included in the list when Edward Trelawny enumerated the grievances of his childhood.

In fact, Charles and Maria seem never to have regarded their offspring as potential saints but always as sinners of the deepest dye and seem to have enforced the "seen and not heard" theory so drastically that the children's lives must have been as uneasy as the lives of frightened rabbits. The only sure way of escaping punishment was to escape notice, and this was a good deal easier for the girls, or a quiet, delicate boy like young Harry, than for Edward; healthy, high-tempered, and impetuous, he was forever in hot water. That he was also tall and strong and, with his clear-cut features, olive complexion, dark curly hair, and blue eyes, must have been extraordinarily handsome, did not make up for noisiness, untidiness, and disobedience—indeed, one suspects that his good looks may have been resented by his parents as being wasted on a younger son. For, by this time, even his mother seems to have lost whatever earlier fondness she had felt; his reminiscences did not record one single act of kindness on her part. Yet there must have been something—some caress in babyhood, some occasion when she stepped between him and his father, for he regarded her with a deep affection that remained unchanged until years of neglect had convinced him she was callously indifferent to his fate.

As for his father: many a better-tempered, more fair-minded man than Charles would have found this passionate, self-willed child difficult to deal with. Charles was both irritable and unjust, and must have had a sadistic streak for he seems never to have doubted that Solomon was right: the rod was the one dependable weapon for eradicating childish faults. "Punishments and severity of all kinds," Edward Trelawny wrote, "were the only marks of paternal love that fell to my share, from my earliest remembrance."

Luckily for the child, with every year it became easier to escape from his father's sphere of influence. A big strong boy of eight or nine could not be kept within bounds if he wanted so much to get out that he ran away regardless of the flogging that might await return—even in manhood Trelawny never considered the result of any action until it was too late!

At first, the park itself would have been enough. There were ferny dells, bird-haunted thickets, deep forest—Shotwick was famous for its oaks—watered by small bright brooks, and the moldering ruins of old Shottewik Castle to explore. He made friends with keepers, poachers, and trespassing village boys. But soon the park was not enough. Young Edward was ranging farther and farther afield. How far would a healthy, nine-year-old boy be able to extend his explorations? Pretty far. Before long the Mersey, on the far side of the Wirral, would have been reached though it would never become so familiar as Shotwick's own Sands of Dee. The sea itself was probably unattainable; but he would have caught tantalizing glimpses from the hilltops and, as he watched the river fishermen drawing their nets, he would have heard tales of drownings and shipwrecks, and compared them perhaps with wilder tales told him by old family servants: Cornish tales of Cruel Coppinger, smuggler and pirate; of disasters, such as the wreck only forty years before described by Baring-Gould,

of "an Algerian corsair, carrying 24 guns, manned by swarthy
mariners with turbans and scimiters, run ashore in Mount's
Bay by her captain who thought he was near Cadiz!"

Such stories would have fired the imagination of any boy.
Did they bring this boy visions of a future where pirates and
corsairs, turbans and scimiters, would have lost their romance
and become part of everyday life? Did they help to turn that
future away from England and the Western world, and slant
it, irrevocably, towards the "gorgeous East"? All guesswork.
But whether or not Edward Trelawny's explorations of countryside and river shore were flavored with a breath of the
Orient that affected his future, these days of freedom gave
him the only pleasant memories of his boyhood and came to
an end far too soon. He was sent to school.

For some time past, a vague discussion as to the children's
education—so far, entirely neglected—had been agitating the
family; probably Charles and Maria could not find a school
that was sufficiently cheap to suit Charles and also sufficiently
smart to satisfy Maria's family pride. When Edward was between nine and ten, however, it became clear that the matter
could not be postponed much longer, and a trivial incident
finally roused Charles to action.

He happened to come upon the boys in the apple orchard
—Edward high up in a tree throwing the fruit down to his
brother—and flew into one of his sudden rages. He ordered
the boys to follow him. They obeyed. In dead silence he
walked them rapidly to the near-by town, reached "a walled
and dreary building and knocked at a prison-looking gate."

The school proved to be as forbidding inside as out. The
schoolmaster, Mr. Sayer, was a dapper little man, powdered
and spectacled, with bright buckles in his shoes; but "there
was impatience in everything he said, and a formal precision,
most fearful to a boy."

In the conversation that followed, Charles made it plain
that he was seeking a penitentiary rather than a place of education for his sons. Both were vagabonds, but the younger

was the ringleader and "would come to the gallows if the devil were not scourged out of him."

Mr. Sayer promised to do his best along these lines, a few minor matters were arranged; Charles bowed to the schoolmaster, and without noticing his sons in any way withdrew.

The months that followed were in some ways the hardest of Trelawny's life. He was to undergo experiences as cruel, but none quite so sordid, or so futile. Yet the school was no worse than a thousand schools of the time. Even in the great public schools a boy who learned anything was the exception. Bishop Trelawny's recommendations for the "children of Winchester" did not include improvement in education. It would be years before Arnold, Trelawny's contemporary, made Rugby a school where "a certain amount of classical or general learning was to be obtained." Shelley learned little at Eton. Byron learned nothing at Harrow and remembered Dulwich as "a damned place." Later on, Anthony Trollope's twelve years at both Winchester and Harrow taught him "nothing whatever." In all schools, little and big, the food was often uneatable and floggings frequent. Trollope was mercilessly flogged. Coleridge, hearing of the death of a former master at the Blue Coat School, remarked that "it was lucky that the cherubim who took him to heaven were nothing but faces and wings, or he would have flogged them by the way."

If the clever, charming Coleridge and the inoffensive Trollope could not escape punishment, Edward Trelawny— passionate, rebellious, fearless, and utterly undisciplined— naturally came in for his full share.

He knew what was in store for him. "When I thought of my father's injunction not to spare the rod," he wrote, "my heart sickened. . . . My school life was one scene of suffering, but the first day was the bitterest. At supper I could not swallow my doglike food, arranged in scanty portions; that night in my beggarly pallet, the rush lights extinguished and surrounded by the snoring of the weary boys, to me a sound of comfort, I gave vent to my overcharged heart in tears. I sobbed aloud; if anyone stirred I held my breath. I sobbed on, and was not heard. . . . I was flogged seldom more than once a day, or caned more than once an hour. I became callous and was considered by the master the most obdurate and violent rascal that had ever come into his hands. Every kind and gentle feeling of my naturally affectionate nature seemed subdued by this savage treatment, I became sullen and vindictive. Finding it useless to attempt to avoid punishment, I vented my rage on the boys and, as I grew in bodily strength, I gained respect by fear, and became the ringleader in all sports and mischief. I thus learned my first lesson as to the necessity of depending on myself, and the spirit in me was gaining strength, in despite of every effort to destroy it, like a young pine flourishing in the cleft of a bed of granite."

The boys in subjection, he turned his attention to the masters, and one peculiarly obnoxious tutor got beaten within an inch of his life. This satisfaction, rather naturally, brought Edward before the head master for judgment. As Mr. Sayer stood glowering down at him from a raised platform, Edward seized the little man by the legs and tipped him over backward. Other masters closed in, and he was locked up in a cold bedroom on bread and water for two days. The second night he set fire to the bed curtains with his candle. This was convincing; Mr. Sayer decided that he had had more than enough of Mr. Charles Trelawny's younger son, and sent him home—without being allowed to speak to anyone, even his brother, and under a guard.

By a lucky accident, his father was not there to meet him. Charles was away from home on business connected with another inheritance—his father, General Trelawny, had just died; and when he returned he was still so absorbed in affairs that Edward's unwelcome reappearance in the home circle was ignored, until Charles happened to ask him how far on he was in Latin. This led to a surprising discovery: Edward not only knew no Latin; the "rule of three" and the multiplication table were also unplumbed mysteries, he could not even spell his own name correctly!

Charles was furious. Until now there had been some talk of sending Edward to Oxford; there was a living in the family that he might as well have. But the Church seemed unlikely to want a young man with so little turn for books, and Edward most certainly did not want the Church. However, the discussion might have gone on indefinitely if a trivial incident had not again brought things to a head.

Ever since that apple-stealing, Charles had suspected Edward of thievish tendencies. Suspicion became certainty; he learned that Edward had actually given a pigeon pie to an old beggar woman, dish and all! Unfortunately for Edward, the woman was so foolishly honest as to return the dish; and though she held her tongue when she was threatened with the stocks, the house of correction, and transportation, Edward could not, of course, let her suffer. He confessed. "But," he wrote, "I hated her honesty and never afterwards could endure old women. . . . My father's wrath was dreadful. I was cuffed and kicked; but I had learned to stand firm, and I neither wept nor asked for mercy."

This shocking pigeon-pie affair, combined with Edward's annoying way of taking punishment, was to have serious consequences. Charles became convinced that the boy was a hopeless case; a nuisance that must be got rid of. The surest way was to put him in the Navy. (Long after this time, according to Thomas Wentworth Higginson, troublesome Massachusetts boys were given a taste of the sea "to cure them of naughtiness.") Charles had observed that the Navy's methods with boys always sent them home chastened in spirit and improved in manners, and often did not send them home at all.

This wise decision having been reached, Charles set about finding a ship and a captain who would take his son as a first-class volunteer. This was the quickest way of getting rid of him. A boy could go to the "Royal Academy established in His Majesty's dockyards at Portsmouth for educating young gentlemen in the sea service," where he would have been taught "the French language, dancing, fencing, and the use of the firelock" as well as mathematics. But Portsmouth was too near—Edward might expect to come home now and then— and he was too young, only thirteen. The Naval Academy did not allow a boy to become a midshipman until he reached the age of seventeen, so Edward would have to stay there four years. This would never do. Better send him straight to sea. Two years' good hard training at sea was supposed to lick a boy so thoroughly into shape that Edward might become a full-fledged midshipman at fifteen.

So a ship was found: the *Colossus,* a 74, commanded by Captain Morris, an old friend of Charles's, willing to take the boy. At the moment, the *Colossus* happened to be out at sea somewhere with Nelson's squadron, but that was not allowed to interfere with Charles's plans. Edward was fitted out as rapidly as possible, taken to Portsmouth and shipped, as passenger, on board the *Superb,* a line-of-battle ship commanded by Captain Keats, to join the *Colossus* wherever and whenever she might be met with.

If Charles had hoped that a ship would prove an even more unpleasant place of education for his son than Mr. Sayer's school, his expectation was not, at first, justified. Edward liked the sea. As a passenger he was free to roam about the ship—a great broad vessel with a tremendous spread of square sails and the raised forecastle, high poop, and quarterdeck reminiscent of those magnificent Elizabethan ships, built "the more for their majesty to astonish the enemy." Her exterior was gay with stripes of color and gilded "gingerbread work"; but within she was painted all one plain deep red, because of the blood that would drench the walls and floors when the wounded were brought down after an action: it would show less.

So picturesque a ship would have kindled imagination. Trelawny must have felt a first stirring of the passion for a seafaring life that neither hardships nor injustices were ever quite able to kill. He would have liked the decks best; to stand gazing up at the great white spread of sails, watching the sailors go skipping about at such dizzy heights, so sure of finding their way among that intricate confusion of masts and rigging. But his insatiable curiosity would have led him to explore the *Superb* from stem to stern. As a passenger he would have been allowed a peep into the captain's cabin under the poop—large but as bare as a barn, for all decoration and any furniture except absolute necessities were "looked upon as Persian and soul-destroying"; he might wander into the ward room, dedicated to the other officers, equally lacking in comfort, though each man had "a little fenced-off cupboard" of his own. But Trelawny would have eaten his meals with the midshipmen, the surgeon and master's mates who berthed in the after cockpit—low and badly ventilated but always a fairly good-sized space, for it was here the wounded and dying were brought to the surgeon and, for the same reason, though the middies had to sit on their sea chests they were always provided with a table, made fast to the floor, to be used for operating as well as dining. That the wood was so deeply stained the diners found it difficult to tell whether the red blots came from blood or gravy, would have affected the appetites of squeamish persons. But the stains might have been currant jelly for all Trelawny cared. He must have enjoyed the bad food and ribald conversation of the midshipmen's mess, for he seems to have given no trouble to anyone, either officers or men. Naturally enough, for he was happy. Liberty was sweet. Everything that went on was novel and interesting.

He liked watching Sir John Thomas Duckworth, Vice-Admiral of the Blue, come aboard at Plymouth with all the precise etiquette of an ecclesiastical function. "Side boys" in white at the gangway; boatswain, glittering with gold anchor-buttons, silver chain, and silver whistle, ready to "pipe the side." Crew rigidly at attention; officers, equally rigid, on the quarterdeck. All eyes fixed on the godlike figure of the admiral moving majestically forward, in a dead silence broken only by the long solemn piping of the boatswain's whistle; saluting the quarterdeck; turning majestically towards his cabin, and disappearing from mortal view.

After this fine show, it was something of a comedown to watch potatoes and mutton being taken on in Cornwall, and the entertainment, such as it was, soon palled. For the *Superb* was bound for Cadiz, and everyone on board was eager to be off and find out what Lord Nelson was doing in those waters. Except the admiral. At the moment, Duckworth was more interested in provisions than in the prospect of glory (though Duckworth could fight when he wanted to—the action off Santo Domingo a few months later when Duckworth succeeded in burning both the *Diomède* and the *Impériale* was a famous victory); he refused to be hurried, even after the *Superb* put to sea, or to take any interest in Nelson—until it was too late!

The first news of Trafalgar reached the *Superb* from the *Pickle,* a schooner in Nelson's fleet, compelled to heave to although her captain was speeding home hoping to be the first to tell England of Nelson's victory and Nelson's death.

Captain Keats received the news with intense excitement, darkened by grief and anger—it was infuriating that mutton and potatoes should have prevented his ship taking part in this magnificent victory—and Duckworth made no attempt to conceal his distress when he realized what his procrastination had cost him, and the *Superb* went on her way wrapped in gloom.

"A deathlike stillness," Trelawny wrote, "pervaded the ship. Sorrow and discontent were painted on every face; and I sympathized with the feeling without any clear knowledge of the cause."

Not long after, they began meeting various ships from the victorious fleet straggling back to England, all more or less disabled. Among them was the *Colossus,* the ship to which Trelawny had been assigned. He was transferred from the

Superb; Duckworth communicated with Collingwood, in charge after Nelson's death, was given six ships of the line and orders to pursue the remnant of the enemy fleet that had managed to escape, and made for the Mediterranean, while the *Colossus* continued on her homeward way.

Trelawny must have said goodbye to the *Superb* with some misgivings, knowing that he would no longer have the freedom of a passenger and would be under orders. But he got on all right. "I found cockpit life," he wrote, "more tolerable than my school and little worse than my home. Besides, I was treated with exceeding kindness, and I began to be delighted with my profession."

Yet "cockpit life," never any too easy, must have been far from agreeable on board the *Colossus.* The old 74 had suffered badly at Trafalgar. "In that sanguinary encounter," Marshall writes, "she sustained a far greater loss than any other British ship, with forty killed and one hundred and sixty wounded; among the latter were her gallant commander, two lieutenants, a marine officer and nine midshipmen." She was limping home, dismasted, half her upper deck cut away by enemy shot, very nearly a wreck and laboring in the trough of the sea. The weather was very bad. Officers and crew alike were frantically impatient to get back to England; provisions were stale; the voyage seemed interminable. That under such conditions the officers found either time or spirit for kindness to a little volunteer speaks well for Captain Morris's regime—though kindness was such a novelty to young Edward that a very little would have gone a long way with him. Much or little, it evidently made up for hard work, poor food, and rough seas, for he responded in a way that would have filled his father with incredulous astonishment. He became a good boy! For the first time in his life, except for the few weeks of liberty on the *Superb,* he was not in revolt and satisfied with himself. That his superiors were equally satisfied with him is proved by a certificate (preserved by his family) from Captain Morris: "Mr. Edwd. jno. Trelawny served

as volunteer of the 1st class on board His Majesty's Ship Colossus under my command from the 20 November 1805 to
the date hereof, during which time he behaved with diligence
and sobriety and was always obedient to command."

The "date hereof" was December 29th of the same year, so
the kind treatment that had worked such a remarkable
change for the better only lasted a little over five weeks. If
Edward could have stayed on under Captain Morris, in all
probability his life would have taken a very different turn.
Unfortunately, the *Colossus* was to be paid off as soon as she
reached home, which meant that Charles would have to un-
dertake the annoying task of finding another berth for his
son.

However, those five weeks ended in a burst of glory that
almost made up for their shortness: Portsmouth's welcome
home of the *Colossus*. Trelawny would by then have been
steeped in stories of Nelson's victory and, as his lively imagination always dramatized a situation and made him a
figure in it, no doubt, for the moment, he was able to feel
himself a full-grown man who had fought bravely at Trafalgar and could accept a share of the welcome as his due.

And it was a great welcome. As the *Colossus* moved slowly
and heavily into the roadstead every ship she passed cheered
her to the echo, and when at length she came to her moorings
at Spithead the water instantly became crowded with boats.

"What a scene of joy then took place!" Trelawny wrote.
"From the ship to the shore one might have walked on a
bridge of boats, struggling to get alongside. Huge bumboats
came bringing fresh provisions, and a circle of boats hung
around us crammed with sailors' wives and children, and
doxies, thick as locusts. These last poured in so fast, that of
the eight thousand said to belong at that period to Portsmouth and Gosport I hardly think they could have left eight
ashore. In a short time they had achieved what the enemy's
fleet had failed to do—taken entire possession of the Trafalgar
squadron. I remember that, on the following day while the

ship was dismantling, these scarlet sinners hove out the three first 32-pound guns; there must have been as many as three hundred of them heaving at the capstan."

Leaving the *Colossus* after all this excitement must have been much harder than leaving the *Superb*. For if Edward had hoped his weeks of good conduct might bring forgiveness from his father, he was disappointed. When Captain Morris communicated with Charles, he received word that the boy was not, under any circumstances, to be allowed to come home, but was to be sent at once to Dr. Burney's navigation school at Gosport to remain until another ship could be found for him.

This was horrible news. A school, to Trelawny, meant only another period of humiliation and suffering almost too great to be borne. But there was no help for it. Captain Morris gave him a letter to be forwarded to his father; put him and two other boys destined for Gosport, in charge of a master's mate; bade the man see them safe in Dr. Burney's hands, and turned his attention to more important matters—such as caring for his wound and, ultimately, receiving a gold medal and the thanks of both Houses of Parliament for his gallant conduct at Trafalgar.

But there must have been more kindness and gallantry than wisdom in Captain Morris's make-up, for his choice of an escort was strangely lacking in discretion. The little party had scarcely set foot in Gosport when their good-natured leader decided that the poor little devils ought to see life and have a bit of fun before getting shut up in school, and suggested letting Dr. Burney wait awhile. The boys were more than willing. The party proceeded forthwith to the Crown and Anchor, enjoyed an enormous breakfast of beefsteak washed down with grog, and started out to explore the town.

After weeks at sea, the mere feel of solid ground under their feet was exhilarating, and to young Trelawny, country-bred, streets and shops and crowds of people were most exciting novelties. They roamed about, staring and exclaiming. In

most places the group would have attracted attention; rollick-
ing master's mate in blue frock coat with plenty of bright
buttons, and gold-laced cocked hat very much on one side,
shepherding three little rosy-cheeked boys, all very smart in
blue tail-coats, white nankeen breeches, white waistcoats,
black neckerchiefs, ruffled shirts, buckled shoes, white silk
stockings, dirks, and three-cornered hats with gold loops and
cockades. Here in this seaport town no one noticed them—except the mate's personal friends of whom there were many,
for his acquaintance, male and female, was wide. They stopped
again and again for a chat, to have another drink, or to do a
trifle of shopping—the mate's pockets jingled with pay that
needed to be spent. Three boxes were engaged for the evening performance at the theatre, and every friend he met was
invited to dinner. So when dinnertime came, a large company, enlivened by the presence of many of the "scarlet sin-
ner" persuasion, assembled to partake of the feast.

It went off extremely well.

"The viands," Trelawny wrote, "miraculously vanished.
Bottles flew about. The empty dishes were cleared away,
dried fruit, and wines of all kinds, with sundry cut-glass bottles of brandy, hollands, shrub and rum, garnished the board.
The memory of Nelson was pledged. Toasts, songs and un-
clerical jests wended away the hours, until it was time for the
theatre and we sallied out into the high street. I remember
nothing of the play, except that the audience was exclusively
composed of sailors and their female companions. About midnight we supped, and again turned out. Watchmen, dockyard
men and redcoats were assaulted wherever we fell in with
them—by this time the houses about me appeared to roll and
pitch like ships. We were taken back to the tavern and entrusted to a fiery, red-faced old harridan who swore she would
care for us as if we were her own children. The mate ordered
a bed, a warming pan, a red herring and a bowl of punch to
be ready for him on his return, and departed."

All the little boys were dead drunk now and only too

thankful to be assisted upstairs and tucked into bed. Trelawny, as the youngest and prettiest, got a kiss from the "flaming harridan" and the pious reminder "not to forget to say
his prayers."

As the next day and night went to the same riotous tune, it
must have been a bleary-eyed group of pupils that the master's mate finally deposited at the school. But he himself
showed no signs of a too lively shore leave, and his deportment so impressed Dr. Burney that he was invited to dinner. But he declined, presented each of his charges with a
couple of guineas, murmured an injunction to "say nothing
to the old hunkses about the past," and went his way, leaving
behind him three small boys as little disposed for the rigors
of school life as boys well could be.

However, Dr. Burney's discipline was not as severe as
Mr. Sayer's; his pupils did pretty much as they chose. But
there was no teaching worth listening to, and no kindness. So
the old rebellious mood, forgotten on the *Colossus,* closed
down upon Trelawny again; worse still, he was picked up by
a boy much older than himself, and of a peculiarly mean
type, who got hold of Captain Morris's letter, opened it and
persuaded Trelawny—as usual, without pocket money—to keep
the money to buy a gun. They went "birding"; found no
birds, argued over possession of the gun. The dispute became
a quarrel. Trelawny threatened the big boy; he ran away;
Trelawny shot him.

This created something of a stir in the school. But the
wound was slight and, as Dr. Burney had just received
word from Trelawny's father that a berth was waiting for
him, he got off with a short confinement and was despatched
to his third ship, a frigate, fitting for sea.

Here in the frigate his "cockpit life" really began. On the
Colossus, a 74, volunteers were consigned to the gunroom,
slung their hammocks among the cutlasses, muskets, and pistols, and were under the supervision of the gunner. But in
smaller vessels they messed with the midshipmen and were

supposed to be kept in order—but never were—by a school-master, usually the ship's chaplain. The midshipmen lived in the after cockpit, a foul hole below the water line, almost dark, with no ventilation to the outer air; so low that a man could not stand upright, so small that "any berth large enough for a fight when the chests were cleared away was considered roomy"; smelling horribly of bilge water—that most horrible of all bad smells—old rope and tar, of rancid butter and rotten cheese, of sweat and dirty clothes; for here the hammocks were swung at night, here the middies slept and washed and dressed; studied and quarrelled and played practical jokes; ate and drank and sang and fiddled, with never a moment's privacy, nor any quiet even at night for the "youngsters"—banished to their hammocks when the talk got too indecent, or the drink too deep—until the "oldsters," the senior midshipmen often middle-aged men, chose to leave off carousing and go to sleep themselves. No wonder that Mr. Midshipman Easy found his quarters "infinitely inferior to the dog kennel which received his father's pointers"; or that another boy, in real life, wrote to his father: "I thought I should like the service, but I hate it most confoundedly."

But Trelawny fitted into cockpit life as if it had been the pleasantest life in the world. He thoroughly enjoyed the noisy society. Of this particular group of boys on the frigate, he wrote: "I learned to love them." For he was that sort of boy; the type described by Marryat (Trelawny's contemporary, born in the same year): "like midshipmen in general, with little appetite for learning, but good appetites for dinner, hating everything like work, fond of everything like fun, fighting *à l'outrance* one minute, and sworn friends the next—with general principles of honour and justice, but with all the virtues and vices so jumbled together that it was almost impossible to ascribe any action to its true motive."

The miseries of cockpit life, he seems scarcely to have noticed! He accepted bad food and bad smells, dirt and noise as all part of the day's work (when he wrote of this time, its discomforts were not even mentioned). From first to last, he had only one complaint to make of the Navy: the inferior character of most of the officers he found himself compelled to obey.

The Navy was full of such men; the war with France that had begun in the year of Trelawny's birth still dragged on and showed no signs of ending—although Nelson had written after the battle of Cape St. Vincent: "I scarcely think the war can last—for what is it all about?" The demand for officers and seamen far exceeded the supply. Shopkeepers and farmers were given commissions; press gangs kidnapped sick men and boys in their teens and ransacked the jails for riffraff, often of such a ferocious criminal type that even an experienced officer was obliged to resort to brutal methods. "Our naval glory," Masefield writes, "was built up by the blood and agony of thousands of barbarously maltreated men. . . . Perhaps no place has contained more vice, wickedness, and misery, within such a narrow compass, than a ship of the line at the end of the eighteenth century."

Now, in 1806, conditions were much the same. The mutinies of Spithead and the Nore (that "dark and melancholy blot" of nine years before) had forced the Navy to become a little more "crew-conscious." But floggings that ended in death were still not unknown; the pay was still pitifully small— about twenty-five shillings a month; the men's share of prize money, pitifully disproportionate to the part they had played —after a great victory an admiral might get some eight thousand pounds and the men have to put up with nineteen shillings each! The food was still vile—biscuit, dusty with weevils and wriggling with maggots; water, "revolting in color and swarming with putrescent life"; during a long voyage rats became a high-priced delicacy.

This treatment naturally developed a peculiarly brutal type of seamen. But these pigtailed ruffians in striped shirts and flowing trousers had their good qualities. They were brave—Nelson said of his sailors: "They mind shot no more than peas." They knew their business. Knew it so well that

the volunteers and other "youngsters" went to the sailors for
their practical instruction in seamanship.

A boy had much to learn in order to "graduate." Christopher Lloyd sums it up: "Before he could pipe out his orders,
he must learn to run aloft with the agility of a monkey, to
scale the rigging of the towering masts from futtock shrouds
to main royal top. He must learn the stays, shrouds, braces;
how to ship the carronades on their slides and lash the gun
carriages securely; how to hand and reef, read the compass
and master the signal code."

For timid boys this sort of "agility" must have been difficult to acquire, and sensitive souls would have found close
association with filthy, foul-mouthed sailors most unpleasant.
But Trelawny was neither timid nor sensitive. He too was
the product of a brutal age. An age trained to disregard suffering and despise comfort.

The Wordsworths submitted to smoky chimneys that ruined
their eyesight, and damp bedroom walls that racked them
with rheumatism, as unresistingly as if these afflictions came
straight from Divine Providence. When Anne Brontë's hero-
ine objected to her pupil's pulling off the wings of live spar-
rows, she was reproved by the indignant parent. Kind Miss
Eliza Pinckney was simply delighted to watch tiny tots of
three years old, happily employed in factories earning their
own living.

So Trelawny did not much mind the brutality of the sailors
and, if he had come straight from the *Colossus* and Captain
Morris, he might have got on well enough with the officers.
For Captain A. (Trelawny never gave the name of an officer
he disliked, or the name of the ship) was an acquaintance of
his father's, inclined to leniency. But the wretched school interlude had increased the arrogance that was his worst fault,
and both Captain A. and the first lieutenant happened to be
men of plain extraction who, having "arrived" by crooked
roads, remained unable to live up to their position; and such
persons Trelawny never learned to tolerate. For, with all his

talk of freedom and equality, he remained, at heart, an aristocrat.

In his writings, the only allusion to his own ancestry is bitterly contemptuous: "I came of a family so proud of their
ancestry that even gout and mortgaged estates were traced
generations back on the family tree, as ancient heirlooms,
and therefore to be reverenced." In an argument he always
ranged himself on the side of the people. Nevertheless in his
description of these two officers the emphasis is on their lack
of breeding.

"The captain," he wrote, "was a red-gilled, sycophantic
Scotchman, the son of an attorney, who had bowed and
smirked himself into the notice of royalty. His first lieutenant was a Guernsey man, a low-bred, mean-spirited, malicious
scoundrel. . . . I soon realized that the navy was not suited to
me, and although my passion for the sea remained undiminished, I longed for freedom. From that time forward, I
brooded over the possibility of breaking my indentures, and
seeking my own fortune, as tales and histories tell us people
did in the olden times."

Tales and histories. Evidently Trelawny had discovered
the world of books. Few boys of his active, restless, adventurous temperament ever make that discovery. He was a real-
ist, an "extrovert"; occupied with the material aspect of life,
endowed with an extraordinarily keen visual sense and a
lively curiosity for everything, little and big, that went on
about him; interested in people; making friends easily; so
physically strong that the mere exercise of his young body
was, in itself, a pleasure. Add that he had learned nothing at
school (he never became what is called an educated man), was
still, at thirteen, very nearly illiterate, the mystery deepens;
that sort of boy usually feels a hearty aversion for the printed
page. Another question: When and where did he make the
discovery? At school? In the crowded noisy life on board
ship? More likely, as a child, on some rainy day in the old
library at Great Saughall. For already, here in his third ship,

the love of literature that would become the most enduring
pleasure of his life was going hand-in-hand with the love of
adventure.

"At this period of my life," he wrote, "an involuntary passion was awakened in my bosom for reading; so that I seized
on every occasion for borrowing and collecting books, and
every leisure moment for reading them. Old plays, voyages
and travels were my principal studies, and I almost learned
by heart Captain Bligh's narrative of his voyage to the south
sea islands and the mutiny of his crew. His partial account
did not deceive me. I detested him for his tyranny, and Christian was my hero. I wished his fate had been mine and
longed to emulate him. The story had a marked influence on
my life."

He was right. Bligh's tale of mutiny undoubtedly helped
to develop the spirit of rebellion that the tyranny of his
father—and the raven—had first aroused. But such tales did
more for him; they taught him to mingle romance with reality, to find a dash of romance in almost everything he did.
Sometimes he needed to do this because real life was almost
too hard and suffering to be borne; sometimes because, subconsciously, his artistic sense was forcing him to create drama
out of the commonplace. Whatever the cause, just as a painter
intensifies the lights and shades of a landscape by looking at
it reflected in a Claude Lorrain glass, so Trelawny, even in
boyhood, learned to heighten the chiaroscuro of everyday life
by seeing it mirrored in the "dark glass" of imagination.

So now, here in his third ship, he was visualizing himself,
not as a naughty little boy, but as Christian, full-grown hero
surrounded by tyrants and resisting to the death. It must
have been less easy to see Captain A. in the role of Bligh; but
the first lieutenant was well fitted to act second villain, and,
as it happened, the ship's company included a still meaner
wretch, the captain's clerk.

In the ordinary course of events Trelawny would not have
come much in contact with the clerk. But the man was dis-

honest and, seeing that the boy owned a good many handsome books, made friends with him and offered to keep the books in his cabin, a pleasanter place to read in than the noisy messroom. Trelawny gladly agreed. For a while all went well. Then one day when he went to get a book the clerk told him sharply that he might continue to read here, but that none of the books were to be removed.

Trelawny stared; took up a book, and was turning arrogantly away, when the clerk caught him back, seized a ruler, and struck him over the head. Trelawny struck back. But the clerk was a full-grown man, twice his strength; he was beaten to his knees. Delighted midshipmen gathered in the doorway and cheered him on. He fought like a wildcat. A table went over, writing materials flew about. Struggling and panting, trying in vain to get from under, he caught sight of a penknife on the floor; stretched for it, got it, and began driving it into the clerk wherever he could reach him. The man let go, and yelled for help. Trelawny staggered to his feet, dropped the knife, picked up his book and walked out of the cabin, blood streaming from his face but his head held high, and sat down in the messroom to await developments.

The affair might have ended the boy's career for good and all—stabbing even a clerk on board ship was a good deal worse than peppering a fellow pupil with birdshot, and he came near being charged with murder. For the first report told the captain that this terrible boy had forced his way into the clerk's cabin and attacked the poor man with a carving knife. Sea law was cruel in those days, and a ship's captain lord of life and death. Brutal captains had been known, though very rarely, to risk ordering a midshipman flogged— stretched on a grating and lashed like a common sailor (a sentence that, with Trelawny, would have been the same as death, for he would never have survived a flogging—he would have jumped overboard); if Captain A. had construed his attack as in any way connected with a mutiny he would inevitably have been hanged. Taken to the cathead, a yellow flag flying at the masthead; gun fired, sailors manning the rope; body jerked up into the air, dangling at the end of the yard arm, and Charles Trelawny's troublesome son would have ceased his troubling.

Fortunately for him, a friendly witness was able to plead his cause; a midshipman named Murray had seen the fight from the beginning. He told Captain A. that the clerk had been the aggressor; the boy was being unmercifully beaten and had used the knife in self-defence. This put a different complexion on the matter; it was almost as bad for a clerk to strike a midshipman as for a midshipman to kill a clerk.

In all probability, Captain A. was more than willing to take the boy's side; Mr. Charles Trelawny's friendship was important to a self-made man, it might be difficult to convince him that his son deserved hanging, and the voyage was nearly over. So the captain relented. Trelawny got off with an imprisonment so nominal that it merely gave him rather more leisure than his messmates.

And they were all so loud in their admiration for his magnificent resistance to tyranny in the person of the clerk—whose cheek showed a nasty scar—that Trelawny felt himself a hero, almost as big a man as Christian! He went ashore much the worse for his cruise with Captain A.; cockier than ever, vainer, harder, more arrogant, more passionate, more on the lookout for insults, readier to snatch at any weapon that came to hand and determined to do exactly as he chose on his next ship.

However, his stay on the next ship, a guard ship, was so short there was no opportunity for bad behavior, and he was immediately re-drafted to a sloop of war making ready for a long cruise, to Spain, South America, and the coast of Africa. In a happier mood he would have enjoyed the prospect of seeing strange lands. But he was hard up and too homesick. As usual he was hoping to be allowed to go home to say goodbye. As usual he was disappointed. No word came from his father. And no money!

Even full-fledged midshipmen were paid too little to get on without private means, and their families were expected to contribute towards their support. Trelawny not being of a saving disposition—thrift was, and remained, an unknown virtue to him—was obliged to start off on a long voyage without a cent of pocket money, although he was in need of many necessaries, for his chest had been rifled on the guard ship by a dishonest midshipman. He went to sea poor—and not only in pocket but in spirit; he was depressed at finding himself, for the first time, among utter strangers. Captain Morris had been a friend of his father's, and Captain A., an acquaintance. But this new captain was a stranger, both to him and to his family, and this seemed to cut him off still more completely from home.

However, the man was well enough in his way. Trelawny despised him for his "pert, pragmatical manner" and his small stature; "he had to jump on a carronade slide to box the men's ears." But the midshipmen turned out to be an exceptionally fine lot of fellows (they always did—he seems to have had no difficulty in getting on with other boys), and the officers must have been fairly kind; for the months went by, and Trelawny was back in England again with no conspicuous bad marks to blacken his record.

By now he was desperately homesick again; all his boastful imaginings forgotten. He was no longer a hero, a bold bad man slashing the cheek of an upstart clerk; he was a homesick little boy so crazy to get home that he could think of nothing else. But no word came from his father. He went on hoping, until the captain wrote for instructions and a message came —not for him but for the captain: Mr. Edward Trelawny was to be transferred to a frigate now making ready for the Orient; in future he would receive a yearly allowance; he was not to come home.

"Who can paint in words what I felt," Trelawny wrote more than twenty years later. "Torn from my native country, cut off from every tie, transported like a felon—at that period, few ships returned from the East under seven years. I was torn away; not seeing my mother, or brother, or sisters, or one familiar face. No voice to speak a word of comfort, or to inspire me with the smallest hope that any human being took an interest in me. Had a servant of my house, or even the old mastiff, companion of my childhood, come to me for one hour I could have hugged him for joy. But I was even to be separated from my messmates, whom I had learned to love —these are things, which some may feel but none can delineate. . . . I knew now that I was an outcast, thrust from my father's threshold in the hope that I should not cross it again. . . . From that time, my father left me to my fate with as little remorse as he would have ordered a litter of blind puppies to be drowned."

CHAPTER III

"From this hour, freedom!
  From this hour I ordain myself loos'd of limits and imaginary
    lines,
  Going where I list, my own master, total and absolute."
                                          —WALT WHITMAN.

But the sea worked its usual soothing spell. Homesickness faded. Life, with India ahead, seemed bright again. Unluckily the captain of the frigate happened to be another of those mediocre men Trelawny found so difficult to respect. "Old Hoofs," as the middies called him, was a strange misfit. Born and bred in the country, feeling a passion for the land as intense as most captains feel for the sea, he had been for years on half-pay, living a contented farm life, when an interfering relation in the admiralty insisted on giving him a ship. He had torn himself away from wife, children, and farm with bitter regret, bringing with him as consolation such a vast quantity of livestock—sheep, pigs, and poultry—that the frigate bore an agreeable resemblance to a farmyard and the captain's days went by pleasantly enough. He busied himself with feeding and caring for his pets and repairing damages after a spell of blowing weather, and unless some infringement of duty happened to draw his angry attention the ship was left in charge of the first lieutenant.

But if Trelawny hoped that this aloofness might prove a blessing, he was soon disabused. They had been only two days at sea when the captain's eye happened to light upon the new arrival, and he flung Trelawny a warning: Captain A. had reported the atrocities—the stabbings and what not committed on his ship—and any smallest act of insubordination would be followed by instant dismissal from the Navy.

It was a new and glorious idea! Bad conduct would lead to escape. For the first time Trelawny realized that this life he hated might be brought to an end—by himself. As a beginning, he joined the other midshipmen in their favorite game of annoying the captain by teasing his pets. The most satisfying method was to run a needle into the brain of some unfortunate fowl; stand grinning in the background during the captain's diagnosis of a mysterious malady and, when the corpse was thrown overboard, retrieve it with such perfect technique that broiled chicken could be counted upon to vary the usual bully beef and biscuit.

Strange to say, these pretty sports did not improve the captain's temper. He grew more fretful every day, more eager for the land, less tolerant of the sea. The middies, unaware of any tragedy in the situation and despising him for a landlubber, continued to plague him; Trelawny, of course, contributing his full share of tricks and often inventing new ones.

The consequences of all this playfulness might have been serious, if Trelawny had not meantime acquired a protector among the officers. Aston, one of the junior lieutenants, took a fancy to the boy and, before long, Trelawny could tell himself that he had actually made a friend!

It was the boy's first friendship; the first of those intimate and romantic relationships that were to become so important in Trelawny's life. Aston's influence was all good. Trelawny remembered him as a man of "stability of character, heroic courage, gentle and affectionate manners and open, manly bearing." That he was also tall and handsome goes without saying—Trelawny never felt attracted by anyone with an unpleasing exterior; he believed that an ugly body always housed an ugly soul. Aston's influence was lasting; years later, Trelawny wrote:

"I had been in his watch and through the tedious nights he had dived into my real character so as to discover that I was not what I seemed to be. His kindness drew me out of the shell in which I had shrunk. He awakened those feelings which had become torpid and called others forth that I had never felt. He became my champion with those above me."

And the boy needed a champion. He had made an enemy as well as a friend; an enemy remembered, like the friend, throughout a long lifetime—but not Trelawny's first enemy; a father and a raven shared that distinction! One of the lieutenants was a "keen, sharp, cunning and villainous Scotchman, whose sole delight was in torturing his subordinates," and Trelawny's spirit made him an ideal victim. The wild beauty of an untamed colt that had bewitched Aston made him offensive to the Scotchman. The colt must be broken. He told the boy that a superior should be saluted by taking the hat entirely off the head. Trelawny, already sensitive to "tyranny," flung back an impertinent objection: no one on earth was his superior; if *superior officer* were intended, then the proper salute would be a mere touch to the hatbrim. The captain, called from his poultry to punish an "act of mutinous insubordination," decided for the boy and against the lieutenant. The war was on. As a rule, the Scotchman got the best of it. But the boy was alert. Before long, he saw his chance and took it.

In the daily routine and calm weather Trelawny was as unsatisfactory a middy as ever irritated his superiors; lazy, indifferent, and impertinent. Storms brought out a courage and presence of mind that set him head and shoulders above his mates. The ship on her beam ends, masts bent like fishing rods, light sails in ribands, sailors swinging to and fro on the bow, no light but the red and rapid lightning, in a wild roar of wind and sea, the boy was in an ecstasy of happiness. The "idle apprentice" became a "son of God shouting for joy."

But a calm lost him the reputation that the storm had gained. Punishments came so fast that he accepted them as inevitable, the bitter that always followed the sweet. Not, however, the persecutions of the Scotch lieutenant; they rankled. He kept a careful score of his grievances and brooded over each mark he set against the man's name.

A punishment most of the boys feared was being sent to the masthead for four or five hours. The danger was nothing to Trelawny, but it was a wearisome business. With his usual ingenuity, he contrived to enliven these hours by making them as unpleasant to the officers as to himself. He would stretch himself nonchalantly along the cross-trees as if glad of the opportunity for a nap and, in hot weather, he sometimes really did fall asleep. Anxious eyes watched him from below; not even his enemy, the Scotch lieutenant, cared for the job of fishing a boy out of the sea.

But the Scotchman, also ingenious, decided to vary the punishment. Trelawny was ordered to the extreme end of the topsail yard for four hours. Nobody—not even this exasperating boy—could fall asleep there!

Trelawny went. Walking along the yard at a dizzy height he got hold of the topsail lift, laid himself down between the yard and studding-sail boom and disposed himself for sleep. The lieutenant, on tiptoe with anxiety, kept hailing him from below. An agreeable lullaby; he was lying there contentedly enough, when an idea came to him, a way of ending this sort of punishment for good and, incidentally, revenging himself on his tormentor.

He could swim like a fish, he had seen a sailor jump from the lower yard arm for fun without being hurt, the roll of the ship was in his favor and the stage set, for it was sunset and officers and men were at their quarters. He stood up, watched for a heavy roll of the ship that brought him close to the crest of a monstrous wave, and dropped, sinking deep into its bosom. He had gone down straight, hands over his head, and he moved his legs and arms as he descended, but the impact brought incredible agony, and he came as near death as he was ever to come during a long life. Insensible to everything but pain, he was dragged on board. The torture of resuscitation was even worse than the torture of drowning, and the next forty-eight hours were pretty bad.

There were alleviations, however. No one dreamed he could have been such a fool as to risk his life merely to annoy the Scotch lieutenant. The captain contributed a fowl to make soup and a bottle of wine, and the invalid revived sufficiently to insist on the fowl being broiled and the wine mulled, averring that he "didn't hold with anything insipid." But the reward that more than made up for his suffering was exactly what he had planned for: the Scotch lieutenant got a severe reprimand for having endangered the life of a midshipman. And before long he won another round, though more by good luck than intention.

The frigate had been cruising for some time between Madras and Bombay, on the lookout for pirates. The coast of the Konkan, which is guarded by a barrier of rocks rising out of the sea like the hill forts from the Indian plain, was a likely place—some twenty years later it was still "the seat of tribes who exercised in piratical expeditions those predatory habits which elsewhere impelled them to inroads by land." Off Goa, a suspicious-looking vessel hove in sight. Dead calm prevented escape; two of the frigate's boats were sent to board her.

The crowded hour that followed was glorious indeed!

"I was in the bow of our boat," Trelawny wrote, "on fire to realize my ardent love of fighting. The instant we touched the bow of the Malay, I seized a rope and swung myself on board and before my foot was on the deck I had cut a fellow across the head. Followed by two or three sailors, we cut and slashed away without mercy. The Malays jumped overboard. Furious at the thought of their escaping, I seized a musket and was about to fire on them in the water when Aston laid hold of me.

" 'Don't you hear?' he exclaimed. 'I have been roaring to you till I'm hoarse. Are you mad? Put down that musket.

You have no right to touch these people. For all we know she is a harmless merchantman—' "

He broke off, for at that moment the savages resolved all doubts by opening fire with their matchlocks from the shore. Aston could order his men to scuttle the ship and return to the frigate.

But the hour that followed was far from glorious for Trelawny. Aston told him he had behaved like a fool, and he knew it. This "running amok"—courage without self-control —was a silly business.

He had learned a lesson, and the affair was to have another good result. If Trelawny had shown too great relish for fighting, the Scotch lieutenant had shown too little. Looked down upon as a coward, he was obliged to moderate his persecutions, and before long another incident put an end to them altogether. An alarm of fire in the powder magazine gave Trelawny a chance to volunteer. He went down a rope into the smoke, put out the smouldering fire, and handed the blue lights up to the deck with such quick efficiency that even "Old Hoofs" began to think well of him; and his enemy knew he was now out of reach.

But this immunity had its drawbacks. The lieutenant, obliged to find another target, selected Trelawny's only intimate friend among the midshipmen, knowing that Trelawny would feel every arrow as keenly as if it were aimed at himself.

Walter was a gentle little fellow, quiet, timid, and studious—as unlike Trelawny as two boys could be. Their friendship depended to some extent on this unlikeness, for the latent tenderness of Trelawny's nature was brought out by pity for a creature as friendless as himself, and without any of his defences of character. Walter could not take punishment with an impudent grin, or return the middies' teasing with a blow. He cried and turned the other cheek. But this did not alienate Trelawny. For he knew Walter's story.

Walter had a right to an inferiority complex. He was not

only illegitimate—the usual rich nobleman and the usual simple country girl were responsible; he had been brought up in extreme poverty and educated at a charity school, and although his mother had made such sacrifices to get him into the Navy he knew he ought to feel grateful, he was as unsuited to the life as a little girl. But there was no escape. He would live and die within the walls of a hateful ship and be buried in the hateful sea.

Two passions were to rule Trelawny's life: an angry pity for the weak and a furious, ungovernable hatred of tyranny. They often dovetail; to Trelawny they were one and the same thing. He had been resisting tyrants and kicking against their pricks almost since birth with varying success. But Walter was the first to need his help; his first object of unselfish devotion. As often as he could he took Walter's punishments on himself. All teasing came to an end when he made it plain that an insult to Walter was an insult to himself. Even the Scotch lieutenant's enmity might have been diverted to another quarter if Trelawny, with his usual recklessness, had not given the man a real grievance to resent.

He persuaded Walter to help him concoct a caricature, "representing the Scotchman's obedience to the recall signal while the other boat was hastening to the Malay ship," added a doggerel poem of his own composition, and when the officers were at mess dropped it down the hatchway on the table. There was a burst of laughter. "The Scotchman's long colorless face turned to a bright lemon hue; festering with suppressed bile, he had an attack of jaundice."

That Trelawny was responsible soon became known, for he took to singing the verses all over the ship at the top of his voice until they became as familiar to the sailors as "Cease Rude Boreas," or "Tom Bowling." But it was some time before it was discovered that Walter was also guilty. When that leaked out, the lieutenant vowed, "by God, to make the sickly boy drown himself before he was a week older," and set about doing it.

Walter was punished and abused till he became desperate and at last, "replying with hasty words and anger, he was degraded from the situation of an officer, turned before the mast and stationed in the mizzen-top. He was compelled to do duty with the mizzen-top boys. His former messmates were forbidden to speak to him, he was obliged to put on the dress of the sailors and mess with them, and the Scotchman exerted his utmost influence to blast his name by the abhorrent infliction of corporal punishment; but the captain, though hitherto cajoled, would not consent. . . . His gentle heart was bruised, he sunk into gloom."

This dumb resignation continued. Trelawny did his best, but Walter would not listen now when he talked. At length, in desperation, he disclosed a secret; he was leaving the ship and the Navy forever at the next port! This roused Walter at last. But when Trelawny urged his friend to come too, Walter hesitated, until Trelawny added that revenge on their enemy was to be part of the programme.

"I pointed out," Trelawny wrote, "the exquisite treat we should have, in buffeting his enemy to death. The hope of this wild justice did what no other hope could do—it made him calm."

Night after night, Trelawny would slip away and join Walter. The boys would crouch there in the swaying mizzen-top in the thick hot darkness—the Indian stars coming and going with the long roll of the ship, the hot wind whistling in the rigging—and talk as boys have talked ever since boys were boys; confiding and sympathizing, complaining of the present and planning for the future. Boys in caves and dugouts and chalk pits, hiding in the heather and the sand dunes, in haymows and apple trees, in tents and garrets and cellars, any corner anywhere that is safe from the uncomprehending, unreasonable interference of grown people. And their talk is always the same talk and always will be. Escape and rebellion; revenge and romance; adventures on sea and land, themselves the chief figures; killing savages, rescuing dusky brides, leading forlorn hopes; always on the right side, always helping the under dog.

The dreams of the boys in the mizzen-top followed these age-old paths, but with a difference. Such dreams seldom withstand the light of common day; Trelawny was bent on making them come true. The future, he insisted, was in their own hands. They were men now; a ship was not the world, nor were they galley slaves chained to the oar for life. The English seemed all-powerful, but were tyrants only of the sea-shore. India with her thousand kings was open to them. As for the risk, lower in the scale of misery they could not sink, and any change to them must be good.

And as the nights went by, the impact of the stronger na-ture made itself felt; Walter lost his fears and began to long for "a land where Europeans dared not follow, to cast off country and caste and find a home amid the children of na-ture. The leprous pariah lived in bliss compared to what a sailor had to endure."

But here Trelawny's common sense would protest; leprosy was no part of his scheme of life; he intended to keep his limbs and make them do him good service. And when, in imagination, they transported themselves to an island of the Indian archipelago and discussed the details of savage life, and Walter exclaimed, "No canoes! I never will look at salt water again, my blood would curdle at it. I will find some sheltered ravine, some river's bank shadowed by trees, and there will I live in brotherhood with the natives, marry and have children and build a hut," Trelawny would break in with a laughing: "What! Be tattooed and naked?" For al-ready Trelawny was sharpening his best weapon in the battle of life: a hard realism that would temper romance and never allow it to degenerate into sentimentality. But there is a touch of homesickness in his looking back at those hours in the mizzen-top:

"We would while away the time," he wrote, "building cas-tles in the air, almost possessing them and forgetting all things else, until our pastoral, innocent, romantic fabric was suddenly annihilated by the cursed, croaking; querulous, sycophantic, broad, vulgar accents of the Scotch lieutenant, bawling out: 'Haud your tongues, ye wearisome rascals in the mizzen-top there, or I wull ha' ye down to the rope's end of the boatswain's mate; I wull, ye ragamuffins!' and we would slink down the rigging, creep into our hammocks and awake to a repetition of our abject slavery during the day and a continuation of our romance at night, both of us looking forward to the nightwatches."

But there was serious stuff mixed in with the dreams; dreams were only a by-product of Trelawny's fixed determination to leave the Navy and take Walter with him. He began planning for that happy day. It was not idle planning. With foresight remarkable in a boy of fifteen he decided to turn over a new leaf and get what he could out of it before throwing the book away for good. So he set himself to learn all that his superiors could teach him of the ways of the sea— leaving the Navy did not mean leaving the sea; love of the sea was an enduring passion. He studied drawing and navigation; read every book he could lay his hands on—he had always been fond of reading, but in a desultory fashion—and talked to the old sailors, drawing from their tales of India and her countless islands much curious information to be stored away for use in the future. For he realized, with a lack of racial prejudice unusual in an Englishman, and wisdom far beyond his years, that the East offered a perpetual puzzle to the West; that if he intended to live in the Orient he must have guidance through the maze, and that no yarn was so fantastic it might not provide a clue. He was more than right. Those sailors' yarns were to color his whole life through and through with all the colors of the rainbow—both his life of action and his life of imagination; light him through many dark adventures and give a wild unearthly glow to his writing.

That this energy was spasmodic and the new leaf did not remain immaculate goes without saying. An active boy can not turn into a student overnight. Luckily Trelawny had friends to help him. Walter's serious turn of mind ("When we were carousing," Trelawny wrote, "he would be at his books") was salutary, and Aston's encouragement often kept him working when he was tempted to play. Even so, Trelawny's determination might have weakened and he might have spent a long life in His Britannic Majesty's Navy and died an Admiral of the Blue, if it had not been for that *idée fixe:* revenge on the Scotch lieutenant for injuries to himself but, much, much more, for the hardships of Walter's life. Revenge, of course, hinged on leaving the Navy; in plain words, on desertion!

It was characteristic of Trelawny that neither then nor later does he seem to have felt any disgrace in the act. Probably he considered his father, not himself, responsible; if family pride suffered, so much the better. Anyway, he never spoke or wrote of it as desertion. He had suffered under a hateful yoke that he should never have been condemned to wear. Yokes were made for slaves. He proposed to get rid of his at the first possible moment.

When he got his chance he took it, instantly and without a qualm.

CHAPTER IV

"The little villages, with their leafy huts, were surrounded and protected by hedge milk bush the color of emeralds. A light veil, as of Damascene silver, hung on each settlement and the magnificent trees were tipped by peacocks screaming their goodnight to the sun."
—SIR RICHARD BURTON.

The frigate was in port at Bombay. Trelawny had been one of the first ashore—on some pretext or other he always contrived to get into the first shore boat and never returned to his ship until the blue-peter was hoisted and the fore-topsail loosed. He made at once for a favorite tavern in the town and "plunged headlong into extravagant pleasures."

Shore leave seems to have implied absolute liberty. Even the midshipmen were left without supervision or restriction of any kind, and Trelawny could "plunge" as deep as he chose. To a modern middy it would seem fairly deep. "What time I could spare from women and wine," Trelawny wrote, obviously with naïve admiration for his wild boyhood, "I devoted to playing at the billiard table, galloping about the country and rioting in the bazaars. My horse was a vicious looking brute, with an ambiguity in his eye that gave him an uncommon sinister expression. But I had a fellow feeling for his independent spirit, and found the excitement of contention a delight—for I loved to stem the stream and have never followed the footsteps of the prudent who keep the high-beaten track of the world. Thanks to a Turkish bit and saddle which I substituted for the mockery of English ones, I, drunk or sober, kept my seat, and my horse and I became a show-lion to the sober natives. I would go galloping about the narrow streets to the imminent peril of men, women and brats. Countless were the complaints of stalls upset, bruises and fractures; notwithstanding a hundred conflicting castes, all joined in a hearty curse against me."

In short, the boy behaved even worse on shore than on board ship, with the same flamboyant delight in seeing himself as an imp of hell—he never outgrew that childish trait—and less fear of consequences. For, in the Bombay of his time, he wrote later, "if you refrained from political interference and presumed not to question the omnipotency of the holy of holies, the East India Company, you could do no wrong. . . . You were never criticized for arrogance and cruelty to the slaves, unless you happened to horsewhip them during the sultry hours of the day, when you were laughed at for a greenhorn."

It was a cruel time. Not many boys of sixteen would have been moved by the sufferings of slaves. Trelawny was not only more sensitive than most boys of his age, he was also more persistent. He never wavered in his determination to get himself out of bondage and take Walter with him.

The wretched Walter had not, of course, been allowed shore leave; but Trelawny contrived to hearten him with frequent messages, and the plan of escape had been perfected in every detail. Walter was to wait until the frigate was on the point of sailing. A canoe engaged by Trelawny would be lying near by; as soon as the sea was dark Walter was to drop himself over the port bow and swim to her; he would be picked up and the boys would be together again with the free world all before them.

There remained one important matter to be attended to—the punishment of the Scotch lieutenant. Trelawny had taken that job upon himself; Walter's part was to be that of the maiden watching from the side lines while the knight engages in mortal combat. That a combat was not necessary to escape and might, indeed, make escape impossible, was of no consequence. A combat had to be. Just how and when it could be brought about gave him a good deal of anxiety.

The lieutenant was often to be seen strolling about Bombay, apparently unconscious that a bitter enemy dogged his footsteps, but seldom alone, never wandering off into some corner where he could be got at. But the fatalistic certainty that was to guide Trelawny so often in after life helped him now to bide his time. Sooner or later, chance would deliver the man into his hands.

But the days went by. The frigate was making ready to sail. Trelawny became increasingly restless and might have taken some risk that would have ruined everything, if it had not been for the soothing influence of a new friend.

They had met at the tavern. The new friend was tall, dark, and handsome; a man of mystery, known in Bombay as the "Stranger." He professed to be a merchant. A merchant of what? Where did he trade? No one seemed to know. He called himself De Ruyter, claimed America as his birthplace and spoke perfect English; but he could "converse with the natives with equal ease whether the tongue happened to be the brutelike grunting of the Malay, the more humanized Hindoostanee, or the soft, harmonious Persian," and all these people paid him deference; even the fat, pompous Armenian merchants stopped their palanquins and got out to converse with him. On the other hand, European residents, including the English naval officers, also found the "Stranger's" society agreeable. These contradictions naturally took a boy's fancy. Almost at first sight, Trelawny realized that he had found the ideal hero of romance. His catalogue of De Ruyter's perfections is rather touching in its extravagance, for it was written long after.

After describing his hero's "majestic stature" and "air of invincible determination," he recalled, one by one, every feature of the handsome face in admiring detail, ending: "His eye was so varying it was impossible to distinguish its color; in a state of rest it was overcast with a hazy film like a gray cloud, but with excitement it gradually brightened till its rays, like the sun, became so bright that your own were dazzled. A long residence in a tropical clime had not affected his energies; the maddening fever of the jungles tainted not his blood, the sunstroke fell innocuous on his bare head, and he alone went the round of his occupations heedless of time or temperature. But he drank little, slept little and ate sparingly. He was approaching his thirtieth year. . . . He became my model. The height of my ambition was to imitate him, even in his defects. For the first time I was impressed by the superiority of a human being."

This careful description is given here almost in full because De Ruyter's character must be studied or Trelawny's cannot be understood. It should not be rejected as too extravagant to be true. De Ruyter was a real man. Only the influence of a real man could have been so lasting. Three persons were to make Trelawny what he was—four, if one counts the raven! A girl, Zela, was to awaken his heart, and a poet, Shelley, impress his mind and soul. De Ruyter formed the raw, restless, irresponsible boy into a man of action and gave him an example of self-control that finished the lesson Aston had begun. Without De Ruyter, Trelawny might never have acquired that magnificent self-control that would take him through so many crises—physical crises, that is. A spiritual crisis seems always to have taken him by surprise—he was never to learn any spiritual self-control whatever.

That the influence of a man like De Ruyter, coming at such an impressionable age, should have been lasting is not unnatural. It was also curiously far-reaching. It would reach across the next fifteen years and touch another new friend, Byron, creator of Manfred, Mazeppa, and a dozen other heroes of romance, all reflections of Byron himself—or, rather, what he imagined himself to be: the "fine flower" of heroland, a sort of boiling down into one splendid whole of every hero that ever took the stage of life. And Byron did possess most of the "outward and visible signs," though not the "inward grace." There was too much *fa figura* in Byron's make-up, base metal that kept him from ringing quite true. But Trelawny might not have realized this as soon as he did, if it had not been for the memory of De Ruyter, a flesh-and-blood *Corsair*. He might *never* have seen through Byron. And if Trelawny had kept his illusions, if he had stayed with Byron at Missolonghi, if, together, they had— Too many *if*'s and too far ahead of the story. They must wait for a later chapter. It is the year 1807, and Trelawny is a boy of sixteen following a tall dark "Stranger" about the streets and byways and through the crowded, many-colored bazaars of Bombay.

To be allowed this privilege by so godlike a guide meant much to the boy. He made no secret of his admiration—Trelawny never made a secret of anything—and De Ruyter must have found it gratifying or he would not have permitted the companionship. As they explored Bombay admiring eyes must have watched them both, for the satellite was as brilliant as the star. Trelawny was already six feet tall and as strong as a man, with a perfectly built body and a beautiful face.

Their sight-seeing took them off the beaten track. Trelawny noted with satisfaction that his friend "was familiar with all the out-of-the-way corners of this most irregular of towns, and entered into many dark abodes without ceremony." But these wanderings were never aimless; there seems to have been a purpose in De Ruyter's every action, even when he retired into the background and posed as an indifferent spectator. "While others"—Trelawny again—"were carousing and keeping midnight orgies, he often joined us, but when we were fired by the juice of the grape or maddened by arrack punch, he drank coffee and smoked his hooka. But he exceeded the youngest of us in the enjoyment of the present hour and, by putting himself on a par with us, he gained an influence that Solomon in all his wisdom could not have accomplished."

The words suggest a picture. You see the dimly lighted, crowded inner room of the tavern, the gaily dressed, turbaned slaves padding noiselessly about a table glittering with

brass and silver, the midshipmen in their tight little blue
jackets, their little cocked hats on the backs of their curly
heads, singing and drinking, making believe they are men,
and the "Stranger" looking on with middle-aged amusement.
Reviving his own boyhood? No doubt. But there was a more
practical reason for good-natured tolerance. De Ruyter, lolling in the background with his hooka, was less nonchalant
than he seemed. Those "clouded" eyes moved calculatingly
from one flushed, boyish face to another, and the silly talk,
that became reckless talk as wine and arrack punch loosened
tongues, was carefully sifted for bits of information that
might be useful later on when a "merchant" began collecting
his merchandise.

So the acquaintance that had begun with a game of billiards in the tavern was deliberately encouraged by the older
man until the explorations of Bombay's out-of-the-way corners could be unobtrusively extended and information collected at the fountainhead.

Visits to the men-of-war lying in the harbor became frequent—for his new friend, the boy noted, "seemed to seek the
society of naval officers." It was the last society that Trelawny
himself would have sought—there was something obnoxious
in the mere sight of brass buttons and a cocked hat. But the
visits were pleasant enough, for the naval officers liked the
society of De Ruyter as much as he liked theirs. So during
the last days of that memorable shore leave, all the men-of-
war lying in the harbor were visited, with one exception;
Trelawny did not take De Ruyter on board his own frigate—
probably because an unexpected meeting with Walter could
not be risked.

Everywhere, the two were made welcome and De Ruyter
was accepted without question as the harmless gentleman he
appeared to be. But Trelawny's suspicions would not down.
De Ruyter was so inquisitive—asking questions about the
ships, their cruises and rates of sailing, the peculiarities of
the various commanders. Could he be a spy? The rajahs were

known to employ spies to keep them informed of all that went on in the Residencies. That he hated John Company was plain enough; when he spoke of the greedy London merchants who were bleeding India white, "his brow would darken, his lip quiver and his eye dilate," and Trelawny would long to do his share in freeing the natives from the cruelty and extortion of Anglo-Indian rule.

Hatred of oppression. Pity for the weak. De Ruyter must have guessed that these were the strings to play upon if he wanted to get the boy. But it is not necessary to suppose him insincere. Cruelty and extortion were everywhere in Anglo-India; one stroll through the streets of Bombay proved he was not exaggerating. The handsome houses of the English quarter stood cheek by jowl with squalid native huts. The poor were always on the edge of starvation, weeds were gathered for food, in a famine year the hedges around the city lost every scrap of green, and dead bodies lay along the roadsides.

And De Ruyter became even more impassioned when he indulged in prophecy. Sooner or later, freedom always triumphed; all dictatorships came to an end. "When goaded past endurance," he insisted, "the most patient animal will turn, armed with the invincibility of despair. The wild-cat will do it with the tiger—I have seen him do it!"

Noble words. Not, Trelawny decided, the language of a spy. There was another possibility; De Ruyter might be the commander of a privateer, a private ship of war. But under what flag? There were no English or American privateers in these waters. If his ship flew a French flag—England and France were at war—how could he be safe here in this English port, on friendly terms with the English authorities?

So this theory also had its puzzling side. But of the two rôles, that of privateer seemed more suitable for De Ruyter; the ideal hero—perfect except for one small flaw: he was inclined to minimize the sufferings of midshipmen! He even remarked that the persecutions of the Scotch lieutenant were not worth Trelawny's notice; the malice of so insignificant a person was "a little thing."

A little thing! Did De Ruyter consider cruelty a little thing? Ruin had been heaped upon Walter, and he, Trelawny, was responsible. Walter had been his scapegoat; he was bound in honor to revenge these injuries. Who touched Walter, touched him! And a good deal more to the same effect, in what must have been a very fair imitation of De Ruyter's best romantic manner.

He was reaching the climax of his tirade—calling down curses upon his own head if the vile miscreant went unpunished, asking pariahs to spit at him and wild dogs to hunt him through the jungle—when the door opened and the miscreant himself came in, alone!

The man hesitated for a moment on the threshold. But a boy's anger was not important. The lieutenant decided to appear unconscious of any ill feeling. There was an ingratiating smile on his long pale face as he came sidling in, with a bow for De Ruyter and a casual reminder to Trelawny that the ship was sailing next day, the officers must be on board before sunrise.

The words were not out of his mouth before the boy was at him.

It was the raven battle over again. Years later, his revenge on the Scotch lieutenant was recalled with the same vividness, the same relish, the same gloating regard for every gory detail:

"I dashed my hat in the rascal's face," he wrote, "with a cry of rage: 'You told me once never to stand in your presence with my hat on. For the last time I obey!' I stripped off my coat and drew my sword. He attempted to pass me. I caught him by the collar and swung him into the middle of the room. 'Draw!' I cried. 'This gentleman and the billiard marker shall see fair play.'

"He appealed to De Ruyter, calmly smoking. De Ruyter advised him to 'draw and fight it out,' adding, 'He is but a boy and you should be a man by your beard.'

"The fellow began whimpering, begging to be let off. He humbled himself, protesting he had never intended me any wrong; asked my pardon, entreated me to put up my sword and go on board with him promising he would never take advantage of what had passed. Disgusted at his meanness, I struck him from me. 'Remember Walter!' I cried 'you cowardly and malignant ruffian. You white-livered scoundrel. Can no words move you? Then blows shall!' And I hit him with the hilt of my sword in his mouth, and kicked him, and trampled on him, I tore his coat off and rent it to fragments. His screams added fuel to my anger, I was furious that such a pitiful wretch should have lorded it over me so long. I roared out, 'For the wrongs you have done me I am satisfied. Nothing but your currish blood can atone for Walter!' Having broken my own sword at the onset, I drew his from beneath his prostrate carcass and should have despatched him on the spot, had not a stronger hand gripped hold of my arm. It was De Ruyter's. He said in a low calm voice: 'Come, no killing.' He took my sword and handed me a billiard cue. 'A stick is a fitter weapon to chastise a coward. Don't rust good steel.'

"I belabored the rascal, his yells were dreadful, he was wild with terror. I never ceased till I had broken the butt end of the cue over him and he lay motionless.

"De Ruyter had stood sentinel at the door. He now left it and a shoal of blacks and whites rushed in."

Among the crowd of eager strangers, questioning and exclaiming, a familiar face emerged. The face of Walter!

Trelawny stared at him in amazement. Walter here? Here on shore? Why, Walter should have been waiting on the ship, waiting for the canoe. Trelawny stared at Walter, but Walter was staring at the body on the floor. The Scotch lieutenant! Was he dead? Walter looked questioningly at De Ruyter. De

Ruyter shrugged his shoulders; but he felt the man's pulse, beckoned to the servants and told them to take the gentleman to a doctor.

The wretched lieutenant was lifted from the ground. He stirred, his eyes opened. But, less plucky than the raven, he did not now "spring up with a hoarse scream"; he lay limp, blubbering like a child, and let himself be carried out.

De Ruyter turned to the boys, realizing, as they did not, that the affair would have serious consequences. Trelawny was told that he must leave Bombay at once, escape before the alarm was given and the town gates closed, and Walter that he was probably safe enough "as he had changed his uniform." Trelawny gave Walter a startled glance and saw that it was true—Walter wore a scarlet coat!

Walter smiled with calm satisfaction. "Yes," he said, "thanks to God and my mother, I have a commission in the Company's service and was discharged this morning from the ship—one of the officers going to England made over his traps to me. I came here at once to consult you, Trelawny, as to how we were to get our revenge—the frigate sails tomorrow. You have forestalled me—"

De Ruyter broke in. "All that can be discussed later. Trelawny, you have no time to lose. Be off, off like the wind!" He lowered his voice. "Go to the bungalow I told you of. Walter and I will join you there as soon as the frigate has sailed and this affair has blown over. Now, no more words. Be off, I say!"

Trelawny obeyed. His horse was brought. He borrowed a white jacket and a sabre from De Ruyter, gulped down a glass of claret in Walter's honor, mounted, and galloped away to the gate. A guard of Sepoys was drawn up under the archway; he set spurs to his horse, dashed through with a wild hurrah, and galloped out on to the plain of sand which lay beyond the town.

"Here," he wrote later, reliving that splendid day of fighting and escape, "I gave vent to my joy and played as many antics as a madman loosed from his chains. I spurred my willing horse to the centre of the sandy waste, hallooing with rapture. I drew the sabre and flourished it about, regardless of my horse's eyes and ears, until the town gate was out of sight. Then I pulled in my foaming steed, looked about me and seeing nothing human anywhere around, I dismounted and patted my horse's neck, exclaiming: 'The spell of my bondage is broken! I will obey no one now. If any dare attempt to replace the yoke around my neck, I'll not yield though pursued by all the men in the fleet and garrison.' "

In this riot of "release," danger of arrest was forgotten. A bungalow in the wilderness might be a good objective, but there was no need to take the shortest route and reach it without delay. Why hurry? Take your time, be on the lookout for adventures. Something amusing might turn up.

Something did—and at once. He had flung away his cap and was about to get rid of all his clothes as emblems of civilization—although the sky was like molten gold and the sand burned his feet, when he saw in the distance "a silvery cloud rising in a bright circle around some dark object on the ground."

This promised well. He postponed undressing, mounted and galloped off to investigate.

The dark object turned out to be a man, flat on his back; the bright circle, a cloud of sand sprayed into the air by a horse, gone mad, circling around and around, tearing with his teeth, striking with his hoofs at the man feebly defending himself with a sabre but almost at the last gasp.

No better opening scene for a life of adventure could be imagined. Trelawny instantly took the centre stage. The horse, so enraged that he could not be driven away, was killed; the man—a cavalry soldier, which added an agreeable touch to the rescue—was revived with arrack; palanquin fetched from the near-by village of Dungaree, bearers paid, grateful invalid despatched to the hospital in Bombay, helpers tipped, and Trelawny, well satisfied with himself, was free to go on his way. To the bungalow? Not yet.

This successful doubling of the Don Quixote and Good Samaritan rôles was too exhilarating. Trelawny "determined to conclude a busy day by a noisy night," and betook himself to the village, which he knew, by experience, offered plenty of amusement.

An extraordinary variety of Oriental faces peered out at him from the doors of the mud-walled huts as he rode into Dungaree. His description of the village is as brilliant a page as can be found in English prose, and is given in part as an example of his style and proof of his extraordinary visual memory.

"The abode of an ancient friend of mine received me," he wrote. "She was the female sheik of the tribe, and united in her person the characteristics of the buffalo of the jungles— its ball-proof hide of dingy hue, decorated with bristly straggling hairs, sunken eye and horny face—with the splay feet and hump of the dromedary. Her name was Muckery. She was a monstrous hag and looked coeval with sin.

"The inmates of her house were heard approaching. I distinguished the little patterings of their baby feet, and presently the jingling of their bangles and rings. Arms, wrists, ankles, toes and fingers glittered with brass, silver and glass, making a most harmonious music, as from aloft they descended a faery-looking bamboo ladder like a continuous stream of ants down an old wall. With flowing trousers and scanty cotton vest, each female was starred on the forehead with yellow or red ochre. . . . Here were the well-greased, black beauties of Madagascar; the ferret-eyed, amber-hued, thickset Japanese, shining like sunflowers; the light and pliant limbed Kubshee, the swollen and blubber-lipped Hottentot, moving like a porpoise, the Hindoo girl with eyes like a stag and form like the antelope; the fair, oily, moon-faced Armenian, fashioned like a turtle, and the soft and fondling

Parsee, like a turtle dove; the Cheechees, a race of Europe
and India, of fire and frost, with the tallowy whiteness of the
English joined to the dark hair of the East. . . . There was
every gradation of colour and caste; muddy, olive, leaden,
copper, and all the family of browns. . . . There were all ages
and every degree of stature; from nine to ninety, and from
the height of my pipe-stem to that of the palm tree."

The "female sheik" gave him a warm welcome. A "noisy
night" must, of course, be ushered in by drink. He ordered
a brew of that "liquid fire called punch" and a vague interval
followed, crowded with strange dreamlike figures; to his intense astonishment, "Old Hoofs," the captain of the frigate,
wandered in, obviously an habitué of the establishment, and
although at first annoyed at finding his lost midshipman in so
unsuitable a spot he soon became mellow. They drank together and banged on the table and sang the song of the old
Commodore:

> "The bullets and the gout,
>   Have so knocked his hull about
>   He'll no longer be fit for sea!"

The nautch girls danced around, shaking their bangles;
the room grew hotter and hotter. Suddenly the atmosphere
became so suggestive of hell that escape seemed necessary. He
tore down a bamboo rafter and had sent a row of kedgeree
pots smashing to the floor when Muckery called out for the
Hurkandazers. Sepoys rushed in. Sobered by danger, he over-
turned a lamp and in the confusion of fire and smoke flung
himself from a window, found his horse, and without waiting
for a saddle galloped off into the darkness.

In a narrow lane he encountered a mob gathering for the
fire, they "fled before him like wild ducks"; he dashed on,
demolished a small mud temple with its little pipkin-bellied
image of Brahma and dish of perfumed rice, cleared
the village, crossed a wide jeel, swam a ford, made for a glit-

ter of light and crashed into a wall. The rein broke, and he
fell.

When he came to some hours later he found himself in
another village, lying on a mat under the shade of a bunya's
shop, the centre of a group squatting on their haunches and
staring at him in silence. He motioned for water; they shook
their heads. Then the bunya came. He spoke English, a kedgeree pot of toddy was brought, Trelawny sipped and felt
better. A bheestie stood near by carrying a palmetto bucket
of water slung on a pole. Trelawny reached for the bucket
and tipped the water over his head; it smoked on his burning
temples, he felt a thrilling sensation of pleasure and sat up.

But he was aching all over and stiff as a mummy, his face
and hands and head cut and bruised. A quiet bungalow in
the country seemed more inviting now. He asked where he
was, found the village was near the Callian road, asked for
his horse. No one knew what had become of it. By the advice
of the bunya—advice seemed less obnoxious than on the previous day—he hired a buffalo hackery and, being for the
moment satiated with adventure, took the shortest route to
the bungalow.

De Ruyter's careful directions brought him at length to a
small village among the hills lying towards the frontier of
the Deccan. The hackery could go no farther. A couple of
coolies were hired as guides, and he was piloted through a
field of Indian corn, across a ford, and up a green trail to the
bungalow.

It was charmingly situated in a grove of coconut palms
backed by a blue mountain, and was set in a garden of guava,
mangrove, pomegranate, banana, and lemon trees drooping
under their load of fruit, that sloped down to a bathing pool
overhung by a sweet-smelling tangle of roses, jasmine, and
geranium.

The old caretaker stood bowing and smiling at the door.
He went in. The place was as pretty inside as out, airy and
tent-like; the roof supported by light bamboo uprights, the

walls painted in blue and white stripes and hung with guns, spears, trophies of the chase and amusing drawings of ships, lion and tiger hunts—De Ruyter had a turn for sketching. A wing sheltered the caretaker and his numerous family, as well as a small wiry-haired yak which, when Trelawny arrived, was squabbling with the children over some fruit.

Saboo, the caretaker, showed him about, pointing out all the various comforts and elegancies with pride. But, at the moment, food seemed more important than beauty. Trelawny ordered tiffin and asked if a message had come from De Ruyter. Saboo fumbled in the folds of his turban, extracted a plantain leaf tied with coir twine, and presented the packet as if it were an offering to a god.

De Ruyter's news was good. The frigate had sailed—one day late, because of having to search for its missing middy; he was safe and Walter was safe. Walter had been placed under arrest, but De Ruyter's evidence had got him off after a very short detention. The report of the Scotchman's condition was most satisfactory; his jaw was dislocated, several front teeth knocked out, two ribs broken, and it was feared there were internal injuries as well. He had been carried on board the ship in a semi-unconscious condition.

Splendid news! Glorious news! The debt had been paid in full, and something over! Trelawny leaped to his feet, tore off his torn, soiled clothes and made for the pool. Splashing and singing, sending the spray into the air in a bright shower, he "played a thousand antics." Emerged refreshed, and lay on the margin, half asleep, watching the reflections of the roses and jessamine come and go in the warm, still water.

An appetizing smell came drifting from the kitchen. He roused himself, twisted a bit of striped cotton around his waist for a cummerbund and went indoors.

Lunch over, an excellent Indian lunch, he ordered a coolie to bring him a hooka, selected a book from De Ruyter's library—the *Life of Paul Jones,* so suitable under the circumstances that one suspects it had been provided with intention

—and, taking his dessert out into the garden, lay there under a shady tree, smoking and reading, and savoring to the full that sense of complete well-being that only material pleasures can give.

Soon all the miseries of the previous day—the bruises and cuts and stiff sore muscles—were forgotten. Saboo's children were climbing trees. He twisted another bit of calico around his head for a turban, greased himself from head to foot with coconut oil and spent a delightful afternoon climbing coconut trees—so much more amusing than climbing masts—learning how to tap them and to hang the toddy pots.

"A lightness," he wrote, "an elasticity and exuberance of joy, such as I had never before known, thrilled through me. It was the first day I could number of entire happiness [a sad saying for a boy of sixteen]. Nor did I then, as in more mature years we do, dash the present hour with thinking on the next."

Night came as flawless as the day; a gentle air drifted through the trees. He sat on a green slope, listening to the hooting of the owls and watching the vampire bats flitting around the pool until old Saboo came to warn him: "*House good to sleep in.*"

And so, climbing trees and working in the garden, bathing and eating and sleeping, three days went by, so beautiful, so easy, so carefree, after the narrow life on board ship, that he was almost sorry when a message came: De Ruyter and Walter were on the road.

But this was only a momentary feeling. He would go to meet them. The idea of showing himself in his present emancipated condition was exhilarating. He mounted the little yak, and with a long bamboo over his shoulder and a vanguard of coolies bearing kedgeree pots of fresh toddy, he rode magnificently down the trail.

Rounding a tope of neem trees, he saw them coming, deep in conversation, their horses close together.

They saw him—a young Bacchus; six feet of supple glis-

tening bronze flourishing a thyrsus, curly head thrown back,
laughing, prodding his strange steed, riding towards them
across a field of yellow corn. They gave him a casual glance.
No hint here of their little brass-buttoned midshipman—an
Indian princeling and his servants setting out for the chase?
They were passing him without a word, when De Ruyter
recognized not the naked rider but his mount, and pulled
up.

"Why, that's my yak!" he exclaimed, and as Trelawny
burst into a roar of laughter: "You madcap! By Heaven,
you'll kill me with your pranks!"

They all dismounted. They sat down on a bank and
laughed and laughed—surely no joke had ever been half so
good as this. They were refreshed with toddy, they talked
and talked—no friends had ever been half so companionable.
They remounted—Trelawny and the yak leading the procession; crossed the ford and went on up the trail to the
bungalow.

A lonely Eden had seemed delightful. Trelawny found it
ten times more delightful with another boy. Walter's Army
uniform went the way of the Navy, and he too adopted the
"habiliments of nature"—with modifications; they wore
jackets because of the mosquitoes, shoes after they had
stepped into a centipede's nest. The boys might have been
six instead of sixteen, De Ruyter said to himself, as he sat
smoking his hooka under a tree, watching his guests gambol
about the garden, splash in and out of the bathing tank,
shin up the coconut trees, make toddy, devour Saboo's tif-
fins with no perceptible diminution of their capacity for
melons, peaches, and bananas, sleep like babies, and wake
like young giants.

"We passed two days of unalloyed happiness," Trelawny
wrote of this halcyon episode. "We climbed the hills; we
chased the jackals, regardless of heat or toil; we sung and
danced—danced, not as in the days of slavery, from the excitement of drink; we were drunk with joy."

The two days, if Trelawny had had his way, would have been indefinitely prolonged. But Walter again developed a streak of independence. Trelawny had never reproached Walter for having ruined their plans of escape at the last minute; his nature was too generous for reproaches. But if he hoped great things from this holiday as a perfect prelude to the life of adventure they had so often discussed together in the hot darkness of the mizzen-top, he was disappointed. When Walter's leave was up, he insisted on returning to Bombay.

Trelawny did his best to hold him. He expatiated on the advantages of a "peasant mode of existence" (made so fashionable by Paul and Virginia and their successors that even midshipmen knew Nature was now spelled with a capital), and contrasted it with that of a soldier, all drill and duty. But Walter could not, or would not see the Army through Trelawny's dark glasses. He spoke of his mother; her sad past, her present satisfaction and confidence in the future. Trelawny gave in—a mother who loved you must be a good thing to have; gave in warmly and wholeheartedly—Trelawny never did things by halves.

But when Walter went on to suggest that Trelawny too should forsake Nature for Bellona and try for a commission, Trelawny let himself go in a burst of invective: What! Resume a badge of servitude, whether blue or red! Serve King and Company and be bribed with gold, honor, and frippery! Give up his freedom! And for what? For bread? Why, bread was to be found here on every bush!

"But you love glory," Walter insisted, "and cannot live without broils and fighting."

This, Trelawny had to admit, was true. He did like fighting. But not Walter's sort. He, Trelawny, did not propose "to fight like a butcher's dog, on compulsion, fed on sixpence a day, slipped from the collar to subdue slaves." No; when he wanted glory he would battle against tyrants and oppressors wherever they were to be found—and that, he had reason to believe, was everywhere!

This magnificent peroration silenced Walter, whose powers of rhetoric were considerably less. But Trelawny agreed to visit him in camp, and the boys went off together. De Ruyter let Trelawny go without protest; there had been a ring of sincerity in that fiery declaration of independence that told him the boy was his and would return.

The visit went off pleasantly. No fear of arrest seems to have disturbed the boys—apparently, the left arm of His Majesty's Service made a point of not knowing what the right arm did! Walter's tent was comfortable; the Army officers, a jolly lot. Walter again began hoping to lure Trelawny away from romance and De Ruyter—Walter's sensitiveness warned him there was a very dark side to De Ruyter—back to a good sane useful life, with no nonsense about it, in the Army. Trelawny would have no difficulty in getting a commission; the Company wanted boys between fourteen and eighteen, healthy, spirited boys like Trelawny, and was not exacting as to education. The regulations read, "A Cadet must be able to write a good legible hand, construe Caesar's Commentaries, be expert in vulgar and decimal fractions and have a good character from the master he last studied under"; but that was nothing (Walter had acquired an education, as well as an inferiority complex at the Blue Coat School); a week's cramming would make that all right.

Trelawny knew better. What seemed so easy to Walter was beyond him. As for a certificate of character from a master—schools, in his experience, were places not for gaining but for losing character; certainly, Dr. Burney's recommendation wouldn't have satisfied the most lenient Company examiner. But all this was beside the point; Trelawny's reputation might have equalled Parsifal's, and his erudition Lord Macaulay's—the influence De Ruyter had acquired was far too strong for Walter to counteract. There wasn't, Trelawny decided, a pin to choose between the red and the blue; the

Army men were as limited in their outlook as the Navy, their amusements as little worth while. Before very long he bade Walter a final goodbye and returned to the bungalow.

De Ruyter was there, waiting for him. De Ruyter was sympathetic; he listened patiently to Trelawny's long-winded praises of Walter—his sweet disposition, gentleness, and touching love for his mother—until Trelawny produced Walter's parting present. There was a hint of mockery in De Ruyter's comment:

"His mother's Bible, I presume? Or a cookery book. Or an Army list." But he glanced at the book with some surprise. It was Volney's *Ruins of Empire and Laws of Nature*—"an essay on the philosophy of history, containing a vision which predicts the final union of all religions by the recognition of the common truth underlying them all." De Ruyter was impressed.

"By the God of Nature," he remarked, "the fellow has some soul in him, after all! By the way," he went on, "I am going back to town tomorrow. In ten days, I am going to sea. What do you intend to do?"

The question was a vital one. With it, Walter faded out of the conversation, as—after the parting in Bombay—he faded out of Trelawny's life. The two friends never met again; each had chosen his own path, and the paths diverged too widely for even chance to bring them together. Had Walter chosen wisely? He was not the stuff of which generals are made; it is to be feared that Walter died, as he was born, under a cloud. Probably he never knew that he would achieve a pale sort of immortality as a friend of Trelawny's. For Trelawny—a most constant friend—never forgot Walter. He wrote of him as a dear friend, and that meant inclusion in a group of immortals so dazzling in their brilliance that, if Walter did know, he would have been satisfied.

But that was in the far future. For the time being, De Ruyter's abrupt: "What are you going to do?" drove Walter and every other thought out of Trelawny's mind. What was he going to do? Why, he hadn't given that a thought—the quiet life here at the bungalow was so pleasant—

De Ruyter laughed. Very well. The bungalow was at his disposal. Also the sixteen coconut trees, the garden, and the yak. Old Saboo, his frow, and half a score of children lived off the coconut grove. Why not Trelawny? He could make toddy from the sap and arrack from the toddy. The fruit furnished oil to brighten his skin and fill his lamps; the shells were useful for drinking cups; the husks for bedding, twine, ropes, and cables that could be sold for rice and ghee. There was the tank to swim in and fruit in the garden.

Trelawny exclaimed, with enthusiasm, that as he could also fish and shoot and go naked, it seemed to him an altogether perfect life. De Ruyter agreed; advised him to relinquish any idea he might have had of embarking on a life of adventure, and glanced out at the night sky—he usually travelled at night; saw that the Great Bear shone on the verge of the horizon, and rose. He threw a bag of pagodas on the table, bade Trelawny deny himself nothing that money could buy. They shook hands. He moved to the door. And paused.

"Remember," he said, "if you should weary of your pastoral life, I have a lovely little craft, well armed and formed for peace or war as occasion serves; she lacks an enterprising young officer. I had thought you might fill the vacancy—"

"You never told me!" Trelawny cried. "Where is she? Let me have a look at her! How is she rigged? Where does she lie? How many tons? How many men?"

But De Ruyter only laughed, raised his hand in a mocking gesture, and was gone.

Trelawny moved to the door and stood looking out into the darkness, listening to the horse going down the trail, chink of hoofs on a rocky ledge, jingle of bit and bridle as the animal tossed his head sniffing the chill night air, the far-off *splash-splash* as he took the ford.

Sound died away; Trelawny flung himself on the margin

of the water tank and lay staring up at the stars with a puzzled frown. The stems of the palm trees, pale and straight as the masts of a ship, mounted up into the sky and lost their tops in its indigo blue. . . . To live like a tree? like a vegetable? Was that enough? Masts . . . The tree trunks disappeared; he saw the masts of a ship, bending this way and that in a salty gale. He stirred restlessly, jumped to his feet, and went indoors.

CHAPTER V

"The wind, the tempest roaring high,
The tumult of a tropic sky,
Might well be dangerous food
For him, a Youth to whom was given
So much of earth—so much of heaven,
And such impetuous blood."
                                        —WORDSWORTH.

Trelawny was now so eager for the sea that when De Ruyter came to fetch him a few days later, old Saboo and the yak, the water tank and the sixteen coconut palms were already fading into insignificance; the pastoral life had lost its flavor.

He turned his horse's head towards the trail, glanced back, waved his hand to the children, and rode out of his boy's paradise, never to return.

De Ruyter's two ships—an Arab grab brig and a dhow—were waiting for them at anchor off a wharf in Bombay, unloading a cargo of cotton and spices purchased, Trelawny was told, by the Company. The grab, a vessel of some three hundred tons, was indeed a "lovely little craft." Trelawny praised her lean, wedgelike, elongated bow, her beautiful water line, and her run aft like a schooner.

They went on board. The captain, known as the rais, could speak English and welcomed them with deference. He was a handsome old man, an Arab, and the crew working on deck were Orientals too; Arabs from Dacca, savage, lean, and wild-eyed, in red jackets and turbans. But down below, out of sight, there were more sailors; Europeans: Danes and Swedes, and a few Americans. All of them good men, De Ruyter remarked; "ready to fly aloft in a squall or board an enemy in battle."

In battle? Trelawny's questioning look was answered with an offhand explanation: the grab was fitted for war as well as peace. So was the dhow. What did Trelawny think of the dhow?

Trelawny thought very poorly of the dhow. That large mast forward and gigger mast aft her head, her stern and raking of bamboo work, gave her a clumsy look; she was "little better than a catamaran or a masuli boat."

De Ruyter laughed. Trelawny was not obliged to admire the dhow. It was not the dhow but the grab that he was to sail in. How would he like to run the grab down the coast to Goa—as captain?

Trelawny stared. It was a joke of course. He had had lessons in navigation; he was a midshipman—but to command a vessel! De Ruyter could not mean what he said; it was a joke.

But De Ruyter meant exactly what he said. Trelawny was to sail the grab to Goa; the crew would be under his command, the rais act merely as his assistant. He was to go on board that evening and sail at midnight. Meantime—De Ruyter's voice hardened—not a word of all this to any soul on shore. If he went to the tavern he was not to drink, for that might lead to talk. For the same reason he was to keep away from Walter.

Trelawny promised. He would not drink. He would not talk. He would keep away from Walter. He kept his promise. Sundown found him on board the grab.

The rais gave him a polite welcome; read a note De Ruyter had sent, and asked for orders. At what hour did the master intend to sail?

It was true then! Until now Trelawny had been half afraid he was to play the little boy given the end of the reins and told he is driving. But he managed a calm answer—modelling his manner on Aston's: they would sail at twelve, the boats were to be hoisted in, everything made ready for sea. He gave the men standing around a kind nod—modelled on Aston's nods—and went below for a careful inspection of his kingdom.

The more he saw of the grab, the better he liked her. Her waist was deep, pierced with portholes for guns, but battened except for the two forward and four after ones, which had six long nine-pounders. Her gunnels were armed with swivels. Her forecastle was raised, the poop low; under the poop was the main cabin. Roomy, well lighted, cooled from the stern ports and with two good berths, it had an air not only of comfort but of the picturesqueness that De Ruyter's taste could give to the most utilitarian surroundings. The walls, and the fore bulkhead ribbed with bamboo spars, were handsomely garnished with arms: muskets, bayonets, jagged Malay creeses and stars of pistols, their butts raying out, muzzles together. But the after part of the cabin was dedicated to peace; its shelves crammed with books, writing materials, drawing materials, nautical instruments, telescopes. Charts were suspended from the ceiling, and from the centre beam swung the transposed compass. As De Ruyter had remarked, the grab was well prepared for both peace and war.

Evening was here now. Lights twinkling yellow in Bombay windows; the peak of the Queen of Maharatta's Knitting Needle dim against the blue; Kanary sending out its warning to the sea. At eight o'clock the gong sounded for the sailors' supper. They gathered on deck, squatting on their heels in little circles, divided by caste, and ate their *messala* with relish, whether it was rice, ghee, dried bumbalo, curry, fresh fruit, or dried chillies. Trelawny, watching them, realized he too was hungry.

His supper over—it was an excellent meal—he disposed himself for a siesta. The couch was soft, a hooka usually induced drowsiness, he was accustomed to napping in the most uneasy spots. Now to his surprise sleep would not come. As he lay staring up at the low ceiling, the reason for this wakefulness occurred to him:

"Not being forbidden to sleep," he wrote later, "nor having the fear of punishment for neglect of duty over my head, I felt wakeful and alert. My mind was occupied with the responsibility with which my friend had entrusted me."

Responsibility. De Ruyter had known what he was about —De Ruyter always did know what he was about. Thanks to hard parents, stupid schoolmasters, and brutal officers, disobedience had become Trelawny's instinctive reaction to any order. Now, a sense of responsibility brought—not humility (he was never to acquire that virtue) but enough reasonableness to make him see discipline in a new light. No ship could be run without orders from above and obedience from below.

He went on deck to see that all was going as it should, and as he paced restlessly up and down, watching the dogvane that would signal a land breeze and departure, Nelson before Trafalgar could not have been more conscious of responsibility or more eager to be off.

The dogvane turned at last; by half-past twelve the grab was on her way. She glided gently out of the harbor—Tullreef on the larboard, Prongs on the starboard—on out into the open sea.

Dawn found Trelawny on deck, his telescope sweeping the horizon; as the mists cleared away he saw the dhow off the bow, a black speck against a pale blue sea. Press of sail brought the grab within hailing distance, and by eight o'clock De Ruyter was on board.

Breakfast over, conversation took the turn Trelawny had been impatiently awaiting: De Ruyter embarked on the story of his life.

It was throughout an *apologia pro vita sua* bristling with high-flown phrases: "conflicting broils of European adventurers and native princes . . . besotted barbarians flying at each other's throats in contention over the pasture while English wolves made off with the cattle . . . The vast monopolies strangling the East were devouring locusts who would squeeze their fathers' eyes out as if they were nutmegs. . . ." But with all its rodomontade De Ruyter's story, being true, was convincing. It was the long injustice and oppression of these "locust-wolves," the East India Company, that had turned him from an honest merchant into a rebel bent on revenge, dedicated to the freedom of India, eager to "drive the European nations back to the sea from whence they came." But that hope too had ended in disillusion. He had come to see that the old system here in the East, hoary with decay, must remain until a new one sprang up to take its place; and that, Time only could accomplish. It was the same everywhere; the same injustice, the same desire for freedom. "Europe was an antique bronze patched and smeared with whitewash; the finger of destruction already upon it." Revolution had done something for America, but not enough; freed her from the British yoke, but left her an oligarchy. France had freed herself only to fall back into the hands of a dictator. The world needed a great moral revolution; an upheaval of society. . . .

De Ruyter at last left the abstract for the practical, the past for the present. All his hope of freeing India at an end, he had turned back to the sea for a living: had gone to the Mauritius, fitted up an armed vessel on credit and, in a few months, had quadrupled his former earnings as an honest merchant. In short, he was a privateer, flying the French flag, ready to rob John Company whenever he got the chance —the cargo he had just sold in Bombay had been seized from a Company ship coming from Amboyna, an enemy of England, ready to fight an English vessel if the need arose.

De Ruyter must have offered this last statement with some trepidation—the boy was English! But Trelawny's face told him he was safe. The boy would accept whatever he chose to teach and follow wherever he chose to lead. He rose, gave a few last instructions: Trelawny was to wear Arab dress at Goa; the rais would see to that. They shook hands; he returned to the dhow; the grab went on her way down the coast.

Trelawny had much to occupy his mind now. He knew the truth at last. De Ruyter was—as he had hoped—a privateer! A privateer like Great-grandfather John Hawkins. A splendid trade—that of a privateer. Ignorant persons might call it by a harsher name—pirate, buccaneer. What did the term matter? Either way, it meant plenty of fighting. That it might mean fighting England did not disturb him in the least. His short stay in Bombay had been long enough to develop a hearty dislike of the East India Company. As for England, his England was limited to a child's acquaintance with a few miles of Cheshire's countryside and a few dull streets in Portsmouth and Gosport. Lisbon and Seville and Rio, he could visualize; London was only a name. He didn't know a soul in England outside of his immediate family, and since the day when he had been transferred from one man-of-war to another, without being allowed to go home and say goodbye, he had heard nothing from any of them; not even from his mother, or his sisters. He would never hear now: desertion from the Navy had ended any hope of that. Aston wouldn't speak to him if they were to meet; Walter had taken another road. East or West, De Ruyter was the only person anywhere who cared a rush whether he lived or died. Where would he be now if De Ruyter had not befriended him? A beggar, wandering through the streets of Bombay, hungry, sleeping by the roadside, always in fear of arrest. Desertion was a crime—they hanged men for desertion! No use worrying about that now. De Ruyter had told him to "become an Arab." He went to find the rais.

The rais proved an adroit costumer, and as Trelawny's features were of an aquiline cast, and his skin, naturally dark, had been burned to deep bronze by the Indian sun, he was more easily transformed than if he had been the ordinary English type, fair-haired and round-faced. In half an hour the rais told him to look in the tiny mirror on the cabin wall. He liked what he saw. His "make-up" was perfect. Loose, dark blue trousers and purple vest; a high black cap of Astrakhan lamb's wool; cashmere shawl around his waist stuck with a small creese; bare neck, arms, and ankles, well greased and highly polished; rough curly hair shorn off except for the one elf-lock on the crown that is preserved by Mohammedans for the convenience of black-eyed houris transporting them to paradise; teeth dyed the color of bright red chessmen; a "chaw" of betel nut in his cheek, he stalked majestically on deck to exhibit himself to the crew. They applauded; told him he could pass anywhere for an Arab. He was as pleased with himself as the heir to a dukedom greeted by the tenantry on his twenty-first birthday. A life of adventure was opening before him, and that was the only life worth living.

The voyage was uneventful. But Goa was ahead, and the thought of seeing Goa again was in itself exciting. It was off Goa that the frigate had met the little Malay vessel and Trelawny had had a first taste of hand-to-hand fighting, gained glory for himself, and humbled the Scotch lieutenant. But this time the rocky, pirate-infested coast of the Konkan seemed quiet enough. Nothing happened. In due time the grab arrived off Cape Ramas, the dhow came up; at sunrise the next day they passed under the fort of Aguada and anchored in the harbor of Goa.

The sun came up in splendor; touched the pale marble of monasteries and colleges with rose color, glittered on the ruined arches and colonnades and pinnacles of the ancient Portuguese town, once crowded and prosperous, now "a city of the dead." Her bunder had been breached by the sea, and only a few insignificant country vessels lay at anchor in her harbor.

The week that followed was devoted to business. The dhow had to be disposed of; the grab's cargo of rice and coffee sold, her supply of water completed. De Ruyter left his purser, the rais and Trelawny to see to this and went off up-country for a conference with the Rajah of Mysore. It was an anxious week. The grab was in imminent danger of being recognized for a privateer in spite of her innocent appearance, and when De Ruyter returned to Goa he had to risk his life every night interviewing secret agents in a ruined monastery at some distance from the town. So the week seemed endless. The grab's crew heaved a sigh of thankfulness when, at last, word came from De Ruyter that all was to be made ready for departure; they would sail that night as soon as he came aboard.

The night wore away. De Ruyter did not appear. It was long after midnight when a faint sound of muffled oars signalled his approach. A bad ten minutes followed. Lights and voices came from the city wharves. As De Ruyter drew near from one direction, a boatload of customs officers arrived from the other. They tried to come on board. But Trelawny had been told what to do in this emergency. He stood waiting, axe in hand, and as De Ruyter leaped onto the deck he cut the cable—that he happened to "take a chip" out of the leg of a sailor who stood too near was not considered important by anyone. They were off. "Oaths and threats, mingled with the rippling of the waves, died away. Crowded with sail, the grab majestically raced from the port and beheld the foe returning from their bootless expedition to the shore!"

Day broke. Harbor and land were blended now in a vague blur of lilac and cream color, enveloped in transparent vapor broken by the fleecy clouds of morning. De Ruyter's glass searched the horizon; the only sails in sight were a few innocent country vessels. They were safe. Breakfast could be enjoyed in peace.

One by one the members of the staff gathered in the cabin. No group of men ever differed so widely in race, religion, character, and appearance. There were five. The rais was an Arab from Madagascar, a devout Mohammedan; De Ruyter, an American and a freethinker; Trelawny, an English boy with neither nationality nor religion. But the three were on a par as far as looks and physique were concerned. The other two, however—Van Scolpvelt, the ship's surgeon, and Louis, purser and steward—might have posed for a medieval carver of miserere seats. They were not only grotesque in themselves; they were still more grotesque seen as a pair.

Louis, a cross of Dutch and French, with a broad, square Holland torso supported by thin French legs, suggested "a hogshead of Schiedam on stilts"; his pumpkin face would have been all Dutch except for a Gallic nose, "like a ripe fig with the stalk uppermost," that had given him the nickname of "Louis le Grand."

Van Scolpvelt, on the other hand, although a Hollander, was a thin, wiry, sinister little creature, his face puckered like a withered shaddock. His head was as bald as an egg; he had no eyebrows or eyelashes, but his long, thin neck and dry, sapless little body were dotted with red bristles, and when stripped for operating, he bore a horrible resemblance to a hairy red caterpillar. His age could not even be guessed at; but his faculties were unimpaired. He had come to De Ruyter from a Dutch East Indiaman because, in that peaceable craft, he could not count on as many cadavers for post-mortems as he needed for the experiments that were his only interest in life. His hands, made for operating, were long and narrow, so fleshless that when he shaded a candle the light would show clear through the palm, with supple sensitive fingers clawed like the talons of a bird of prey. He was as cruel as a vulture, too; if he imagined himself to be on the track of something new in surgery or medicine, he would vivisect anything—man, woman, or child; bird, beast, or fish—that he could get his clawlike fingers upon. He knew the value of those fingers. "Wherever a ball goes," he would say, "I can follow it!" And that skinny forefinger, quivering like the antenna of an insect, would prod the air with an eagerness that made Trelawny shudder.

Trelawny, of course, hated the surgeon. The man's hideousness was repulsive—Trelawny could not abide even moderately ugly people. He loathed the cruelty that, in his ignorance of science, seemed to him both senseless and revolting. Even the surgeon's books were unreadable, couched in strange jargon and illustrated with disgusting plates of organs, entrails, and deformities in crude reds and blues.

But he liked Louis. Louis was good company when he was not too drunk, an excellent cook if he could get the proper materials and ingenious if he could not.

Today, Louis's breakfast, from the fresh provisions laid in at Goa, was relished by everyone. There was no talk until it was over; then conversation turned to last night's adventures. It was agreed that it had all gone off extremely well. Everyone praised Trelawny's presence of mind—except, perhaps, the chipped sailor nursing a bandaged leg. The present voyage was discussed. It developed that De Ruyter had changed his plans. The grab was now making for the Isle of France (until recently known as Mauritius); he was the bearer of important despatches from certain persons in India to the French government at Port Louis. Wind and weather permitting, they would reach the Laccadive Islands, the first port of call, in time to permit a detour farther on if any very rich merchandise were reported in the neighborhood.

But the wind soon died. For four days the grab lay "a painted ship upon a painted ocean." In similar conditions on the frigate, Trelawny would have fretted away the time in grumbling, mischief, and sleep. Now to his surprise he found himself "transformed," as he wrote later, "from a drowsy boy to a most active and energetic man. Time seemed to go like the swallow."

For De Ruyter was too wise to let a calm get on the crew's nerves; he kept them busy. The grab must be given a more warlike trim. Four verdigrised brass nine-pounders, secreted under the ballast on the keelson, were hoisted up and mounted; shot lockers on deck fitted and filled; two furnaces prepared for heating shot red-hot; a good supply of cartridges, rockets, and blue lights manufactured; the magazine put in order, and between-decks cleaned and whitewashed. The men were mustered and quartered, exercised and practiced with guns and small arms, and Trelawny was instructed in the use of the spear and creese by the rais.

In all these activities De Ruyter himself took the lead. He was a born leader of men; never tired, never out of temper. Trelawny copied him in everything; easily in physical matters, less easily when it came to evenness of temper.

These days of calm weather were not all activity. There were talks on deck in the warm still blue evenings, the Southern Cross swinging overhead; endless discussion of freedom and revolution; prophecies that dictators would soon vanish from the earth. De Ruyter's library was that of a well read man; it gave Trelawny the only education he was ever to experience. Shakespeare would have been there, of course, for De Ruyter was a Shakespearian scholar; Plutarch's *Lives,* and biographies of modern soldiers—Cromwell, Marlborough, and Clive; Hume's *England,* Gibbon's *Decline and Fall;* a few novels—Defoe, Smollett, Fielding, Sterne; a little poetry—Pope, Ossian, Milton; Trelawny's old favorite, Bligh's *Mutiny of the Bounty;* the works of Bentham and Malthus, and the apostles of socialism and the "return to nature"—Volney, Rousseau, Bernardin de Saint-Pierre (who had, as it happened, laid the scene of a pretty tale, *Paul and Virginia,* in the very island to which the grab was making her reluctant way—the Isle of France), and many technical books on mathematics and navigation.

So, take it all around, Trelawny's youth was provided with such a balanced ration of mental and physical improvement that he could have echoed the Reverend Isaac Watts, D.D.:

> "In books, or work, or healthful play,
> Let my first years be past,
> That I may give for every day
> Some good account at last!"

Would Dr. Watts have approved of the "account" to be rendered at the end of this voyage? Not altogether. He would have deprecated the lack of godliness only too evident on board—daily prostrations of Mohammedan Arabs not coming under the head of worship. The grab's decks were never, of a Sabbath morning, spread with awnings and white hammock cloths fore and aft, her capstan covered with a Union Jack, as was the invariable custom on the East Indiamen, where, as a contemporary of Trelawny's noted, "Sunday was strictly observed; the captain being liable to a pecuniary penalty for failure to perform divine service. The crew, for the most part, were very attentive." Nor was De Ruyter accustomed, like Lord Nelson, to invoking the protection of a Higher Power before going into action, or to falling on his knees after a victory and returning thanks for the vast number of enemy corpses that strewed the sea.

Dr. Watts would, of course, have objected to De Ruyter's letters of marque—France being England's hereditary enemy and also a notoriously frivolous and papistical nation—but not to privateering in itself. Pacifism had not yet been discovered by the clergy, and privateering not only was legal but would remain so until 1858, when the Treaty of Paris remarked, with admirable terseness: "Privateering is and remains abolished."

Although the days of calm were not ill spent it was a relief when, at last, a thunderstorm cleared the air and next day a northwest wind brought the grab in sight of the Laccadive Islands at sunrise.

The approach needed daylight. For the little palm-tufted coral islands had never been accurately surveyed, and the bones of many ships—from Phoenician galleys to Dutch, French, and English East Indiamen—strewed the surrounding reefs. But De Ruyter knew these waters like the palm of his hand (Trelawny must have been getting useful lessons in practical as well as theoretical navigation), and the grab drew near in safety.

Now the sea became gay with proas, darting from island to island, marvels of speed and efficiency, more like birds than boats. One of them came up to windward of the grab, and passed her as if she had been stationary, though she was driving along under a staggering topgallant breeze. The men standing on the proa's outrigger seemed skimming on the waves or plunging straight through them. Glimpsed for a second, then enveloped in a shower of spray heavy as a breaking waterspout, the canoe flashed past like a swallow and vanished.

A marvellous sight. As usual, De Ruyter improved the occasion (in peaceful moments, he seems to have been more like Rollo's Jonas than Mr. Abbott would have been able to believe), delivered an interesting little lecture on proas, whipped out a sketchbook—he was handy with his pencil—and made all clear with a drawing; and when Trelawny had learned all there was to know about proas he sent him ashore to buy bananas and vegetables for supper.

Next morning Trelawny was given another errand. Sunrise showed three large Persian vessels lying becalmed some two leagues to the westward, and he was sent with a guard of ten armed men to pick up information. The information he brought back was exactly what De Ruyter wanted. It seemed the Persians had just been attacked by a Malay pirate cruising off the Persian Gulf, plundered of a rich cargo, and the crews treated with extreme cruelty. Wind and weather permitting, the pirate might be intercepted on her way home through the Straits of Malacca. The grab prepared at once for sea.

A long chase followed, tedious, and coming to an unsatisfactory conclusion. They caught sight of the pirate in the "misty dawn of a shining day." The tricolor of France went fluttering to the grab's masthead, and Trelawny, as a final touch of preparation, was given her letters of marque to read. But the Malay was foolishly bent on escape. It was useless; six o'clock found her within long shot. She was hailed, in Malay, and ordered to send an officer to the grab bringing her ship's papers—a French commission gave the grab this right. But the Malay would not give in. A warning shot was fired over her. She returned it with a volley of scrap iron, nails, and bits of glass that rattled in the grab's rigging, spattered on the deck, and wounded three of her men. De Ruyter's warning changed instantly to a long, low, well directed fire.

But the Malay, torn to pieces, still refused to give in. Boats were sent to board her, and were driven back. A last summons to surrender brought no response. A pirate could not be left to roam the sea, a menace to shipping. At last, with extreme reluctance, De Ruyter decided she would have to be sunk, treasure and all.

It was dark now. With sunrise the grab's big guns opened fire with red-hot shot prepared during the night. The fiery hail brought puffs of smoke from the wreck. The smoke became a cloud, streaked with scarlet. Sparks ran up the rigging. Sails caught. And now the men, smoked out like bees, began crawling up from below—an immense number of them, two or three hundred, crawling up on all fours until the decks were thick. Red tongues licked out from hatchways and portholes; the men jumped into the sea, and through the rents in her sides her cargo came pouring out. The grab's crew yelled that they could see the glitter of gold dust, pearls and rubies, the sheen of silk, and smell the scent of attar of roses as that rich cargo slid out into the sea. But Trelawny saw only the drowning men. The firelit water was dotted with black heads bobbing about, rising and falling with the waves . . . A tremendous explosion burst from the Malay. The grab shuddered, and as the wind, hushed in the concussion, let her sails go they flapped against the mast like clapping hands. The pirate ship went down stern foremost. A swirling ripple glimmered through the smoke screen; became bordered by wreckage. A confusion of spars, tackle, and dead bodies, drifting about, slowly widened to a vast circle. Only one head was left now; a feeble war cry rang across the water, a fist was raised in defiance; vanished; a few bubbles rose to the surface . . . The smoke lifted, gathered itself into a cloud that rose majestically higher and higher. High overhead it paused, hung motionless. It seemed to Trelawny—his eyes following it awestruck as it rose—that "the pirate ship was changed not destroyed. Her crew were pursuing their vocation in the air."

De Ruyter, seeing the look on his face, remarked, with intentional matter-of-factness, that it had been a painful sight, but the pirates had deserved their fate; and told Trelawny to get the crew to work. The grab must return to her proper course as soon as possible; there were still those despatches for the Isle of France to be delivered.

The boats were hoisted in, the grab's sails spread, she turned southward. But her crew were a good deal the worse for wear, and no one felt any elation over their recent victory. Even Van Scolpvelt was disappointed with the result of the fight. Only two men had been seriously wounded—a Swede and an Arab—and just as he was preparing to take off the Swede's foot with a neat little instrument of his own invention—a "hexagonal, transverse, treble-toothed, revolving saw" that could tear through flesh and bone as easily as through the leg of a table—De Ruyter interfered: "they had better wait a while and make sure"; and although the Arab was so obliging as to die, De Ruyter would not let him have the body for a post-mortem. It seemed that Arabs did not like post-mortems. This indifference to scientific research was enraging, but De Ruyter's word was law. Van Scolpvelt had to watch a fine cadaver go down to the sharks entirely unexplored.

The man was buried in the sea. No detail of Mohammedan ritual was omitted. The head was shaved; eyes, nose, mouth, and ears stuffed with cotton and camphor; the body washed, anointed, and bound into a mummy; and with a twelve-pound shot tied to his feet, the Arab slid overboard.

His comrades could see him go with satisfaction. It had been a nice funeral, and there was no need to worry about the ghost. All his joints had been broken, so the ghost would be unable to "walk" and come back to make trouble on the ship.

But Trelawny had watched the proceedings with growing distaste. Burial at sea was a horrible business. He thought of the sharks, he visualized that mummy tiptoeing in an eternal chassé back and forth across the ocean floor, and decided that, if he ever had to bury a person he loved, it should not be in the sea. He would find some better way.

These gloomy anticipations were gone almost as they came. Before the bubbling ripple on the water had been wiped out by a wave, he was back again in the cheerful present, searching the horizon for some promise of adventure exciting and more profitable than the last.

But the days went by, and only innocent country vessels dotted the sea. They reached the Laccadives again, moved on to Diego Rayes, and put in there for food and water, passed that long cluster of islands called the Brothers and, keeping more to the south, took a fresh departure from Roquepez. And still no prizes! It began to look as if those important despatches for the Isle of France might actually reach their destination.

Then one gray morning adventure came. Not, however, the sort the grab was after. Two vessels showed through the mist. Another long, long chase began. But with the parts reversed. Now it was the grab that was making frantic efforts to escape, for the vessels were English frigates come to these waters for the express purpose of catching French privateers on the way to the Isle of France.

Day after day that chase went on. De Ruyter succeeded in shaking off one of the frigates too slow to keep up with the grab, but the other refused to give up the pursuit. She seemed to anticipate his every move. Evening might see her fading into a safe distance; when morning broke there she would be again, nearer than before. At last, he decided to run for an island he knew well surrounded by dangerous reefs and maneuver the grab into a cove "scarcely larger than an albatross's nest," reached by a channel so narrow and tortuous that the frigate could not follow except with boats; and that, she might not dare to try.

The grab reached the island, pierced its ring of reefs and made for the channel. Not even De Ruyter would have attempted to take a ship through that labyrinth in bad weather; fortunately, the sea was like glass. Slowly, slowly the grab was angled in and came to anchor in the cove.

The crew stood about the decks, listening for the sound of oars. The frigate's boats had been in close pursuit when the grab left the open. If they followed in, they might at any moment come in sight around a headland at the entrance to the channel.

A long half-hour of tense silence followed. The heat was fearful. Everyone stared at the headland. No one spoke. Now and then, Van Scolpvelt would emerge from the hold where he had been preparing gratings for the wounded, ask hopefully when the carnage might be expected to begin, and disappear—"like a carrion kite smelling blood!" Trelawny muttered angrily. De Ruyter gave him an anxious glance—the strain was getting on the boy's nerves. If the boats followed in —English boats flying the Union Jack . . .

The silence broke suddenly. A groan came from the crew. The bow of a boat was rounding the point! It flew the Union Jack. Other boats followed close. The Englishmen, as they saw the grab, broke into a cheer.

It was answered by an Arab war cry. The French tricolor fluttered to the grab's masthead; she opened fire. The fight was on!

And it was a splendid fight. Trelawny had never enjoyed himself so much in all his life. The red and blue flutter of the Union Jack had held him for a second. Then loyalty to De Ruyter took him into the battle, and, once in, he forgot everything else—what or why he was trying to kill—in the wild exhilaration of the game. He was wounded in the arm, cut and bruised by a pistol butt thrust into his mouth. He felt no pain. . . . It became a hand-to-hand encounter. . . . British boats were stove in, water and shore strewn with wounded men, the grab's deck spattered with blood . . . At what seemed the very height of the turmoil—all at once—the end came.

De Ruyter shouted an order. Trelawny stood still, his cutlass dropped to his side. He stared about him incredulously. Yes, it was over. English boats in retreat, English seamen laying down their arms. It was over. . . .

He became aware of pain, sharp pain, of blood trickling down his face; he was bleeding like a pig. . . . He stood swaying a little, swabbing at the blood with his sash. . . . A tall English officer came running along the deck, brandishing a cutlass. De Ruyter ran to meet him. There was a flash of steel. But the Englishman was no match for De Ruyter; his cutlass bent like a hoop. He flung it from him with a curse, and surrendered.

As the cutlass went slithering along the deck, Trelawny's heart gave a sickening thump and turned over inside him. The man was Aston!

They came towards him. He got out a faint "Aston—don't you know me!" Aston gave him no answering look of recognition. He staggered. De Ruyter caught him as he fell. He went off into a dead faint.

When he came to, Aston's face was bending close to him. For a moment it was the "drowning frolic" over again. He was coming up—up—up—through deep water, struggling for breath, calling to Aston for help. He gave Aston an imploring look. Aston smiled. He closed his eyes and let himself drift out on a wave of unconsciousness.

Two days later the grab was on her way again. The English wounded had been returned to the frigate, with Captain De Ruyter's compliments, in the grab's long boat flying a flag of truce. The prisoners had been made as comfortable on board the grab as narrow quarters would permit. In spite of Van Scolpvelt's scientific experimentation his patients were recovering. The weather had cooled off. Even the English officers—Aston, a midshipman, and an officer of marines —were in fairly good spirits when they assembled in the cabin for supper that evening. They had put up a good fight—it was the fortune of war.

An appetizing smell of roast fowl drifted in from the galley. The result proved as good as the prophecy. De Ruyter brought out his best Madeira. Louis added a bottle of Schiedam, "of the proper bamboo color, with the taste of flame mellowed by juniper smoke." Cigars were lighted; hookas bubbled; conversation turned to discussion of the fight. It was agreed that the grab's position had made her impregnable; that the English captain (not "Old Hoofs"; Aston had left that frigate soon after Trelawny's desertion) had been a fool to send his men into such an obvious deathtrap. Compliments were exchanged. De Ruyter was thanked for his consideration; he remarked that it was an honor to entertain such gallant enemies. Take it all round, it was an extremely jolly evening.

Trelawny had enjoyed every minute of it. His arm was sore and stiff, he had a nasty unhealed wound in his side, his head was bandaged, and his face a mass of contusions; but he was as gay as a lark. Aston had forgiven him—or, at least, intimated that bygones would be bygones—and a feast was the proper finish to glorious victory. He remembered that evening, and the days that followed, as among the best of his life.

"Everything went by pleasantly and merrily," he wrote long after. "I was associated with the two men I most admired and loved, Aston and De Ruyter. Although, to a casual observer, no two men could seem more dissimilar, at the core they were the same; they had the same stability of character, heroic courage, gentle and affectionate manners and open manly bearing. They soon grew fast friends. I now wanted only Walter; and then, if a deluge had swallowed up all the world and the grab had been our ark, I should have lost nothing to weep for."

A merry existence on the grab had, however, one drawback. She was too crowded, the presence of so many unexpected visitors made food and accommodations difficult, and Louis was beginning to wonder how long his chicken coops would stand the strain, when just in time, before Franklin's aphorism "In three days guests, like fish, begin to stink" could come true, a strange sail hove in sight.

She proved to be a French corvette. De Ruyter went on board her for a conference. The captain was an old friend of his, a man who could be trusted. So De Ruyter's prisoners —with the exception of Aston and four seamen who preferred their present quarters—were handed over to him. This accomplished, the French captain, "a young man of engaging manners," came to return De Ruyter's call. Introduced to Aston and Trelawny, he invited them to dine with him at four o'clock on the corvette.

The dinner went off very pleasantly. De Ruyter and Aston both spoke French, and Trelawny could follow the conversation, having already picked up a little French from Louis as well as a smattering of Arabic and Malay from the crew— this facility for languages was to be very useful to him in after life. He listened with growing excitement. It appeared that the corvette was on the way to Madagascar to investigate recent depredations of the Maratti pirates, and her captain wanted De Ruyter to join the expedition!

But De Ruyter hesitated. He was taking despatches to the Isle of France; he was not at all sure that he wanted to fight for Europeans against natives—whether Dutch, French, or Portuguese, they were all, he remarked, in the habit of "slaughtering natives whenever they wanted a salad or a fresh egg." But when the French captain reminded him that the Maratti were slave traders, which lowered them in his estimation, and urged him at least to follow alongside for a while in the hope of meeting some vessel bound for the Isle of France that would deliver his despatches, he consented.

The grab was headed for Madagascar. "The weather," Trelawny wrote, "being particularly fine, with little wind stirring, we passed our evenings very pleasantly in giving parties alternately on board the grab and the corvette." By day, however, he was watching the sea for friendly sails as eagerly as he had been used to watching it for possible prizes. But the sea remained empty. He was beginning to despair when a beautiful swanlike vessel hove in sight, an American schooner.

As soon as her captain realized that the grab and the corvette were French she hove to, lowered a boat—evidently her captain was coming to call. The grab and the corvette paused, awaiting his arrival.

As the boat approached, Trelawny stood with De Ruyter and Aston at the grab's rail admiring the graceful ship with a starred flag waving over her taffrail. They praised "the arrowy sharpness of her bow, the gradually receding fineness of her quarters; the raking masts that seemed to taper to nothing, the swallow-tailed vanes fluttering above like fireflies." De Ruyter remarked that the schooner was "a nautical wonder, surpassing all other vessels in beauty and exquisite proportions as the gazelle surpasses all animated nature," and she was, he added, with pride, "an exclusively American product; strange to say no other nation seemed able to build or work a schooner." This vessel, he went on, appeared to be the fast-sailing, well-armed sort that drove what was known as a "forced trade" for drugs and spices. On leaving home, they usually made first for a French port in order to secure a commission and letters of marque, or at least take on a French captain who could serve, temporarily, as commanding officer if they happened to be stopped and questioned by an English man-of-war; the United States and Great Britain being for the moment at peace, all American privateers were obliged to fly a French flag.

Meanwhile the schooner's boat had been drawing near. The captain came aboard the grab and was warmly welcomed by De Ruyter, who was eager for news of Boston, his "home town."

The news was not any too good. It seemed that relations between the United States and Great Britain were becoming strained almost to breaking point. Britain's "orders in council" and her insistence on the "right of search" had caused bad feeling. It looked like war. But New England was opposed to war. In fact, Massachusetts went so far as to say that if President Madison took the country into war, she would secede—after all there was such a thing as States' Rights. But it might all blow over. The captain sincerely hoped it would. He most certainly did not want to have to go home and fight England—or any other country for that matter. This war going on now between England and France was bad enough. He had narrowly escaped from an English squadron in the Bay of Biscay and from another at the Cape of Good Hope.

This last remark brought a question from De Ruyter: Was the captain aware that the Isle of France was being blockaded by the British?

This was news to the American—very bad news. What, he asked, did De Ruyter advise him to do?

De Ruyter was reassuring: If the schooner avoided Port Louis and made for the insignificant little town of Port Bourbon on the opposite side of the island, she would get in without difficulty—and he added some instructions that might be useful in entering the rather intricate harbor of Port Bourbon. The captain thanked him warmly, made no objection to taking De Ruyter's despatches, gave him a pipe of cognac, a hogshead of claret, and a supply of edibles, shook hands all round, and returned to his ship.

Within a few hours the schooner had faded from sight, making straight for the Isle of France. Grab and corvette, still in company, went on to Madagascar.

CHAPTER VI

"Deep, deep below the bay, the seaweed and the spray,
Embalmed in amber every pirate lies."
—Vachel Lindsay.

The Maratti were a peculiarly savage tribe of native Africans; warlike, cruel, and hitherto unconquerable even by Europeans. From time immemorial they had lived off the natives of eastern Madagascar and the near-by islands; raiding their villages and plundering their vessels, but meeting with occasional reverses until they formed an alliance with the pirates of Nossi Ibrahim and could venture to attack the Europeans of Madagascar, the Isle of Bourbon and the Mauritius, where they slaughtered, burned, and looted with such success that the Dutch in the Mauritius, weary of their forays, finally allowed the French to take over their beautiful island and rename it the Isle of France, and sailed away to South Africa, finding Hottentots more tolerable than pirates.

When, one by one, other promising settlements had to be abandoned, a punitive expedition sent by the French, Portuguese, and Dutch succeeded in wiping out a fleet of war canoes, and the brigands were driven back from the seacoast to the mountains. But the looting soon began again. And now it was far worse, for slaves became the prime object of their raids. The business was well organized, and the Madagascar pirates soon had a monopoly. They specialized in slaves as the Dutch specialized in spice and the English in tea. The islands were divided into districts, their population counted, and estimates made as to the probable rate of breeding. Every spring and autumn a fleet of proas was sent to visit the islands in rotation; the latest crops of healthy boys and girls were harvested, marked with a red-hot iron and black powder, and carried back either to Nossi Ibrahim or to St. Sebastian, another pirate stronghold at the northern end of Madagascar where the island stretches a long finger out into the sea. Here in these mud-walled towns, the captives were held until a profitable sale could be arranged with English, Dutch, French, and Portuguese traders, who shipped them off to foreign markets; some of them, no doubt, in the end finding themselves weeping like Ruth "amid the alien corn" of Carolina and Georgia and Virginia.

As Europeans had no smallest objection to the slave trade, the business might have gone on unchecked if the Maratti had not made a bad mistake. They seized a French ship carrying a load of sheep and poultry the French had looted in a raid of Madagascar, slaughtered every man on board, and made off with the sheep. This was too much for French honor to stomach. At first a total extermination of the inhabitants of Madagascar was considered necessary. But as most of the French fleet was busy elsewhere fighting the English it was finally decided to despatch a corvette—the corvette commanded by De Ruyter's friend, the "young man of engaging manners"—to "investigate this act of piracy" and do whatever seemed necessary under the circumstances—or rather, whatever the corvette was capable of doing.

This was not very much. The nearer the French captain got to Madagascar, the less he liked the prospect of engaging the Maratti singlehanded, and he naturally did his best to enlist De Ruyter's sympathies. But although the despatches had been provided for, De Ruyter still hesitated to commit himself to taking sides. His hesitations annoyed the captain and, of course, exasperated Trelawny, by now so eager for a fight that he did not care a sou marquee which side was in the right so long as he could fight somebody.

In the meantime the two vessels continued to companion each other, separating by day in order to avoid observation and coming together again at night for an exchange of hos-

pitality. But the most delightful dinner party was a poor substitute for adventure. Trelawny continued to hope that De
Ruyter would see things in a properly belligerent manner before it was too late, and just before they reached Madagascar,
De Ruyter's last scruples disappeared.

They fell in with a bunch of Arab trading vessels that were
limping home after an encounter with a fleet of Maratti
proas, eighteen of them, each carrying from eighteen to forty
men. Two of the Arab ships had been seized, the rest plundered of their cargoes and all their able-bodied men taken for
slaves, leaving a handful of old, sick, and wounded to get
home as best they could, starving on a meagre supply of rice
and water. Then the proas had made for Madagascar, in order to unload their captives, probably at St. Sebastian, and
then go on to visit the islands in the Mozambique Channel.

De Ruyter and the French captain met at once for a conference. If the Arabs were right, many of the pirates must be
absent from the nest, and this would be a good moment to
strike. It was decided to land near St. Sebastian, surprise the
town during the night, plunder and burn it, destroy the forti-
fications, and rescue the prisoners. This arranged, the corvette lent the grab two brass cannon and fifteen soldiers, and
they moved on towards Madagascar.

Early one morning they came in sight of mountains and a
rocky shore, the coast of an enormous island, the second
largest in the world, a thousand miles long: Madagascar. A
land of marvels and monstrosities; its forests grew the "man-
eating tree" which lures human beings up into its top and
squeezes them to cider with its branches; there the dodo
once lived in reality and the roc in imagination; its beaches
saw the ventures of Sindbad and the old Man of the Sea, of
the Cid and Vasco da Gama. There most of the great pirates
began their careers. When Captain Avery, mate of the *Charles
II,* seized his own ship, he made for Madagascar before he
pounced on a vessel of the Great Mogul and other rich prizes
whose cargoes of silks and jewelry and spices, despatched to

New England, were welcomed as a godsend by pious house-wives. It was in Madagascar that Captain Kidd, in the *Adventure* galley, decided to change from privateer to pirate, beginning the career that ended, in the course of time, with a noose around his neck. For the depredations of "robbers upon the sea" came under the same head as acts "done within the body of an English county," and though land thieves occasionally got off, pirates, considered *hostis humani generis*, were never given the benefit of the doubt or of clergy.

In Kidd's day Madagascar was the "worst nest of pirates in the world," but from time immemorial the island had bred pirates. A thousand years before Christ, her vessels had harassed the fleets of Hiram of Tyre carrying gold of Ophir to King Solomon for the "lily work" of his temple at Jerusalem, and two thousand years later—on into the end of the nineteenth century—the pirate trade was still going on briskly and profitably between Africa and the various ports of the Indian Archipelago.

For centuries Nossi Ibrahim on the east coast had been Madagascar's chief market; and De Ruyter knew that it must, of course, be crowded with slaves in need of rescue. But he was too wise to attack it with inadequate forces. So the grab and the corvette moved cautiously northward towards the smaller town of St. Sebastian, piloted by De Ruyter who knew every inch of the coast. In the dimness of twilight a narrow, tortuous channel was safely navigated; at midnight they reached the end of the island and came to anchor near shore, but behind a cape that hid them from the town.

The night was cloudy, with gusts of rain. In thick darkness, a hundred and twenty well armed men and officers landed on the beach. De Ruyter was in command; the French captain, unaccustomed to savage warfare, was remaining on board his vessel, but keeping watch on the operations. As the town had three entrance ports in its mud walls, the invaders were divided into three parties: De Ruyter, with fifty men, was to attack the main entrance; a French lieutenant, with thirty-five, approach from the beach; Trelawny, with only thirty—but they were De Ruyter's best Arabs armed with lances and short carbines—was to climb the cliffs ready to come down on the town from above. De Ruyter gave his orders: the town was to be taken with as little bloodshed as possible; only armed men who refused quarter were to be killed, women and children were to go free. The parties were to proceed to their posts in silence, and wait. At dawn he would fire a rocket, and at that signal they were all to attack at once. This clear, he sent them off.

Trelawny and his men went scrambling up a steep cliff only to find themselves on the edge of a ravine with the sound of rushing water coming from below. They lost time finding a better approach; but he hurried his men on at a furious pace, and it was not yet dawn when they emerged on a hilltop and discovered a narrow stony sheep path overgrown with prickly pear and tangled shrubs that seemed to lead down to the town.

Trelawny and two men descended the path. The ground gradually smoothed underfoot; they could hear the surf beating on the rocky shore. At last, close below them, they made out a huddle of low white huts, like beehives, barely visible in the first pale light of dawn. He sent his men back to bring up the rest of the party and went on alone to the wall. It was low and crumbling; a mud hut not much larger than a swallow's nest clung to the side, below it was a hole, evidently the entrance he was expected to take.

The men arrived. They crept down and waited in the shadow of the wall, waited restlessly, for dawn was glimmering through the falling rain, but no signal came from De Ruyter.

At last, a rocket curved hissing over the town. Trelawny answered, and his rocket was scarcely alight before he was crashing through the hole in the wall. A guard sprang up from under his feet; he grappled with him, killed him, and hurried on. His men followed, chopping and slashing their way into the heart of the town.

The surprise was complete. In a wild confusion of war cries, Arab and French, of screams and flying feet, the pirates scurried about like rats. Some tried to climb the walls, others tried to burrow through them. None would surrender. They were killed like rats.

It was a brutal business—Trelawny was to remember it with disgust and shame. De Ruyter's orders were disregarded; the excuse for attack—rescue of the Arab prisoners—forgotten even by Trelawny, until De Ruyter called to him. The prisoners, he shouted, were over there in those huts on the sand hills.

Trelawny was only just in time. The pirate women were stabbing the prisoners as they lay bound hand and foot in heaps on the ground. His men despatched the hags, he went on into an inner tent. Here he found an Arab flat on his back, bound and fastened to a stake driven into the earth. He was covered with blood, half dead, feebly warding off the attack of an old vixen humped on his chest jabbing at him with a coconut knife and trying to reach a young girl who was crouched at his feet.

Trelawny caught the old woman by the twist of cloth about her waist, pulled her off, killed her, and threw her away. His men unbound the old Arab. Trelawny lifted up the girl, untied her hands, wrapped a cloak around her, turned to the Arab. There was a desperate question in the dying eyes. Trelawny knelt down and drew his creese. The girl screamed. But Trelawny placed the weapon in the old man's hand. It was a sign of friendship; the old man understood, and relaxed. Trelawny spoke reassuringly:

"We are friends, Father," he said. "Fear not. We are friends."

The old man gave him another searching glance and seemed satisfied. He caught Trelawny's hand and put it to his cold lips; with infinite difficulty, he drew a ring off his own hand and placed it on Trelawny's, fumbled for his daughter's hand, joined it to Trelawny's, held them together for a moment, mumbled a blessing, and fell back dead. The girl clung to him sobbing. Trelawny left her and went out of doors, faint with loss of blood—he was badly wounded—and gasping for air. He was trying to bandage his leg when De Ruyter appeared with Aston—who had come on shore not, of course, to fight but to see the pirate town. De Ruyter was shouting an order as he came: the town was to be evacuated at once. The Maratti were rallying on the hills outside the walls.

Trelawny dashed back into the tent, followed by Aston. The poor girl still lay shivering and sobbing and clinging to her father, imploring him to speak to her; refusing to believe that he was dead. But the Maratti war cries were sounding nearer; there was no time for persuasion. He snatched her up in his arms, wound his abbah around her, gave her to Aston, and told him to carry her to the beach; he would come behind and guard her—not from the pirates but from their own men, all half crazy now with pillage and bloodshed, the French soldiers drunk as well, making their way out of the blazing town—it had been set on fire—down to the shore quarrelling with one another over the treasure, bent double under the bundles of loot they carried on their backs.

Trelawny forced a way for Aston through the confusion. They reached the beach. It was strewn with booty; gold and silver, spices, India muslins and Persian shawls, armlets and anklets and necklaces, maize, corn, rice, salt fish, turtles, and rakee lay piled in heaps on the shore. The best treasure, the slaves—male and female, of all ages and countries—were being loaded into the longboats to be rowed out to the corvette waiting with the grab outside the reef.

There was not a moment to lose now. The beach was so exposed to the fire of the Maratti ranged along the cliff tops, shooting down at the invaders with bows and matchlocks, that the grab and corvette's men suffered more during the embarkation than in the sacking of the town.

But at length the last boat was loaded. It shoved off. At once the Maratti came down like a flock of crows. Bullets, arrows, and stones rattled on the boat, and the fiercest savages even swam out to sea in pursuit, yelling defiance and retreating only when the enemy were far out of reach.

But no one from either vessel had been left behind. Aston and Trelawny had managed to get the Arab girl on board unhurt, though half dead with fright. Trelawny told Louis she was to have his cabin—he was giving it over to her; asked the rais to see to her comfort, and straightway forgot the girl's existence.

The mountains of Madagascar faded on the sky line. It was suppertime. Louis provided a magnificent supper: turtle soup, callipash and callipee, and an egg dish of his own invention so choice that burgomasters and ambassadors had, he declared, offered him vast sums in vain for the recipe.

But Trelawny was soon satisfied. The victory had left him depressed rather than elated. It was his watch; he went on deck and stood at the rail gazing at the sunset. It faded; the sea changed from blue to dusky olive, and the moon rose amidst a flock of little fleecy clouds like lambs grazing on the hills of heaven. The sea was empty, only the corvette's black hull and white wings broke the vast horizon. He sighed as he looked at her swaying gently in the soft night air, thinking of the slaves in her hold; not, of course, destined for freedom; chained now like beasts, in that worst of all dungeons, a ship's hold below the sea . . .

De Ruyter appeared on deck. Trelawny became suddenly aware that the wound in his leg was paining him, that he was stiff and bruised from head to foot and heavy with sleep. He went below, tumbled into a berth "without troubling to unrig," and fell asleep as his head touched the pillow. "Perhaps," he wrote years later, "it was a magic pillow—I wish I had it now."

Whether or not the pillow were enchanted, strange to say, night brought no dreams of the little captive Arab maid. Nor did daylight remind him of her. In fact, Trelawny never thought of her at all as the grab scudded merrily along with a favoring wind, accompanied by the corvette. They were both bound for the Isle of France, for De Ruyter was intending to enjoy a few weeks' holiday there; he had a country place in the hills. They were not, of course, making for Port Louis because of the British blockade, but for Port Bourbon on the southeast coast, whose harbor was so little frequented the grab could be sure of lying out the monsoon there in safety.

The prospect of dry land and country-house life was agreeable. Meantime, the weather held good and the days on shipboard went pleasantly by. Madagascar lay five hundred miles behind, and the Isle of France was almost in sight before Trelawny remembered that he had rescued a girl and it might be a good idea to find out how she was getting on.

He went in search of the rais. The old man was only too glad to talk about the little Arab lady. He knew all about her and her family. She was of high rank. Her father had been Sheik of the Island of Sohar, a beautiful island in the Persian Gulf; his tribe, the Beni-Bedar K'urcish, was a noble tribe ancient as the sands of the sea. The rais felt it an honor to be allowed to care for the lady. One of her waiting women had been found and was in attendance upon her; both had been provided with suitable garments, the best food and every luxury that the rais had been able to procure.

Trelawny nodded his approval, and added that a present from himself might be appropriate under the circumstances. The rais agreed. It was decided to send the lady a slave; there were some nice little Malay girls among the prisoners. This arranged, the rais remarked that the lady would wish to thank her liberator in person as soon as she was strong enough for an interview; but that was not possible as yet; she was still suffering from the shock of her father's death.

Trelawny signified his perfect willingness to wait and was turning away when Aston and De Ruyter came up, and the latter stopped him with a most surprising remark, addressed to the rais.

"I don't know whether you agree with me, Father," he said with extreme seriousness, "but I am inclined to think this Arab girl is the lawful wife of our young friend here. Was she not affianced to Mr. Trelawny by her father according to the customs of your country?"

Married? Trelawny stared at De Ruyter. Was this a joke? If so, it was a poor one! But the rais's answer banished any such hope.

"You are right, Malik," the rais said solemnly. "Who can doubt it? Yet it sounded strange to my ears when the men present at the sheik's death told me of the betrothal. Old as I am, never before have I heard of an Arab sheik, whose generations are as countless as the grains of sand on the desert, giving his daughter to a giaour belonging to a country so newly discovered that our ancestors knew not of it, nor could her father have heard of its existence, and an infidel!"

"Why do you say that?" De Ruyter protested. "No doubt the sheik thought the young man was an Arab. Does he look like a Christian? Does he not wear the Arab dress? I know that he has a Koran in his cabin. He can say his *namaz*."

The rais nodded. "Wise are you, Malik, and that is the truth. For my part, I feel sure that the father of this boy was an Arab, or at least Arab-descended. I never saw any of your Western people sun-dyed and featured like this boy. He is honest and brave, loves our people, fights with our weapons, and uses our customs. Now that he has, by the blessing of Mohammed our holy prophet, married an Arab wife, I hope he will search out the tribe of his ancestors and not like unto his foolish father go from his own country to dwell on white rocks in the sea."

Trelawny had listened to this discourse with growing uneasiness. The rais was obviously in earnest. But he believed

that De Ruyter was teasing him, until the rais remarked that
a marriage should be acknowledged by an interchange of
rings, and there was not the vestige of a smile on De Ruyter's
face as he advised Trelawny to select a ring for the bride
from the treasure chest—she might like a ruby—and added
solemnly that he believed a marriage arranged, as this had
been, under the shadow of death was peculiarly binding.
The rais agreed. Moreover, deep-hidden secrets were often re-
vealed to dying eyes. The sheik most certainly knew what
he was doing when he gave his daughter into the hand of
a stranger, together with all the hopes of his house and the
care of his children.

"Children?" Aston inquired. "Are there other children?"

Trelawny shuddered. What responsibilities were descending upon him! A wife, children, and Heaven knew what
else— But the rais reassured him. "Children," it appeared,
was merely the Arab term for the members of a tribe, and
very few of the sheik's were left. After years of depredations
from various marauders, the tribe had become so weak that
their village had been wiped out and most of the inhabitants killed. The final blow came when Maratti proas took
the sheik's vessel and carried him, his daughter, and a few
servants to slavery in Madagascar.

"He was a brave and desperate warrior," the rais added
with a sigh, and walked away.

Trelawny stared at his friends. They were laughing. But
his face told De Ruyter that this was no laughing matter, and
Trelawny's question—was the rais speaking the truth?—was
answered with proper seriousness.

"According to Mohammedan ritual and Arab custom the
marriage was legal," he said, "but you are not bound. The
Koran means nothing to you, my boy. You are not an Arab.
Their law is not yours."

"But how will it affect her?" Trelawny demanded.

"Well, as her father has affianced her to you, she cannot
marry anyone else. So you must provide for her and convey

her and her Arabs to their native land. You have feeling as well as honor, you will do what is right. Now come down to the cabin, and we'll continue our talk over a bottle of claret."

Aston, however, was not so easily satisfied—the boy was too young for such responsibilities! As De Ruyter walked away he asked Trelawny what he intended doing.

"Doing?" he answered. "Why, man, the thing is done!"

"Done?"

"Yes, I am married—without bans, or any fuss and feathers. It's like the first shock in bathing; the timid who creep in by degrees suffer more than the bold who plunge in head-foremost. If I must go in, give me deep water and a height to leap from. Then the shock will be soon over."

"But consider, my lad; she is only a baby and you have scarcely seen her."

"No Arab sees anything of his wife until after he is married."

"But you can't take her home! You don't intend passing all your life with Arabs?"

"Why not?" There was bitterness in the exclamation. Trelawny was thinking of that house from which no letters ever came, where his existence was by now forgotten. "I have no home. Old Father Rais says that I belong here in the East, and I like it well enough—I like the sun better than snow. Now, Aston, don't pucker up your face like a parson in the pulpit. I hate preaching. Come, shake the wrinkles out with claret. This is my wedding day. Let us spend it in rejoicing."

The claret was excellent, the cheroots and calleans soothing. Trelawny had begun to forget his marital anxieties when Louis contributed a remark:

"I had a frow once. But she was never good for much. When I went to sea she drank all my gin."

But drink, Trelawny knew, was not a failing one need fear in an Arab wife. He finished a last glass of claret pretty well reconciled to his fate and ready to face the future with courage, although somewhat uncertain as to what sort of husband he wanted to be. That a wife must be taught instant and unquestioning obedience went without saying. But how did a man get it? By severity? By kindness? He wished he knew more about women. He had never talked to a girl in his life, never even seen a respectable girl since he was ten. . . . Was the sheik's daughter pretty? . . .

He was wakened by Van Scolpvelt tugging angrily at his leg. One of the Arab prisoners was dying—the damn fool, after being most skillfully treated—and insisted on seeing him. Some silly nonsense about Trelawny being his "father"! Realizing, with something of a shock, that tribal duties were descending upon him and that a wife's relations might be as burdensome as a wife, Trelawny doused his head in a bucket of water and followed Van Scolpvelt to the sick bay.

The Arab was almost gone. But his "father's" presence revived him for the moment. He urged Trelawny to be kind to the sheik's daughter and offered to carry a message from her to the sheik, whom he would soon be meeting, "for the blue angel of death was hovering near"; gave a word to his own family—two wives and five children, now Trelawny's charge—they should be frequently reminded of their feud with the Maratti, for so long as a single Maratti remained alive he himself could not enter Paradise, and came to the really important point: his funeral. The rites must, of course, be performed according to Arab custom and, above all, his body must be carefully guarded from "that old white Indian"—he pointed feebly to Van Scolpvelt. "If he is permitted to cut anything away from me and eat it," he moaned, "I am no more fit for a warrior in the other land!"

Van Scolpvelt's yell of rage at this accusation was too much for the dying man. He shuddered—and died.

So now there was a funeral to arrange. De Ruyter and Aston must have felt some amusement as they watched their young friend taking the part of undertaker, but they did not interfere, and the elaborate ceremonies that consigned the Arab to the deep went off with due solemnity.

At last it was over. Trelawny turned away with a sense of duty done, but feeling strangely unlike himself, and both restless and impatient. This transformation was too sudden, too complete. A week ago he had been a carefree boy of the West, homeless to be sure, but with all the world before him. Now here he was tied down—a sea sheik, an Arab, a Mussulman—and married! Married to a girl whose face he wouldn't recognize if he saw her; whose name, even, was still unknown to him. Reluctantly he told himself that it would be a good idea to find out a little more about her. But that could wait. Till after breakfast anyway—he called to Louis to hurry breakfast, and went below.

But, breakfast disposed of, the tiresome duty of seeing his wife's duenna, if not the lady herself, became insistent. He sent for the old woman. She appeared, polite but distant in manner, inclined to postpone an interview with her mistress rather than further it. She had, of course, no objection to revealing the lady's name—nor her own, Kamalia. This was easy to pronounce, but the lady's name, Zela, was very difficult for a Western tongue. Kamalia smiled grimly as Trelawny tried to get the sibilant Arab z and he had to repeat it again and again. At last, she was satisfied, and they returned to discussion of an interview. She finally agreed that it might be arranged provided the proper formalities were observed. Rings must be interchanged—had he provided himself with two rings? Trelawny assured her that the sheik's ring and a handsome ruby ring for the bride were in his pocket. But she still hesitated, gazing at him with such anxiety that he knew she was asking herself whether any giaour, even this pleasant-spoken young man, could be trusted to behave like a gentleman. But she finally consented to give him his instructions. He must not touch the lady's veil or her garments and not, of course, her person. He must not talk too much, or ask questions. He must not stay too long. He must remember that the Lady Zela was in deep mourning, her thoughts were communing with her father's spirit; all her love had died with him. Her eyes, which outshone the stars when she was happy, were now lustreless; her face, fairer than the moon, darkened by clouds of grief; her lips, redder than henna, pale with sorrow; all her loveliness under eclipse now that tears were her only food and sleep had fled her pillow, since she had been left alone in the world.

Trelawny agreed that it was a sad case and promised to carry out instructions to the best of his ability. The old woman bade him wait here on deck while she prepared her mistress for what, she implied, was bound to be an unwelcome visit; she would return shortly and escort him down to the cabin.

"O stranger," she ended tearfully, "be good to her and all good will be yours!"

She waddled away. Trelawny looked after her with some misgiving. The prospect was not alluring. He felt no enthusiasm for a doleful orphan mourner, with red eyes and a white face.

In the meantime, it was pleasant here on deck. Old Kamalia delayed her return. But he was in no hurry, and sat contentedly enjoying his callean, inhaling whiffs of the fragrant tobacco of Shiraz filtered through the rose water of Benares, and was so nearly asleep that he started when a voice spoke sharply behind him.

"The Lady Zela is waiting for you," Kamalia announced. "If you do not come at once the coffee will be cold and the sweetmeats turned sour."

She marched off. Trelawny followed meekly.

The door of the cabin was opened by the Malay slave girl Adoo, his wedding present to his wife: a swarthy girl, broad and squat and low-browed, with tiny black eyes and coarse, straight, black hair hanging over her flat dark face like the foretop of a wild horse. He entered hesitatingly, took a step forward, and paused.

A low couch faced him, and from among its cushions a heap of yellow draperies emerged—Arabs mourn in yellow—innumerable veils and shawls wrapped around a figure sitting cross-legged; hands hidden; feet tucked under her, only the tips of small pink toes peeping out—"like nestlings," he thought, "from under the mother bird's wing." He could not see her face, for long soft dark hair fell over it and covered her like a cloud. She sat motionless; her attitude breathed modest resignation verging on indifference.

But those downcast eyes saw more, of course, than they appeared to see, and what they saw must have been pleasing to the young person hidden inside that apathetic bundle.

A fine figure of a man stood there in the doorway: so tall that his turban brushed the ceiling, with broad shoulders, narrow hips, aquiline features, olive skin and wearing Arab dress; like, yet unlike, an Arab. For the eyes were blue—a thrilling oddity!—and there was a sparkle in them, an ingenuousness in the expression of his face, very unlike the remote imperturbability of an Arab.

But whatever pleasure the bride may have felt was well concealed. She continued to sit: silent, immobile as a sphinx carved out of stone. No one spoke. The cabin seemed under a spell. Trelawny, too, might have been a statue—a statue of the King of the Black Isles turned to marble by enchantment; struck dumb, not by sorcery, but by a sensation he had never before experienced: shyness. . . .

Another moment, and he would have turned tail and made for the deck. Kamalia, no doubt, realized this, for she made a sign. The bundle of shawls quivered.

Zela emerged. She rose, slipped her bare feet into embroidered slippers, and came swaying towards him. She took his hand, pressed it gently to her forehead and to her lips, and gently let it go, her head still bent under its cloud of hair.

The light touch of her lips stirred him. He forgot that he was a man of the world—an Englishman, a privateer, slayer of pirates—and stammered like a little boy as he begged her to resume her seat.

She obeyed. Folded her hands, tucked in her feet, became a heap of yellow shawls.

Kamalia fetched him a cushion. He sat down at a respectful distance. Wishing that he could see his bride's face, wishing she would speak, trying to think of some remark that would lead to conversation. . . . Nothing came to him. . . . Silence fell again. . . . Again, Kamalia came to the rescue.

She brought a tray of refreshments: coffee in cups no bigger than a nutshell set in silver filagree stands; jellies of mangosteen and guava, various "syrups tinct with cinnamon."

Zela rose—Trelawny would have risen too, but Kamalia motioned him to sit still—and taking a cup from Kamalia, she presented it to him with graceful humility. He saw her hand as he took the cup—delicate and very white. His eyes on the hand, he took the cup awkwardly and spilled the coffee. "A bad omen," Kamalia muttered. But Zela calmly removed the cup, presented a dish of conserves, and resumed her seat on the divan.

He nibbled a sweet, absently, scarcely tasting it. . . . Kamalia gave him a significant nod and pointed to the ring he was wearing—the ring of betrothal given him by the dying sheik, a massive gold band bearing an inscription in Arabic and bound with two strands of camel's hair.

He got to his feet, approached the divan, and offered the ring to Zela. To his dismay, she shivered—he could see her bosom fluttering under its silken vest, as she recognized the signet of her tribe that made wrong right, that gave and took away, according to the will of the owner. But Kamalia whispered. She accepted the ring, held it close for a moment, then replaced it on the forefinger of Trelawny's right hand and pressed it to her forehead and to her lips.

At this second touch of her lips he stood entranced, forgetting his next move. Again Kamalia's nod reminded him.

He fumbled in his pocket and brought out the ring chosen from De Ruyter's treasure—a hoop of gold so small that a fairy might have worn it, set with a ruby the size and color of a wild grape; felt for her right hand among its draperies and slid the ring on the forefinger with such deference that old Kamalia smiled approval. But as he ventured to hold the hand and kiss the palm, not once but over and over again, the old woman frowned and shook her head. He took the hint; laid the hand gently down, and summoned his best Arabic for a word of reassurance.

The Lady Zela had nothing to fear either for herself or for the tribe; every one of her father's people on board had been released and would be well taken care of. Nor must she give way to loneliness. Although he himself was a stranger with foreign ways, he was willing to learn the customs of her country if she would be his teacher; and the rais, she must remember, was an Arab, a good old man, who would love her like a father.

But this handsome speech failed to give the consolation he had hoped for. His bride continued to weep, and Kamalia motioned him to go. He moved to the door and paused.

"Dear sister," he said imploringly, "moderate your grief. Command me in all things. Am I not your happy slave?"

He bowed, with his hand on his heart. The Malay girl opened the door. He left the cabin. Old Kamalia looked after him with a satisfied smile.

She would have laughed aloud, if she could have watched Trelawny that day. He went about his work in a haze of unreality; ate, drank, and smoked as if in a dream. As he thought of that poor girl down there in the cabin crying her eyes out, his heart swelled with a new sensation, new and alarming, but not altogether disagreeable. Pity, such as he had felt for Walter, was mingled now with tenderness and love, and whether he was working or idling he still felt the touch of soft lips on his hand.

A week went by. Every day Trelawny tapped at his bride's

door and was admitted. Found an immobile silent heap of yellow shawls waiting passively on the divan. Tried to rouse it to life, to make himself agreeable, but, so far as he could see, without any success whatever. De Ruyter's treasure chest, overflowing with Oriental jewels, was at his disposal; he brought her presents; searched the Maratti plunder for silks and ornaments that had been stolen from her father and returned them to her. She still hid her face, still wept, still refused to speak.

His impatient nature felt the strain, his pride suffered. Left to himself, he might have flung out of the cabin after one of these annoying calls and never come back. But old Kamalia was keeping him exactly where she wanted him to be—hovering on the edge, stimulated but unsatisfied. According to Kamalia, the Lady Zela was much less insensible than she appeared; etiquette demanded this show of maiden modesty. She was, in fact, beginning to think very highly of her spouse. Yesterday she had remarked that she liked the sound of his voice; today, that he was gentle and kind and "as handsome as a zebra."

This was good news. He determined to make one last attempt.

And Kamalia had been right. Things went better from then on. First he was allowed a glimpse of his lady's cheek, smooth and sweetly curved. Next she gave him a word of greeting soft as the warble of the birds that live in the cinnamon groves. At last, he was permitted to hold her hand in his for a moment and, as he let it go, she raised her head. He saw her eyes. They were large and dark and gentle, shaded by long dark lashes. The eyes completed the spell the pressure of her lips on his hand at their first meeting had begun. Twenty years later, he wrote:

"That silent pressure wove the first link of a diamond chain which time nor use could ever break or tear away. Love was ignited in my breast; pure, ardent, deep and imperishable. Zela, from that day, was the star I was destined to worship, the deity at whose altar I was to offer up all the incense of my first affections. I consecrated my heart to Zela. When dull mortality returns to dust, when my spirit wings its way like a dove, it will find no resting-place, no olive branch of peace, till reunited to Zela."

CHAPTER VII

"The fig tree putteth forth her green figs, and the vines with
the tender grape give a good smell. Arise, my love, my fair one,
and come away."   *—Song of Solomon.*

The Isle of France was to lose her musical name and revert
to the old Dutch name, Mauritius, not long after that warm
winter's day when Trelawny saw for the first time the place
that was to bring him both happiness and sorrow. Revert to
the Dutch name but not to Dutch ownership. The French
occupation of fifty years was almost at an end; the island was
to change hands for the third time and become English. Not
because England particularly wanted the island, though it
was both rich and beautiful; but because it was a base for
French privateers operating in the Indian seas, and their
attacks on England's merchant marine had become an increasingly serious feature of the war. Their prizes were
usually conveyed to Port Louis, and they refitted there before
starting out on another raid.

So England decided that the island must be taken and a
blockade of Port Louis began, and continued, but only by
fits and starts. Not long before this first visit of Trelawny's,
Robert Surcouf, the famous corsair of St. Malo, had run the
blockade with such success that fourteen cargoes of rice had
been slipped through for the relief of the inhabitants, and
when the grab and the corvette drew near the coast the island
was still French without fear of immediate change. For no
one, not even the well informed De Ruyter, realized that the
arrival of Lord Minto in India meant a more aggressive eastern policy; that Minto would soon give the *coup de grâce;*

the island would be taken by the British and would remain British.

The island was well worth taking and keeping. Very small, only thirty-six miles long, but proverbial for beauty and fertility. Bernardin de Saint-Pierre had chosen it as the Eden for his Paul and Virginia, that anemic little pair so unworthy of an Eden; so unfitted for the "great outdoors" where they were condemned to wander, forever losing their way, hungry, thirsty, bursting into tears, and in every way demonstrating their dislike of Nature, the benevolent goddess made fashionable by Rousseau and his disciples.

Yet Nature was at her best in the Isle of France. It seemed to Trelawny, as he stood at the grab's rail with Aston and De Ruyter watching a blur on the horizon sharpen to mountain peaks, that this was a fairy island conjured up out of the sea by a genie for the delight of mankind.

The coast they first approached was rugged: its cliffs, honeycombed with vast caverns where the surf went booming in and out with ceaseless fury; its peaks, tossed up into fantastic shapes by volcanic fires. The tallest, to which the whole island seemed to lift itself, was Pieter Both—named after the first Governor General of Netherlands India who had helped to make the Dutch supreme in the Indian archipelago for nearly two hundred years. It rose some three thousand feet from a high plateau ringed about by lesser *pitons*—the Morne, Brabant, Signal Mountain, le Pouce, De Ruyter pointed them out; he said the plateau was the choicest part of the island. Down below on the shore, heat and humidity, storms, fevers and sunstroke made life unbearable from November to April. But up there on the plateau, where he had built his house, the air was always cool and pure, with just enough rain to keep his gardens green.

Green valleys were striping the mountainsides now. The glass showed huge trees emerging from primeval forest, streams cutting their way to the sea: a sea stilled by reefs, changing with the iridescence of shallow water that ripples

over white coral sand. The two vessels moved on; passed
Amber Island, where the wreck of the *Saint Géran* that had
brought Virginia to her death was still to be seen, and the
Golden Sands where Paul had found her body; came in sight
of Port Bourbon, and began feeling their way through the
rocks and shoals that guarded the harbor.

Whiffs of flower scent and spice drifted from the shore;
already canoes piled high with fresh fish, fruit, and vegetables
were hurrying out from the town. But any sort of land with
any sort of climate would have been welcome after a five-
hundred-mile voyage, and any town—even this little huddle
of whitewashed cabins—promised relief from the monotony
of sea life unbroken by adventure. The crews let their anchors go with a shout, "sprang aloft like birds, and furled
the sails in an instant."

And of all those waiting to set foot on shore Trelawny
was, of course, the most impatient. This Eden would see a
pair very unlike poor frustrated Paul and Virginia. Trelawny had none of Paul's morbid timidity, nor Zela any trace
of Virginia's morbid affectation. But neither were they in
the least like the Adam and Eve Byron created for his Eden
of the South Seas: Torquil and Neuha. Neuha is too buxom,
Torquil merely a rather silly young Englishman. The Greeks
might provide a Zela. Zela could be Atalanta, beautiful and
swift of foot. Or Nausicaä, running along the seashore, playing ball with her maidens. But Trelawny was not a tricky
Hippomenes nor a cold, calculating Ulysses. A Lancelot or
a D'Artagnan, perhaps? Young D'Artagnan meeting Nausicaä there on the seashore, taking her hand, wandering off
with her into the primeval forest? Too farfetched! Let them
remain Trelawny and Zela, waiting, not in fiction but in
real life, on the deck of an Arab grab as she comes to anchor off the wharves of a sleepy half-deserted town in the
Isle of France.

For, by this time, Zela too was on deck. As the grab entered the harbor Trelawny had hurried below, and she had

let him lead her up into the sunlight. Dazzled by the glare, alarmed at seeing two strange men come to speak to her, she had drawn back; but only for a moment. The men spoke gently; she recovered her self-possession. De Ruyter made her welcome, in fluent Arabic, to his ship, his country house, and everything that was his. She thanked him. Trelawny sent for a carpet and cushions. She seated herself. Enthroned there on scarlet silk encircled by her waiting women against a background of blue sea and sky, she might have been the Princess Jehaun-ara and her court in some old Persian illumination for the Thousand-and-One-Nights.

Trelawny would have welcomed a little leisure just then, to be able to take his place beside Zela and play prince to her princess. But he was too busy. One of the first canoes that came from shore had brought De Ruyter a message from his secret agents. The English blockade of Port Louis had been abandoned for the time being, probably because the southwest monsoon was about to set in and the frigates had to get back to safety at Madras, and also because the English merchant fleets were, by now, past the Isle of France and out of danger. This was important news for the French corvette. Her captain decided to stay in Port Bourbon only long enough to get water and fresh provisions and take on board the prisoners and wounded from the grab, and then proceed to Port Louis to make his report to the French commandant. De Ruyter was to meet him there; he would go by land, riding across the island on horseback. Meanwhile, Trelawny was to unload the grab's cargo and get her ready for overhauling; she was to stay here in the harbor until the monsoon had blown itself out. In three days De Ruyter hoped to be back again and escort his friends to his country house for a long pleasant holiday in the uplands.

Trelawny set to work and worked hard. The plunder collected from the pirate town and De Ruyter's recent voyages was all to be transferred to the French authorities at Port Louis, except for the share to which De Ruyter and his crew were entitled, and the grab emptied of pretty much everything she contained. Magazines of spars, boards, and matting were erected on the shore to shelter the cargo while it was being loaded onto the backs of the mules and slaves that were to carry it across. It would have been a difficult job in cool weather at an English port. Here, in this suffocating heat, most Europeans would have broken under the strain. The bearers—animal and human—were lazy and stupid; a babel of strange tongues added to the confusion. But Trelawny, in a way, was enjoying himself. He wrote of this experience:

"With a nature ardent, active and enterprising, my soul was in what I undertook, and with unwearied diligence I executed De Ruyter's orders. Watching and toil were to me pleasure, for my body was strong and my spirit winged."

Order gradually came out of chaos. The heaps of merchandise on the shore dwindled, party after party of bearers climbed the trail behind the town. At length the beach was clear. De Ruyter returned. Preparations for the trip to his country house could begin.

One morning before dawn a procession lined up on the beach; a long procession, for De Ruyter was taking everything that might be needed by guests differing widely in tastes and requirements. One of them was Aston; De Ruyter had brought the necessary permission from the commandant at Port Louis, and Aston and his four men were to stay with De Ruyter as long as they liked. Aston was, of course, delighted at the prospect of a country holiday. So was everybody else. Chattering, laughing, and singing—some mounted, some on foot—they got under way just as the sun appeared on the horizon.

De Ruyter and Aston headed the procession. Then came Zela and Trelawny, followed by Van Scolpvelt, old Kamalia and Adoo, the little Malay girl; servants and bearers and a long string of pack mules brought up the rear. The mists of early morning were still drifting in from the sea as they moved along the pebbly beach paved with bright-colored shells, crossed an arid plain, and came to the foot of a rough trail that angled steeply up the cliff side so narrow that two animals could not go abreast. Trelawny dismounted, gave his horse to a boy, and walked on beside Zela, ready to help her if she needed it. But he realized at once that fears for the horsemanship of an Arabian girl were absurd enough. She had ridden since babyhood—spirited horses, in rocky desert passes so dangerous that this trail seemed to her as safe as a caravan route. No stream was too deep for her to ford, no precipice could try her nerves. She would halt her pony on the rim and lean so far out to gather a flower that he would clutch at the scarf around her waist and she would laugh at his alarm.

She was laughing and talking so easily now that he had begun to feel safe with her, when a misunderstanding suddenly destroyed his self-confidence. He realized, with a shock, that she was as sensitive as she was fearless, and that they were still strangers.

They had reached the plateau; below them the sea fog spread a thick white blanket, pierced here and there by rocky peaks. The ground was smoother, and they were riding side by side at a good pace when, without warning, Zela jumped from her saddle and went running up a sand-bank like a fawn. She was back again in a moment, offering him a flowering branch she had broken from a little tree. It was a coarse-leaved plant, with blowzy red blossoms, yellow berries, and a disagreeable musky scent. He laughed, thinking she was in joke; but as he waved it away and bent to lift her into the saddle, she shrank, and he saw to his horror that she was crying. But why! What had happened? She only shook her head. At length he got the answer: he had despised her favorite tree, the yakoonoo—a tree sacred to the Arabs, emblem of all that her tribe held dear. It grew beside her father's tent, sheltered it from the sun, drove away the flies. Arab maidens wore its blossoms wreathed in their hair, and when they died it was strewn over their graves. Her heart had rejoiced when she saw it growing in this far country. She had brought him a branch. An Arab would have welcomed the gift. But he was a stranger. She belonged to a stranger!

The lament filled him with pity. He was afraid to touch her, to kiss her. Cursing himself for his stupidity, he ran to the shrub, pulled it up by the roots, and brought it back to her.

"You were right, dear sister," he said. "The tree, now that I see it nearer, is very beautiful, and the smell is delicious. We will take it with us and plant it in our garden."

She smiled at him. He tied the little tree to his saddle, and they rode on.

The mists were fading now; the whole island lay spread out before them clear and shining in the sun, and bordered with blue sea. De Ruyter joined them. They were to break-fast beside that lake—he pointed; the servants were already unpacking the baskets.

They dismounted in the shade of a group of rose-apple trees that encircled a grassy space on the edge of a little lake. The water was diamond-clear, broken by the gleam of golden fish, centres of silver rings as they rose snapping at the many-colored dragonflies—green and blue and yellow—that darted and dipped over the still water. Deep as well as still, De Ruyter remarked; prawns as big as lobsters lived there, and monstrous eels fifteen feet long. The air and the land too were crowded with life. Every tree was noisy with parrots; two deer crossed a glade and vanished into the forest as they approached; wood pigeons and doves, busy with their morn-ing shower baths, fluttered indignantly up and away; water hens dived; and gray partridges hurried to hide among the swordlike leaves of the vacoa that bristled along the far side of the lake. At a little distance a baboon sat placidly—and continued to sit—eating his breakfast, stuffing himself with bananas.

The picnic was spread on the grass. A cool air, sweet with

TRELAWNY

By MARGARET ARMSTRONG

CHANCE meetings are the exciting ones. One hot summer day in 1820 a remarkable young Englishman — twenty-eight, though he had lived incredible adventures — was wandering on an acacia-shaded terrace near Lausanne, above the Lake of Geneva. He was in a mood of ennui and discontent; after years of romantic seafaring he had tried to settle down to well-bred life in England; had married ouside his gamut, and divorced. On the terrace he met a bookseller friend who sat reading *Queen Mab*. The bookseller told him about its author, a young poet called Shelley. The wanderer found something strangely provocative in what he learned about the young poet. He determined to meet him.

This, which happened under the same trees where Gibbon strolled the night he finished the *Decline and Fall*, was the prelude to one of the most unexpected friendships in English letters. The adventurous young buccaneer was Edward John Trelawny, whom we remember most often for his account of the last days of Shelley and Byron, and the scene of the burning of Shelley's body on the Italian beach. Once read it is not forgotten. Through the glassy waver of flame-troubled air we see the iron cage over the embers, those figures on the sand, and Byron swimming out to sea to cleanse himself. It is one of the many episodes which Miss Armstrong revives, or brings fresh for a younger generation of readers, in this admirable book. And though her biography might seem the quintessence of escape, a tale of adventure from quite a different world, it seems also queerly of today.

He went to sea, at fourteen or so, when the 'tweendecks of naval vessels were painted solid red so that the blood of the wounded wouldn't be too conspicuous. He revolted against bullying discipline and read about the *Bounty* mutiny; he hated Captain Bligh. He ran away and went privateering with the mysterious De Ruyter, a roving adventurer. Made up as an Arab he commanded an Arab *grab* (which seems to be a kind of brig) and made war on French and English impartially. He found himself married to a beauteous Arab girl, his adored Zela. These adventures Miss Armstrong faithfully retells from that great find of our boyhood, *The Adventures of a Younger Son*, in which Trelawny's early life lost nothing in his own telling. Miss Armstrong wisely does not advise us to put too much confidence in Tre's autobiography for matters of fact. It never made the slightest difference to any reader how that book was mixed of truth or fancy. Old Tre's life was so astonishing that exaggeration could never make it more odd.

We need to remember two things: that he was himself the incarnation and actuality of what became known and fashionable as "Byronism"; and was the exact contemporary of Captain Marryat,

from whom we can check Trelawny's naval reminiscences. But he lived, a figure of astonished reverence to his juniors, until 1881. I myself knew well a distinguished old gentleman (Sir Sidney Colvin) who well remembered having gone to call on Trelawny and had shaken the very hand that still bore the scar of snatching Shelley's heart from the red-hot embers.

The seafaring and privateering, the Arab bride muffled in silky draperies, even the voyage to America and the attempt to swim Niagara above the falls (he was "bitterly mortified," he said, when the river was too strong for him, and only a fluke prevented him from going over the fall; his description of the adventure is one of his greatest passages) are all thundering good adventure stuff, and in fullblooded romantic tradition.

But it was the friendship with Shelley, whose character evoked something finely sensitive and unselfish in our Cornish giant, that makes him most enduringly memorable. The life of the Shelley household on the Italian shore often seemed comical enough to the salty old corsair; the duplication of females and the nudist bathing parties on the beach aroused his mirth, but like all genuine adventurers he had done his own thinking, and he recognized and saluted intelligence.

From the time he fought with the raven as a child, he decided to live his life his own way, and he did so, wilfully and happily, for more than eighty years. "Personality," that mysterious essence so widely publicized nowadays, is probably rather less frequent than a hundred years ago. It is good to find Miss Armstrong's clear eye and skilful hand going back to one of the most genuine originals of our race. Biography that includes all the charms and vivacities of fiction remains the best entertainment in print.

CHRISTOPHER MORLEY

In accordance with a suggestion made by a number of our subscribers, this monthly reprint from the Book-of-the-Month Club *News* is printed in this format so that it can be pasted, if desired, to the flyleaf of the book.

the scent of guavas, citrons, wild mangoes, and a thousand
aromatic herbs and shrubs, came drifting up from the valleys
below. Again the scene was worthy of a Persian painter.
Only a Persian could have immortalized the pattern of this
Oriental "conversation piece" in all its gay minute detail.
Background of blue sky and emerald-green leaves enamelled
with flowers and small bright-colored birds; foreground of
blue water, and emerald-green grass scattered with fruit in
flat baskets—melons, peaches, grapes—a fit setting for the
bright figures. Zela and her women in pale clear tints—pink,
turquoise, lilac—seated on scarlet cushions; De Ruyter and
Trelawny—orange, red, brown—reclining beside them on the
grass. The only European touch contributed by Aston, fair-
haired, in a dark blue uniform—unaccustomed to reclining,
he stood leaning against a tree—and the dingy figure of Van
Scolpvelt, too absorbed in watching an unfamiliar beetle
alight on his hand to be aware of either good food or beautiful surroundings.

But they were still some miles from home. Reluctantly De
Ruyter gave the signal for departure. The horses were saddled, they took the trail again. Dipping into green valleys,
rising to stretches of primeval forest where tangles of jasmine,
wild grape, and trumpet flower hung thickly interlaced making a dark, moist, green tunnel carpeted with moss that
muffled the sound of their horses' feet. Too dark—too silent!
Trelawny caught Zela's hand. It was a fairy place; she must
take care! A demon might be lurking here in some hollow
tree ready to snatch her from him forever—

But as he spoke the trail broke into a clearing, dazzling
with sunlight. It sloped to a river. They crossed a bamboo
bridge—first sign of civilization—and reached a path that
took them zigzagging up through shrubs and trees to a high
open level space and De Ruyter's house.

It was large and very white, only one story high, with a
touch of the baroque in its architecture; an agreeable combination of French and Oriental taste. The roof, broad and

steep, overhung the façade, making a veranda supported by a long row of white columns; wings stretched out at either side. It sat in the midst of a garden crowded with flowers and shrubs.

As they approached, servants came out to take their horses. They dismounted in the shade of the veranda and followed De Ruyter into a large cool hall paved with stone flags, shaded by Persian blinds. A stream piped from the mountains fell tinkling into an oval pool lined with blue tiles where goldfish swam, and hurried out of doors to fill a bathing tank and water the grounds before it escaped and became a waterfall mingling its music with the countless birds singing their hearts out in the garden. Flowering plants in pots bent over the pool and scented the air of the patio; cushions and divans invited repose; its walls were ornamented with trophies and drawings, as in De Ruyter's bungalow in the Deccan; but this was far more luxurious, a country house fitted with elegance and comfort.

Trelawny and Zela stood looking about them like children. Zela, though accustomed to luxury of a barbaric sort, had never before stepped inside the walls of a house, and Trelawny not since leaving home. A door opening from the hall bore an inscription in Persian characters: *The Zenana.*

"A whim," De Ruyter told Trelawny with a smile, "not of mine, but of the artist who arranged and painted the interior. So far as I know, your lady is the first to enter it."

He ushered Zela through the door; Kamalia and her servants followed, the door closed. Trelawny found himself shut out. But there were luxuries to pass the time: a refreshing wash; a siesta; tiffin.

Zela did not appear when the gong rang—Arabian ladies dine in private. But De Ruyter lamented the absence of their "queen bee," and Trelawny sent for her. She came. They gave her a low couch—she had never sat on a chair, never even seen a chair, nor eaten with a knife and fork. Trelawny laughed at her attempts to manage a fork; she laughed when he tried to eat rice and curried chicken with his fingers, daintily, as she did.

The afternoon slipped lazily away. As the sun sank behind the mountaintops, a sea breeze sprang up. Zela emerged from the zenana. They all went out of doors to admire the garden. In this fertile, irrigated soil plants from Europe and the Orient grew as happily as native flowers and fruits. Pineapples and mangoes, melons and aubergine, asparagus, and pumpkins—even strawberries and raspberries, clingstone peaches and grapes were here, and stocks, sweet basil, violets, and roses as well as purple passion flowers, and huge yellow morning-glories, and the pretty shrub called Bois de Demoiselle mingling its red berries with the heavy clusters of Persian lilac, feathery grasses, and dark clumps of bamboo. Behind the garden a winding path mounted to a white summer house fitted with couches and cushions. Servants brought trays of refreshments; cool drinks of fresh pomegranate juice, fruit and sweetmeats in little silver filagree baskets. They ate and drank. De Ruyter and Trelawny took their calleans, Aston a cigar.

Zela wandered away. The three men sat smoking, watching her light figure wrapped in gauzy veils move about among the flower beds on the slope above them. She paused under a drooping Indian tree and looked down at Trelawny from its shadow.

Years later, he could record every feature, every grace of her figure, as clearly as if she stood before him. He wrote:

"Her face was small, oval and pale of hue; contrasted with the date-colored women about her the soft transparency of her complexion was striking, heightened by the cloud of dark hair that grew in a silky line low over her broad, smooth forehead. Her eyebrows, straight and well defined, waved at the outer tips but were not arched; her large dark eyes were full but neither sparkling nor prominent, the whites tinged with blue, and soft as a thrush's unless she were moved by

joy, surprise or sorrow when the starlike iris dilated with
magical effect. The eyelashes, long and dark, curled up at
the tips and shadowed her cheeks when she looked down. A
line of ineffable grace descended from her chin to her white
throat and thence to her bosom, high and just developing
into form; her limbs were long and rounded; her motion
quick but not springy, light as a zephyr. Her mouth was
harmony and love."

That mouth smiled back at him as he gazed. But he felt
again as in the forest a sense of her elusiveness; a premonition that his possession of her could not last, she would fade
away from him like a sea wind. He wrote:

"As she stood there canopied under the dense shade of that
sacred Hindoo tree, in whose every leaf a fairy is said to
dwell, I ran to her and caught her in my arms.

" 'I have you now, dear sprite!' I cried. 'Promise me that
you will never fly away and leave me for a leafy dwelling in
some fairy tree!'

"She trembled and begged me to let her go. I placed her
gently on the ground. She ran to take refuge with her old
attendant. And this was my first embrace of my Arab maid."

CHAPTER VIII

"Thou wast that all to me, love,
    For which my soul did pine—
A green isle in the sea, love,
    A fountain and a shrine,
All wreathed with fairy fruits and flowers,
    And all the flowers were mine."
                                —POE.

The warm clear still days drifted idly by. Trelawny and
Zela wandered about their Eden, undisturbed by thoughts of
the past or plans for the future; living from hour to hour,
immersed in that haze of serene indifference to the world
outside possible only to lovers. Sometimes they remembered
to come indoors when the gong rang for a meal; more often
they ate fruit instead, arguing as to the rival merits of mangosteen and custard apple, dates and peaches. They planted
the yakoonoo tree. They made wreaths for Zela's hair, taught
each other new words in Arabic and English, punished stupidity with kisses, spelled their names in pomegranate seeds,
drew hearts and darts on the sandy garden paths, and, in
all the usual immemorial ways, amused each other and bored
their friends.

Aston could watch the comedy of young love unfold with
sympathetic tolerance. De Ruyter soon became impatient. He
reminded Trelawny there was a world outside the garden;
Port Louis was a picturesque little town, the shipping was
worth seeing. But Trelawny felt no need of any society but
Zela's; he always found some excuse to stay behind when De
Ruyter and Aston rode to Port Louis.

A suggestion that the island should be explored met with

more success, for Zela was persuaded to make one of the party. They climbed the lesser *pitons,* penetrated the depths of primeval forests, discovered new lakes and waterfalls, bathed in clear pools, fished in brooks, hunted wild boar and finished the day with a picnic. This life suited Zela; she was as tireless as the men, as reckless, and far quicker and lighter on her feet. Trelawny provided her with a short, light spear for boar hunting. She learned to shoot and fish. She was afraid of nothing.

And when bad weather kept them indoors gathered about the hall fire—reading, drawing, and fencing—while fierce wind tossed the garden trees like feathers and torrential rain beat against the blinds, they would send for Zela to sing to them and tell them stories. It was pretty to see her, perched cross-legged on a divan, wrapped in her spangled gauzes and embroidered silks, twanging an odd little zither or guitar, singing the "songs of Araby"—the love songs of Ibn Quzman the wandering minstrel, the sad songs of widowed Laila ul-Akhyaliyya, the heroic verse that celebrated the victories of Islam—and her story-telling was still more entrancing. Even De Ruyter would look up with a smile from his drawing board when she gave them a tale from the *Nights:* the tale of Prince Camaralzaman and Badoura, Princess of China; of Gulnare of the Sea, daughter of "the most potent prince of the ocean," bride of Mirza, King of Persia, whose brothers— "tall, handsome and incredibly agile, with whiskers of a sea-green color"—came up from their vast empire in the bottom of the sea to visit her; or described the "terrestrial paradise" prepared by the Princess of the Isle of Ebene for her lover.

But although De Ruyter was becoming sincerely attached to Zela and less critical of Trelawny's infatuation, he was not sorry when an invitation came from the commandant too tempting for Trelawny to resist. The authorities at Port Louis were giving a banquet to celebrate the victory at St. Sebastian; Trelawny was asked and was to receive his full share of compliments for the part he had played in the taking of the pirate town.

So a few days later Trelawny and De Ruyter in their best Arab costumes and Aston, discreetly inconspicuous in mufti, rode away down the trail to Port Louis, Zela waving good-bye from the veranda. The forest was soon left behind; they reached the rich, cultivated fields of De Ruyter's plantation dotted with the whitewashed cabins of his farm hands—all free men, of course; De Ruyter would not employ slave labor on his plantations. The trail mounted again to the plateau, crossed it, and began to descend to the coast, broadening as it neared the town.

It was a green and white town: green trees and hedges, white houses. French taste had given it a touch of elegance and as much neatness as could be exacted from slave labor in a hot climate, swept away most of the rickety wood and mud of the Dutch occupation and substituted solid baroque buildings that provided everything necessary for comfortable provincial life: theatre, hospital, reading room, magazine for storing the East India Company's goods, aqueduct to bring mountain water for the canal, and a turtle pond—replenished now with turtles from the island of Rodriguez, for the huge turtles of Mauritius, so large that six men could sit inside one shell, had long since been exterminated.

Religion had provided a very small whitewashed baroque church; and government, as befitted Imperial France, a large and imposing residence for the commandant; built of stone, two stories high and colonnaded, with a flat roof used as a terrace ornamented with awnings, shrubs, and plants in pots.

The interior was as handsome as the façade. Trelawny, new to large establishments, might well have felt overawed. But as usual he was too interested in new surroundings to think of himself. The commandant welcomed them with discrim-inating politeness: De Ruyter was greeted as an intimate friend, Aston with the respect due to a fellow officer in ad-

versity, and Trelawny got a special word of commendation
for his bravery in the St. Sebastian affair, intended no doubt
to put a shy boy at his ease. This tact was unnecessary. When
an introduction to the lady of the house was suggested he
agreed with his usual smiling self-confidence.

His host took him through a long white corridor into a
boudoir where a lady reclined on a couch. He stared at the
room and its occupant with eager curiosity. It was his first
sight of either a boudoir or a fine lady, and both were worth
looking at.

The room was shaded to a greenish light that suggested
coolness, but gay with flowers, dishes of fruit, bright silk curtains, graceful furniture, and small birds hopping restlessly
about in gilt cages. The lady was dressed in the extreme of
Paris fashions—as extreme, that is, as could be expected of a
lady in exile: hair elaborately arranged in a curly topknot
à la Grecque; India muslin frock revealing every curve of
slightly overripe charms; bare feet encased in silver sandals.
She lay reclined in a Madame Récamier attitude, waving a
palm-leaf fan back and forth with an air of extreme languor.
But as the two came in she sat erect, returning Trelawny's
stare with unfeigned interest.

The commandant introduced him—to Trelawny's surprise, merely as "a young Arab chieftain"—and hurried away.
More surprising still, the lady at once developed traits
strangely reminiscent of the girls in old Muckery's bungalow
at Dungaree. She drew him down beside her on the couch,
stroked his cheeks, exclaimed at their smooth olive tint, the
fire in his eyes, the length of his curly black eyelashes. She
admired his shawl—*un vrai kashmir!*—the intricate folding
of his turban, the texture and color of his scarves, and, discovering that he understood French, began a lively catechism:
Had he ever loved? Did he believe in the Virgin Mary?
Would he like to be christened? Would he like to go to
Paris? Were Arab women as handsome as French women?

He nodded and smiled, amused by her mistake, keeping

up the farce. But her chatter soon palled. He suppressed a
yawn as she began lamenting her sad fate. A Parisienne. Exile
in a barbarous island. So hot, so unhealthy, so remote. No
opera. No theatre. No balls. No shops. Nothing but scenery!
She hated mountains—nasty jagged black peaks frowning
down at you. Forests scared her to death. The sea made her
sick.

He stared at her now in honest bewilderment. (Trelawny
was to become insensitive to many things as he went on
through life, but never to natural beauty. When he came to
write of these early years, he gave pages to the beauty of the
Isle of France, describing its landscape with the accuracy of a
painter. He would lose much as he went on, but beauty
would stay with him to the end.) It was a relief when De
Ruyter's entrance broke into her monologue.

De Ruyter was an old friend of Madame's and a favorite—
she declared he was "the only gentleman on the island." He
spoke fluent French. She discussed Trelawny, as freely as if
he were not sitting there beside her. A handsome fellow.
Strange that an Arab chieftain, brought up on the sands
among lions and tigers, should carry himself with such distinction. Think what a winter in Paris would do for him—
and dancing lessons. She would teach him to waltz. He would
make a sensation in Paris. Did he belong to De Ruyter?
Might she have him? She was going home in a few weeks—
might she take him with her?

This was too much! He was on the edge of laughter that
would have given him away and ended the farce, when a
servant came in to announce tiffin.

After tiffin, a sumptuous affair, the commandant took his
guests to a reading room, "built by the merchants for the literary pursuits and improvement of the island," where the
captain and officers of the corvette and various island digni-
taries—military, civil, and mercantile—were awaiting them.
The ceremonies got under way. The commandant led off
with an address well turned and flowery, thanking the heroes

of St. Sebastian for the great service they had rendered France in abating the pirate pest. The captain of the corvette disclaimed any share in the capture of the town: the glory was not his but Captain De Ruyter's. De Ruyter made the proper rejoinder. He bowed. The captain bowed. Everybody bowed. Next came the rewards for valor. The commandant presented each of the heroic captains with a handsome sword, and the corvette's first lieutenant and Mr. Trelawny with fine silver-gilt goblets engraved with suitable inscriptions. Aston, of course, got nothing—the best they could do for him was to ignore him entirely. No reference was made to the encounter with the English frigate—for which tactful omission Aston was, no doubt, properly grateful—and after another round of refreshments, the commandant took his guests home to prepare, with a long siesta. for the dinner that was to complete the day.

But Trelawny could not waste time in sleep. The American schooner was lying at anchor in the harbor, and he wanted to have another look at her.

She was as lovely as ever. He stood on the wharf for a long half-hour, admiring her birdlike beauty, watching her white reflection come and go in the blue-green water, with no premonition of the part she was to play in his life, unaware that the schooner cast a shadow as well as a reflection; a shadow that would lengthen and, in the end, darken all his memories of the only two people he was ever to love with constancy: Zela and Shelley.

But Trelawny's present was too cheerful for premonitions. He stood there contentedly, admiring the little American, wishing she were his, and would have stayed much longer if a gang of slaves had not happened to be unloading a ship in the dockyard. The cruelty of their drivers filled him with an indignation he was never to forget.

"To every appeal they are deaf as crocodiles," he wrote long after. "While you are talking of humanity, they will lash the bare and festered back of an overloaded female slave, her tender nature one animated mass of ulcers and cancers, half consumed alive by flies and maggots, death her only hope and coming like a bridegroom. I have seen men with their spines knotted like pine trees and their skins as scaled and callous, the flesh cracked into chasms from which the blood oozed out like gum. I have seen hundreds of these poor wretches undergoing their daily toil in the dockyards of Port Louis, and the pity and pain I felt at the sight of these poor slaves could only be equaled by the deep and overwhelming damnation I invoked on the heads of their oppressors forever. Surely such monsters are annihilated, they cannot be immortal. Yet they should have an eternity to torture them. What they have done to others should be done to them and I defy the invention of hell's demons to be more cunning in cruelty than themselves."

But when he left the water front and went for a stroll about the town he could not, of course, escape the slaves. The proportion of slaves in the island population was overwhelming. No animals were employed except a few buffaloes and an occasional saddle horse. There were no carts or carriages in Port Louis; the ladies used palanquins. For slaves were much cheaper than animals. According to the Vicomte de Vaux, who recorded the tariff a little before Trelawny's time, a healthy man or woman, from thirteen to forty, was worth "two muskets, two cartouche boxes, ten flints and ten balls; or a fat capon and a knife; or seven balls and ten needles; or a pair of scissors"—rates which would have excited the envy of planters in Carolina and Virginia. For Americans had to pay not only for longer transportation, but for the loss of much perishable merchandise during the voyage across the Atlantic—slaves had such a disappointing way of being found dead in the hold when a slave ship came into port.

But the trip from the markets in Mozambique or Mada, gascar was short enough to ensure a cargo arriving in fairly good condition. Slaves wore out very rapidly, of course; but

no one cared. There were plenty more where they came
from. A pair of scissors would buy you another one just as
good.

So Trelawny's stroll gave him little pleasure. He was glad
to return to the commandant's house and forget the slaves
in the pleasure of dressing for dinner. It was a prolonged
pleasure. He draped his shawl, folded his turban, adjusted
the jewelled dagger in his belt a dozen times before he felt
satisfied, and was not half done admiring himself as he re-
volved in front of the looking glass when a smell of turtle
soup drifting through the corridors reminded him that he
was hungry.

The dinner was fine, but there was too much of it; too
many courses, too many wines to be tasted and appreciated,
far too much French chatter. These Frenchmen! How tall
and ruddy and dignified Aston seemed, surrounded by these
"bilious little monkeys with their sallow skins, bald heads,
yellow eyes and noses like squashed figs"! How infinitely
superior was any Englishman to any Frenchman—or Dutchman or Portuguese, for that matter! He was whispering his
contempt for these "vain, gasconading harlequins" to Aston
when one of them, warmed by too much good Burgundy,
happened to remark that Paris was as superior to London as
Calcutta to Port Louis. This was too much! The whisper
would have risen to loud indignation, if Aston had not laid
a firm hand on his arm. However, Aston added a smiling
nod that showed he approved these patriotic sentiments and,
being a kind man, did not add the obvious reminder that
an Englishman who had deserted from His Majesty's Navy,
who had fought hand to hand with His Majesty's soldiers
and sailors, who was forever praising the Oriental way of
living and the Mohammedan faith, who wore Arab dress
and had married an Arab wife, would do well to forget his
English blood once for all. For Aston knew boys. He knew
England. England had a way of letting her children wander
through many crooked lanes before they reached the turn-

ing that would bring them home. This hearty British contempt for foreigners was wholesome. It might not only take
the boy home, but keep him there.

So Aston sat enjoying the commandant's excellent cigars
in placid British silence, and the chatter went on, and Trelawny fidgeted, longing to escape. He wanted to get back to
Zela. It was late. Zela would be anxious. . . .

At last it was over. They were out of the hot crowded
room. On horseback, but with the commandant still in polite
attendance. He insisted on their making a tour of the Champs
de Mars, a fine open space in the outskirts of the town used
as a parade ground and promenade; it seemed to Trelawny
that the last adieu would never be said, the final bows interchanged. But at last they were really off; out of the stagnant,
suffocating heat of the coast, mounting up into the clear
freshness of the plateau, and free to discuss the day's doings.
They were all in fine spirits, especially Trelawny, childishly
delighted with his silver-gilt goblet. It was his first prize.
No red and gold volume of *Rasselas* or *Paradise Lost,* stamped
with the school arms, had ever come his way. Presents were
rare at Great Saughall. The Christmases of Trelawny's youth
never brought presents to children, and birthdays only to
the very pampered from very doting parents. As Charles
and Maria neither pampered nor doted, in all probability
the cup was his first present.

He took it out of his pouch to admire as they rode along,
and became so anxious to show it to Zela that when they
reached the foot of the path to the house he set spurs to
his horse and rode up the ascent at a gallop.

It was dark now; but, to his dismay, no lights shone out
from the hall. All the blinds were closed. Closed? On a
warm evening like this when the breeze that sprang up
after sunset must be allowed to cool the house? Something
wrong! Where was Zela?

He leaped off his horse, gave him over to a boy, found

the hall door locked, forced open a closed window, jumped into the dark room—and paused, startled by a cry:

"Take care! Shut the window! They will escape! They will escape!"

For a moment he could see nothing. Then a twinkle of light advanced across the hall. It was a candle carried in a cadaverous hand. Van Scolpvelt came shambling toward him, waving a white wand and muttering angrily as he came. The window was shut with a bang; he pointed dramatically to the ceiling.

Trelawny looked up—and shuddered. Three large ink-black creatures were weaving back and forth, up and down, in darts and swoops, like swallows possessed by demons.

"Birds?" he asked, gazing stupidly at the creatures.

"Birds! Bats, you simpleton!"

"Bats? Why not let them escape then?"

"I am conducting a valuable experiment. Not altogether new. The great Spallanzani led the way; he tested the common bat to determine whether their flight is guided by eyesight or by some other sense. These are rare species of the same genus. Look at them. Observe their flight. Do not all three fly alike? Yet two are blind."

"Blind? How do you know they're blind? What happened to them?"

But before Van Scolpvelt could answer, Zela came hurrying in. She was crying. Trelawny caught her in his arms.

"I am so glad you're home again," she sobbed, clinging to him. "This horrid yellow Indian has been busy all day catching the poor little animals that live in the ruined well and putting out their eyes with hot needles!"

Van Scolpvelt nodded, grinning from ear to ear. "The cornea," he said proudly, "is entirely destroyed. A most delightful experiment.* My notes will be a valuable contribu-

* Ivan Sanderson made the same experiment, more than a hundred and twenty years after Van Scolpvelt, with African bats blinded with adhesive tape, and proved that ears and nose leaves, not eyes, were their centres of direction.

tion to science. I must also discover whether or not these bats are vampires." He laid a pleading hand on Trelawny's. "You could be of great assistance, my boy. You are juicy, your veins large and full. Will you oblige me by sleeping near the well tonight? I shall be near to see they do not suck too long."

But Trelawny refused; he would, he said, see Van Scolpvelt in a good deal worse place than a well before he helped him with his nasty tricks! Van Scolpvelt sighed, and resigned himself. He must tempt the vampires with his own lean person.

No one made any objection. The servants were ordered to prepare a bed on the brink of the ruined well. Trelawny and Aston put their heads together. Trelawny insisted that the old beast ought to be well punished for his cruelty—he had made Zela cry!—and Aston agreed. They concocted a practical joke of the robust sort popular in His Majesty's —and, no doubt, every other—navy.

The well was deep, built in the Eastern fashion with steps leading down to the water, crumbling now and overgrown with rank vegetation, blackened with bat dung and slippery with the slime of many toads. Trelawny poked about with a long bamboo, found there was not too much water in the bottom; a cot was brought, ropes placed under it and fastened to the branch of a pipul tree that overhung the mouth of the well. Next came the most amusing part of the joke: preparing costumes for the black boys who were to take part in the affair. Aston and Trelawny spent a delightful evening absorbed as schoolboys preparing a booby trap for an usher. They mixed chenam and lime to make paint, and manufactured flapping wings out of blackened paper stretched on Malayan bows, and stole some needles from Kamalia's workbasket. The giggling boys were summoned, and coached. Their bodies carefully painted with white lines that transformed them into skeletons, their shoulders furnished with wings, they were provided with needles and sent to hide among the bushes in the garden.

It all went off exactly as planned. No funnier joke was ever conceived or better carried out. The old man came shambling from the house, found his cot and lay there, looking up at the bats hanging thick in the pipul tree overhead, and waiting.

He did not wait long. The skeletons rushed out, danced around him, pricked him here and there, and then lowered the cot down into the well; while Trelawny and Aston laughed their heads off in the background. They laughed and laughed. It was simply rich to hear the old fellow groan, wallowing in the water, trying to crawl out, falling back, cursing the bats, the toads, the well, and all its devils in Dutch, Latin, and English.

But it was late, almost midnight now, and the most entertaining farce must come to an end sometime. So, reluctantly, a boy was sent down to jerk Van Scolpvelt out with a rope. He stood dripping-wet, staring at his grinning persecutors, blue with cold.

"Too exhausted to articulate," Trelawny wrote later, still relishing the joke, "he shook as if palsied, his thin legs knocked together like bamboos in a gale, his skin was stained with bats' dung and green slime, his face of a clay-cold blue mottled with spots of blood, and his long thin hair hung down like a mermaid's. He was sullen and snarling as a jackal entrapped, and scowled malignantly as I asked him how he got down into the well and if the vampires had bled him. A tumbler of Schiedam, a dry shirt and a bed were prepared for him indoors. He sullenly and silently lay down."

Trelawny and Aston soon followed his example. They bade each other good night, agreeing that it had all been tremendously jolly. Trelawny remarked that it was the best fun he'd had since beating the Scotch lieutenant to a jelly and knocking out his teeth, and hurried off to tell Zela all about it.

He went over the events of the day for her benefit with much satisfaction. It had been a good day, crowded with flattering incidents—perfect, indeed, except for those cruel slave drivers in Port Louis. And how amusingly it had ended! Van Scolpvelt deserved all he got, and more. Hideous old beast—no one with a face like that should be allowed to live! Scientists were a queer lot. Forever looking back to see what others had done in the past, looking forward at each step to make sure they were on the right road. That didn't get you anywhere. Live dangerously—and to hell with the consequences!

But this spirited peroration was blurred by a yawn. Sleep came down on him. In another moment, the day with all its strange contradictions—pity and brutality, love of country and hate of country—was over.

Meanwhile the grab was lying idle in the harbor of Port Bourbon. De Ruyter had given himself wholeheartedly to agricultural pursuits. He was a country gentleman now, dressed like a planter in white linen and broad-brimmed hat; his talk was of soils and crops, of rainfall and drought, never of the sea.

Of all his household only one remained aloof. The rais had no intention of turning his spear into a pruning hook, and was merely waiting for the day when the malik would put to sea again. But he waited patiently; experience had taught him that these agricultural interludes were apt to be brief. He would come up from Port Bourbon now and then to report; call on Zela, for whom he felt a tribal responsibility; accept a cup of coffee from old Kamalia; glance with some disgust at Aston and Trelawny lolling about under the trees in the garden, and hurry back to his quarters on the grab.

But one day the rais's visit lasted so long that Trelawny had begun to suspect important news when De Ruyter hailed him from the house. He hurried in. The hall was strewn with maps, charts, and instruments. The rais stood bending over a map. De Ruyter knelt measuring distances with a pair of compasses, but sprang to his feet as Trelawny entered, and while he told the news—a rich English prize had been seen near the Mozambique Channel—was already getting out of his white linen and into a blue coat. In half an hour the three were on their way to Port Bourbon and the grab.

There was no time to lose if the English vessels were to be intercepted, and much to do. The grab was to undergo one of her frequent transformations. She was to be a corvette. New masts, spars, and sails were ready—the rais had seen to that, but the elongated bow must be unshipped and the upper works lowered, and she was to be camouflaged: one side painted all black, the other black with a broad white stripe. The work got under way at once. A crew was hired in Port Louis. A few days later a neat corvette was sailing out of the harbor of Port Bourbon.

Trelawny stood watching her for a while from a cliff top —rather to his surprise, De Ruyter had told him he was to stay at home and look after the plantation. She dwindled. Became a speck. Was gone. He returned to the house, and for the moment country life seemed a trifle tame.

But Zela was waiting for him. Their days fell back into the usual pleasant routine. Now and then guests dropped in on them from Port Louis. Now and then, very unwillingly, they accepted an invitation from the commandant's lady, who had taken a fancy to Zela when she found Trelawny was not only married but an Englishman. She raved over Zela's beauty. A twist of the curling tongs in her hair, a touch of paint on her face, a smart French frock, and a hat with plumes, and the child would be ravishing!

Zela could dismiss these suggestions with a smile. But Trelawny found them infuriating (his dislike of European dress was to be lifelong), and all the way home he would amuse Zela with angry comparisons between "gentle wood pigeons and squawking peacocks," and Aston with his tirade on a subject of which he knew nothing whatever: the iniquities of polite society.

But visits to town were seldom allowed to intrude on their placid country life. The days drifted by. De Ruyter had been gone for nearly a month when one morning, before sunrise, the peace of Eden broke. A message came from Port Louis: De Ruyter was back.

Trelawny jumped out of bed and hurried down the trail. Before it was fully day he had come in sight of the harbor. The grab lay there at anchor. But she was not alone. A cable's length astern, he saw another familiar shape—the American schooner! What was she doing here? When she left the Isle of France she had been bound for Manila. As he stared at her, she hoisted a flag—a *French* flag—and an English ensign was unfolding beneath it!

Half an hour later, he was scrambling on board the grab and shaking hands with De Ruyter—wounded but jubilant. The wound was nothing, he said impatiently. What did Trelawny think of his prize? He pointed to the schooner, laughing at Trelawny's astonishment.

The mystery was soon explained. The schooner had been captured by an English frigate, and her American officers replaced by Englishmen; but while she was being conveyed to a British port a storm had disabled her and separated her from the frigate. When De Ruyter came across her, she was in such distress that he had gone to her assistance only to find her sailing away from him. A shot brought English colors fluttering to her masthead, and a fight had followed: sharp, but brief because of her condition. He had taken her. Here she was!

Trelawny had been listening to this story with growing excitement. He had coveted the little American from his first sight of the starry flag at her taffrail. Gazing at her that day a few weeks ago from the wharf here in Port Louis, he had told himself he would give an arm or a leg, anything, everything

—except Zela—to possess her. Could the dream be coming true!

He began to hope, and, as he listened, hope grew. De Ruyter was describing an expedition he had in mind, and taking for granted that Trelawny was going too. Then hope became certainty. De Ruyter told him they were to be companions; De Ruyter and the rais in the grab, Trelawny as captain of the schooner.

At once triumph gave way to a fever of impatience. When De Ruyter spoke of certain legal formalities that must be observed before repairs could begin, Trelawny could not conceal his contempt. The schooner was not yet De Ruyter's property? Absurd! Hadn't she been taken in fair fight? All this legal etiquette made him sick. To hell with the laws of salvage! Why not run her quietly round to Port Bourbon, put her in shape, let her slip out and away? Who could stop her? Give the little lady a few miles' start and she'd show a clean pair of heels to any ship in the harbor!

But De Ruyter only laughed and told him to go home and wait. Officials loved red tape and were never in any hurry to unwind it. The moment that things were in order, he would be sent for. In the meantime he could talk it all over with Zela and Aston, and tell them what was in prospect.

Trelawny went indignantly home. He told Zela and Aston all about everything, and kept on telling them. With every day that passed his indignation grew. He fretted and grumbled unceasingly.

"How I loathe the tardy transactions of these grovelling serpents!" he would growl, striding up and down the veranda. "To my mind arithmetical calculations do far more mischief than earthquakes. All this wanton wasting of time while De Ruyter gives securities and signs deeds and enters bonds—and even, it appears, pays money—to get possession of property that already belongs to him! It's outrageous! I believe these lawyer fellows do it on purpose!"

Even Zela had become a little weary of his jeremiads, and

the whole household rejoiced when, at last, the message came. Everything was in order. The schooner belonged to De Ruyter. Repairs could begin.

This news was steadying. The fretful boy became a competent superintendent. Within an extraordinarily short time the schooner was as good as ever and ready for sea.

One bright morning, as the sunrise breeze came ruffling across the water, a gay cavalcade took the trail that led down to Port Louis, where De Ruyter and the rais were waiting. Most of the party were in fine spirits: Trelawny singing at the top of his not very melodious voice, Zela smiling and serene, Kamalia and Adoo content to follow wherever their mistress chose to take them, and Louis looking forward to the delicious stew he would make out of a turtle tied behind him on his saddle. Van Scolpvelt was, as usual, indifferent to his surroundings, and too intent on preserving his cases of specimens from rough handling to care whether the next year were spent on land or sea. Of them all, only Aston felt either foreboding or regret.

These past months in the Isle of France had been the happiest of Aston's life. They were over. For even the complacent commandant could not allow him to stay on here after De Ruyter left. His friends might return, work in the garden, watch the flowers bloom and fade, fruit ripen; picnic beside clear streams and hunt the wild boar through the forest. He would not be here. These months had taught him he had been meant for a peaceful country life. But De Ruyter was bent on letting him escape. Before long he would be back in the Navy again; enduring storms, close quarters, and the fighting he hated. This French war, that had lasted nearly twenty years now, looked as though it would never end. He would go on fighting until he was killed or, at best, crippled and worn out, would find himself a derelict in Greenwich Hospital. He rode away from the friendly country house sad at heart and looked back at its shuttered windows with a sigh.

But Trelawny and Zela neither sighed nor looked back.

There had been no farewell picnics, no last tour of the garden—Zela had not even said goodbye to her yakoonoo tree.
Why say goodbye when they would be back so soon? They
exchanged laughing glances as old Kamalia was hoisted into
the saddle, warned Louis to take good care of the turtle,
touched up their horses and rode away. Rode out of Eden—
"garden east of the sun and west of the moon"—without one
backward glance. They would see it all again so soon.

By noon they were all on board, the two vessels weighed
anchor together: the rais, Van Scolpvelt, and Louis in the
grab; Aston with Trelawny, to their mutual satisfaction. But
Trelawny was satisfied with everything; with his crew—Aston's four Englishmen had volunteered, as well as several of
the schooner's Americans, including her first mate, a capable
New Yorker named Strong; with his equipment—six twelve-
pound carronades and four long six-pounders; he had provisions and water for ten weeks.

"Zela was with me," he wrote later. "Nothing could have
induced her to remain behind. With all my wishes gratified,
my joy was boundless as the element on which I floated and
I thought it would be everlasting. I went to sea with an
exulting heart."

CHAPTER IX

"In the morning, at break of day, we were clear of all our enemies, and so shaped our course along the coast for a bay, where
we proposed to trim our pinnace, and to renew our wood and
water, and so depart upon our voyage with all possible speed."
                                              —SIR RICHARD HAWKINS.

The voyage began well. They picked up several good prizes:
a Dutchman sailing with English papers yielded a fine haul
of pearls, corals, and carnelians; a flock of little country vessels belonging to John Company were looted of their cargoes
of ghee, bumbalo, paddy, betel nut, arrack, pepper, salt, silk,
and gold moidores, and her convoy, an English frigate, driven
on a rocky shore.

But before long De Ruyter decided they would do even
better if they were to make for the Far East by different
routes; he would go by the Straits of Sunda, and Trelawny
by the Straits of Malacca, and they would rendezvous at a
certain island off Borneo on a given date.

So now De Ruyter and Aston had to say goodbye. For after
some discussion Pulo-Penang had been chosen as a favorable
place for Aston to make his escape, and Trelawny was to see
him safe ashore at Georgetown before going on. De Ruyter
wished Aston the best of luck, presented him with several
ancient Oriental weapons as souvenirs, and returned to the
grab. In a few hours she was out of sight.

The depressing business of landing Aston came next. The
schooner found safe anchorage off the Malabar shore at some
distance from Pulo-Penang. Trelawny hired a fast-pulling
proa, and he and Aston set off for Georgetown.

All went well at first, and exactly as De Ruyter had

planned, Aston's explanation that he had been landed from an American vessel farther up the coast—which happened to be true—was accepted without question by the English governor. He was invited to dinner, excused himself and rejoined Trelawny. They took a room at a hotel, enjoyed an excellent meal, and started out to see the bazaars. But the meal had begun with sangaree and ended with brandy, with claret and Madeira all the way along; so they were both exhilarated and Trelawny, though not drunk, too light-hearted to remember that he was in an enemy town.

While Aston stood watching some dancing nautch girls, more redolent of rancid oil and garlic than Trelawny fancied, he wandered on, came to a jeweller's shop, stepped in to buy a present for Aston, and instantly became involved in a brawl.

It followed a familiar pattern—it may be that the sight of a bazaar caused him to revert to his quarrelsome boyhood. When the jeweller tried to cheat him he knocked the man down. There was a scuffle. He contrived to get out by a back door, reach the hotel room, leave a note for Aston and a present of twenty gold moidores, get out of his Arab dress and into a white suit of Aston's, and dash out again; sober, and disgusted at his folly, thinking only of getting back to the schooner and Zela, and in mortal fear of arrest.

The hours that followed were a nightmare of escape. He had eluded a sentry and almost reached the shore when the jeweller, bent on revenge, caught up with him. They fought —on the edge of a wharf. Trelawny was stabbed in the arm, staggered, caught at a spar, and recovered himself. But the wretched jeweller lost his balance, went down into a black pit of mud and offal, and sank. Trelawny was too far gone even to think of rescue. He was lying exhausted on the bank, wiping blood from his face, and wondering whether the jeweller's dagger were poisoned, when a near-by "All's well!" brought him to his feet. The shore was patrolled! He ran across the muddy beach, reached the sea, and plunged in.

Swimming with one arm was not easy, but he regained the proa. The mat sail was raised.

Towards evening they came to an uninhabited cove and camped for the night. The Malays speared fish and lighted a fire. It was raining; Trelawny wrapped himself in a sail and fell asleep, to awake cold, stiff, sick, and terribly anxious for Zela. The day seemed endless. But at length they rounded a point and saw the schooner. Zela was on the deck looking out over the water with a spyglass. She cried out in horror at his condition as he came clambering on board. Old Kamalia brought soothing lotions of oil and camphor. He was bathed and bandaged and anointed; fed with roast chicken and claret, guava jelly and coffee, until he was sufficiently re-vived to order the anchor hoisted. The men demurred. It was Friday. No one ever put to sea on a Friday. But supersti-tion could not be respected at the moment; for the authorities in Georgetown would have got wind of his escapade by now, and begun searching the neighborhood for suspicious stran-gers. The schooner got under way at once and turned east-ward, making for Borneo.

Again the voyage was broken by adventure. The first was a meeting with an odd craft, rigged snow-fashion, with ropes of dark grass and purple sails, and her hull so high out of the water that, as she rolled, it showed overgrown with bar-nacles, seaweed, and green slime. A shot from a musket brought her to, and Trelawny went on board merely to gratify his curiosity. He found a crew of the wildest sort of savages, naked except for palmetto hats, and a captain very nearly naked and tattooed from head to foot with red and green serpents, but an Englishman! The story he told in explanation was as strange as Sindbad's. As he was finishing the tale, a cry came from below. It appeared that one of the captain's wives was lying-in and not doing as well as she ought to. So old Kamalia was sent for and the poor lady as-sisted. Then the vessel's rudder was repaired; the captain presented with a chart and a compass, a bottle of brandy and

a bag of biscuit, and Trelawny could return to his ship
pleased with his new rôle of benefactor and this unusually
charitable ending to an encounter.

The next vessel was less fortunate. She was a Chinese junk
out of her course, and so fantastic in appearance that again
Trelawny's curiosity took him aboard. Flat-bottomed and flat-
sided with double galleries and an immensely high, ornamental head and stern; decorated and gilded all over with
green and yellow dragons, she looked more like a floating
tea chest than a ship. Her interior was still more grotesque,
for it was a bazaar swarming with merchants and customers,
and workmen busily making paper out of straw and glass
out of rice, forging iron, chasing ivory fans, embroidering
gold on muslin, barbecuing fat pigs and hawking them about
for sale on bamboo poles in a din like Noah's ark. Animals
and birds were everywhere; monkeys and apes, parrots, paro-
quets, macaws and lories, dozens of pigs, hundreds of ducks,
all chattering and squawking at once.

In the cabin he found two merchants, a Tartar and a
Chinaman, enjoying a meal of fat dog roasted whole, stuffed
with turmeric and garlic; side dishes of shark's-fin jelly, sea
swallow's nest, salted eggs and pilaff, with a huge china bowl
of hot arrack as the centrepiece. They looked up with a grunt
and offered Trelawny a bite of dog. He hurried away. Where
was the captain? No one seemed to know. At last he was unearthed in a cubbyhole over the rudder, but heavy with
opium and unable to concern himself with mundane affairs.
The opportunity was too good to lose; Trelawny sent to the
schooner for some men, intending to exact a good ransom
and let the vessel go.

But the Tartar merchant turned out to be spunkier than
he looked and put up a fight. He thrust a fowling piece in
Trelawny's face, but it missed fire. Trelawny shot him dead.
Other Tartars joined in, and a skirmish followed. It was
brief enough; but Trelawny chose to think that resistance
justified plunder and ordered a thorough search. Every bale

was ripped up and every chest broken open. The bulkier cargo—camphor, dyewoods, spices, pigs of iron and tin—could not be taken; but silks, diamonds, gold dust, copper, drugs, and tiger skins were transferred to the schooner, and she sailed away with the richest cargo she had ever carried and a captain in the best of spirits.

For if Trelawny suspected that the line between pirate and privateer had been overstepped, or that De Ruyter might disapprove of the day's doings, he was not acknowledging it even to himself. He thought of the affair as a crazy impromptu, spiced with danger and laughter: the sort of farce he most enjoyed. He had brought the Tartar merchant's gun away with him from the junk—an antique fowling piece, lock, stock, and barrel inlaid with gold roses carved and chased—and as he examined it that night, admiring its curious ornamentation, he decided to keep it (and did keep it, all his life) as a souvenir of the most entertaining adventure that was ever likely to come his way.

But there had been one flaw in the entertainment; several Chinamen had been inadvertently killed during the search. He regretted this; and his later comment is illuminating, for it harks back to that long-ago struggle with the raven. He wrote:

"An English earl told me the other day that killing a hare on his property was as bad as killing a man. I have done both —killed many of the earl's hares and a leash or two of Chinamen in my time, and for the same reason; I was instigated by excitement, because the acts were forbidden."

The crew were also in excellent spirits; so satisfied, indeed, with their share of plunder that the dangers of a Friday sailing could be forgotten—for the time being; and the schooner moved serenely on her way to Borneo.

Each day took her deeper into fairyland, each night seemed more magical than the last. The sea was dotted with islands now. Islands were everywhere. Arabian Nights islands, green and gold; each with its ring of coconut palm and border of silver sand, rising at the centre to a tall glistening tuft of shining emerald-green trees and tangled vines. Morning pricked them out sharp and bright against a cobalt sea; sunset mellowed them to amethyst and rose-color fading imperceptibly into opalescent blue-green water. At night, they receded, were only silver clouds, drifting, almost lost; but not quite. The sea was never empty. As one group vanished in the schooner's wake another rose on the horizon.

Night or day, Trelawny and Zela scarcely left the deck. They sat there, watching the tropic panorama unfold; sometimes talking of the future—Zela was expecting a baby now, and the future had become important—but more often silent, too contented with life and each other to allow either past or future to intrude on the peace of the present.

The voyage was almost over, their island rendezvous only a few miles away, when the first warning came. They were becalmed. Trelawny had sent a man over the side to nail a loose sheet of copper on the bow. He dangled a careless leg too close to the water. A shark rose, snapped. The man screamed, was hauled up. But too late; he bled to death. At once a murmur of unlucky Friday sailings began, and soon swelled to loud foreboding, for before long they lost another man. Anchored off the marshy shore of Borneo, the crew went up a river to bathe; one of them dived, and never came up again. They dragged and searched, in vain. Cramp? An alligator? Entangling tree roots? No one knew. But the crew, stirred by this second warning, prepared for the worst. It came.

The day began cloudless and fiery hot; water so still that shells and seaweed on the bottom, twelve fathoms down, looked within reach; air so clear that every reed in the swamps could have been counted. A red moon rose into a night so soundless that the roar of a tiger in distant jungles seemed close by, and a candle burning on the schooner's deck sent its flame up without a flicker into stagnant darkness. But with all this stillness, the schooner seemed drifting towards the shore. Trelawny ordered the anchor let go and her sails furled.

As he stood with Zela on the deck, both of them uneasy, sensing danger, uncertain from what quarter it would come, a thunderbolt leaped out of the darkness. The simoom struck. Down came the masts; spars, yards, and rigging flew away like thistledown; guns broke loose, the anchor cable snapped, and the little ship drove out into a sea of boiling foam help-less as a clamshell.

Trelawny had caught Zela to him and was holding her close when a cry came from the sea—men overboard! He thrust her under cover, ran to a boat, and got it lowered. The men were picked up, but as they tried to board the schooner, she lurched and the boat capsized. Trelawny, rising on the crest of a wave, saw a white wisp running along the footropes of the mainboom—Zela! He shouted. She flung him a line, aiming so well that he caught the bight and hauled himself on board. As the other men were dragged up after him to safety, he turned to Zela—she fell unconscious in his arms.

Her body was cold as ice, her dress wringing-wet. There was not a dry spot anywhere on the ship. Decks awash, cabin full of water. Where could he take her? As he stood dis-tracted, another cry came—from the cabin; the dying cry of old Kamalia. When they reached her she was dead. No time to think of the old woman, no time even to think of Zela. The ship might go down any moment. He laid Zela in Adoo's lap, and hurried back to the deck. The simoom was whirling off to sea. In rain coming down like a waterfall, the wreckage was chopped away and makeshift canvas got up. The more immediate danger over; but when the men were mustered, the second mate, the steward, a Swedish boy Trelawny had become attached to, and seven others failed to answer.

Ten men and old Kamalia might have seemed enough to satisfy any storm. The simoom wanted more. When Trelawny

got back to Zela he found her conscious but in great pain.
They worked over her all night. At sunrise her baby was
born—born dead.

The American captain would not have recognized his
smart little schooner if he had seen her limping along to
the rendezvous past the hideous mangrove swamps of Borneo
tangled with roots and branches writhing up out of evil-
smelling slime. She was a crippled ship, with a crew as sick
and sorry as herself and a captain in the depths of depression.
Trelawny's moods were always either black or bright. These
days were the darkest he had ever known, as inky black as
the mud flats they were passing—and passing so slowly that
each day seemed more endless than the last. Zela was still
ill, still mourning her baby. The storm had taken so many of
the crew that he felt as discouraged as Jehan de Mandeville,
whose men "went into the Valley Perilous fourteen and
came out nine." The rich plunder from the Chinese junk
had been injured, and their provisions were water-soaked.
Worse yet, the rendezvous proved extremely difficult to find.
Day after day the schooner went nosing in and out of one
melancholy bay after another only to find an empty harbor
and no sign of the grab.

But on the fifth evening, rounding a red cliff, they saw
three small islands close to shore, and found a harbor well
hidden and not empty. The grab lay there at anchor with
two fine prizes alongside.

That was a grand sight! The schooner came in with her
crew hanging over the rail cheering and singing—surely the
Friday curse was lifted now—and before Trelawny had finished shaking hands with De Ruyter he was up in the sunlight again, misfortunes forgotten as if they had never been.
After all, Zela was alive—nothing else mattered!

And De Ruyter was both sympathetic and encouraging.
The schooner could easily be repaired. There was plenty of
good timber on the mainland and the natives would help—

luckily, he had happened to rescue a number of Bajaus from a fleet of pirate proas, and their chief was grateful.

The Bajaus proved most obliging. They built huts, chopped wood and carried water, and brought supplies of fruit, fish, goats, and poultry. The repairs got under way, and Trelawny was free to explore the shore with Zela. Resilient as one of her own Arabian colts, she had already recovered and was eager as he was to see this strange new country of Borneo.

The prevailing black marsh of the coast happened to be broken here by rocky cliffs topped by magnificent forest. They would pack a picnic basket, land in a cove, gather oysters, make coffee, and sleep away the afternoon in drowsy peace, unless Van Scolpvelt happened to come along the beach with his vasculum looking for specimens, or a cobra de capello raised its black square hood. Once the call of a bird brought Zela to her feet.

"The faoo bird!" she whispered. "That means a tiger is near!"

Trelawny loaded his carbine with ball, for a large creature was crawling down the cliff; not a tiger, but a strange, hairy, lean old man, bent double with age and carrying a club.

"Jungle admee!" Zela shivered. "Very dangerous!"

She was right. The old man advanced menacingly, and Trelawny shot him. Zela was sorry he had to die. They found his little hut under a blossoming tree; it was neat and pretty; he must have been happy there. But Van Scolpvelt exclaimed with delight when he saw the corpse. He had always wanted an orangutan for the museum in Amsterdam and this was the first full-grown specimen he had ever seen.

Meanwhile repairs had got so far along that Trelawny could leave them to the ship's carpenters, and as De Ruyter had decided to stay here in hiding until the China fleet came past, homeward bound, there was time to accept an invitation from a friendly Malay chief who offered to take them on a hunting trip.

It was a fine adventure. Mounted on elephants, they pushed deep into dark, tangled, orchid-hung forests; crossed the Plain of Elephants—a vast treeless tract overgrown with weeds and rattan marked by the paths of wild elephants; they saw birds and beasts no white man had ever seen before. When they had to turn back to the coast again they were sorry, Zela even sorrier than Trelawny; for she had become very fond of the little elephant that had carried her gently and safely through a week of danger.

She cried as she kissed him goodbye and cut off a tuft of bristly hair from his ear for a memento. Trelawny twisted the strands around a ring, and told her he would wear it always in grateful memory of a friend.

A few days later grab and schooner were once more at sea. But not together. De Ruyter had postponed the attack on the China fleet. He was going to Pulo-Penang with the friendly Malay chief to harass the English before they were reinforced by an expedition now preparing in Bombay against the pirates of Sambas; Trelawny was to go to Batavia, deliver despatches to the governor, and lay in fresh provisions, taking Louis along as buyer; the two vessels were to rendezvous at Seahorse Island off the Philippines.

Trelawny had avoided sailing on a Friday this time; but the voyage was to be almost as unfortunate as the last. It began well enough. They picked up a small prize carrying a load of bird's-nests, and Louis could try his hand at bird's-nest soup: a mixture of pigs' feet, sharks' fins, deer's sinews, plovers' eggs, mace, cinnamon, and red peppers that turned out to be even better than his turtle stew. But that was poor Louis's last treat. Cholera was raging in Batavia, and Louis was too fat to escape. He died and was buried at sea. They gave him a good funeral—Trelawny would have read the burial service over him, but unfortunately no one on board happened to own a Book of Common Prayer; his body was wrapped in a French flag, and they fired three volleys as he went over the side. But he would not stay under water—like Prince Caracciolo, who ten years before rose up out of the sea to confound his executioner, Lord Nelson, but for a less sinister reason. The sharks ate the weights off Louis's feet and he came up, not once, but twice. At last they were obliged to bury him on the shore.

Poor Louis out of sight, the crew could forget him in the hurry of getting away from Batavia at the earliest possible moment. But the tragedy was to make a lasting impression on Trelawny. It strengthened his determination never to bury anyone he loved in the sea; it proved that interment of a moldering corpse in the sand was even more repulsive, and it gave him a slant towards asceticism in the matter of eating and drinking that was to grow with the years.

"Keep thin!" became his motto. Poor Louis's fat had destroyed him by weakening his resistance. It was the "greyhound" race—the long-limbed, gaunt, and spare—who escaped fevers and plagues, regardless of their diet, while the fat and red-faced died like flies. Recalling this time, he wrote:

"I rejoice in the extermination of the great feeders and fat-buttocked—all except poor honest Louis, the beating of whose warm heart no mounds of suet could impede. I loathe greasy and haunchy brutes as Moses and Mohammed loathed swine. I salute and revere gout, apoplexy and the stone, for they are in their nature fierce radicals; slayers of kings and priests, the grasping wealthy and the greedy gluttons."

The abstemious Arab way of living seemed to him now the right way. He gave up drinking, except for a "carouse" on some festive occasion, and adopted Zela's light diet of fruit, vegetables, coffee, and sweets. From then on, he would have accepted with alacrity the first half of Middleton's advice to Macaulay, "Live strictly and think freely." The other half, however, "Practice what is moral and believe in what is rational," would always remain, for him, a "counsel of perfection" to be groped for but never attained.

His experience in the Batavia epidemic bore out his theory. Zela and her Arabs, and he himself, remained immune; but as soon as they got out to sea the European sailors began coming down with the fever. A horrible week followed, for Trelawny's surgeon had deserted, and Van Scolpvelt was out of reach on the grab. But he found an old medical book, and dosed his patients with ether, opium and calomel in the early stages of the disease, and quinine bark and wine in convalescence. Some got well. But some died.

The weather added to the ship's misery. Day after day of dead calm and burning heat went by, and the idleness was as bad as the heat. The men became restless. Trelawny set them firing at the fleets of Portuguese men-of-war drifting about on the stagnant water, and a square sail was lowered over the side so that they could bathe. But for some time a French boatswain had been making trouble, telling his friends that the captain was too young, favored natives, and hated Frenchmen. Mutiny was in the air. Trelawny was already on his guard when angry voices on deck brought him from Zela's cabin at a run.

He got there just in time. The boatswain was attacking Strong, the first mate, with a long knife. Trelawny caught the Frenchman by the throat and killed him, "Malay-fashion"— the creese driven over the man's left shoulder, through the back into the heart.

The affair was over almost as it began; the boatswain was thrown to the sharks, peace reigned again, and for once Trelawny could look back on a killing without regret. He knew that he had not killed on impulse, or for the love of killing. He had been patient and done his best to conciliate the man. When the right moment came, he had killed without anger, as he would have killed a snake.

Soon after, a gentle breeze sprang up, and the schooner moved on along the Java coast, now and then stopping at a village to buy provisions. One day Trelawny bought a Malay child as a present for Zela. She cost him a gold moidore; but the mother threw in a sack of tobacco, four fowls, a dozen eggs, and a basket of fruit for good measure. She was a lively little creature and came skipping on board the schooner gay as a lark, delighted at leaving her mother, enchanted with her new home, and was welcomed by Zela and Adoo as an amusing plaything.

Another stop, however, was to have a less agreeable ending. Trelawny had made friends with a Javanese prince—a handsome fellow riding a pretty little red horse—who was so attractive that when a hunting trip was suggested Trelawny yielded to temptation. But the handsome prince was after bigger game than deer and wild swine. He was after foreigners. The trip culminated in a fight on the seashore that came near putting an end to Trelawny's hunting for good and all.

Luckily, Zela was on deck watching the shore. She brought a boatload of men to the rescue; set fire to a carronade with her own hands, and blew the handsome prince and his little red horse to Kingdom Come.

But Trelawny had not come out of the fight any too well. A pistol fired at close range had caught him in the leg and the wound was foul with powder. Zela saved his life a second time. The yolks of raw eggs were applied to draw out the powder; the wound was poulticed, and washed with hot wine. The treatment was efficacious (years later in Greece, he was to recall Zela's raw eggs and try them with the same success). He began to mend. He was allowed a bit of roast kid for dinner. He was himself again.

Meanwhile the schooner had been making for Seahorse Island. She arrived there safely, only to find a message from De Ruyter giving directions for another rendezvous off the coast of Cochin China. On the way, however, grab and schooner came together accidentally during a storm, and being in need of repairs turned about and went on side by side to their old harbor behind the three little islands off Borneo.

They were received with enthusiasm by the Malay chief—more grateful than ever now because of De Ruyter's help at Sambas; the English had been discouraged for the time be-

ing, and after their long voyage everyone was thankful to set
foot on land again. Zela and Trelawny could revisit all their
favorite picnic places. They found the orangutan's hut on
the cliff in ruins and built themselves a little house under his
blossoming tree—only four bamboo stakes thatched with
palm leaves, but it was their own. Trelawny began planning
a bungalow, marked out a garden, and even spoke of staying
here for good. But Zela shook her head. No country—not
even Arabia—was as beautiful as the Isle of France; none
would ever seem so like home.

It was a peaceful holiday time, unbroken except for an
occasional business trip. The grateful Malays were keeping
watch on the neighboring seas. When they brought word of
an English ship likely to pass within reach, grab and
schooner would dash out from their hidden harbor and often
return with a prize. Only one of them, however, was of any
great value: a handsome copper-bottomed brig on her way
from Bombay to China, owned by Parsee merchants and
carrying a rich cargo of cotton, opium, bird's-nests, and
pearls.

A prize of this importance could not be disposed of legally
without difficult negotiation, so the holiday had to come to
an end. De Ruyter decided she must be taken to Batavia.
Trelawny and Zela bade goodbye to their hut on the cliff
top. Grab and schooner and handsome copper-bottomed brig
set sail, making for Java.

CHAPTER X

"O the palms grew high in Avès, and fruits that shone like gold,
And the colibris and parrots they were gorgeous to behold;
And the negro maids to Avès from bondage fast did flee,
To welcome gallant sailors, a-sweeping in from sea."
—CHARLES KINGSLEY.

Batavia was less unhealthy now. Fever and cholera had worn themselves out for the time being, and Zela could go ashore. They walked about the town—two hundred years old, sprung from a factory built by that same Pieter Both who had given his name to a peak in the Isle of France—admiring its massiveness, amused by the sharp contrast between the solemn square stone houses with gabled ends, the canals and stiff rows of the trees of the Dutch, and the peaked roofs, the gilt and paint of the Chinese quarter, picturesque but unbelievably overcrowded. Only sixty years before, twelve thousand Chinese had been massacred in a "pogrom"; but here they were back again, owning the best shops, doing the best business.

But the Dutch were traders too—in the grand manner. All the wealth of the Orient drifted in and out of the port of Batavia. Her merchants traded from Paris to Peru. Napoleon's Marie Louise and Lord Nelson's Lady Hamilton glittered with Batavia's diamonds; Pauline Borghese might wear her embroidered muslins; Mrs. Siddons and Abigail Adams, drink her tea.

And, for the moment, Java was feeling secure in her prosperity, strengthened by Napoleon's recent union of France and Holland. If anyone spoke of the new English governor of India, Lord Minto, as likely to adopt a more aggressive pol-

155

icy in the East, and suggested that he might be casting covetous eyes on their rich island, the remark would have been ignored as in bad taste, unwelcome as a British fleet.

But the town acknowledged one drawback: epidemics—its epidemics had killed a million in thirty years during the previous century. For the Dutch were neat but not clean. Their canals were choked with the garbage and filth of ages, and the native quarter still squatted in a bog made long ago by an eruption of Gunong Salak that had drowned it in mud, although deadly "miasmas" (mosquitoes not yet labelled guilty) were known to rise from swamps at night. Trelawny feared them; he remembered that the natives of Borneo always lighted smudges if they made camp in low ground. He would not let Zela spend a night in the town; they lived on the schooner, and when they came ashore usually rode off on horseback to explore the interior—Java is the most beautiful of all the beautiful islands of the Indian archipelago. Now and then they spent a few days with the governor at his country place in the mountains, or with some other friend of De Ruyter's.

Batavia was most polite to the young couple. Anyone introduced by De Ruyter would have been accepted, for he was known to be very rich and his successes as a harrier of the English were a legend throughout the Eastern seas. But Trelawny and Zela, young and good-looking, were attractive in themselves, and before long Trelawny was also being admired as a young man with a brilliant future in the privateering line. When he took Zela through the bazaars to buy her a present—a batik scarf, a filagree necklace from Sumatra, or a pair of red velvet slippers embroidered in gold such as the Javanese ladies wore—merchants were apt to nudge each other. That tall young fellow, with the little wife on his arm, was a privateer; owned the schooner anchored out there in the harbor; was said to be De Ruyter's son and heir; a young man on the upgrade and bound to succeed.

But, apart from reputation, Trelawny and De Ruyter

would have been conspicuous in this country of fat Dutch-men and dwarf Javanese. No one turned to look at Zela pass-ing by; her beauty was too delicate to attract attention. But all eyes followed the two captains, six feet tall, lean as leop-ards, with their fascinating, rolling sailor way of walking, their bold dark eyes and fierce moustaches; and every lady in Batavia—old or young, Dutch or native—soon became eager to make their acquaintance.

One of the first to succeed was a Javanese who happened to be staying in the lodging house where De Ruyter had taken rooms—business affairs prevented his staying on board ship. She was a great belle, a rich widow from the province of Jug. Being a Mohammedan, she should have been too modest to seek masculine society, but much marrying had robbed her of shyness. She had had ten husbands: one dead, two mur-dered, one missing, six divorced (divorce is easy in Java; the couple go before the priest, break a ring, or cut a bit of cord, and they are free). This wide experience had added to her fame, and although she was twenty-four and therefore no longer young her apartments were crowded with suitors, for she was known to be looking for an eleventh parti. When De Ruyter first appeared on the scene she decided he would do very nicely. But he proved too cool; she transferred her atten-tion to the other captain—as tall and handsome and much younger—and De Ruyter was commissioned to inform his friend of the honor she proposed to confer upon him.

De Ruyter ventured to remind her that the young captain already had a wife. This was waved away as unimportant. She had seen the girl: a white-faced, sickly creature, slim as a fish. Everything wrong about her—eyes too big; mouth too small; no style; wore her hair wound around her head like a turban without a single jewel. In short, not the sort of girl that would appeal to men.

"Look at me!" the widow ended, and flung off her veil—she had been peeping out from behind a scrap of gauze. "Look at me!"

De Ruyter looked. The lady was short—not much over four feet—very, very plump, and orange-yellow. A glistening yellow; polished with oil, her skin shone with the brightness of a gilded ball on a cupola which, indeed, her curves also suggested. Her face was another ball; the dot of a nose and tiny, twinkling, shoe-button eyes were buried in fat, only the lips protruded; they were broad, thick, red slices of blubber that pouted invitingly and with confidence. Her head was bald, except for a tuft no bigger than De Ruyter's moustache and as bristly, gathered into a knob on the crown and stuck all over with jewelled pins.

Take her all around, De Ruyter said to himself—watching her posture and revolve and wriggle—the widow was as unlike Zela as two human beings well could be! So unlike that he found it difficult to preserve his gravity as he thanked her for the exhibition, promised to deliver her message to the young captain, and rose to go.

But the lady's matrimonial experience had taught her that husbands like money as well as beauty. She added another inducement. The man who succeeded in winning her heart would become a prince—Prince of Jug—and owner of vast estates: huge plantations of rice, sugar, coffee, and tobacco; houses and tenements, and hundreds of slaves. With this reminder she let him go, and he hurried away to share the joke with Zela and Trelawny.

They all three laughed and laughed at his description of the Javanese Salome. When De Ruyter went on to tease Trelawny about his conquest, Zela joined in so wholeheartedly, advising him to accept the widow's offer and praising the pretty title, "Prince of Jug," that Trelawny became piqued by her indifference. He called on the widow, and brought back a tale of amorous adventure calculated to rouse Zela's jealousy. But Zela remained calm. She knew she had nothing to fear from any woman. Trelawny would not have turned from her to Scheherazade or Badoura, most certainly not to any ball of yellow fat.

He went again and again. Each time his story grew more highly colored. He described the delicious refreshments provided by the widow; her sugared green nutmegs preserved in syrup—a *spécialité de la maison*—were the best he had ever tasted. He described the widow's caresses in warm detail, and implied they were returned. Zela only laughed. He gave up trying to arouse Zela's jealousy, and the house of the widow saw him no more.

The lady would not, of course, admit defeat. She tried other weapons. The schooner was bombarded with delicacies. Boatloads of provisions arrived; the decks were strewn with bags of coffee and tobacco, baskets of fruit and flowers, jars of preserves, cakes, and sugar candy. The hard-hearted captain remained aloof.

News came that the schooner was on the point of departure. The widow, too desperate now to regard rough water or convention, hired a rowboat and appeared alongside just as the crew began getting up the anchor. She called to Trelawny; raised imploring hands; wept and screamed and begged to be taken on board. The captain only waved good-bye. The anchor came up. The widow toppled over into the bottom of her boat and lay there, upside down, in kicking hysterics. The schooner's sails filled slowly. She moved out of the harbor. Trelawny and Zela looked at each other with a laugh, glad to see the last of the silly Widow of Jug.

They were glad too to get away from Batavia's dirty harbor streaked with oil and garbage, out into the open sea again, all infection blown away by clean sea breezes. But Trelawny was aware of a feeling of depression. One of those black moods of his was upon him. He could find no cause for it. Zela was here beside him on the deck. Her cheeks were pink, her eyes bright. He felt her hand; it was warm. The voyage before them promised well; they were to move still deeper into the East and explore new islands of the archipelago. He tried to shake off the blackness. He could not. That night he had a dream.

It was a horrible dream: a confusion of faces and figures, hurrying back and forth busy with some savage rite, weaving a dazzling zigzag pattern of red and yellow and blue. The Javanese prince on his little red horse, the yellow Widow of Jug, hand in hand with the Blue Angel of Death, evil and menacing. Kamalia and Adoo, weeping and reproachful. All circling about, closing in on a small white frightened little creature—Zela! Zela—in danger—calling to him for help— He tried to answer, tried to reach her— The yellow widow's claws caught him by the throat— He beat them off—and woke.

For a moment he was afraid to move. Then he stretched out his hand. Zela was there beside him! Warm, breathing softly, alive—safe. The Javanese prince could not harm Zela— he was dead, blown to atoms; the Widow of Jug's hate could not stretch across miles and miles of blue water. It was a dream—to be forgotten with daylight.

But the dream was never to be entirely forgotten. "That vision," he wrote long after, "has haunted me through life. Often since then I have arisen from bed, haggard, sick, suffering such agonies as only devils can inflict. Ever, as it recurs, it is the more frightful. Always, it assures me of some horrible change."

But the next day brought an interruption that helped him to forget the dream. They fell in with three vessels of the French navy and went on board one of them for a talk. The Frenchmen were in a cheerful mood, for they had nearly— though not quite—captured an English ship, a frigate that Trelawny recognized at once from the description as his own: the frigate commanded by "Old Hoofs," which he himself had, as he put it, "abandoned." With his strange ability to reconcile conflicting emotions, to remain excessively loyal to England while fighting her tooth and nail, he was scarcely off the French ship before he began expressing his satisfaction that "Old Hoofs" had succeeded in escaping from the "lubberly Frenchmen," went on to condemn the boastfulness of the French race (forgetting that all Trelawnys, himself included, were more given to blowing their own horns than to hiding their lights under bushels), and ended with a contemptuous comment on the slovenly appearance and bad manners of French officers compared to British captains and lieutenants (forgetting now that he had found a certain Scotch lieutenant singularly deficient in both neatness and deportment!).

A later note on the incident is even more suggestive of his split patriotism. "This same beautiful French frigate," he wrote, "was afterwards captured in an action with one of the smaller English frigates and now carries the British jack. In her first cruise, under the victorious flag of England, she added to our naval force by taking, after a very sanguinary and gallant action, another of France's finest frigates in the Indian seas."

These three French vessels were the last they met with. Each day was taking grab and schooner deeper into "Island India," they passed only small craft carrying paltry cargoes not worth taking. One of these insignificant vessels, however, they were obliged to stop for; an open boat with five shipwrecked Englishmen—a master's mate and four sailors—adrift for seven days and dying of thirst. They were picked up and cared for; but, in spite of all Van Scolpvelt could do, two of them died. The mate, Darvell, pulled through; and the sailors told such a story of his courage and unselfishness that Trelawny felt drawn to him at once, and they became friends. They had much in common: both were daring to recklessness; both easily fired with pity for the wrongs of oppressed people and eager to engage in almost any "forlorn hope" that presented itself. What was still more important to Trelawny, Darvell was English.

For although Trelawny might admire primitive man's character, praise the comfort of native dress or lack of dress, the healthfulness of simple food, and sneer at the conventionality, money-grubbing and gluttony of Europeans, when he chose a friend, he chose one of his own race. Of the five friends of his young manhood, De Ruyter was an American; Walter, Aston, Darvell, Shelley were all English, all men of some education—and all, strange to say, short-lived. "By the time I was thirty," Trelawny wrote, "not one was left me," and added—thinking most of Shelley, last of the five: "Friendship is dead to me; nothing is left to me but its memory."

But all these sorrows were in the far future as grab and schooner moved serenely on their way, weaving in and out among the Sunda Islands. "They spangle the eastern ocean," Trelawny wrote, "thick, bright and countless as the fleecy clouds of a mackerel sky in summer; Edens where nature yields spontaneously all man could want. As we approached in our boats, the listless islanders seemed to gaze on us with wonder at the folly of these strange people who could wander restlessly about on the waste of waters in barks built of trees, and when, by signs, we made known our need of wood and water they pointed to the forests and streams; they neither aided nor opposed our landing."

Sometimes they would find an uninhabited island, and while the crews were cutting wood Trelawny and Zela could wander about admiring a new world. "Even the sand, the shells and rocks," he wrote, "resembled nothing seen before. Beasts, birds, lizards, insects—the very sea around us, the noise of the surf, the sky, the clouds above, the air we breathed, appeared new and strange. Zela would exclaim in girlish delight at some little unknown floweret, while I stood entranced gazing at a titanic tree on whose wide-spreading branches monkeys and parrots had formed their kingdom and under whose shade an army might have sheltered. We often thought ourselves to be, and perhaps we were, the first intruders on these solitudes. Birds and beasts viewed us with wonder, but fled not."

More often they could only skirt a beautiful shore, near enough to smell the spicy breezes and see trees crowded with birds: blue minas with golden crests and feet; lories, brilliant and variegated as a tulip bed; hundreds and hundreds of tiny scarlet hummingbirds. "Zela would scream for joy," he wrote, "and weep to be taken ashore; but the wild islanders forbade it."

Sumbawa, however, turned out to be inhabited by still another variety of islanders, neither fierce nor listless. Schooner and grab were anchored offshore taking in provisions. One evening Trelawny and Zela had been having supper on board the grab and were rowing home. The night was clear and still, the water like glass. Suddenly they caught a strange sound, a blowing and splashing coming from the shore, and gleams of light slitting the dark water. A school of giant fish? Dolphins? Seals?

"Savages!" Zela cried. "Swimming out to take us by surprise!"

Trelawny passed the warning back to the grab, and hurried on board his ship to rouse and arm the men.

They stood along the rail, watching. The splashing was louder now. They could see a multitude of heads, with long black hair streaming behind, approaching rapidly. The men wanted to fire, Trelawny forbade it. There was a tense moment. Then a laughing cry came from Zela and Adoo—the savages were all women!

The men dropped their pistols, cutlasses, and boarding pikes, and looked at one another with a foolish laugh—there was no doubt as to the sex of the enemy. Chirping and twittering like a flock of Mother Carey's chickens, the women surrounded the ship; they came climbing up the chains, the gangway, the bow, the stern.

"Some of these aquatic ladies," Trelawny wrote, "were young, sleek-skinned and of pretty Moorish features; but I was so entirely devoted to Zela that my thoughts never veered for an instant to any other. . . . With the dawn of day, they assembled on deck bedizened in various trifles gleaned from the sailors—buttons, beads, nails, odds and ends of discarded clothing, and went strutting up and down; one sporting a checked shirt, another a white jacket; some with only a solitary shoe or stocking, or a gaudy handkerchief instinctively applied to the head. Then a frightful old squaw appeared wearing an ancient scarlet waistcoat that had once helped my quartermaster to win the hearts of Plymouth belles, and at sight of this robe of honor, the other water nymphs clapped their hands in envy and admiration, and plumped overboard, hastening to hide their inferior decorations in the water, and went chattering and clattering back to shore. To avoid a repetition of these nocturnal orgies, we got under weigh."

They wandered on again, weaving in and out among new islands; apparently without any particular end in view, and without hope of profit—the cruise had brought them only a few cargoes of spice. No doubt De Ruyter suspected that the privateering business was becoming too dangerous because of increasing English aggression and was avoiding, rather than meeting, any English vessels.

Anyway, when they reached the Dutch Spice Islands, whatever suspicions he may have had were confirmed, for they found Amboyna in all the bustle of preparation for defence; it was rumored that Lord Minto intended to take the island. Not a new experience; Admiral Rainier had made it English for a time. But it was Dutch now and the inhabitants were arming, and everybody in a state of alarm—except the Governor. The Governor assured De Ruyter that he believed the rumor to be without foundation. De Ruyter could not agree, but he kept his opinion to himself. He had no intention of being detained for an indefinite time helping the Dutch fight off the English. Grab and schooner laid in provisions and sailed away from Amboyna at the earliest possible moment.

They moved westward now, making for the island of Celebes. Darvell and his sailors were still with them, and must be disposed of. As De Ruyter had hoped, they found a neutral vessel in the harbor of Macassar and the three Englishmen could be started safely on their way home.

Darvell, like Aston, seems to have enjoyed his taste of privateering life and been an agreeable guest, for Trelawny wrote that he and De Ruyter "parted from the gallant young officer with deep regret."

But, the farewell once over, Trelawny could enjoy strolling about the town with Zela. The European look of the place seemed a pleasant change after a sojourn among savage peoples; it was cleaner and healthier than Batavia, and even more Dutch—the old church must have reminded De Ruyter of New York, for it boasted a stoop and green blinds. There were pretty little gardens gay with flowers, and, more important than prettiness, there were Dutch ships in the harbor on their way to the Spice Islands carrying delicacies long unknown to grab and schooner. They loaded up with wine and cheese and biscuit, and laid in a supply of most excellent Schiedam—thinking of poor Louis—and then the crews got a holiday, for navigation among coral reefs and islands was difficult and everyone was tired out.

By now both vessels were in need of repairs. So before long they moved eastward again; rounded the southern tip of Celebes; went on up into the huge Gulf of Boni, and came to anchor near shore. They had to stay here some time. The grab's bowsprit was badly sprung; good spars were not to be found at once; sails, casks, and rigging were in poor shape, and both vessels swarmed with rats. Nobody minded rats in moderation; in fact, the monotony of a sailor's life could be pleasantly broken by a rat hunt, and the monotony of sailor food by a tasty dish of rat. Later on, Trelawny would shock his squeamish friends with a gloating description of "the Borneo breed of rat; long-bodied, short-legged, sleek-skinned and fine-eared, that, when skinned, split open, sprinkled with pepper and salt and nicely broiled furnished a salubrious and piquant relish for breakfast." But rats, either as game or as food, could be dispensed with here in Celebes, and Van Scolpvelt was told to do his best. His best was good; not a rat, scorpion, centipede, cockroach, flea or bug could withstand his fumigations of "kill-devil hell-paste." When the hatchways were opened again, the ships were as clean as whistles from stem to stern.

CHAPTER XI

"Cover her face; mine eyes dazzle: she died young."
—JOHN WEBSTER.

De Ruyter had chosen a perfect setting for their villeggiatura; Celebes offered every attraction that the most exacting holiday makers could desire. Far more beautiful than Borneo, perfect in climate and wildly picturesque, its peaks and forests, lakes and rivers invited exploration; and Trelawny made the most of his leisure time. Before long he happened upon a small, round, bright blue bay that promised good fishing; and one day he brought some of his men to draw a seine and Zela to admire its color and gather shells.

The beach curved around the blue water in a belt of golden sand, satin-smooth without a single pebble and sprinkled with shells of every imaginable tint, fantastically twisted, spiralled and scalloped. It was backed by a wall of jagged rocks, prickly as a hedge of petrified cactus, that rose menacingly to the plateau above. But Trelawny found a level spot for Zela's tent, and set it up. They wandered along the beach, gathering shells. They watched the seine come in, overflowing with fish—gold and silver, pink and purple and green. They chose a fish, and broiled it.

When lunch was over, he left her with Adoo and the Bali slave child, to climb a peak where he could command a wider view. Zela begged to go too, but he would not take her; the climb was stiff, and she was safe here in this quiet bay. The natives of Boni were good people—their Rajah was a friend of De Ruyter's, and men from the ships' crews were busy all about.

The climb was very stiff. But with the help of a boar spear

he managed to reach a ledge where he could survey a vast
landscape. In one direction the huge Gulf of Boni stretched
on and on to the sea. Behind him were mountains, extinct
volcanoes. Looking straight down, far below, he saw the little
bay, a blue sapphire set in a rim of gold; the white square
that was Zela's tent; the ship's boat drawn up on the shore—
with the seine spread over it to dry, it might have been a
black spider veiled in a gray web. He had taken an Arab
sailor with him. As they stood there looking out, the man
gave an exclamation, and pointed.

"Sharks," he said. "When they come in like that, it means
bad weather."

A line of dots was moving in from the ocean. With a glass,
Trelawny could see they were sharks—blue sharks, eight of
them. They came on in single file. As they reached the mouth
of the little bay the water suddenly thrashed to foam; one of
the sharks had met a swordfish. The fight was fierce; when it
was over a dying shark lay near shore, and his seven companions were slipping unconcernedly back to sea again.

Trelawny pocketed his glass, and returned to the bay. He
found the sailors firing at the shark with their muskets, left
them there, and walked on up the beach to Zela's tent. As he
drew near, wild moaning cries hurried him to a run. He burst
into the tent. Zela lay there on the sand, unconscious, shivering, white as death and covered with blood from a dozen cuts
on her neck and arms. Adoo crouched beside her. The Bali
child screamed and wailed and wrung her hands in a corner.

He dropped on his knees and felt Zela's heart. It was beating. He kissed her. She opened her eyes, tried to smile, lost
consciousness again. He tore up his shirt, bound her wounds
as well as he could, bathed her face, gave her wine. She
pointed feebly to Adoo. The poor girl was almost gone, bleeding to death from a gash in her leg. He did his best for her
too. The Bali child kept on screaming. He worked in a nightmare—not the Widow of Jug nightmare; a nightmare of repetition, a sense that all this had happened before. Zela, half

dead, lying in a tent—a tent in Madagascar—covered with blood, not her own, her father's— This was worse! What had happened? What had happened?

The sailors gathering anxiously outside the tent were as puzzled as himself. He ordered them to launch the boat at once—he must get Zela back to the schooner. They shook their heads. He dashed out indignantly; one glance told him they were right. The storm signalled by the sharks was here. Sky black, waves mountain-high; no boat could live in that sea for a moment.

The wind was tearing like a mad thing at the tent, trying to uproot it, drive it out to sea. The men fetched a sail and spread it over the roof; weighted the guy ropes with stones, drove the tent pegs tight, dug a trench; brought water, dry wood, a lantern. Night fell: a hideous night, noisy with wild shrieking wind and torrents of rain. The canvas flapped and strained ominously; rain beat in, soaked the sand. He sat on the ground propped against the tent pole, holding Zela in his arms, trying to shield her from the wet, watching her white face. She lay limp and lifeless. Hope died within him.

"I knew," he wrote later, "that the spring tide which had borne me on to perfect happiness was turned, ebbing back to the sea, and that mine and my happiness would be left a stranded wreck. I wished that the lightning would rend the rocks about us till they crumbled down, filled the bay, and buried us together. The invocation I made then I have never revoked—would that it had been accomplished!"

But towards morning faint color came seeping back into her cheeks and lips. She spoke. Bit by bit he found out what had happened.

She had gone swimming with Adoo. The Bali child was perched on the cliff top, ready to warn them if the sailors came too near. They were diving from a ledge of rock, diving for branches of pink coral, when the child screamed: "Sharks! Sharks!" There was a noise of splashing coming in from sea, men shouting. Adoo managed to scramble up on the ledge.

Zela tried to follow, slipped on the seaweed, caught at Adoo's hand, pulled her over. Both fell. The rocks were sharp as knives. She fainted. When she came to, she was here in the tent.

He heard the story with momentary relief. But her wounds, though painful, were not serious enough to account for her condition. Had she been hurt internally when she fell? He began longing for Van Scolpvelt as he had never longed for anyone in his life. Old Van Scolpvelt, whom he had always disliked and teased, now seemed an angel of wisdom and mercy. Would the storm never end? Would day never come?

Day came at last; with sunrise, the storm died. They got Zela and Adoo back to the schooner. Van Scolpvelt came from the grab. He shook his head. There was no sign of grief on his wizened face, but he took off his spectacles and wiped them as if they were misted over, and the skinny fingers Trelawny had always dreaded touched her with unexpected tenderness. There might, he said, be some internal hurt; he could not tell. But his bandaging made her more comfortable; Adoo was cared for. He gave Zela a dose of opium, and she went to sleep.

Trelawny resumed his watch. Hour after hour, he sat beside Zela, his eyes on her face, without speaking, refusing food; sunk in a brooding lethargy so unlike him that De Ruyter became alarmed and called him away to communicate a piece of news that ought to act as a counterirritant and make him forget his anxiety for a time at least: Lord Minto was preparing to take the Isle of France!

The news came from a reliable source—an Armenian merchant in Bombay. Minto's expedition was already in active preparation. It would comprise a huge fleet and some ten thousand men and was expected to reduce Port Louis before the year was out. The authorities there must be warned; grab and schooner were sailing at the earliest possible moment. There was work to be done; Trelawny had better get busy.

Trelawny nodded, and did as he was told; but listlessly, far more interested in a present of healing oils and and unguents that had come for Zela from the friendly Rajah of Boni than in anything, good or bad, that could befall the Isle of France.

However, the thought of it as their destination was vaguely cheering when, two days later, they set sail. Zela had been so happy there. Once back in De Ruyter's garden, under the shade of the lucky yakoonoo tree, refreshed by cool flower-scented breezes, Zela might recover her strength. Then hope faded again. That garden was miles and miles away! The voyage by the shortest route, with the best weather, would take more than a month. Could she live till then? He began wearying Van Scolpvelt with questions and importunities, trying to make him promise to keep Zela alive until they reached the Isle of France.

The irritable old man—patient now, and very kind—gave what little encouragement he could. That Macassar oil of the Rajah's seemed to have a remarkably soothing effect—Celebes was as famous for its healing oils as Java for its poisons; Macassar oil might cure as well as soothe. He counselled patience and hope; life was not yet extinct. Country air might well prove beneficial; every day brought the Isle of France nearer.

Patience and hope. Of the two, Trelawny found hope easier to hold than patience. This fixing of a goal—the conviction that De Ruyter's garden was a wonder-working place as sure to heal as the Pool of Bethesda, helped hope to live, but made patient waiting impossible, and the voyage seemed to stretch endlessly ahead.

But the first lap was the worst. They had to make one stop —off Batavia—to lay in provisions and give the governor their alarming news of Lord Minto's activities; but after that, once through the Straits of Sunda, and moving resolutely on out into the vast spaces of the Indian Ocean, the feeling of being really on the way pointing straight for the desired haven, helped to make the next few days more bearable, and another week brought true consolation: Zela began to get better.

Her strength came back slowly, so slowly that Trelawny would not let himself hope too much. But every day saw some slight improvement. At last, she was able to sit up for a while and they could talk; talk of their little Borneo hut under the old orangutan's blossoming tree, of Sumbawa's "mermaids" and, most often, of the Isle of France. They would recall their first picnic beside the mountain lake and the fat baboon eating a banana; her finding of the yakoonoo tree; the fresh coolness of the swimming pool in De Ruyter's garden, its flowers and fruit. And the days before they had learned each other's language, when she would pick the red seeds from a pomegranate and make letters on the moss, and he would understand.

The voyage was almost over. An evening came when she looked so like herself, perched on a scarlet cushion, dressed in her best spangled gauzes, singing him an Arab song, that he felt he could leave her for the night in Adoo's care and went to his own cabin to enjoy the first unbroken sleep he had had since her accident.

He did not enjoy it long. Almost as his eyes closed, nightmare came down on him; the nightmare of the yellow Widow of Jug, the Javanese prince on his little red horse, and the Blue Angel of Death. He woke in a sweat of horror, aroused by a cry, and staggered to his feet. Adoo was calling—

He found Zela fallen back on her couch, half conscious, in pain, dying. Adoo, sobbing wildly, pointed to a jar of sweetmeats—little green nutmegs preserved in syrup. And he knew! Knew, now, that hate's arm was longer far than love's. The hate of the Widow of Jug had stretched across miles and miles of sea and caught, not himself, but Zela!

From the first there was no hope. Van Scolpvelt could only say that the nutmegs must have been poisoned—Adoo had happened to find them in the storeroom, and Zela had eaten several; perhaps with the venom distilled from the upas tree, perhaps not—the Javanese were skilled in poisons. He did what he could. He gave her a sedative. She seemed easier, lay quiet. Trelawny took her in his arms. . . . The night wore away. At sunrise a hail came from the lookout on deck:

"Land! The Isle of France!"

He saw from her face that she heard. She was speaking. He bent close.

"I am glad, love. But I am too weak to walk," she whispered, "you will have to carry me ashore in your arms"—and died.

News of the English attack had already reached the Isle of France, and Port Louis on the farther side of the island was feverishly preparing to withstand a blockade when the schooner came to anchor in the quiet harbor of Port Bourbon. Even here in this remote spot something of the dread and commotion of the doomed capital could be felt; Port Bourbon's few inhabitants lived in fear of what the next hour might bring, and the French sailors in the schooner's crew went about their work muttering angrily of the iniquities of "perfidious Albion" and the Emperor's strange neglect of his Eastern possessions.

But Trelawny noticed little of all this and cared less. He remained as stonily indifferent to the island's fate as the Sentinel Peak itself, even when De Ruyter came hurrying back from Port Louis and reported the approach of an English force too overwhelming to resist. De Ruyter was in a gloomy mood. He prophesied surrender, not only of the Isle of France but of French power in the Orient. This was the beginning of the end; when England's new broom finished sweeping, France's navies—and her privateers—would have vanished from the Eastern seas!

He spoke with intentional emphasis, hoping to rouse Trelawny from his stupor of grief; but the boy scarcely heard what he was saying, and broke in with the question that so often follows death: where was Zela to be buried? Dig a grave for her in De Ruyter's garden among the flowers, under the yakoonoo tree? No; there were crawling beetles in that rich

moist earth. Bury her in the sea—clean and cold and pure?
He shuddered, remembering poor Louis. A funeral pyre,
such as the Greeks prepared for their dead? Let the body
vanish in flame, the spirit return to the elements. What did
De Ruyter think? Could that be done? Could De Ruyter
arrange it?

De Ruyter, gentle and pitying, assured him that it could
be done. He and the rais and Van Scolpvelt would see to
everything. By midnight the pyre would be ready; he would
signal from the shore.

All day, Trelawny watched beside Zela. "The utmost human nature can endure and survive, I suffered," he wrote of
this time. "Ours were no common ties. She had been as a bird
driven by tempest from the land that sought refuge in my
bosom, and like a darling bird too delicate to be entrusted to
others' hands, I alone fostered and cherished her." Night
came. The signal flared from the shore. A boat was in readiness.

"I had robed Zela," he wrote, long after, "in the richest costume of her country. Her yellow vest was spangled
with little rubies, and her chemise and flowing drawers, of
sea-green Indian crape, edged with gold; her outer garments
were of the finest muslin of India; her slippers, and the embroidered kerchiefs which bound up her hair and concealed
her bosom and the lower part of her face, beaded and em-
bossed with pearls. I preserved one braid of her long, dark,
silken hair, I placed it in my breast, and kissed her eyelids,
cheeks and lips. Carefully folding her in a large Arab barican
of white camel's hair, I conveyed her into the boat. I was a
mere machine. The blood in my veins was stagnant. I got
over the boat's quarter into the sea, and pressing my precious
burden to my breast and warily preventing the water from
touching her, I walked through the surf to the shore. Its coolness strengthened me and I was enabled to stagger to the spot
where stood the funeral pile. A black iron furnace, like a coffin, was placed upon it; figures flitted about like spectres. I

paused, realized the necessity of going through what I had undertaken, and placed the body within the iron shell as tenderly as a mother lays her sleeping child in its cradle.

"De Ruyter drew me back. Oil, spices, musk, camphor and ambergris were thrown in. Dry bamboo and reeds covered all. Smoke rose in a dark pyramid. I sprung forward, stumbled, and fell unconscious on the sand so near the fire that my hands were burned. What followed I know not."

The next few days were sad enough for everyone who had known Zela. The most hardhearted men in the crew felt a touch of pity for the death of one so young and so beautiful, remembering that "she had never spoken but in kindness, or come amongst them but to confer a favor." Adoo was ill with misery, the rais inconsolable. Zela's twelve Arabs—all that were left of the tribe—mourned the loss of "the last blood of their family, the utter extinction of one of the purest Arab tribes, whose pedigree went back thousands of years to the fathers of the human race, and gave vent to their grief in loud and clamorous yells."

As for De Ruyter, he had come to love Zela like a daughter, and his grief was sincere. But as the weeks went by and fear and tension increased at Port Louis, he must have found Trelawny's apathy more than a little trying. He had come to depend on the boy's energy, courage, and intelligence: qualities badly needed in this time of uncertainty. For De Ruyter knew that, with the fall of Port Louis, his career as a French privateer was at an end, and also his life in the Isle of France. If he left the East for good, and returned to America, he must get rid of the grab, sell his country place, provide for his servants and farm hands, pension the rais, and dispose of Zela's dependents: her Arabs, Adoo, and the Bali child.

He tried to discuss all this with Trelawny; it was useless. He got only languid assent to whatever plan was suggested, until it came to the question of Adoo. When De Ruyter remarked that the rais, who was returning to his home in Arabia, had offered to adopt not only Zela's Arabs but Adoo and the Bali child, Trelawny suddenly woke to indignant protest. Let Adoo go? Certainly not! He would not allow that for a moment. Adoo would die of grief. No; it must be distinctly understood that whatever happened—whether he stayed in the East, or went to America, or returned to England—Adoo was to go along. Adoo had loved Zela; she was all of Zela that was left to him. He would *not* be parted from Adoo!

De Ruyter was at his wit's end. This unforeseen complication must have seemed the last straw. After long consideration, he had decided against taking Trelawny with him to America. For one thing, the boy was not well enough, physically or mentally, to start life in a new country. For another, friction between England and America was increasing, and if war came an English boy would be far from welcome in the States. He had decided that Trelawny would have to go home, back to his own family in England. The plan was not altogether satisfactory. His family were, by all accounts, a hardhearted lot of snobs, conventional, purse-proud. They scarcely ever wrote to him; at long intervals he received a very small sum of money. None of them seemed to care whether this second son of the house lived or died. Even his mother would probably resent the reappearance of a prodigal so long out of sight on the other side of the world that he was also comfortably out of mind—and a prodigal who looked the part!

A handsome, healthy prodigal could expect a fairly kind welcome, but Trelawny was neither healthy nor handsome now. He was only a rough sailor boy with a thin, haggard, grief-lined face; wild eyes, shaggy hair, work-worn hands, unkempt dress, skin burned to a Moorish blackness. A strange figure to come shambling into an English drawing room. Strange enough, in all conscience, without this last preposterous addition: a young Malay slave girl hanging on his arm!

De Ruyter did his best, he protested and argued. Trelawny remained firm. Adoo was a good faithful soul. If his people didn't want Adoo he would take her somewhere else. Adoo would die of grief if she were parted from him. He would not let her go.

De Ruyter tried another tack. Was it wise to take a Malay girl to cold, wet, sunless England? Could she be happy in a land where everything—food, dress, customs, religion—would seem not only unfamiliar but horrifying? Why, Adoo would die of cold and misery in a week! Arabia was hot, the rais was kind. Trelawny gave in.

This question settled, preparations could begin for the long voyage to Europe—in the schooner; a frail craft for the rough Atlantic, but better than the grab. Trelawny took her around to Port Louis; she was put in apple-pie order, provisioned, a European crew engaged—not a difficult matter; every English sailor in Port Louis wanted to get away before Lord Minto's fleet closed in on the island.

The day of departure arrived. Friends came to say goodbye. Not Adoo—Trelawny could not face that farewell. Adoo had been staying contentedly with the rais in Port Louis expecting to be taken on board the schooner as soon as she was ready for sea; everyone felt it would be kinder to let the rais tell her after the schooner had sailed. At sunset, the schooner spread her wings and sailed out of the harbor for the last time.

De Ruyter and Trelawny watched the Isle of France fade on the horizon in silence. It was De Ruyter's home. Trelawny knew that he would never again experience the happiness he had found there with Zela; such happiness never came twice in this world. Both men were sad enough; they would have been sadder still if they had guessed that a little boat was following in the schooner's wake.

Adoo had watched the sailing with incredulous anguish. The rais had tried to console her, and she seemed resigned. But as soon as it was dark she had swum out to a country craft anchored in the harbor; stolen its little boat, and paddled desperately out to sea, hoping, poor thing, to overtake

the schooner. All next day the rais and his people had searched
for her. When news came of the missing boat, the search
widened. At last they found the boat, wrecked on a far-off
reef, but not Adoo. Neither England nor Arabia would have
to take care of Adoo's future.

Fortunately for Trelawny, knowledge of this tragedy did
not add darkness to the voyage. (It was more than a year before he heard of Adoo's death. "When the news came," he
wrote, "it was like a sword thrust through my body." He
blamed himself bitterly for having given in to De Ruyter,
vowed that never again would he take advice—not even from
so wise a man as De Ruyter, and was considerably strengthened in his belief that, for him at any rate, impulse was a
better guide than reason.) The voyage was dark enough without that cloud of regret; very long and very hard; monotonous, except for the usual storms and an occasional threat of
capture from an enemy vessel that ended in escape. But the
strain of those hard, cold, wet, anxious days and nights was,
in itself, healing. Before long, Trelawny found he could sleep
without the opium he had needed ever since Zela's death.
Slowly, perfect health came back to his body, and a sort of
numbness to the spirit that was almost peace. After hours of
merciless fatigue on deck the warm quiet cabin seemed like
heaven. De Ruyter's companionship must have been comfort-
ing. (Van Scolpvelt seems to have gone home in another ship.)
No doubt he talked and Trelawny listened, as in the old days
of their first voyages in the grab. Talked of Eastern affairs; of
France's prospects; of the personal interview with Napoleon
he intended to ask for in the hope that the Emperor might
be induced to take a more aggressive policy by convincing
him that the Isle of France would be the first of a long surrender, that Java would come next—Java, the richest jewel of
the archipelago—and within another year the British jack
would reign supreme over the Eastern seas.

This abstract talk would have been soothing. Reading must

have been an even better anodyne. No doubt there were many new books on the cabin shelves now, for De Ruyter acquired books as a ship's hull grows barnacles. No doubt Trelawny read them all and re-read the old ones; and, as poetry would have suited his mood, it was probably during this voyage that he became so saturated with poetry that lines of verse were apt to find their way into his correspondence often with odd effect. One line of Shakespeare, found perhaps at this time, he took for a motto he was to hold to all his life:

> "Come what come may,
> Time and the hour runs through the roughest day."

The roughest voyage must also have an end. The schooner's came near ending badly, for enemy ships "lay as thick in the English Channel as coral islands in the Sulu archipelago." But De Ruyter contrived to slip her through, and one gray morning she came safely to anchor in the gray harbor of St. Malo.

CHAPTER XII

"Seeinge (most mercyless Misteris) neither my person can please you, neither my calling content you, neither my singular affection towards you cause you to requite it with lyke love, I mean utterly to abandon the place of your abode, and to bestow myselfe in some such fare country, whyther not so much as ye report of your beauty shall come."   —GEORGE PETTIE.

Trelawny sat crouched on a low bare rock out at sea off the coast of Jersey, staring at the dark water, waiting impatiently for sunrise and the turn of the tide, but with no desire for what day might bring. A few feet away the two smuggler-fishermen bribed by De Ruyter to carry him across the Channel and set him safe on the English shore lay stretched out beside their boat drawn up on the rock, fast asleep and snoring contentedly, having already earned their money. This rock was English. Just before sunrise the tide would turn; their passenger could be landed in a cove on the island itself and this rather chancy job would be finished. Meanwhile they slept and snored.

Trelawny could not sleep. He was tired and cold and wet and hungry—a supper of shellfish washed down with Nantz had failed to satisfy him. He was sunk in one of his blackest moods. Bidding goodbye to De Ruyter had meant bidding goodbye to the only human being in the world whom he loved, or who cared a rush whether he lived or died. It had snapped the last tie that held him to the past; to Zela, to all that warm, bright, sun-drenched East where he belonged. For he knew now—shivering as the fog closed down sour with the smell of mud and seaweed—that he was a child of the East, not of the West. What was he doing here in England? Chilly, damp, inhospitable England. If he were to jump off into the next wave that came curling in, who would care? His family? He laughed aloud, remembering that homesick little boy turned out by his father "with as little remorse as he would have ordered a blind puppy to be drowned."

The sun rose, painted the fog with a pale yellow eye. The fishermen stood up; stretched, yawned, bent over the boat, beckoned to him. He glanced at the incoming wave. Shook his head. A prodigal who has made his way half across the world and is almost in sight of home must risk the last few steps, no matter how poor a welcome he may get at the end of the road.

The boat pushed off into the fog. A few hours later he was on dry land, making his way to the nearest village.

What happened next? Did the prodigal go straight home just as he was, ragged and forlorn in his dirty sailor's slops? Or did he go first to a good tailor—he had a liking for handsome clothes—and make himself presentable before submitting to family inspection? What sort of welcome did he get when he knocked at his father's door?

Trelawny himself left these questions unanswered. He ended the story of his adventures in the East with that night on the cold rock off the coast of Jersey, and did not begin the account of his European experiences until some seven or eight years farther on.

But the last question can be answered easily enough. Trelawny's correspondence of this time and later makes it plain that, after this first home-coming, he never broke with his family again; and he appears to have got on fairly well even with his father. So the welcome must have been kind. This granted, the answer to the other question follows almost as a matter of course.

In the Bible story, the welcome depends on the father—a father so indifferent to appearances that he seems to have found his son's rags endearing rather than repulsive. In real life, with a father like Charles Trelawny, it would have been just the other way. The welcome would have depended chiefly on the son—what the prodigal looked like when he turned up again. As a poverty-stricken young Edward would have been kicked out in short order, it is safe to assume that he had made himself presentable before venturing into the home circle.

The decision may have been arrived at only after some hesitation. The desire to shock would have fought with the desire to impress. Which would be more amusing? Act the dirty, ragged sea dog, with rolling gait and strange oaths on his lips, clapping his father on the back, laughing grimly as his mother shrank and his sisters shrieked in horror? Or should he overwhelm them with admiration? Saunter in, very elegant indeed; the neglected son transformed; rich and handsome now, a credit to his family?

Granted that the latter picture must have proved the more fascinating of the two, and that Trelawny never did things by halves, it is safe to assume that when he rejoined his family he not only had discarded the sailor's slops he found so comfortable, but was dressed in the very height of the fashion (perhaps the most becoming that men have ever worn); a less foppish figure than Beau Brummel, less dignified than Jane Austen's Darcy, but as well turned out and as good-looking with a devil-may-care recklessness that both Brummel and Darcy would have condemned as ungenteel—and envied in their hearts. For a new type of hero was stepping into the limelight.

In other words, the classic was giving way to the romantic in literature and architecture, manners and dress. Byron, the high priest of romance, had arrived in London, and smart society was watching the noble lord create heroes in his own image with breathless interest. Girls were already dreaming of world-weary Childe Harolds; soon they would dream of Manfreds and Mazeppas, of Laras and Don Juans. A suitor must have wild eyes, a black moustache, a long cloak and a wicked past and be on the lookout for some sweet pure English girl who would help him to forget, or remain disconsolate.

The Byronic influence spread like a plague; by now, even country belles would have caught the infection. So, whether his family were in London or in Cheshire when he returned, he found himself welcomed by his sisters with open arms as a gift from heaven, and every girl he met overwhelmed him with attentions and hoped to become the "bandit's bride." For no young man in all England was better fitted, in appearance and reputation, for the glamorous rôle of hero-villain.

Unfortunately, he was less well fitted for it in reality. If he had been half as wicked as he looked, the girls would have suffered and he himself have got off scot-free. But all his wild adventures had left him as ignorant of the ways of the world as a shepherd boy fresh from the moors. The "vine leaves in his hair" were worn only for ornament. He was very young—not yet twenty. He had never so much as spoken to a girl of his own class and took for granted that all "good women" were like Zela: simple, loving, and sincere. The very look of his father's house—brocade curtains, thick carpets, ornaments, mirrors, silver, and china—must have seemed strange to him. He had never sat in an armchair or dined at a well appointed table in his life. It was an unkind fate that sent a creature so ignorant, so foolhardy, and so susceptible into a new world utterly unaware of the dangers that surrounded him; never suspecting that he might better have ventured unarmed into the hold of a pirate ship, or a tiger-haunted jungle, than into the drawing rooms of his sisters' friends, innocent little blue-eyed angels, listening wide-eyed to his tales of adventure, every one of them intent on binding him hand and foot and making him her own for life. So he talked and flirted and enjoyed himself, and strolled as carelessly along the flowery path as the child in the allegory, and never guessed his danger—until it was too late!

Disaster was inevitable. It came soon. Not long after his return he found himself engaged to one of the wide-eyed English angels.

Her name was Caroline Julia Addison *—usually called Julia. She was the youngest child of "John Addison of Calcutta in the East Indies esquire," and had been born in India. She may have been staying in Bath when she and Trelawny met, for he had intimate friends there, the family of Captain White, who were also friends of hers. She was only nineteen; she must have been pretty, for Trelawny could never abide anyone, man or woman, who was not good-looking; her having been born in India may have added a touch of romance and reminded him of Zela. Anyway, on the 17th of May (May is not considered a lucky month for marriages) in the year 1813 (thirteen is an unlucky number) Edward Trelawny and Caroline Julia Addison were married. They had two little girls, Maria Julia and Eliza; everything seemed going on well enough.

Then on the last day of December, 1816, Trelawny got the shock of his life. He discovered that Julia had a lover, one "Thomas Coleman, esq., Captain in his Majesty's 98th Regiment of Foot."

At this distance of time it would be futile to guess at the original cause of the disaster or to distribute the responsibility. Zela's lovely little ghost may have come between them— she had set a standard a second wife might well have found hard to emulate. Trelawny could never have been easy to live with. He was fickle, fell in and out of love with extreme rapidity. Whether or not he was in any way to blame, he suffered, he was horribly mortified, and started divorce proceedings at once.

All divorces in those days were intentionally intricate affairs, intentionally hedged about with technicalities, and intentionally prolonged. Trelawny had a clear case; he won at every move. But the law refused to be hurried, there was no

* Authority: Rouge Croix, College of Arms, London.

escaping one jot of wearisome routine. His very small stock of patience must have been exhausted before he had signed the first of the necessary documents and when, at the end of two long years, he was given the last petition to sign, he must have read it with mingled rage and amusement, for he—hater of princes—was obliged to adopt an attitude of unwonted humility if he was going to get what he wanted.

"Humbly Sheweth and Complaineth to Your Most Excellent Majesty Your true and faithful Subject," it began, and continued on the same abject note, "That on or about the 17th of May, 1813, your said Subject was married . . . That on or about the 31st December, 1816, Your Subject first discovered . . . That Your said Subject did, in the Easter Term in the 57th year of Your Majesty's reign, bring his action on the Court of King's Bench at Westminster against the said Thomas Coleman . . . That Your said Subject exhibited a libel in the Consistory Court of the Bishop of London against the said Caroline . . . That Your said Subject stands deprived of the comforts of Matrimony . . . May it therefore please Your Most Excellent Majesty (out of Your Princely Goodness and Compassion to Your said Subject's misfortune and calamity) that it may be enacted . . . By and with the Advice and Consent of the Lords Spiritual and Temporal and Commons in the present Parliament assembled. . . ." And so on and so on, for several pages and, at last, in the "59 year of Geo. III, Session 1819," Trelawny got his freedom.

It does not need much stretch of imagination to realize the purgatory his proud and undisciplined nature must have gone through in those few years. Caroline Julia's name does not appear in any of his writings. All direct mention of either the marriage or the divorce was omitted. But there is an occasional bitter allusion to the miseries of "double-harness," and a tirade in his first book gives a pretty good idea of the torture he suffered—or believed he had suffered—at Julia's hands. "The fatal noose was cast around my neck, my proud crest humbled to the dust, the bloody bit thrust into my mouth, my shaggy mane trimmed, my hitherto untramelled back bent with a weight I could neither endure nor shake off, my light and springy action changed into a painful amble—in short I was married."

However, once the affair was over he naturally did his best to forget it—he never recalled anything painful if he could avoid doing so, and probably for this reason he left the years before and after his marital failure, as well as the affair itself, completely blank when he came to write the story of his life. His first book ends with that cold rock off the coast of Jersey, and the second begins a year after his final divorce.

Fortunately the gap can easily be filled in from other sources both private and public. For the years immediately after his return from the Orient were among the most eventful in European history. England herself had gone through a dreadful alternation of hopes and fears, ups and downs. No sooner had the Allies got Napoleon safely shut up on the isle of Elba than he was out again, on the warpath. Everyone grumbled, "I told you so," and complained, like Wordsworth's little daughter: "Oh, when they had him, why didn't they kill him!" The Hundred Days brought an even more dreadful suspense. Cornwall and Devon feared invasion and waited, looking shudderingly out to sea with an apprehension they had not felt since the Armada hove in sight (and would not feel again for another century). Then came the glorious relief of Waterloo, England could relax. Cornwall and Devon could watch a ship—H.M.S. *Bellerophon*—come to anchor off Plymouth; watch with triumphant satisfaction, for the ship was a cage and it held a wild beast that, this time, would not be allowed to escape. Little boats pushed out from shore, circled about as near as they dared, came back to boast of having caught a glimpse of the beast or heard him roaring. It was a fine show, and it lasted for days and days. For Bonaparte was "waiting his destiny," as Creevy wrote, "at the hands of the Prince at Torbay," and George was slow in making up his mind. But, at last, the final curtain came down. Bony was transferred to the *Northumberland;* she vanished below the horizon; Bony was off to St. Helena; "the land had peace."

And during these years so troubled both for Europe and for Trelawny, what had his relations been doing? Nothing much, except grow richer and more important. Charles, having long since retired from the Army, had not been obliged to help the Allies catch Bony and could devote himself to looking after his Cheshire estates and the fortune left him by his father, General Trelawny, who had died in 1800. The general must have "cut up" pretty well, for Charles was rich enough to get into Parliament in 1809 as member for Mitchell, a rotten borough owned by his brother-in-law, Sir Christopher Hawkins—still alive and, no doubt, still practicing his little economies at Trewithen. Charles had also squeezed out enough money to buy Harry, Edward's elder brother, a commission in the family regiment, the Grenadier Guards. So in 1817 Harry was enjoying life at Woolwich; which meant he could congratulate himself on two escapes: he had escaped being killed at Waterloo and also—what he probably considered almost as important—had got away from home. The women of the family—Edward's mother and sisters—were less fortunate. They could not escape; and home must have been a pretty terrible place, for Charles still kept his household in complete subjection. In fact, to judge from an incident of the time described by Edward later on, Charles was harder than ever to live with; his cruelty and miserliness had increased rather than diminished with the years.

"In his London house," Edward wrote, "my father had devoted a room on the ground floor, under a skylight, to the conservation of choice wines, foreign preserves, and cordials. One day a neighbor's child at play next door happened to lodge a ball on the skylight, and my youngest sister * stepped out of a back window to seek for it, slipped and fell through the leaded glass down onto the bottles and jars below. She

* Charlotte: she married a brother of Henry Trevanion, husband of Byron's niece, Georgiana Leigh.

was dreadfully bruised, and her face, legs and hands so badly cut that she retains the scars to this day. My mother was called. Her child screamed out for God's sake to open the door, she was bleeding to death. But the door was locked and my father had the key. My mother dared not break the lock —had I been there my foot should have picked it! Will it be believed that my sister, in that state, was compelled to await my father's return from the House of Commons? At last he returned, my mother informed him of the accident and tried to allay the wrath she saw gathering on his brow. He took no notice of her but paced to the closet; the delinquent awed by his approach hushed her sobs. He opened the door, found her trembling and weeping, scarce able to stand. Without a word, he cuffed her out of the room, and then gloomily decanted what wine remained in the broken bottles."

This unpleasing anecdote told by Trelawny as "an instance of my father's ferocity," was the last allusion to the family in his books. But something of what was going on at the time of the divorce and later may be gathered from his correspondence with a friend, Augusta White.* She was one of a large family living in Bath, the daughter of Captain George White of the Royal Navy, who had known Julia, but who took Trelawny's part when the break came. Her sympathy meant much to him during the mortifications and delays inevitable in a divorce case, and she may have hoped to take Julia's place after the divorce. But though Trelawny wrote to her freely and with grateful affection, his letters are not quite love letters; and Augusta must in the end have decided not to allow disappointment to spoil a friendship, for the correspondence beginning early in 1817 continued off and on for more than fifty years; she preserved many of his letters, and they were handed down to her descendants as relics of a romantic episode.

The earlier letters, written from London, are wretchedly

* Letters from Trelawny to Augusta White; unpublished, inherited by the Misses Draper of Montreal.

unhappy; sprinkled with bitter and very youthful comments on the vanity of human affairs and quotations from Shakespeare and, as usual, with many oddly misspelled words such as *quight* and *roughfest*. He speaks of his "poor orphans" and his "dear baby"; of his wife, "the unfortunate woman who might have been respectable but is now—" He apologizes to Augusta for having sent her a certain box, as a souvenir of her former intimacy with Julia, not realizing that it had been a present to Julia from that "wretch, Coleman." He remarks that experience has taught him a lesson: "I have studied your sex too closely during the past three years to be again deceived. Had I known them half as well one year previously I had not been the wreck I am." But the dominant note is frantic impatience; he is longing to be free, to escape, to forget. He talks wildly of "chains that bind my spirit downward," and of caged larks, "winging their weigh on high after tedious bondage"; of being unable to plan his future: "Till this rock is weathered I will not alter my course."

But the divorce proceedings had scarcely begun before Trelawny's thoughts were turned in another direction: Augusta's father died, apparently under tragic circumstances. Always a most pitying person, his long letter of condolence was warm with the same generous selflessness that, later on, was to make it possible for another bereaved woman—Mary Shelley—to revive again after a tragedy. It ends: "My heart is heavy, my own sorrows no longer remembered. . . . If your mother does not use me in this time of her distress I shall doubt her loving her son."

Then came another change in the tone of his letters. Trelawny's dark moods could never hold him very long. He wrote: "Cheer up, sweet little Aust. Take the world as 'tis, not as you would wish it to be. You know my motto,

" 'Come what come may,
Time and the hour runs through the roughfest day.' "

He began to tell Augusta what he was doing in London: His family had left Soho Square for the summer and taken a large house near Southampton. "I hold quight a levy for the actors," he wrote, "in my lodgings; many of them are well red [Byron spelt it *redde*] and clever, and men of talent are always desirable companions be their rank in life what it may. . . . Drury Lane and Covent Garden both open in a few days. . . . I am practicing cadriles, and all the fashionable figures." He writes of having had "tolerable sport" while staying at Mr. Campbell's country place near Lincoln for the shooting, and complains: "I find myself sadly at a loss for horses in London, not caring to borrow from the guardsmen."

But these distractions were soon supplemented by a more enduring pleasure. He discovered the pleasure to be found in art. It was a strange discovery for a young man of his wild restless nature to make. Since childhood he had knocked about the world, consorted with sailors and savages; he was without education—that is, he was self-educated. Until his return to England De Ruyter's cabin bookshelf had been his only contact with literature; he had probably never stepped inside an art gallery in his life. Yet he wrote to Augusta from London: "I have received extreme delight from an exhibition of pictures at Bullock and from seeing a magnificent window of stained glass, of which I am a great admirer. 'Tis an exquisite piece of art and I have viewed it many times." And from Lincoln: "This town is famous for its old, venerable, grand, magnificent, far-famed, beautiful Cathedral— but the ladies have yellow skins and thick legs."

Meanwhile the divorce case was dragging on. He became increasingly restless. He wrote to Augusta, "I form a thousand plans to dispose of myself," and then: "My father has offered me a Commission in any Regt. I choose, not wishing me to go to South America or Australia. . . . I am busily engaged with the South American affairs. . . . It is Sir Rob't

Wilson who talks of going to South America—he is one of the gallant men who saved Lavalette, if he goes I shall join him."

These South American plans must have been connected with Bolívar, or some of the other patriots whose struggle against Spanish tyranny was exciting the admiration of all modern-minded Europeans. Sir Robert Wilson would have been an ideal leader for an expedition of this sort. He had a brilliant record as soldier, traveller, and writer—"his work on the defects of the British army system is remembered as the first protest against flogging." Though he seems to have been more chivalrous than wise, Lord Ilchester said of him: "Seldom were high courage, enthusiasm and lack of judgment so singularly mingled in one individual." But that was a blend Trelawny would have admired rather than distrusted, so Wilson's withdrawal may have been the reason for his staying on in England.

On the other hand, a remark to Augusta suggests an even more likely reason: "I have had a packet of letters from Allsop at Buenos Ayres; he is well, not coming until next year."

This mention of a friend in South America named Allsop links the year of the divorce with Trelawny's past, and probably explains both his original interest in some South American expedition and his final abandonment of the project, whatever it may have been; for, in *Adventures of a Younger Son,* Trelawny makes it plain that Allsop was the real name of Darvell, the young officer the schooner had met with adrift in the Indian Ocean after a shipwreck.

"Darvell's life was a short one," Trelawny wrote; "it has been so with all those to whom I have linked myself. His riper judgement shook off the fetters that had manacled him in boyhood; his daring spirit forced him on from danger to danger. On his return to Europe he became a leader of the forlorn hope of the heroic few who are to be found in the van of those fighting for liberty. No sooner was the flag of freedom unfurled in the New World by spirits like his own, than he hastened to join their ranks. His bleached bones may

still glitter on the yellow sands of Peru, where the small vessel
he commanded was driven on shore and wrecked, in a chivalrous action he fought with a Spanish force ten times his
superior."

These English years were to be clouded by other losses.
Aston, Trelawny's first friend, and De Ruyter, his best—except Shelley—also came to their deaths at this time. Aston was
drowned, and De Ruyter killed in a fight off the Barbary
coast between an English frigate and a French corvette in
which he happened to be travelling. "De Ruyter was standing on the taffrail," Trelawny wrote later, "sinking his despatches over the stern, when the halliards of the French
ensign were shot away. . . . His body was found enveloped in
the folds of the tricoloured flag under which he had fought
so long victoriously."

The news of these three deaths was not to reach Trelawny
for some months to come, which was fortunate. Life was depressing enough without bad news. The divorce case was
dragging on. His children's bringing-up had become a complication; he wrote angrily to Augusta: "Ill or not, I wish the
child not to be christened. What does it signify being buried
in consecrated ground—all humbug!" The remark is less callous than it sounds, and means more than it would nowadays.
Feeling was running high among the intelligentsia in this
matter of christenings. Freethinkers had decided that christenings were almost as wicked and quite as vulgar as marriages and were ready, like Shelley, to suffer martyrdom
rather than permit their offspring to be contaminated by
priestly ministrations—unless, of course, some practical reason came in, such as inheriting money. Now, in 1817, Shelley
had just "bowed down in the House of Rimmon" enough to
get married to his Mary, but he still stood firm in defence of
their children. Not long, however; the next year—for a practical reason—he gave in. The register of St. Giles' in London
noted a triple baptism: the christening of "William and
Clara Everina, children of Percy Bysshe Shelley, Esq., and

Mary Wollstonecraft his wife . . . . Also Clara Allegra, reputed daughter of Rt. Hon. George Gordon, Lord Byron, Peer, of no fixed residence, travelling on the Continent, by Clara Mary Jane Clairmont."

Those names were to mean much to Trelawny later on; they make a link with the future just as Allsop's name linked him to the past. But that time was still three years ahead. All through 1817 he kept on dallying with the idea of adventure. Then he lost interest in South America. When at last he won the first round in his suit for divorce and got his decree nisi, instead of dashing across the world to join a forlorn hope and die for freedom he decided to live and—always in extremes— to live in the country. So he rented a little cottage, Cannon Farm near Pinner in Middlesex, and let himself sink deep into the bosom of the soft green English country, hoping to relax and to forget.

It was a mistake. He had come back too late, he was too dissatisfied with himself, too restless. South America might have finished him. He might, like Darvell, have left his bones to glitter on the yellow sands of Peru. But he had been meant for that sort of death—his tragedy was to come not from dying too soon but from living too long.

The rural experiment amused him for a time. He wrote cheerfully to Augusta of his life at "Trelawny Villa," and quoted:

"Fatigued at last, a calm retreat I chose
And soothed my harass'd mind with meet repose."

Then restlessness returned. Now his quotations took a different turn:

"He travels and expatiates as the bee,
From flow'r to flow'r—so he from land to land,"

and before long he had decided to follow the bee's example.
The year 1820 took him to the Continent. In August he

was staying in Ouchy on the Lake of Geneva near Lausanne, seeing something of a more cosmopolitan society than he had ever before encountered. For at this time "Lausanne," he wrote later, "was one of the inland harbors of refuge where wanderers from all countries sought shelter." Most of these exiles were gathered here—as so often before and since —because they were "free thinkers," and Switzerland allowed them to talk, as well as think, freely, and even to read books forbidden by less progressive governments. Trelawny soon made an acquaintance—one of those chance acquaintances not personally important whose influence may be far-reaching: a young bookseller, graduate of a German university, "more interested in literature than in lucre," and trained to express himself with eloquence and exactitude. He was probably the first highly educated man Trelawny had ever met, and it must have been extraordinarily exciting to hear put into well chosen words theories that De Ruyter had often presented, but in too half-baked a form to be altogether digestible. De Ruyter's character—his courage, tolerance, and hatred of tyranny—had been more impressive than his talk. The young bookseller was a linguist; bits of Goethe and Kant and other great foreign writers were translated for Trelawny's benefit; their philosophy, religion, and politics, exhaustively discussed in the light of modern thought. Then one memorable day a new name "swam into his ken," a name that was to echo all through Trelawny's life on and on into extreme old age—the name of Shelley.

It was a midsummer day, hot and sunny; Trelawny had happened to pass a terrace shaded by feathery acacias, saw his friend sitting there absorbed in a book, and joined him. The book turned out to be *Queen Mab,* Shelley's adolescent arraignment of the enemies of mankind—religion, government, and war—which the bookseller had just come across by accident.

"I might never have noticed the book," he remarked, "if a priest had not chanced upon it in my lumber room. When

I saw him read a few lines and fling it from him with a cry of horror, I thought of the old proverb: 'No one throws a stone at a tree that does not bear fruit.' "

"Priests do not," Trelawny said. "I too must have a bite of that forbidden fruit. What do you think of it?"

"It is crude, but well flavored. They say the author is but a boy; if that be true we shall hear of him again."

Trelawny nodded. He was already reading, already excited by what he read.

No setting could have been more perfect for an introduction to *Queen Mab*. The terrace was the terrace in front of Gibbon's house where, thirty years before, the *Decline and Fall,* his story of "the triumph of barbarism and religion," had been finished. "I wrote," he said, "the last lines of the last page in a summer house in my garden. After laying down my pen I took several turns in a covered walk of acacias which commands a prospect of the country, the lake and the mountains. The air was temperate, the sky was serene, the silver orb of the moon was reflected from the waters, and all nature was silent."

If the two young men reading there had looked up they would have seen the same landscape—sunny now, not silvered with moonlight; and ghosts are not supposed to "walk" by day. Nevertheless, *Queen Mab* might have drawn a ghost of Gibbon's turn of mind back to his old haunts, to peer over Trelawny's shoulder with a tolerant but pessimistic smile as he read of a future

> "When poverty and wealth, the thirst of fame,
> War with its million horrors, and fierce hell
> Shall live but in the memory of time."

Queen Mab was of course an appetizer. Other poems by Shelley were unearthed in the bookshop lumber room, and the more Trelawny read the more admiring he became. Before long he had yielded so entirely to the charm of Shelley's song and Shelley's preaching that it was something of a shock to be brought up with a round turn, as he was floating happily along on the full tide of enchantment, by the adverse criticism of a poet whose opinion could not well be ignored, and who was, incidentally, the first of his tribe Trelawny had ever encountered.

The meeting came about through an English friend of Trelawny's who happened to be staying at a hotel in Lausanne. Captain Daniel Roberts—a son of that "stout fellow" Lieutenant Roberts who had gone around the world with Captain Cook and was in command of the pinnace at the time of Cook's murder—was at loose ends now, like so many Army and Navy men after the Peace, and travelling for pleasure on half-pay. A rough diamond, not especially interesting in himself, he and Trelawny had much in common. For one thing, Roberts had met both Byron and Shelley some years before in Geneva, had dined at the Villa Diodati and seen Byron later on in Venice, and Trelawny listened eagerly to all he had to say of the two poets. It was disillusioning to hear Roberts speak of Byron as not really a handsome man, too short and stout; but delightful to find him a wholehearted admirer of Shelley. According to Roberts, "Never were manly wit and sense combined with such ingenuousness, or trust in mankind and unacquaintance with the world, as in Shelley." Then too Roberts loved the sea and everything connected with ships and knew a lot about boat building. Both he and Trelawny were keen sportsmen, ready to put up with any discomfort if they could get good shooting; yet both were sensitive to the beauties of nature, and Roberts had a pretty turn for sketching.

Nevertheless, an intimacy under the circumstances seems a trifle odd, for Roberts was a captain in the Navy and Trelawny a deserter. Odder still, Roberts was not alone in being able to take a lenient view of Trelawny's past; that abrupt departure from His Majesty's Service seems to have had singularly little effect on Trelawny's friendships and none on his future career. One would have thought that a deserter might have faced disgrace, if not arrest, on his return home, and most certainly would not have found a welcome in Army and Navy circles. But nothing of the sort happened. His father could suggest buying him a commission in the Army without fear of any inconvenient discussion of the past; he saw a good deal of Harry's brother guardsmen, and not only the Whites but most of his other intimate friends of that time were Navy people. Yet one may be sure that Trelawny had made no secret of either his desertion or his privateering—he never made a secret of anything. He was much too proud of his adventurous past to keep the story to himself, and from the moment he set foot on English soil he must have been telling everybody all about everything with a readiness that might have been boring if the stories had been less exciting or the story-teller less good-looking. Perhaps this frankness was disarming; anyway, the vitality and charm that had first drawn De Ruyter's attention and brought forgiveness from his first Navy friend, Aston, were still potent. Men as well as women listened spellbound when he talked of his adventures, and it seems to have been agreed that the prelude might be forgotten as an unimportant boyish peccadillo.

So here he was waiting for Captain Roberts one clear shining September morning, in a hotel in Lausanne, having been invited to breakfast and wishing his friend would return—Roberts had gone sketching—for he had walked in from Ouchy and was getting hungrier every minute. At last the captain came in, but not alone. He was accompanied by three travellers whom he had happened to meet on their way to the hotel: a man and two ladies.

"I saw by their utilitarian garb," Trelawny wrote later,* "as well as by the blisters on their cheeks and noses that they

---

* *Recollections of Shelley and Byron*. Here as elsewhere in extracts from Trelawny's books, the writing is condensed and simplified; but the sense never in any way altered.

were pedestrian tourists fresh from the blazing sun and frosty
air of snow-covered mountains. The man was evidently a
denizen of the north; his accent harsh, skin white, of an angu-
lar and bony build, and self-confident and dogmatic in his
opinions. But the precision and quaintness of his language,
and his eccentric remarks on common things, stimulated my
mind. Our icy islanders thaw rapidly when they have drifted
into warmer latitudes. These, flushed with health, delighted
with their excursion, and with appetites earned by bodily
and mental activity, were in such high spirits that Roberts
and I caught the infection of their mirth. We all talked as
loud and fast as if under the influence of champagne instead
of café au lait."

Breakfast over, a carriage arrived to take the travellers
on their way. As they were leaving, Roberts whispered to
Trelawny that they were the Wordsworths—the poet himself, his wife, and his sister—and Trelawny could not resist
an eager question: What did Mr. Wordsworth think of Shelley as a poet?

"Nothing," he answered shortly. "A poet who has not produced a good poem before he is twenty-five will never do so."

"*The Cenci?*" Trelawny ventured.

"Won't do," William shook his head and got into the carriage, followed by a rough-coated Scotch terrier.

"This hairy fellow is our flea trap," he shouted, and they
drove away.

Trelawny was left staring after them, wondering if it were
jealousy or lack of poetic taste that had prompted the verdict.

Nevertheless, Trelawny was to remember that breakfast
party with pleasure, and the feeling must have been mutual.
For Dorothy Wordsworth's record of their Swiss trip—that
had been flavored all through with remarks such as, "The
air invigorated our spirits and we were gay as larks"—noted
that evening: "Lausanne, September 19th. We met with some
pleasant Englishmen."

Soon after Trelawny went on to Geneva, and here at "Plongeon," a large country house belonging to an old Cornish friend of his, Sir John St. Aubyn, he met three young Army men, George Jervoice of the Madras Artillery, Edward Ellerker Williams, and Thomas Medwin—the last a captain, the other two lieutenants, on half-pay travelling for pleasure, like Captain Roberts. They were all living together at a villa prettily named "la Maison des Grenades," the House of Pomegranates, and Trelawny spent many pleasant hours there as well as at "Plongeon." All were young and lively; Edward Williams had a talent for drawing; Jane Williams was a sweet creature and played charmingly on the piano and the harp. All of them were just back from India, and this in itself would have made them interesting to Trelawny; but with Shelley so in his mind—Wordsworth's harsh remark had made no impression—it was extraordinarily exciting to discover that Medwin was actually a cousin of Shelley's and a schoolfellow.

"Medwin had known Shelley from childhood," Trelawny wrote later. "From all I could gather, Shelley lived as he wrote, the life of a true poet, loving solitude but by no means a cynic. Irrespective of his genius, we all longed to meet him."

Medwin turned out to be a terrible bore, given to long-winded anecdotes of personal experiences; but Trelawny put up with his chatter, hoping that through him a meeting with Shelley might come about, for Medwin after long separation was now corresponding with his cousin. He had found a copy of *The Revolt of Islam* in a Bombay bazaar (how well Trelawny knew those bazaars, their smells, hot dust, and garish color!), had written to him and received an invitation to visit the Shelleys at Pisa when he went on to Italy.

All his listeners were soon fired with the idea of meeting the poet, and for a time it looked as though the "Pisa circle" —that group of innocent instruments of Fate that were to bring Shelley to his death—might forgather in Pisa that winter. But Fate must have decided to wait. For one reason or another, having converged they drew apart again. Edward and Jane Williams decided to spent the winter in Chalon-sur-Saône, and Trelawny got word that his father had died and he must come home at once. (Harry, the elder son, of course inherited the Cheshire estates; but Charles must have been able to provide well for his wife and his other children. For Edward Trelawny seems never to have felt the pinch of poverty except when generosity got the best of him and he found he had given away more money than he could afford at the moment.) Only Jervoice went south with Medwin. Trelawny offered to drive Edward and Jane Williams and their baby to Chalon, some seventy-five miles away, in a light Swiss carriage he had bought and they set off. The weather was bad; the trip took four days; they were all thankful to arrive at Chalon. But it turned out to be a damp, unattractive hole; Trelawny bade his friends goodbye and hurried on to Paris by *malle-poste*.

England seemed prosaic after Switzerland; the air heavy, his friends dull. He was always fretted by anything connected with business—anything, in fact, that involved thinking about money. His dissatisfaction with London society that winter of 1821 was increased by hearing from Edward Williams. They had outrun him, as far as meeting Shelley was concerned. Chalon had soon proved intolerable; they had gone to Pisa and at once become intimate with the Shelleys.

The poet, according to Edward, looked the part to perfection. He was young, amiable, full of life and fun, and could talk brilliantly on any abstract subject; but even his ordinary conversation was "akin to poetry; for he saw everything in the most singular and pleasing light."

The liking was mutual. When they settled down at Pugnano although the Shelleys' villa at the Baths of S. Giuliano di Pisa was five miles away, the two families met nearly every day, dining, sketching—Mary was sitting to Edward for her portrait, a miniature she intended to give Shelley on his birthday—talking, making music.

But the poet's chief pleasure was boating. When Edward Williams wrote that Shelley had had a little boat built at Leghorn and they expected to enjoy delightful trips exploring the various streams and canals in the neighborhood, Trelawny was filled with envy, tinged with the contempt all sailors feel for soldiers who venture on the water. In Edward's case this contempt was justified. Edward wrote:

"A few nights ago I nearly put an end to the poet and myself. We went to Leghorn to see after the little boat and, as the wind blew excessively hard and fair, we resolved upon returning to Pisa in her, and accordingly started with a huge sail, and at 10 o'clock P.M. capsized her."

This time, Fate let them off with a ducking. Edward Williams caught cold; but his confidence remained undiminished, and neither he nor Shelley thought of their escape as a warning. Yet it was not their first. That winter while they were sailing on the Arno in an even smaller boat, Williams stood up suddenly, caught at the mast to steady himself, and tipped the boat over. He could swim a little and managed to struggle ashore; but Shelley could not swim a stroke and would have sunk like a stone if a more competent friend had not been with them.

"I caught hold of Shelley," Henry Revely wrote, "and told him to be calm and quiet, and I would take him on shore. His answer, characteristic of his undaunted courage, was: 'All right; never more comfortable in my life; do what you will with me.' But as soon as I set him down on shore he fell flat down on his face in a faint."

These experiences, however, only increased Shelley's romantic passion for the water, and the correspondence between Edward Williams and Trelawny must often have touched on boat-building for at the end of 1821 Williams wrote: "Have a boat we must, and if we can get Roberts to build one so much the better."

But this letter had begun with an odd reproach worth noticing as an extreme instance of that extraordinary disregard for dates, bordering on a complex, that was to disconcert Trelawny's readers later on and even throw doubt on his veracity. Williams wrote from Pisa, the day after Christmas, 1821, but it was in answer to a letter that Trelawny had dated January 1, 1822!

Williams was amused. "Forty years hence, my lad," he remarked, "you will treat the present with more respect than to *antedate* the coming year. But I hope that time with you will always fly as unheeded as it now appears to do." He ended, "Pray remember me to Roberts." (To Roberts, who was to be remembered by posterity only as the man whose talent for boat building brought about the death of Williams and Shelley!) "Tell him he must be content to take me by the hand, though he should not discover a pipe *in* my mouth, or mustachios on it,—the first makes me sick, and the last makes Jane so.

"Bring with you any new books you may have. There is a Mrs. B. [Beauclerc] here with a litter of seven daughters, who is the gayest lady, and the only one who gives dances, for her young squaws are arriving at the age when, as Lord Byron says, they must waltz for their livelihood. When a man gets on this strain, the sooner he concludes his letter the better. Addio."

In the meantime Trelawny had left England. "Having become tired of society," he wrote later, "I determined to pass the winter [of 1822] in the wildest part of the Maremma, in the midst of the marshes and malaria, with my friends Roberts and Williams; keen sportsmen both—that part of the country being well stocked with woodcocks and wild fowl. For this purpose, I shipped an ample supply of dogs, guns and other implements of the chase to Leghorn. For the exercise of my brain I proposed spending the summer with Shelley and Byron, boating in the Mediterranean."

This agreeable combination of sport and poetry decided

upon, he had gone to Chalon to get the horse and cabriolet
he had left there with the Williamses; to Geneva, where Captain Roberts was waiting for him, and at last after long antici-
pation found himself actually headed for Italy.

"In my Swiss carriage," he wrote, "we could go on or stop,
where and when we pleased. We could sketch, shoot, fish and
observe everything at our leisure. If our progress was slow,
it was most pleasant. We crossed Mount Cenis and, in due
course, arrived at Genoa. After a long stop in that city of
painted palaces, anxious to see the Poet, I drove on to Pisa
alone."

CHAPTER XIII

"I reckon, if I count at all,
First Poets—then the Sun—
Then Summer—then the Heaven of God—
And then the list is done."
                              —EMILY DICKINSON.

When Trelawny arrived in Pisa, January 14, 1822, the Shelleys had been drifting from one Italian town to another for nearly four years. They both knew that a mild climate was better for Percy's health, and Italian scenery more stimulating to his mind than the quiet English landscape, and Mary had accepted a roving life in foreign parts for his sake. But those four years had not been as happy for her as for Percy. She had lost two children; she was often desperately homesick; she distrusted the strange Italian way of living; she was not strong enough to share Percy's long walks and rides and dangerous excursions on the water; she found his liking for solitude and dislike of society very hard to endure, and although she still loved him and still believed in him wholeheartedly as a poet, she was beginning to wonder whether it had been worth while to sacrifice so much for those wild radical theories that had banished him—the gentlest, kindest soul that ever lived—from his father's house and made him "a scorn and a hissing" to his compatriots. In short, this daughter of Mary Wollstonecraft and Godwin, the advocate of women's rights and the philosopher, was suffering—as reformers' children are so apt to suffer—from reaction.

With a brilliant mind but a conventional heart, fed from birth on radical ideas and not much else, denied the amusements usually enjoyed by a pretty girl, Mary was mentally

stimulated and emotionally starved, and she found Shelley—
young, charming, grandson of a baronet—irresistible when he
came to sit at Godwin's philosophic feet. When he fell in love
with her and suggested they should practice what her father
preached—scorn the "slavery of marriage," forget he had a
wife already and elope—she joyfully agreed, and off they went.

That had all come about years ago—in 1814, soon after
Trelawny's marriage to Julia Addison. Now, in 1822, the first
fine careless rapture that had snatched Mary away from her
father—leaving him more shocked than a radical philosopher
had any business to be, for Godwin had "a horror of the public papers"—was of course less careless. But though Love had
often fluttered perilously close to the window sill he had
never actually flown away; and here, in Pisa, Mary was as
contented as it was in her nature to be, and Shelley was
happy—the first six months of 1822, except for one unhappy
interlude, were probably the most serene of his life.

Both the contentment and the serenity of this time came
largely from the presence of those amiable, slightly commonplace young persons, the Williamses, Edward and Jane; "tem-
peramentally," according to Miss Glynn Grylls, "the most
normal friends the Shelleys ever had." At first they had both
liked Edward better than Jane. But Percy soon discovered
that Jane—for all she was so simple, shallow, and cheerful—
stimulated his poetic imagination to a quite extraordinary
degree. Mary, realizing this was true, accepted the situation
as just another of "Percy's Platonics," and found Jane's liveliness a relief from the intolerable boredom of Tom Medwin
(he stayed on and on—Mary wrote to a friend, "The burden
of Tom grows very heavy!"); and even when Percy gave Jane
a guitar, with some pretty lines calling himself "Ariel" and
Jane "Miranda," she was only a very little jealous, for she
knew that Percy was only a very little in love.

So the intimacy flourished, and when autumn made village life impossible Shelley had found apartments for both
families in the same house in Pisa: the Tre Palazzi di Chiesa

on the Lungarno. The Shelleys with their one small Percy Florence and Medwin moved into the top flat; Edward, Jane and their two babies, into the one directly below; and they were scarcely settled in before another friend—a friend less soothing than the Williamses—Lord Byron, arrived to take up his residence on the opposite side of the river.

It was Shelley's doing. For various reasons, he had wanted Byron to come to Pisa; had made it easy for him (Shelley could be efficient when he chose—Matthew Arnold's nickname, "ineffectual angel," had little foundation in fact) by choosing a palace that even Byron would think suitable for his way of living—the magnificent Palazzo Lanfranchi, supposed to have been built by Michael Angelo, on the Lungarno; and here in due time the great man had arrived from Ravenna "with his servants, his horses, his monkey, bulldog, mastiff, cats, peafowl, hens and other livestock"—as well as that still more indispensable article, his mistress, Countess Guiccioli, lodged, however, at a discreet distance in another quarter of the town and chaperoned by her complacent family, the Gambas—to give sleepy Pisa a taste of the noisy, bright-colored, pompous comedy that a Byronic entrance on a new scene always provided.

Trelawny's arrival two months later was a very different affair. He came alone—having left Captain Roberts in Genoa, probably to see about that little matter of building a boat for Mr. Shelley. It was late, almost dark, when he drove in from the north in his little Swiss carriage, and Pisa's marble palaces and towers stood up white and ghostlike in the twilight. He found an inn, stabled his tired horse, ate a hurried dinner, and then made his way through empty, ill lighted streets, depressed by the sadness of the ancient town—a faded Gulnare long since deserted by the sea—glad to reach the Tre Palazzi, mount the stone staircase and find himself at last in the cheerful apartment of his friends, the Williamses.

Their welcome could not have been warmer. The three

had much to talk about and were laughing and telling one another all that had happened since they had parted at Chalon a year ago, when Trelawny became aware of eyes—glittering eyes—looking in at him from the dark passage with disconcerting intentness.

Jane laughed. "Come in, Shelley!" she called. "It's only our friend Tre, just arrived."

"Swiftly gliding in, blushing like a girl, a tall thin stripling held out both his hands," Trelawny wrote thirty-six years later, still able to recall the meeting as if it had been yesterday.

For the "stripling" who came into the room that winter's evening was to become the one great romantic figure of Trelawny's life. Of the three persons who shaped his character —De Ruyter, Zela, Shelley—Shelley's mark was the most enduring. The remembrance of De Ruyter's courage would come to strengthen him in crucial moments; no other of his many loves could ever rival Zela; but he was to accept every one of Shelley's beliefs and denials, theories and practices—sensible and fantastic, little and big—and make them his own. The friendship was to color his whole life through. Yet it had only six months to ripen. The shadow of the little American schooner—the shadow that had been lengthening from across the world for so long—was taking shape in the mind of Roberts, the boat builder. Another six months and it would become reality, and Shelley would go the way that "golden lads and girls all must." But that six months was enough. When Trelawny reached the last of his nearly ninety years he was thinking and talking and writing about Shelley as if he still saw him as on that evening in Jane's parlor, "gliding in with outstretched hands."

He did not of course realize this at the time. His first feeling as he saw Shelley's "flushed, feminine and artless face" was merely incredulous surprise. Could this be the rebel poet—"this mild-looking, beardless boy, dressed like a boy in a black jacket and trousers he seemed to have outgrown"?

Was this "the veritable monster at war with all the world, excommunicated by the Fathers of the Church, deprived of his civil rights by a grim Lord Chancellor, discarded by his family and denounced by rival sages of literature as the founder of a Satanic school"? He could not believe it; it must be a hoax!

Jane, seeing Trelawny's bewilderment, broke in with a tactful question:

"What book is that you have in your hand, Shelley?" she asked. "Calderón's *Magico Prodigioso?* Oh, read it to us!"

"Shoved off from the shore of commonplace incidents," Trelawny wrote, "and fairly launched on a theme that interested him, he became oblivious of everything but the book in his hand. . . . His lucid interpretation of the story, and the ease with which he translated the most subtle and imaginative passages of the Spanish poet, were marvellous. . . . I no longer doubted his identity."

There was a pause. Trelawny turned to Jane with a word of comment. When he turned back again, Shelley was gone.

Jane smiled. "He comes and goes like a spirit," she said, "no one knows where or when."

Almost as she spoke he returned, this time accompanied by his wife. Trelawny liked Mary's looks—her fair hair, delicate complexion, calm gray eyes and slim figure; he knew she was Godwin's daughter and the author of *Frankenstein;* he admired her wit and animation. "Like Shelley," he wrote, "she could express her thoughts in varied and appropriate words, derived from familiarity with the works of our vigorous old writers." But that evening "she brought us back from the ideal world in which Shelley had left us, to the real, welcomed me to Italy, and asked me the news of London and Paris, the new books, operas and bonnets, marriages, murders and other marvels. The Poet vanished and tea appeared."

By this time Trelawny, always quick as a flash in his likes

and dislikes, knew with conviction that he admired both the
Shelleys and wanted them for his friends. How did they feel
about him? What impression did he make that evening?
Mary's reaction seems to have been excitement mingled with
doubt. Her journal of January 14th noted "Trelawny ar-
rives," as an important event, but a few days later: "Trelawny is extravagant—*un giovanni stravagante*. . . . He tells
strange stories of himself, horrific ones." And she wrote to
a friend:

"He is a kind of half-Arab Englishman, whose life has
been as changeful as that of *Athanasius,* and who recounts
the adventures as eloquently and as well as the imagined
Greek. He is clever; for his moral qualities I am yet in the
dark; he is a strange web which I am endeavouring to unravel. I would fain learn if generosity is united to impetu-
ousness, probity of spirit to his assumption of singularity
and independence. He is 6 feet high, raven black hair, which
curls thickly and shortly like a Moor's, dark gray expressive
eyes, overhanging brows, upturned lips, and a smile which
expresses good nature and kind-heartedness."

Obviously Mary was too conventional to give immediate
approval to this exotic newcomer. Shelley, on the other hand,
aware of the admiration in the "dark gray expressive eyes"
gazing at him with such intentness as he read from Calderón,
must have felt an answering wave of friendliness. For admiration seldom came Shelley's way. No great poet ever
lived so entirely without applause—the *Literary Gazette* had
dismissed *Adonais* as "a mere collection of bloated words"—
and no man of so sweet a nature ever had to get along with
so few friends. Here in Pisa he was living in strange isola-
tion cut off from the great world—the world of publishers,
readers, critics; living in a "glass house," hearing the stones
of the Philistines rattling on the roof and eager to reply, but
always finding his sling too weak; for no publisher dared to
take his poems; they were "forbidden fruit," printed at his
own expense, read on the sly. The little praise that drifted

in from outside came muffled, "horns of Elfland faintly blowing," and for friends he had only Medwin, a bore; Edward
Williams, merely a nice fellow, and Byron, a genius and intellectually his equal, but too moody, too cold-hearted, too
fickle for real friendship—Shelley had discovered long since
there was more torture than pleasure to be derived from
"companionship with a demiurge."

So Shelley was not so overrun with friends that he could
not find room for another. But whether or not he returned
Trelawny's liking at once, their first evening together was
cut short. Jane's tea tray appeared, Shelley vanished; not,
however, before making an appointment for the following
day. Mr. Trelawny would like to make Lord Byron's acquaintance? They would go together.

So next afternoon found the two, so oddly unlike—fair,
slight, boyish Ariel; tall, dark Pirate—strolling along the
Lungarno to the Palazzo Lanfranchi. They entered a vast
marble hall, mounted a vast marble stairway, were ushered
through a vast salon and on into a small billiard room empty
except for Byron's bulldog, Moretto, who was welcoming
them with a growl when his master came in from an adjoin-
ing room.

The usual politenesses were exchanged. But Trelawny—
himself always at ease in any society—realized with some
amusement that the great man was feeling a little embar-
rassed at meeting a stranger and was trying to cover it with
an affectation of nonchalance. Neither embarrassment nor
affectation, however, could live long in Shelley's presence;
both soon wore off. Byron asked Shelley to look over a poem
he had been writing, Shelley instantly became absorbed;
Byron picked up a cue and suggested a game of billiards.
Trelawny agreed, they began knocking the balls about. But
neither was interested in the game. Byron was too occupied
in talking—telling anecdotes likely to impress this new acquaintance, such as the story of his swim across the Helles-
pont—and Trelawny much too intent on listening and watch-

ing, making the most of this interview with a famous poet, hero of a thousand scandals.

Those "dark expressive eyes" of Trelawny's never missed anything they wanted to see, and he was blessed with an ex· cellent visual memory. The portrait he drew of Byron in his *Recollections* is as vivid as if he had used paint instead of words: "In external appearance Byron realized that ideal standard with which imagination adorns genius. He was in the prime of life . . . regular features, without a stain or fur- row on his pallid skin, his shoulders broad, chest open, body and limbs finely proportioned. His small highly finished head and curly hair had an airy and graceful appearance from the massiveness and length of his throat; you saw his genius in his eyes and lips. In short Nature could do little more than she had done for him, both in outward form and in the in- ward spirit she had given to animate it. But all these rare gifts, to his jaundiced imagination, only served to make his one personal defect the more apparent . . . he brooded over that blemish as sensitive minds will brood until they mag- nify a wart into a wen. His lameness certainly helped to make him skeptical, cynical and savage.

"There was no peculiarity in his dress, it was adapted to the climate; a tartan jacket braided—he said it was the Gor- don pattern, and that his mother was of that ilk. A blue velvet cap with a gold band, and very long nankeen trousers, strapped down so as to cover his feet: his throat was not bare as represented in drawings."

The portrait is a handsome one. Byron happened to be thin at the time. The months in Venice that Mary Shelley mildly termed "the gaieties and incorrectness of his Vene- tian life," had taken off some of the fat that was the plague of his life, and he had adopted a slimming diet—cold pota- toes and vinegar, biscuits and soda water—that kept him looking as a poet should look. "By starving his body," Tre- lawny wrote, "Byron kept his brains clear; no man had brighter eyes, or a clearer voice."

Lady Blessington's description a year later is much the same. She also noticed a certain *gaucherie,* due to his trying to conceal his lame foot, and she too was surprised at Byron's "want of that natural self-possession and dignity which ought to characterize a man of birth and education. . . . A bad and vulgar taste predominated in all Byron's equipments, whether in dress or furniture. . . . His carriages and liveries were in the same bad taste, having an affectation of finery, but *mesquin* in the details, and tawdry in the ensemble."

Trelawny, of course, also perceived Byron's lack of taste; but, being a few years younger than Byron and coming straight from London, it seemed to him merely old-fashioned; Byron had lost touch with present-day society. "The character he most commonly appeared in," he wrote, rather pityingly, "was of the free and easy sort, such as had been the fashion when he was in London and George IV was regent, and his talk was seasoned with anecdotes of the great actors, boxers, gamblers, duellists, drunkards, etc., appropriately garnished with the slang and scandal of that day. Such things had all been in fashion and were at that time considered accomplishments by gentlemen, and of this tribe of Mohawks the Prince Regent was the chief and allowed to be the most perfect specimen. Byron, not knowing the tribe was extinct, still prided himself on having belonged to it; of nothing was he more indignant than of being treated as a man of letters, instead of as a Lord and a man of fashion."

Lady Blessington and Trelawny were very unlike, yet both of them were conscious of Byron's innate vulgarity and both found it puzzling—though for very different reasons. Trelawny, with eight hundred years of ancestry behind him which he never alluded to, could not understand why Byron should derive so little support from his noble lineage and yet be forever talking about it. Lady Blessington studied the question from another angle. As she had climbed very high indeed without either ancestors or virtue to help her along, but never felt secure because of the first handicap (the latter did not matter so much—strawberry leaves can cover a multitude of sins), she must often have reflected that her perch would have been more comfortable if she could have boasted just one fairly respectable forefather with any chance of being believed. In consequence the contemplation of a baron who got so little good out of his noble birth never ceased to fill her with envious astonishment. On the other hand, as she herself was grateful to the Muses for a small gift and only wished it were larger, another discovery was almost as amazing. This really great poet considered social position far more important than genius! "Were he but sensible," she remarked sadly, "how much the *Lord* is overlooked in the *Poet* he would be less vain of his rank; but, as it is, this vanity is very prominent and resembles more the pride of a parvenu than the calm dignity of an aristocrat."

Neither she nor Trelawny seems to have realized that Byron's bringing up was responsible for the traits they found so puzzling. To all intents and purposes he *was* a parvenu. The wave that had washed him up from mean poverty-stricken obscurity into bright sunlight had come too suddenly and too late. He never ceased being surprised at finding himself safe on shore, never ceased wondering whether he looked quite like the others who had always been safe, and never felt at home in the world of smart society which, incredible as it may appear, was the only world where he cared to shine.

So it is scarcely surprising that Trelawny should have found Byron at first sight as disappointing as Wordsworth, though in a different way. As he watched this pale young man with soft white hands, brandishing a billiard cue, bending languidly over the table, chattering of nothing, boasting of everything, he told himself that, having "come prepared to see a solemn mystery," he seemed likely to be bored with a rather dull farce. But he was wrong—very wrong, as he soon found out.

Shelley rejoined them, and almost at once Byron's cloak

of affectation fell from him. It was always so. Byron could sneer at Shelley behind his back, he could be unutterably false to their friendship,* but he could never resist Shelley's charm when they were face to face. Now, as the two poets talked of their trade Trelawny listened in wondering admiration—surprised at first to find the great poet not only inviting criticism from the little one but accepting it, then astonished by the brilliance of Byron's defence, his mental agility, and a memory for apt quotations that would have floored most opponents. This was the real Byron, creator of Childe Harold and Don Juan, the man he had travelled so far to see!

Interruption came too soon. A servant appeared; his lordship's horses were at the door. They all went down. The animals stamping impatiently in the hot dusty street, jingling, shaking off the flies, were unworthy of a noble lord; "sorry jades," in Trelawny's opinion, and encumbered with superfluous trappings—holsters, martingales, breastplates, and the like—that gave a comic effect to English eyes. Byron's horses were, indeed, something of a joke to his friends. Captain Roberts went so far as to call them "dog-horses"; but then Roberts was terribly plain-spoken. Having first met Byron during a plump interval, he went on describing the poet as "grossly fat"!

So Trelawny was glad that he was not obliged to accept the loan of a jade. He sent to the inn for his own Swiss horse. They were joined by Count Taaffe, an Irish poet, conspicuous in Pisa but a bad rider and almost as great a bore as Medwin. They all set off. Rode for an hour or so out into the country—Byron talking with wit and animation, for he was in good spirits—reached a *podere,* drank wine and ate cake; wandered out into the vineyard, and amused themselves pistol shooting—the marks, five-paul pieces stuck in the tip of a cleft stick.

"Byron, Shelley and I," Trelawny wrote afterwards, "fired

* See Byron's letter to Hoppner, Oct. 1, 1820.

at fifteen paces and one of us generally hit the cane or the coin; our firing was pretty equal." (But Roberts, describing a similar occasion, said that Byron's hand shook, while "Shelley's was firmness itself. . . . He was like a child, so excited at making a good shot, running forward like a child to see where they had hit," and added that he, Roberts, had not only practiced pistol shooting with Byron, but with "a more famous shot even than he, one of the most extraordinary characters of the age": Trelawny.) "After five or six rounds, Byron pocketed the battered money and sauntered about the grounds. We then remounted."

As they rode slowly home in the cool of the evening, the conversation again turned to discussion of poetry, and again Trelawny "was pleased and surprised at Byron's docility in listening to Shelley—but all who heard him felt the charm of his simple earnest manner; while Byron knew him to be exempt from egotism . . . that he was the truest and most discriminating of his admirers." Even when Byron remarked that Murray, the publisher, was urging him to resume his "old *Corsair* style, to please the ladies," and Shelley came near losing his temper as he insisted that "a book-seller's logic" should not be allowed to influence an author, and "that time would reverse the judgement of the vulgar," Byron only smiled tolerantly.

Then, without warning, Byron suffered one of those disconcerting changes of mood that were the despair of his friends. As they rode towards the setting sun, he quoted Coleridge,

> "Gazing on the Western sky,
> And its peculiar tint of yellow green,"

with sneering contempt. "Who ever saw a green sky!" he demanded.

Shelley was silent, knowing Byron to be as insensitive to the half-tones of a landscape as he was to subtle gradations of character. Trelawny was surprised into a protest:

"The sky in England is oftener green than blue."

"Black, you mean," Byron snapped, and they rode on in silence.

But his sense of humor soon came to the rescue—it must have been as diverting to find a swarthy, moustachioed sailor-man discussing the exact tints of a sunset sky as to hear Satan quote Scripture! He began talking of poetry again, and as he dismounted at the door of his palace he mentioned two words that made an odd rhyme. Trelawny was able to cap them with two lines from *Don Juan* that were still cleverer, and Byron, always easily flattered, laid that soft white hand of his on the crest of Trelawny's horse with a kindly smile.

"If you are curious in these matters," he said, "look into Swift. I will send you a volume; he beats us all hollow, his rhymes are wonderful."

On this amicable note they parted, and as Trelawny rode on to his albergo he must have felt that his visit to Pisa had at least begun well. He had never spent a more entertaining day—intellectually stimulating, varied by agreeable exercise.

It was only the first of many pleasant days he would spend in the old Italian town during those halcyon months of 1822 while Fate was holding her breath, waiting to strike: days made especially satisfying by a ripening friendship with Shelley. There was no disillusionment here; the more he saw of Shelley, the more he admired. Shelley had but one fault: he worked too hard. "He would set to work on a pyramid of books, his eyes glistening with an energy as fierce as a gold digger who works at a rock of quartz, crushing his way through all impediments, no grain of pure ore escaping his eager scrutiny. . . . He had seen no more of the world than a girl in a boarding school, and his habit of brooding on his own thoughts, in solitude and silence, damaged his health of mind and body." After leaving him one morning, standing in front of the fireplace reading a book open on the mantel-shelf, and returning at night to find him still there, still standing; having forgotten to sit down, forgotten to eat the food that had been brought to him, Trelawny decided that "the dreamy bard needed glimpses of rough life," and took it upon himself to drag poor Shelley away from books as often as possible.

Trelawny's naïve comment, "He disliked it, but he could not resist my importunities," illustrates his amazing self-confidence; for Shelley must have found this ruthless interference with work rather trying. Perhaps he did not have the heart to refuse, when Trelawny came breezing into the study, hearty and confident as a trainer who is bent on making a strong man out of a weedy boy. Perhaps the physique of this big sunburned sailorman excited his emulation. Anyway he seems to have submitted to the "glimpses" fairly often and to have accepted a certain amount of training with a docility that, on one occasion, came near putting an end to him for good and all.

Trelawny had been bathing in a deep pool in the Arno while Shelley sat watching him from the bank, and had been showing off, "exciting the astonishment of the poet by a series of aquatic gymnastics learnt from the natives of the South Seas." As he came ashore, Shelley asked mournfully:

"Why can't I swim? It seems so easy."

"Because you think you can't," Trelawny answered. "Take a header off this bank, and when you rise turn over on your back; you will float like a duck."

He obeyed on the instant; stripped himself of jacket and trousers, kicked off his shoes, and plunged in. But, to Trelawny's horror, he did not come up; "he lay there stretched on the bottom like a conger eel, not making the least effort to struggle or save himself," and would have drowned if Trelawny had not dived in and fished him out at once.

He was not grateful; when he recovered his breath, he said wistfully:

"They say Truth lies at the bottom of the well. In another minute I should have found it, and you would have found an empty shell. It is an easy way of getting rid of the body."

"What would Mrs. Shelley have said to me if I had gone back with your empty cage?"

"Don't tell Mary—not a word! But it's a great temptation; in another minute I might have been in another planet."

The experience must have given Trelawny a shock. But he was not discouraged. He was forever coming in with tempting proposals, and one day, finding the poet already flown, consented, at Mary's suggestion, to follow him to his remote sanctum in the *pineta*.

A calash took them out of Pisa through the gate of the Cascine, and on for two or three miles to the vineyards and farm buildings of the Grand Ducal estate, where they dismissed the carriage, told the driver to return for them in the afternoon, and walked on towards the sea. But Mary soon found the loose sand and hot sun too much for her. Trelawny left her under a pine tree and went on.

"Before long I came upon the open sea," he wrote, "at a place called Gombo, from whence I could see Via Reggio, the Gulf of Spezia, and the mountains beyond. After bathing, seeing nothing of the Poet, I penetrated the densest part of the forest, ever and anon making the woods ring with the name of Shelley, and scaring the herons and water-birds from the chain of stagnant pools which impeded my progress.

"With no landmarks to guide me, I was bewildered in this wilderness of pines and ponds; so I sat down and smoked a cigar, reflecting that a red man would have known his course by the trees themselves, their growth and color; or if a footstep had passed that day, he would have hit upon his trail. As I mused upon his sagacity and my own stupidity, the braying of a brother jackass startled me. He was followed by an old man picking up pine cones. I asked him if he had seen a stranger.

"'L'Inglese melancolico haunts the woods maledetta,' he answered. 'I will show you his nest.'

"As we advanced, the ground swelled into mounds and hollows. By-and-by the old fellow pointed with his stick to a hat, books and loose papers lying about and then to a deep pool of dark glimmering water, saying 'Eccolo!' I thought he meant that Shelley was under the water. The careless, not to say impatient, way in which the Poet bore his burden of life, caused a vague dread amongst his family and friends that he might lose or cast it away at any moment.

"The strong light streamed through the opening of the trees. One of the pines, undermined by the water, had fallen into it. Under its lee, and nearly hidden, sat the Poet, gazing on the dark mirror beneath, so lost in his bardish reverie, that he did not hear my approach. There the trees were stunted and bent and their crowns were shorn like friars by the sea breezes, excepting a cluster of three, under which Shelley's traps were lying; these overtopped the rest. To avoid startling the Poet out of his dream, I squatted under the lofty trees, and opened his books. One was a volume of his favorite Greek dramatist, Sophocles—the same that I found in his pocket after his death—and the other was a volume of Shakespeare. . . . He had been writing verses on a guitar. I picked up a fragment, but could only make out two lines:

> " 'Ariel to Miranda.—Take
> This slave of Music.'

"It was a frightful scrawl; words smeared out with his finger and all run together. It might have been taken for a sketch of a marsh overgrown with bullrushes and the blots for wild ducks. . . . I then hailed him, and, turning his head, he answered faintly:

" 'Hello. Come in.' "

The interruption must have been sufficiently annoying. A less sweet-tempered man would have protested at being roused so abruptly from his "green thought in a green shade."

But when Trelawny told him his wife was waiting for him, he crept obediently out of his pine-scented arbor though he gathered up his books and papers with a sigh.

"Poor Mary," he murmured, "hers is a sad fate; she can't bear solitude, nor I society."

As they left the sea and turned inland, Trelawny spoke of the scrap of verse he had found and tried in vain to read. Shelley nodded; his first draft of a poem was always very nearly illegible.

"When my brain gets heated with thought," he explained, "it soon boils and throws off images and words faster than I can skim them off. In the morning, out of the rude sketch, as you justly call it, I shall attempt a drawing. If you ask me why I publish what few or none will care to read, it is that the spirits I have raised haunt me until they are sent to the devil of a printer. All authors are anxious to breech their bantlings," he ended sadly—almost as if he had known he would not live to see that bantling breeched. The lovely lines, "With a Guitar, to Jane," were not published until after his death.

Nor was that still more perfect poem—perhaps the most perfect thing of its kind in the English language: "The Invitation," also written for Jane. Sweet, commonplace, unimportant little Jane Williams, to live forever as Shelley's "best and brightest"!—extreme proof of how trivial a spark is needed to fire poetic imagination.

All three poems were among the fugitive verse gathered together by Mary and published two years after her husband's death. Trelawny must have read them, especially the last, with a constriction of the heart and a nostalgic sense of loss. For here was the *pineta*, his "wilderness of pines and ponds," glorified, preserved forever by Shelley's magic:

"Best and brightest, come away!

. . . .

Awake! arise! and come away!

To the wild wood and the plains,
And the pool where winter rains
Image all their roof of leaves,
Where the pine its garland weaves
Of sapless green and ivy dun
Round stems that never kiss the sun;
Where the lawns and pastures be,
And the sandhills of the sea—

.   .   .   .

And the blue noon is over us,
And the multitudinous
Billows murmur at our feet,
Where the earth and ocean meet,
And all things seem only one
In the universal sun."

But after all the birth of a bantling is more important than the breeching. No doubt Shelley was telling himself this, as they walked rapidly on through the forest, for his mood of sadness was soon shaken off. He greeted his Mary with a smile as she left her tree and came to meet them, and parried her complaint—"It was late; they were going to the opera; she had a new frock for the occasion"—so sweetly that, in a moment, she too was smiling. They turned homeward; retraced the dark forest paths; emerged at last into the cool purple twilight of the open country. All three were talking and laughing now; Shelley in such high spirits and laughing so gaily that when they met the pine-cone gatherer the old man beat his donkey and hurried past them in alarm convinced that *il melancolico* had become a raving lunatic.

Trelawny was delighted. Having discovered that Shelley "would, when the spell that bound his faculties was broken, shut his books and indulge in the wildest flights of mirth and folly," as well as that the poor fellow worked much too hard, he took it upon himself to lure the poet away from books as often as possible by suggesting what Shelley called "distractions." Now and then he would succeed. One memorable day they drove to Leghorn, probably in Trelawny's little Swiss carriage, and spent a delightful morning examining the ships that crowded the water front.

"The nationalities of all the world are here," Trelawny remarked; and as they strolled along he named the vessels one by one: "An English cutter, a French chasse marée, an American clipper, a Spanish tartan, an Austrian trabacolo, a Genoese felucca, a Sardinian xebec, a Neapolitan brig, a Sicilian sparanza, a Dutch galiot, a Danish snow, a Russian hermaphrodite, a Turkish sackalever, a Greek bombard.

"I don't see a Persian dhow, an Arab grab, or a Chinese junk," he ended—wistfully, no doubt; these names would have revived many bittersweet memories! "But we have enough variety without them. What do you say to taking a closer look at that Greek ship over there, the *San Spiridione?* You are writing a poem about Hellas. You ought to see something of the Greeks of today. Here comes the Capitano Zarita; I know him."

The captain was introduced. They went on board his ship; stood for a moment on the deck surveying the crew, crouched about in small groups, shrieking, gesticulating, smoking, eating, and gambling. Then the captain invited them to his cabin for coffee and pipes. They went down. "Over the rudder-head there was a gilt box enshrining a flaming gaudy daub of a saint, with a lamp burning before it; this was *Il Padre Santo Spiridione,* the ship's godfather. The skipper crossed himself and squatted on the dirty divan. Shelley talked to him about the Greek revolution, but the captain was opposed to it; it would interrupt trade."

By this time Shelley had seen all he wanted to of the modern Greek. "There is not a drop of the old Hellenic blood here," he muttered, and they hurried away.

But there was another vessel that Trelawny wanted to see —and not only, one may be sure, on Shelley's account: the American schooner.

"You must allow," he said as they approached her, "that graceful craft was designed by a man who had a poet's feeling for things beautiful."

Shelley agreed. They went on board, examined the ship from stem to stern. This skipper too was most polite. He offered them "a chaw of real Virginia cake, and a cool drink of peach brandy." Shelley was persuaded to drink a glass of weak grog—the first and last he was ever known to taste—on the plea of drinking to the memory of Washington. He wrote a few lines of verse in the logbook—that logbook would be worth its weight in gold today; they bade the captain goodbye, and were soon on their way back to Pisa.

Both had enjoyed the expedition. Trelawny noted with pleasure that Shelley "was in high glee and full of fun. He talked of ships, sailors and the sea. . . . He regretted having wasted his life in Greek and Latin instead of the useful arts of swimming and sailoring, and resolved to have a good-sized boat forthwith. I proposed we should form a colony at the Gulf of Spezia. I said, 'Get Byron to join us, and with your family and the Williamses, and books, and horses, and boats, undisturbed by the botherations of the world, we shall have all that reasonable people require.' This scheme enchanted him. . . . During the rest of our drive we had nothing but sea yarns."

Sea yarns? Did Trelawny let his memory drift back to a day more than ten years ago now when, younger and more lighthearted, he had strolled along another water front—the water front of Port Louis—admiring the ships of many nations? Did he spin Shelley a yarn of a crazy Chinese junk? or of storm and adventure in an Arab grab? Or did he weave a tenderer pattern and speak of love and death in an American schooner?

We shall never know. For when Trelawny wrote of this Italian year he was too interested in Shelley and Byron to speak of himself except in relation to them and the other members of the Pisa circle. Anyway, the yarns were sea

yarns, and they brought Shelley home more eager than ever
for a boat of his own. And it must be a schooner, like the
graceful American schooner they had seen in Leghorn. Williams had spoken of a friend in Genoa, a Captain Roberts,
who could build boats. Trelawny must write to him at once.
And Byron ought to have a boat too; Trelawny must speak
to Byron at once. Byron was more likely to listen to him, as
he was new; Byron was always influenced by his last acquaintance. Would Trelawny see about all this at once? Trelawny would, and did.

Byron needed no persuasion. He liked the idea of the Pisa
circle transferring itself in part to Lerici or some such little
seashore village for the summer. He would of course need a
boat: a large comfortable yacht fitted up with every luxury.
Trelawny would please communicate with Captain Roberts
at once.

Trelawny did so. But not at once. Already aware of Byron's vacillating temperament, he "allowed some days to pass,
in order to see if Byron's wayward mind would change." But
this time Byron held to his purpose. Captain Roberts was
written to; he got permission to build the boats in the government dock yards at Genoa, and soon the two schooners
were under way—a small open boat for Shelley, a larger
decked one for Byron—and estimates came from Roberts.

"Like all estimates," Trelawny wrote, "they were a delu-
sion, which made Byron wroth but did not ruffle Shelley's
serenity. . . . Shelley's boyish eagerness to possess the new
toy was pleasant to behold. Williams was inspired with the
same enthusiasm. We used to draw plans on the sands of the
Arno of the exact dimensions of the boat, dividing her into
compartments (the forepart was decked for stowage) and
then, squatting down within the lines, I marked off the
imaginary cabin. With a chart of the Mediterranean spread
out before them, and with faces as grave and anxious as those
of Columbus and his companions, they held councils as to
the islands to be visited, coasts explored, courses steered, the

amount of armament, stores, water and provisions which would be necessary. . . . We would relate instances of the daring of the old navigators; of the extraordinary runs and enterprises conducted in open boats, of equal or less tonnage than the one we were building, from the earliest times to those of Captain Bligh; Byron, with the smile of a Mephistopheles standing by."

For all his affectation of superiority, Byron must have been listening to these tales: his next long narrative poem, *The Island,* was founded on that old favorite of Trelawny's, Bligh's story of the mutiny of the *Bounty,* and he remained sincerely interested in the building of his yacht. Early in February a long letter went from Trelawny in Pisa to Roberts in Genoa giving the minute latest directions for "Lord B's boat." She was to have an iron keel and copper bottom, a high roomy cabin, and four guns "as large as you think safe— to make a devil of a noise." No expense was to be spared "to make her a complete beauty." Directions for Shelley's schooner followed: Roberts was to "lay us down a small beautiful one, seventeen or eighteen feet . . . single banked oars, say four or six . . . three lugs and a jib—backing ones. She will be used for fishing, shooting and as a tender for the other." He ended that it might be a good idea to have a dinghy as well, but made it plain this was only a suggestion; Roberts was not to build a dinghy unless he thought best. This respect for Roberts as the final authority seems to have been maintained throughout the boat-building operations and shows that on occasion Trelawny could make vanity give way to common sense. He knew that Roberts possessed the technical knowledge he himself lacked, and behaved accordingly.

But humility must have been something of a strain. Luckily he could let himself go with the other three. Byron and Shelley were amateurs too ignorant to offer more than tentative suggestions, and even Edward Williams, although as a Navy man he naturally considered himself a nautical authority, was willing to listen when Trelawny held forth. For, after all, a man who had not only commanded a schooner in the Indian Ocean but taken her through typhoons and pirate attacks, ought to know what he was talking about. (As a matter of fact Trelawny did know what he was talking about when it came to the building and handling of a schooner. It should be remembered that, although his knowledge was merely empiric, it had been acquired in a hard rough school and in boyhood, the time when anything thoroughly learned is never forgotten.)

Meanwhile the wives, Mary and Jane, were of course putting up with a good deal more nautical information than they either desired or deserved. But they seem to have borne their husbands' increasing absorption in boat building with a fair amount of patience and to have rather liked the prospect of a summer drenched in sea spray. Nor did they blame Trelawny although, according to Mary, his enthusiasm was largely responsible. She wrote to a friend: "Trelawny came in one afternoon in high spirits, with news concerning the building of the boat, saying, 'Oh, we must all embark, all live aboard; we will all "suffer a sea change," ' and dearest Shelley was delighted with the quotation, saying he must have it for the motto of his boat."

The exact spot where this watery existence was to be enjoyed was left vague. But it had been agreed that some village on the Gulf of Spezia, where the coast rose above the low fetid Maremma, might provide a suitable setting. So one winter's morning Trelawny and Edward Williams started off on horseback to explore the shore, hoping to find modest but comfortable accommodations for the Shelleys and Williamses and even some country house large enough for Byron's more luxurious requirements. They were disappointed. Only a few miserable fishing villages dotted the margin of the bay. They rode on, Trelawny grumbling his usual complaint: if "tyranny had not paralyzed the energies and enterprise of man," this stretch of coast would be as prosperous as the Bay of

Naples. But it was very unlike that populous shore, very desolate. They had almost given up the search when they came upon a ramshackle building called the Casa Magni, near the village of Lerici, unfurnished and forlorn enough except for its situation, which they thought Mary and Jane might consider habitable for a few months. Anyway there was nothing better for them, and nothing whatever that "Milord Inglese" would tolerate for a moment.

The report was not encouraging. Mary's heart sank. Why move to a horrible little fishing village when life was so pleasant here in Pisa! However, the question need not be decided at once, and a week of really hot weather might dissipate her reluctance. She determined to postpone the thought of a prolonged villeggiatura and make the most of urban society while it was within her reach.

In this pursuit she found, rather to her surprise, that Trelawny could be made useful as an escort. That black-browed piratical aspect of his was deceptive; he had a kind heart and, strange to say, no objection to society. In fact he actually liked parties! Such a contrast to poor dear Percy! When the invitations had come for one of Mrs. Beauclerc's balls and Percy's lamentations were, as usual, threatening to take the edge off her pleasure, and Trelawny had offered to accompany her, she had accepted. But with misgivings. Unnecessary misgivings. Trelawny's dancing was not at all bad—it seemed he had practiced the latest quadrilles in London; it was amusing to have a big bad wolf for a partner, see everyone staring at him, coming to be introduced. But she found him more than a good dancing partner. Her journal noted: "I am glad to have met with one who, among other valuable qualities, has the rare merit of exciting my imagination. . . . His company is delightful, he excites me to think." And her timid qualification, "If any evil shade the intercourse, that time will unveil,—the sun will rise or night darken all," seems soon to have been forgotten. She no longer thought of him as "a strange web which I am endeavoring to unravel," but accepted him with confidence as a friend; and when he took to dropping in of an evening to listen while Percy read aloud she realized with pleasure that Percy not only accepted him but, like herself, found Trelawny's personality "exciting to the imagination."

That winter Shelley began a drama, "undertaken," according to Mary, "for the amusement of the persons who composed our intimate society." Edward Williams's diary notes: "Trelawny dined and passed the evening. We talked of a play of his singular life, and a plot to give it the air of a romance." Shelley's hero was "a Pirate, a man of savage but noble nature"; the scene was laid in "an island of the Indian archipelago."

The "intimate society," including Trelawny himself, must have been more than a little amused by the description of the Pirate:

> "He was as is the sun in his fierce youth,
>   As terrible and lovely as a tempest.
>
>   .   .   .   .
>
>   Some said he was a man of blood and peril
>   And steeped in bitter infamy to the lips."

But amusement would have faded when Shelley struck another note and sang of the island as only he could sing, so that they saw it rise before their eyes out of a blue-green sea and hang there hovering like a mirage; an island "paved with flowers and moss" with a garden and a "glassy pool" set in "old hoary stones," sweet with "unblown violets," and lilies peeping "from their bright green masks": one lovely word flowing out of another until his hearers sighed with delight.

And Trelawny? One may be sure that Trelawny was listening with pain and longing and a sense of irrevocable loss. As Shelley read,

"Alas! Why must I think how oft we two
Have sate together near the river springs,
Under the green pavilion which the willow
Spreads on the floor of the unbroken fountain,

.   .   .   .

While the musk-rose leaves, like flakes of crimson snow,
Showered on us, and the dove mourned in the pine,"

he drifted back into the past. The Shelleys' fireside vanished.
He was far away, in an island garden . . . Zela bent over a
glassy pool, watching her reflection come and go in the blue
water. They sat together under the yakoonoo tree; she made
patterns on the sandy garden path, embroidered the white
sand with crimson pomegranate seeds. . . .

The drama was never finished. Shelley was extraordinarily
sensitive to atmosphere. It is just possible that he felt he had
cut too near reality. Anyway the drama was left a fragment.

Another dramatic project of that winter also came to
nothing. Mary wrote later: "Lord Byron talked vehemently
of our getting up a play in his great hall of Lanfranchi; it
was to be Othello. He cast the characters thus: Byron, Iago;
Trelawny, Othello; Williams, Cassio; Medwin, Roderigo;
Mrs. Shelley, Desdemona; Mrs. Williams, Emilia. 'Who is to
be our audience?' I asked. 'All Pisa,' he rejoined. He recited
a great portion of his part with great gusto; it exactly suited
him,—he looked it too."

Society was not to see a performance of *Othello* in the
Palazzo Lanfranchi, but Byron entertained there a good deal
and every Wednesday gave a dinner for what Medwin called
the "convives" of Pisa and any distinguished travellers that
happened along. Even poets were made welcome—if they
were not too modern; Byron considered Rogers, next to Scott,
the foremost poet of the day, immeasurably superior to "that
dirty little blackguard, Keats," and far above Wordsworth
and the other "Pond Poets," all of them a mere "puddle of
water worms." But Shelley disliked dinner parties and sel-

dom attended them; he wrote to a friend: "My nerves are generally shaken to pieces by sitting up, contemplating the rest of the company making themselves vats of claret, etc., till three o'clock in the morning."

This aversion of Shelley's to society was growing upon him. Trelawny wrote of a day when the Poet came hurrying into the Williamses' apartment with such a woebegone face that Jane became really alarmed.

"Mary is threatening me!" he cried.

They exclaimed. He explained.

"Mary says she will have a party; there are English singers here, the Sinclairs, and she will ask them, and everyone she or you know— Oh, the horror!"

They laughed. He went on: "For pity go to Mary and intercede for me. I will submit to any other species of torture than that of being bored to death by idle ladies and gentlemen."

Ned Williams kindly offered to see what he could do. Shelley remained "in a state of restless ecstasy; he could not read or sit," till Ned returned.

"The lady," Ned announced sadly, "has set her heart on having a party and will not be baulked. But," he added, seeing the poet's despair, "it is to be limited to those here assembled and some of Count Gamba's family; and instead of a musical feast we are to have a dinner," and the Poet, Trelawny wrote, "hopped off rejoicing, making a noise I should have thought whistling but that he was ignorant of that accomplishment."

So the weeks went by, and winter warmed to spring, and the boats were nearly done, and Byron named his the *Bolivar*, and Trelawny agreed to captain her, and Shelley bought Byron's share of the smaller boat—paid eighty pounds to make her all his own, and rode to Lerici and decided the Casa Magni might do; and Mary read Greek and drove every afternoon with Countess Guiccioli, whom she found "a nice pretty girl, without pretensions, good-hearted and amiable," and saw something of that agreeable lightweight Count Gamba—Byron's brother-in-law in the sight of Heaven, known as Pierino; and Shelley and Jane wandered in the *pineta* picking violets, and life was slipping along in idle pleasant fashion for all the little Pisa circle when in April their peace was broken. Clare came.

CHAPTER XIV

"She turned away, but with the autumn weather
Compelled my imagination· many days."
                                        —T. S. ELIOT.

Clare* Clairmont was another of those puzzling women who, unimportant in themselves, manage to achieve a vicarious immortality. Her name would long since have been forgotten if it had not been linked with the great names of Byron and Shelley and, less closely, with the lesser name of Trelawny.

The connection with Shelley had come about accidentally. Clare would never have met him if her mother had not happened to marry William Godwin, Mary Shelley's father, which made her to all intents and purposes Mary's sister and, in the end, Shelley's sister-in-law. Unfortunately the girls were too unlike for a sisterly bringing-up to draw them together. Mary, thoroughly English, intelligent, refined, palely pretty, and Clare, of the Mediterranean type, with a brilliant mind, dark, passionate, quick—outwardly reckless but, one suspects, cold at heart—had never been sympathetic, and it was one of the many crosses of Mary's life that the elopement which had taken her away from home had not freed her of Clare. When she and Percy started off on that unblessed honeymoon of theirs, Clare had insisted on coming too. She had stuck to them all through the six weeks' walking trip in France, where she was not altogether *de trop*: her liveliness amused Percy, she spoke French and helped to carry the fourth member of the party, a minute donkey, when Percy decided the poor creature was too weak to walk. After

*Often spelled *Claire;* but as Byron and Trelawny wrote *Clare* this form is used throughout.

their return to England, finding the Godwin household uncongenial, she had transferred herself to the Shelleys' and
remained there for the most part until Byron provided a
brief interlude, which the Shelleys—free lovers and freethinkers as they were supposed to be—could not approve, but
which they were unable to ignore: Mary was too conscien-
tious, Percy too compassionate. Clare's sufferings, Byron's
hardheartedness, the disposition of the child Allegra never
ceased to trouble and annoy the Shelleys and darkened their
last years of married life.

In a way the situation would have been easier to handle
if Byron had been more to blame. Having, like most girls
of the time, fallen madly in love with him, Clare had set out
to get him; had hunted him down with the same single-
minded persistence that had let her play gooseberry on a
honeymoon; had harried him and coaxed him and, almost
literally, sat on his doorstep, until, fascinated in spite of himself by her daring and her brilliance, he took her in. She
became his mistress. Her voice was "like a string of pearls,"
her liveliness amused him; for a time it seemed that she
might, as the phrase goes, "hold him." Byron's best love poem
was written for Clare, and a girl who inspired the lines,

> "There be none of Beauty's daughters
>   With a magic like thee,"

might well feel herself secure.

She did not know her Byron. Within a few weeks he was
writing from Geneva to his sister, Augusta Leigh:

"As to all these 'mistresses,' Lord help me—I have had but
one. Now don't scold; but what could I do?—a foolish girl,
in spite of all I could say or do, would come after me, or
rather went before—for I found her here—and I have had all
the plague possible to persuade her to go back again; but at
last she went. Now dearest, I do most truly tell thee that I
could not help this, that I did all I could to prevent it, and

have at last put an end to it. I was not in love, nor have I any love left for any; but I could not exactly play the Stoic with a woman who had scrambled eight hundred miles to un-philosophize me. . . . And now you know all I know of that matter, and it's over."

But it was not over. In May, 1817, he wrote again to Augusta, from Venice: "By the way, it seems I have got a daughter by that same lady. . . . I mean the one who returned to England to become a Mamma incog. and whom I pray the Gods to keep there. I am a little puzzled to know how to dispose of this new production (which is two or three months old, though I did not receive the accounts till at Rome), but shall probably send for it and place it in a Venetian convent, to become a good Catholic, and it may be a *Nun,* being a character somewhat wanted in our family. They tell me it is very pretty."

Now the bargaining began. If Byron wanted the child it seemed best from the worldly point of view to let him have her. Clare backed and filled—refused—consented. . . . The child was sent to Byron in Venice. . . . Clare changed her mind, wanted her back. The Shelleys offered to take her, Byron would not consider this for a moment; it turned out he disliked Shelley's vegetarianism almost as much as Shelley's atheism. He wrote from Rome to John Murray:

"The Child shall not quit me again to perish of starvation, and green fruit, or be taught to believe there is no Deity. Whenever there is convenience of vicinity and access, her Mother can always have her with her; otherwise no. It was so stipulated from the beginning. . . . She goes out daily with M. Guiccioli in her carriage to the Corso."

But in spite of this concession on the part of the mistress who had taken her place in Byron's affections, Clare, to Byron's extreme annoyance, continued restless and dissatisfied. In April, 1820, he wrote to Hoppner, the British consul in Venice:

"Clare writes me the most insolent letters about Allegra;

see what a man gets by taking care of his natural children. . . . She may see her, under proper restrictions; but she is not to throw everything into confusion with her Bedlam behavior. To express it delicately, I think Madame Clare is a damn bitch." Beauty's daughter had indeed lost her magic!

Meantime Shelley had gone shuttling back and forth between the antagonists; pleading with Byron, arguing with Clare. Both were incapable of keeping to any agreement. The situation grew worse rather than better. At last Byron, tired of the struggle, ended it. Allegra was sent to a Capuchin convent at Bagnacavallo, near Ravenna where he was living at the time. She was only four. She went alone, in charge of a Guiccioli servant. But she was safe; in the hands of pious nuns. Byron could almost forget that he had a child.

And Clare? The news overwhelmed Clare with a despair deeper than she had ever known. The situation of the convent could not have been worse. Surrounded by high stone walls, it stood on the edge of the marshes of Romagna, never free from malaria, often ravaged by "wandering typhus." She knew what those places were like—horrible food, no comfort, no heat whatever; gloomy, dark, and damp even in summer. She sent Shelley hurrying off to Ravenna. Byron declared himself entirely satisfied with the convent; Allegra was to stay there until she was sixteen. Shelley hurried off to Bagnacavallo to see for himself. His report was on the whole encouraging. Allegra was too pale; but the nuns were kind, she seemed happy. Her eyes were as blue as ever, she was still full of vivacity, "a sweet creature."

Then Byron left Ravenna for Pisa. All Clare's anxieties revived. No one anywhere near now to go to the child if she were ill; Allegra was left entirely to strangers. Winter was coming; Allegra had always suffered from the cold. . . . Winter came. Clare, in Florence, brooded; pictured her child hungry, perishing with cold. The Shelleys worried too, remembering a comment of Mrs. Hoppner's, "La pauvre petite est toujours gêlée. Les mains sont comme des morceaux de glace."

Mary seems to have made no objection when Percy suggested Clare's spending a month with them in Pisa, and in Lerici when hot weather took them to the seashore.

So that April of 1822 Clare arrived. She must have been greeted with mixed feelings by the Shelleys' friends in Pisa. Everybody knew her story. But Byron's aura of romance could glorify even his discarded loves, and one may be sure that the most strait-laced as well as the lax regarded Clare with furtive interest.

Trelawny was most certainly not strait-laced. Clare's type— dark, passionate, exotic—would have appealed to him; she might have been a daughter of the desert, born and bred under the black roof of an Arab tent. He found her exciting. But admiration might never have ripened to love if sorrow— unforeseen and overwhelming, a bolt from the blue—had not crowned her with a tragic dignity that aroused his pity; and, with Trelawny, pity was often the prelude to love. In April the child Allegra died of typhus fever at the convent of Bagnacavallo.

Fortunately, when the dreadful news came Clare was not in Pisa. She had written to Byron begging to be allowed to see her child and, while awaiting his reply, had gone to Lerici with the Williamses to help them find a house, as Casa Magni was too small for two families. The Shelleys received the first shock. They were appalled. They grieved for Allegra as if she had been their own child, and could not forgive Byron for his share in the tragedy, although his sorrow was obviously genuine (at the moment; it soon became tainted with an hypocrisy that could quote texts suited to a bereaved parent), and, foreseeing Clare's wild despair, agreed that she must be kept away from Byron—no one could tell to what lengths this sudden realization of her worst fears might take her!

They were still discussing how best to prevent Clare's return to Pisa when she and the Williamses walked in. Shelley instantly took hold of the situation—as Mary wrote later: "Like a torrent hurrying to its course he carried all before him." No one was given time to think or argue. They were moving out to Lerici at once! Why wait? The heat here in Pisa was unbearable. No house for Jane and Edward? Casa Magni too small? Nonsense—there was a large sala overlooking the sea and a terrace. Hadn't Trelawny said they were to suffer a sea change? Mary had better start packing up. She and their little son, Percy Florence, and Clare could go first; Trelawny would see them safely to Lerici, and he and the Williamses would follow as soon as possible. Mary, only too well aware of the reason for this insistence, offered no objection. Trelawny approved. And in the bustle of departure from Pisa and arrival at Lerici they managed to keep the news from Clare.

But that ignorance could not last. When the others arrived, some look, some whisper—"Does she know? Have you told her?" passed from Mary to Jane, and, in a flash, Clare knew. She knew that Allegra was dead.

The hours that followed were pretty bad for everyone in that ramshackle, comfortless old house, Casa Magni. But Clare had pluck. She soon pulled herself together. No one could help seeing that Casa Magni was too small for so many people; she told them she was returning to Florence. A last appeal went to Byron, through Shelley; she would be grateful for a portrait of Allegra, and "a lock of her hair, however small." In a few days Clare was gone.

But in that brief time she had made Trelawny hers. He would have been more than a friend if she would have let him and, just at first, her feeling for him may have verged on love—Trelawny could be very tender with a sorrowing woman, as Mary Shelley was soon to discover, and his open admiration would have been soothing to Clare's wounded pride. But experience had given her caution. She would promise nothing and went away, leaving Trelawny very much in love but by no means hopeless, ready to fling himself with enthusiasm into the seafaring life his friends were enjoying at Lerici.

For living in Casa Magni was almost like living on board ship. Originally merely a boat-house and bathing pavilion built for a large villa never completed, it stood four-square among the rocks on the edge of the shore; behind it rose a steep hillside dark with walnut and ilex. Across the front of the lower story stretched a long portico of columns and arches used only for boats and fishing tackle as bad weather sent the waves splashing in. A sala ran the length of the second story, opening on the roof of the portico, which made a terrace commanding a magnificent view of the blue Bay of Lerici and Monte Venere. But a view did not make up to Mary and Jane for Casa Magni's housekeeping drawbacks. Only the second story was habitable; there was only one chimney, only four, small, whitewashed bedrooms. Mary hated the place; its loneliness, the wild look of the fisher people, the noise of the winds and waves. Jane agreed that it was extraordinarily uncomfortable. But they tried to make the best of things for the sake of their husbands. Percy and Edward considered Casa Magni an ideal residence. To be sure, they were scarcely ever indoors. They spent the day and often the night bathing and fishing and sailing in Percy's little skiff, and Mary, realizing she had never seen Percy in such good health and spirits, so gay and carefree, tried to forget Lerici's deplorable lack of society.

Their only constant visitor was Trelawny, a very welcome visitor to Mary. Long after, she was to recall with pleasure his loud, cheerful, "Ship Shelley, ahoy!" and the ring of his horse's hoofs on the rocks as he came down the steep trail to Casa Magni. Now and then some lady from Pisa would brave the rough trip and stay to lunch. But Shelley's unconventionality was apt to make such occasions distressing. The ocean seemed to have washed away all his sense of propriety; he behaved as if he were a merman or a fish! One day they were all sitting around the dining table in the sala when he came gliding in trying to hide behind the maidservant's protecting skirts, and had almost reached the door of his room when a lady cried: "Oh, my gracious!" He stopped indignantly. Everyone turned, and there he stood, "naked as a needle," glistening with salt water, bits of seaweed tangled in his hair! He vanished. Everyone laughed—except Mary; she was not amused. Nor would she join the bathing parties at Lerici.

"The natives," Trelawny wrote, "reminded me of the South Sea Islanders. At sunset the whole population of men, women and children took to the water like wild ducks. . . . Shelley especially delighted in this sport."

But Mary disapproved; and Shelley shook his head, puzzled by her inconsistency. He complained to Trelawny:

"At Pisa, Mary said a jacket was not proper, because others did not wear them, and here it's not proper to bathe because everybody does. Oh! what shall we do?"

But even Mary had no fault to find with another pleasure that soon came to make Percy's happiness complete. May was not half over when, one never-to-be-forgotten day, the long awaited new schooner came rippling sweetly into the Bay of Spezia and dropped anchor off the beach of Casa Magni for all to see and admire. Trelawny had despatched her from Genoa in charge of two competent men and a boy, advising Shelley to keep all three for the time being. But neither Shelley nor Edward felt the need of expert assistance; Edward knew all there was to know about sailing, they both wanted the little beauty to themselves. They engaged the boy, but the men were sent back to Genoa. Edward's diary noted, "We have a plaything for the summer," and Shelley wrote ecstatically to Trelawny, "Nothing can exceed the admiration she excites."

But Trelawny himself was less enthusiastic. For, in the end, Ned Williams had insisted on some ideas of his own. "When she was finished," Trelawny wrote, "it took two tons of iron ballast to bring her down to her bearings, and then she was very crank in a breeze, though not deficient in beam. She was fast, strongly built, and Torbay rigged. . . . The sailors

I had sent told me they had been out in a rough night, that she was a ticklish boat to manage but had sailed and worked well, and with two good seamen she would do very well, and they had cautioned the gents accordingly."

The "gents," however, were entirely satisfied with themselves as sailor men and found only one small flaw in their new plaything. Her mainsail bore Byron's name, the *Don Juan,* not the poetic *Ariel* which Shelley had chosen for her when she became all his own. Casa Magni was indignant. No one at Casa Magni wanted to be reminded of Byron in any way whatever. Percy and Edward set to work. They scrubbed and scraped and scoured—the "mark of the beast" still showed. They had to buy a new sail. Now she was perfect. Byron could be forgotten.

Not entirely. It was impossible for Shelley to cut Byron loose as easily as a discarded sail. Loyalty to another old friend forbade. Leigh Hunt was coming to Pisa as editor of a brand-new magazine, financed by Byron, to which they would all three contribute, and as that bright idea had originated with Shelley he was obliged to keep on good terms with Byron, although the tragedy of Allegra's death had killed the last spark of a friendship once dear to both.

Trelawny too was to find his relations with Byron affected by Allegra's death. Having championed Clare with his usual hot-headed, passionate confidence, he would naturally have preferred to cut loose from Byron. But Clare's troubling presence had been removed; he had agreed to captain the *Bolivar,* and could not back out for what would seem to others a sentimental reason; and he decided to try it for a time at any rate—though Shelley had his doubts, and wrote to a friend: "How long the fiery spirit of our pirate will accommodate itself to the caprices of the poet remains to be seen." But the *Bolivar* was a handsome yacht, too fine to give up without regret; a trifle overluxurious, perhaps—marble baths and Genoese velvet cushions seemed to Trelawny out of place on a ship. Her cabin was very unlike the cabin of the "little American" where he had been so happy. Perhaps it was as well. He was in love with Clare now. Why think of Zela? Forget Zela. Forget a funeral pyre on the shore—libation of wine and frankincense—flames rising red and gold—sparks blowing out over the water. He was in love with Clare —she would soon relent. Shelley was his friend. A splendid yacht was his to rule and sail. Life was good—so good that he determined to ignore the one drawback: Byron!

They had never really liked each other. Their first meeting had left Trelawny uncertain whether to admire or condemn—awestruck by the genius, bewildered by the man. The awe remained: Trelawny was never to feel at ease with Byron, creator of immortal verse. The bewilderment cleared, in part: no one ever succeeded in understanding Byron; like Oscar Wilde he remained a puzzle to his generation. But familiarity gave Trelawny useful glimpses behind the mask, and before long he could surprise Shelley with an estimate of Byron's character so shrewd that Shelley passed it on to Mary with the wistful comment:

"Trelawny has found out Byron already. How stupid we were—how long it took us."

And Byron? Did he too modify his first impression? Not very much. He never lost his contempt for Trelawny's single-track mind, his quixotic affection for underdogs and lost causes; his breeziness, bluntness, and rather primitive sense of humor; his lack of respect for the aristocracy—to hear the fellow talk one would think he hadn't a drop of good blood in him! And his hands were so rough, his voice so hearty, his spirits so high—altogether a most fatiguing person. But he knew his business—the *Bolivar* and her crew were well handled, and Byron's contempt would soon have faded to indifference if it had not been spiced with envy. Byron envied Trelawny his physique—his height, strength, and vitality.

When the *Bolivar* came to anchor for their morning swim and the two dived overboard into the warm blue sea—a sea almost as warm, almost as blue as the Indian Ocean—Byron, vain of his swimming, would observe with annoyance that no increase of speed could trouble his companion. Trelawny came on, lazily, always abreast. When they reached the rocks and sat there naked in the sunshine, Byron would glance at the powerful figure at his side—a Greek bronze, or his own Corsair come to life—forget that he himself was a great man, a peer, and a poet, and remember that he was a cripple. Cursing the twisted foot that he believed to be the cause of all his misfortunes, in an access of self-pity, he would fling himself into the sea and swim as if the Furies were after him.

But, as he swam, peace would return—the sea was Byron's Pool of Bethesda. Byron was at his best when he was swimming. He walked with a strange, tiptoeing gait verging on the ludicrous; he could not mount a horse without assistance. But he swam like a fish. Swimming was the only sport not affected by his deformity. Trelawny, watching that beautiful body, slipping easily and swiftly through the water, would wonder and speculate. If the deformity were as bad as Byron thought it was—his friends said it had affected his whole life for the worse—why did it show so little when he was swimming? You could see that the right foot was a little twisted and both legs were too thin. But that was all. Another question. What had caused the twist? A malformation? The tendon Achilles drawn too tight? Byron made no secret of having suffered tortures from treatments and braces and cruel boots: why had he never found a surgeon who could straighten that twist? These questions of course remained unanswered. Trelawny might be blunt and reckless to a degree, and prone, like Samson, to use the jawbone of an ass for a weapon; but in common with the rest of the world he stood too much in awe of Byron to make any allusion to that lame foot.

However, for the most part the owner and the captain of the *Bolivar* got on well enough. Byron liked yachting, he was very proud of the *Bolivar,* and he could be a delightful companion—witty and entertaining if he happened to feel like talking, keen to listen if the story were worth hearing. He enjoyed making plans for future travels, and Trelawny's tales widened his horizon. One day they would talk of desert countries; he would envy Lady Hester Stanhope and remark, "Her way of life would just suit my humour." Or South America might come up for discussion; he had often thought of buying "a principality of auriferous soil in Chili or Peru," and going in for mining. But, most often, he talked of buying an island in the Greek archipelago. Islands were cheap there: a charming island could be bought for nine or ten thousand pounds, and of all countries he had known Byron loved Greece the best—he looked back at the two years he had spent there when he was twenty-two as the least unhappy of a tormented life; and Trelawny of course found no fault with the idea of buying an island—he looked back at the Isle of France as the one perfect spot on earth.

But Trelawny lost interest when Byron went on to speak of the wrongs of Greece, of a certain Prince Mavrocordato, an agreeable young fellow who had spent the previous winter in Pisa, given Mary Shelley Greek lessons, and inspired Shelley to write his *Hellas,* a fine thing though too modern in style. Mavrocordato was out there now, helping Greece to throw off the Turkish yoke. If the revolution lasted long enough, Byron had a great mind to take a hand in it himself: fit out an expedition and strike a blow for liberty. What did Trelawny think?

Trelawny shook his head, murmuring that fighting was always enjoyable but the modern Greeks were not worth freeing: their revolution would fizzle out and come to nothing. He would have liked to add, but did not, that Byron's fight for freedom would also fizzle out and come to nothing. Byron take an active part? Byron fit out an expedition? *Byron*—so slack, pampered, inert, procrastinating! The idea was supremely absurd. Byron was too infirm of purpose. Trelawny yawned and changed the subject.

Awe mingled with contempt does not make for friendship.

The summer wore away without bringing Trelawny nearer to Byron in spirit, and before long he was seeing very little of Byron in person. No amusement could hold Byron long. Shelley and Ned Williams had scarcely begun to enjoy their "new toy" before Byron tired of the *Bolivar*. Trelawny, pitying Byron for his ill health and morbid disposition, and convinced that salt water could cure every ill of mind or body, was sorry that Byron so seldom came aboard. By the middle of the summer the *Bolivar* was left pretty much to the captain to sail when and where he chose, alone.

This had its advantages. The *Bolivar* could come curtsying into the Bay of Lerici whenever her captain felt inclined to visit Casa Magni. He was always welcome there, always enjoyed himself—except for his honeymoon with Zela in the Isle of France, this was the happiest summer of Trelawny's life. Before long Clare returned to Lerici for a visit; he found himself more in love than ever. Shelley's delight in the *Ariel* was a joy to see; his blundering attempts at seamanship, his misuse of nautical terms, his tendency to fall overboard when anything went wrong, provided spectators with endless amusement. He became so absorbed in the new plaything that, before long, "he put his beloved Plato in his pocket," Trelawny wrote, "and gave himself to fun and frolic."

This change of heart was approved by his friends. Everyone was sorry when, in late June, a message came from Leigh Hunt that meant a break in the pleasant life of Casa Magni. Leigh Hunt and his family were in Genoa and hoped to arrive in Leghorn within a few days. They would, of course, have to be met.

Unfortunately the Hunts had been so long on their way that everybody was tired of thinking about them. Even Shelley's welcome was wearing a trifle thin, and Byron's first enthusiasm for the new magazine entirely evaporated. If Hunt had come sooner, struck while the iron was hot, the magazine might have amounted to something; but, what with storms and illnesses and one thing and another, the Hunts had managed to take more than eight months getting from England to Italy, and by that time Byron was sick of the very name of Hunt; and if Shelley had been less persistent the *Liberal* would have died before it was born. But Shelley would not give in: he went on praising Hunt and flattering Byron, and at last Byron agreed not only to start the magazine, but to let the Hunts occupy a floor in the Palazzo Lanfranchi.

So the message came. The Hunts were arriving at Leghorn. They must be met. Trelawny and the *Bolivar* left Lerici at once. The married men could not get away so easily: their wives did not like being left alone in this desolate place—especially Mary. Mary had been ill, she was still in low spirits; recent dreams and visions of Percy's had filled her with foreboding. A dream of Edward, calling: "Get up, Shelley, the sea is flooding the house and it is all coming down!" Vision of a naked child, Allegra, rising from the sea, smiling at him. Vision of himself, coming towards him, asking: "How long do you mean to be content?" Such warnings, Mary insisted, should not be disregarded: he must not go.

But Percy could not listen to her. He spoke of the Hunts; the poor Hunts needed him even more than she did. She gave in, she had to. The wives were kissed, and told to cheer up. The *Ariel* spread her sails to a fine breeze, danced gaily from the Bay of Lerici, and rounded the point, out of sight of the three women—Mary, Jane, and Clare—watching from the terrace of Casa Magni.

The Hunts arrived—Mr. and Mrs., six children and promise of another, and a goat. They came straggling down the gangplank: children, forlorn and dirty; Marianne Hunt ready to drop from exhaustion; Hunt himself as lively as a cricket (Dickens's Skimpole caricature was not overdrawn in externals), gratified that Lord Byron, unable to come in person, had sent a representative. "Mr. Trelawny," Hunt wrote later, "of the old Cornish family of that name, was standing, with his knight-errant aspect, dark, handsome and mustachioed, in Lord Byron's boat the *Bolivar* of which he had taken charge for his lordship."

Trelawny, as it happened, was also expected to take charge of Hunt (though not of the family: that was Shelley's job!). He escorted Hunt to Monte Nero, near Leghorn, where Byron was staying at the time in a villa he had rented for the Gambas—the silly creatures had become involved in one of their frequent street brawls and been obliged to leave Pisa. But, this short trip over, Trelawny's responsibilities were at an end.

Shelley's, on the other hand, were only beginning. He had fully expected to bid the Hunts goodbye as soon as he had seen them settled in their flat in the Palazzo Lanfranchi. But the poor souls were too homesick—the flat was so very Italian, the furniture Shelley had bought for them and the wine and food he had provided were so excessively un-English—and he could not bear to leave them. Then Byron arrived, his greeting was cool to the point of insolence; his bulldog took a dislike to the goat and bit off its ear. Hunt's spirits sank to zero, for Byron seemed to have lost interest in the *Liberal*. What with cheering Hunt and soothing Mrs. Hunt and coaxing Byron, if not the bulldog, into a less poisonous frame of mind, Shelley could not abandon his protégés nearly as soon as he had hoped.

When at last he felt he might return to Leghorn, two days had gone by; and by this time poor Edward was so tired of waiting and so anxious to see Jane he had very nearly hired a felucca and left the *Ariel* and Shelley to get back to Lerici in charge of Trelawny.

That was not to be. Just in the nick of time, Shelley arrived. The *Ariel* made ready to sail at once. So did the *Bolivar;* Trelawny—never sure of his friends' seamanship—was going along to see them safely started. Both boats were under way. At the last moment, the Fates interfered—perhaps the dead child, Allegra, beckoned a second time from the sea, warned them the hour, so long postponed, had come at last. The *Bolivar* was held up; a port official demanded a paper that Trelawny had never before been asked for and did not realize was necessary. He could not sail. Percy and Edward would not wait. He had to let them go without him.

CHAPTER XV

"The people gathered much wood and they laid Hector upon the pile, and lit fire beneath it. And when it was burnt they quenched the embers with wine. Then his comrades gathered together the white bones, and laid them in a chest of gold."

HOMER.

At two o'clock in the afternoon of Monday July 8, 1822, the *Ariel* with Shelley, Edward Williams, and a boy, Charles Vivian, sailed away from Leghorn leaving Trelawny, anxious and frustrated, on the deck of the *Bolivar,* and Captain Roberts mounting a lighthouse tower to watch the schooner on her homeward way, for he too was uneasy.

"Sullenly and reluctantly," Trelawny wrote later, "I re-anchored, furled my sails and with a ship's glass watched the progress of my friends' boat. . . . She was soon enveloped in the seafog, we saw nothing more of her. Although the sun was obscured by mists it was oppressively sultry. There was not a breath of air in the harbor. The heaviness of the atmosphere, and an unwonted stillness, benumbed my senses. I went down into the cabin and sank into a slumber. I was roused by a noise overhead and went on deck. The men were getting up a chain cable to let go another anchor. There was a stir amongst the shipping; shifting berths, getting down yards and masts, hauling in of hawsers, letting go anchors, hailing from the ships and quays, boats sculling to and fro. It was almost dark, though only half past six o'clock. The sea was of the colour, and looked as solid and smooth as a sheet of lead, and covered with an oily scum. Gusts of wind swept

over without ruffling it, and big drops of rain fell on its surface, rebounding, as if they could not penetrate it. There was
a commotion in the air, threatening sounds coming from the
sea. Fishing craft and coasting vessels, under bare poles,
rushed by us. . . . The crashing voice of a thunder squall burst
right over our heads. . . . When the fury of the storm, which
did not last for more than twenty minutes, had abated, I
looked to seaward anxiously, in the hope of seeing Shelley's
boat, I watched every speck on the horizon. . . . I sent our
Genoese mate on board some of the returning craft to make
inquiries, but they all professed not to have seen the English
boat. During the night lightning flashed along the coast. At
daybreak, I resumed my examinations of the crews of returning boats. They either knew nothing or would say nothing.
. . . Another day was passed in horrid suspense."

Meantime the women at Casa Magni were becoming increasingly anxious. When a letter came from Hunt speaking
of the storm and asking Shelley whether he had reached home
safely, Mary and Jane decided they could bear uncertainty no
longer. Leaving the children with Clare, they were rowed
across the bay and at Lerici hired a carriage for the long
rough drive to Pisa. It was midnight when they reached the
Palazzo Lanfranchi; Byron had to be roused from sleep. He
was kind, for he shared their fears—Trelawny had come from
Leghorn to bring the bad news to the Palazzo Lanfranchi.
But he could tell them nothing they did not already know.
Without stopping to rest they hurried on to Leghorn to find
Trelawny and Captain Roberts. Their coachman took them
to the wrong inn; the sun was rising, and they were half dead
with worry and fatigue when they finally succeeded in meet-
ing their friends at the Globe.

Trelawny, his heart wrung with pity, consoled and encouraged as best he could. They must not give up hope. The
Ariel might have been driven far out of her course—to Elba,
or Corsica. A message might be waiting for them now at Le-

rici. He persuaded the poor things to go home; saw them back there himself, and returned to Leghorn to join Roberts in a careful search of the coast. A courier was sent in the direction of Genoa to make inquiries as far as Nice; the *Bolivar* began cruising back and forth along the shore; Trelawny and Roberts mounted their horses and started out to interview and question and search every rocky bay and strip of sand for what, by now, they feared to find.

The first news came from Viareggio, halfway between Lerici and Pisa: a body had been found on the shore. Trelawny hurried there at once.

"My worst fears," he wrote, "were confirmed. The face and hands were fleshless, but the tall, slight figure, the jacket, the volume of Sophocles in one pocket—and Keats' poems in the other, doubled back as if the reader, in the act of reading, had hastily thrust it away, were all too familiar to leave a doubt in my mind; this corpse was Shelley's."

Another body, washed ashore some three miles farther up the coast near the tower of Migliarino, had been buried before Trelawny could get there. It was less easy to identify, for most of the clothing was gone; but the description satisfied him it was that of Edward Williams. A third corpse was found a few days later at a still greater distance from Viareggio, and buried at once in the sand above high-water mark. Trelawny was told that it was unrecognizable, a mere skeleton; but he knew it must be Charles Vivian, the boy who had gone down with the *Ariel*.

Hope extinguished, it remained for Trelawny to take the news to Mary and Jane.

"I mounted my horse," he wrote, "and rode off to the Gulf of Spezia, put up my horse, and walked on until I caught sight of the lone house on the seashore in which Shelley and Williams had dwelt and where their widows still lived. I paused—I had ridden fast to prevent any ruder messenger from bursting in upon them, and my memory reverted to our parting only a few days before.

"They had all been in the verandah, overhanging a sea so clear and calm that every star was reflected in the water; the young mothers singing some merry tune with the accompaniment of a guitar. Shelley's shrill laugh—I hear it still—rang in my ears, with Williams's friendly hail, the general *buona notte* of all the joyous party, their entreaty to return as soon as possible, and not to forget the commissions they had given me. I was in a small boat beneath them, slowly rowing myself on board the *Bolivar* at anchor in the bay, loath to part from what I verily believe to have been the most united and happiest set of human beings in the whole world. And now, by the puff of an idle wind . . .

"As I reached the threshold the nurse Caterina crossed the hall and shrieked as she saw me in the doorway. Unannounced I went on up the stairs and entered the room. I neither spoke, nor did they question me. Mrs. Shelley's large grey eyes were fixed on my face. I turned away. With a convulsive effort, she exclaimed:

" 'Is there no hope?'

"I did not answer, I left the room and sent the servant with the children to them. The next day I prevailed on them to return with me to Pisa. The misery of that night and the journey the next day, and of many days and nights that followed, I can neither describe nor forget."

Back in Pisa, one would have thought the forlorn women would have turned to older friends. Strange to say, they continued to depend entirely on Trelawny. They seem to have come to him for everything: for advice in the innumerable difficulties in which they at once became involved, for comfort in sorrow—pity had given him a tact that knew just when to speak and when to be silent. "He did not attempt to console me," Mary wrote later, "but launched forth into an overflowing and eloquent praise of my divine Shelley, till I felt almost happy." It was Trelawny, not Hunt or Byron (Medwin had left Pisa in the spring), who identified the "re-

mains," and shouldered the whole responsibility of the funeral arrangements: no easy undertaking because of the
Italian quarantine regulations.

For a time it seemed as if the official red tape would never
be unwound. The bodies had been temporarily buried at
once where they had been found. Mary and Jane—thinking,
one of a green English churchyard, the other of the cemetery
in Rome where Percy had buried their little son, William—
refused to leave them on that desolate foreign shore. The authorities would not allow them to be disinterred and taken
out of the country. It was against the law. Everything washed
up on the shore must be burned for fear of the plague; on
the other hand, Catholic piety disapproved of burning human bodies, even the bodies of heretics. Trelawny intervened
and argued and explained and pulled wires and answered
questions and signed papers; the English officials at Leghorn
and a friend, Captain Shenley, intervened on his behalf. At
last a compromise was arrived at. The bodies were to be
burned, under proper military supervision; the ashes, in
proper receptacles, might be given to the widows and taken
out of the country.

Meanwhile, Mary and Jane had been persuaded to agree
to cremation. The idea must have come as something of a
shock, especially to so conventionally minded a woman as
Mary. But Trelawny spoke of the ancient Greeks—Shelley's
favorite Hellenes; he described the dignity and beauty of a
funeral pyre. Mary realized that this was the right way for the
body of a poet to return to the elements; Jane gave her consent. But how, they asked, was it to be done? Could Trelawny
attend to it? Had he ever seen a funeral pyre?

He nodded—and, in his mind's eyes, he saw a funeral pyre
on a still more alien shore, flames rising red and gold, sparks
flying out over the dark water. Yes, he had seen a funeral
pyre. He would attend to everything. All should be done
with reverence and beauty. When it was over, he would take

charge of the ashes and bring them a careful account of the funeral ceremonies. They were satisfied. They trusted him, and let him go.

By this time, Trelawny's patience must have been pretty well strained, and one may be sure that he set about his preparations with a sick reluctance. Not only was this the second time he had built a funeral pyre for the person he loved best in the world; in spite of all he had said to Mary and Jane, he knew that this ceremony would be horrible rather than beautiful—he had seen one of those poor mutilated corpses! Zela's little body had been still perfect, she had been wrapped in spangled gauzes and embroidered silks when he had laid her on the pyre. He had watched the flames for only one agonizing moment and fallen unconscious. Now, he would have to see the whole thing through from beginning to end.

But when Trelawny wrote of this time his own grief, his own sensations were never mentioned. The endless negotiations that must have fretted his impatient nature almost past endurance were summed up in a few dry sentences. He described the iron frame he had had made by Nella,* a blacksmith in Leghorn, like that which De Ruyter had provided for Zela's funeral; "five feet long, two broad, with a rim around it, supported by legs two feet high"; and the two boxes to receive the ashes, "covered with black velvet and fastened with screws, a plate of brass attached to the top with a Latin inscription stating their loss by shipwreck, age, country, etc." He procured incense, wine, honey, salt, and sugar to use in accordance with the classic ritual. But the preparations had taken so long that it was more than five weeks after the wreck of the *Ariel* before the *Bolivar,* with Trelawny and Captain Shenley, finally set sail for Viareggio.

At Viareggio there was further delay. The local officials had to be placated; wood sent to the beach near Williams's grave

---

* Nella's receipt ends: "of Edward Trelawny Esq. the amount in full of the above mentioned account.—viz. four hundred and thirteen Tuscan livres in silver."

—his body was to be cremated first; men engaged to dig, and soldiers to keep sight-seers at a distance. These matters attended to, they began waiting for Byron. Byron had promised to come, with Hunt, to help identify Williams's body, which he was sure he could do by the teeth—he said he always noticed a person's teeth. They waited all day. Byron did not come. At six o'clock Trelawny sent a courier to Pisa and received word from Byron that he would attend the following day. Meanwhile the officials and helpers had gone home, and Trelawny and Shenley to an inn to spend the night.

Early the next morning the same party reassembled and proceeded first by boat and then on foot to the beach where Williams's body had been found.

"We were joined by Lord Byron and Mr. Hunt," Trelawny wrote, "in their carriage, an officer from the Health Office at Leghorn, a sergeant and four soldiers, dismounted dragoons, having mattocks, spades, boat-hooks and other instruments, along with the iron furnace and the box for the ashes, and my men with sails to guard against the wind. We proceeded along the beach to a spot marked by the large old root of a fir-tree, near a hut rudely built of boughs and covered with reeds, a shelter for soldiers on the coast patrol. The sergeant exclaimed: 'This is the place!' We halted. He pointed out the exact spot, at high water mark about twenty paces from the sea as it was then, nearly calm, breaking on the beach. We were facing the gulf where my noble friends' bodies were found. The situation was well adapted for a Poet's grave, fronted by a magnificent extent of the Mediterranean Sea with the Isles of Gorgona, Capraia, Elba and Corsica in sight and on the other side an almost boundless extent of sandy wilderness, uncultivated and uninhabited, covered with wood stunted by the sea breeze and the poverty of the sandy soil. At equal distances along the coast stood high square towers with flag staffs on the turrets, for the double purpose of preventing smuggling and enforcing the quarantine laws. This view was bounded by an immense extent of the Italian Alps which are here particularly beautiful; those in the vicinity being composed of white marble which gave their summits an appearance of being covered with snow. As a foreground to this romantic scene was an extraordinary group—Lord Byron and Hunt seated in the carriage, the horses jaded and overpowered by the intensity of the heat reflected from the deep loose sand, which was so hot that Lord Byron could not stand on it. Captain Shenley and myself, with the officer and sergeant commanding the nearest lookout tower, stood around the grave; four soldiers were employed uncovering it. The sergeant with a boat-hook first pulled out a black handkerchief, then a piece of shirt—by the collar of the last being peculiarly formed, I knew it to be Williams's. Presently we came to some loose wood; on this being removed, the head appeared. With a spade I bared the whole of it. The body, dreadfully mutilated, was now wholly palpable. . . . Having placed the furnace near the grave, I went and collected wood on the lee of the little hut to prevent the wind blowing away the ashes. Then with instruments made for the purpose of dragging wrecked seamen out of the sea—for you are on no account allowed to touch a body (a long pole with a round iron in the form of a sickle), we dragged the remains out of the grave and then, with poles shoved under, lifted him into the furnace. I now called Lord Byron. The moment he saw the teeth he exclaimed, 'That is him!' It was a humbling and loathsome sight—mutilated not by time the destroyer, but fish eaten—a livid mass of shapeless flesh. . . . After the whole had been placed in the furnace, I placed two poles under it and carried it behind the hut and placed it on a pile of wood, surrounding it with dry wood and placing some green branches on the top. I set fire to the whole. The fire was immense, and to add to its fierceness, Lord Byron, Hunt, Shenley and myself kept throwing incense, salt, sugar and wine—the soldiers, superstitiously fearful, had withdrawn as far as possible. Lord Byron went to try the force of the waves that had overpowered his friend and swam a long way to sea. Myself and Shenley, having replenished the fire, followed him. Lord Byron was dreadfully sick after swimming about a mile, but I could not persuade him to return. Shenley got the cramp and was nearly drowned. We returned and again gathered about the fire. The body had been about two hours burning; it was still not near consumed. We placed large pieces of timber upon it, the shed caught fire and burnt most furiously. At four nothing remained but a quantity of blackish-looking ashes, mingled with a quantity of white and broken fragments of bones. The furnace was carried into the sea; by sprinkling water on it we cooled it by degrees. Then taking one of the jaws, which was the only whole bone, I shovelled the rest into the small desk-sized coffin, screwed it down and placed it in the carriage. It being too late to commence on Shelley's body, Lord Byron and Hunt returned to Pisa and Shenley and myself to Viareggio."

After a day of such prolonged horror it must have been very nearly unbearable to face another that would be even more trying, for now it was the body of Shelley that had to be burned; but there was no escaping it. At ten o'clock on the morning of the 16th of August, 1822, Trelawny and Captain Shenley were rowed along the shore in the direction of Massa and landed on a strip of beach nearer Viareggio than where Williams had been found but facing the same magnificent view of sea and sand and mountain. Byron's carriage arrived, and the guard, two mounted dragoons and four foot soldiers, which Trelawny had sent for, as spectators were already gathering and threatened to be even more intrusive than on the previous day. The men began to dig. They worked hard for more than an hour, cutting trenches in various directions. At last they came to traces of lime in the sand.

"A spade struck upon the skull," Trelawny wrote. "The body was dragged out of its shallow bed of sand and placed in the furnace. . . . His dress and linen had become black, the body was in a state of putridity. The skull was black. No flesh or features of the face remained; the clothes had in some degree protected the body, the flesh was of a dingy blue. The poem of *Lamia* and *Isabella,* which had been found in Shelley's pocket and buried with him, I was anxious to have but we could find nothing remaining but the leather binding. Lord Byron wished to have the skull, but it broke to pieces— it was unusually thin and strikingly small. Although we made a tremendous fire, the body burnt exceedingly slow. It was three hours before the body separated—it then fell open across the breast—and the heart, which was now seen, was likewise small. The body was much longer consuming than the other—it was nearly four o'clock before the body was wholly consumed, that part nearest the heart being the last that became ashes—and the heart itself seemed proof against fire, for it was still perfect and the intensity of heat—everything now, even the sand on which the furnace stood, the furnace itself being red hot and a fierce fire still kept up, the largest bones reduced to white cinders and nothing distinguishable except the heart, which, although bedded in fire, would not burn. At length we gave over, by mutual conviction of its being unavailing, all exclaiming, 'It will not burn!' *—there was a bright flame around it, occasioned by the moisture still flowing from it, and on removing the furnace nearer to the sea to immerse the iron, I took the heart in my hand to examine it—after sprinkling it with water; yet it was still so hot as to burn my hand badly and a quantity of this oily fluid still flowed from it. We now collected the dust and ashes and placed them in the box made for the occasion and shipped it on board Lord Byron's schooner. There had been, during the whole ceremony, a solitary sea bird crossing and recrossing the fire—the only intruder our guards had not kept away. We then returned slowly to the Inn in a carriage

* Byron wrote to Moore: "All of Shelley was consumed. except the heart, which would not take the flame."

drawn by buffaloes—Lord Byron proceeding to Pisa, and weighed anchor for Leghorn."

The voyage home, with all that was left of Shelley in a "desk-like box," must have been dreary enough, and Trelawny seems not to have let himself think, or rest; for he began writing an account * of Shelley's funeral that same evening on board the *Bolivar*—it is headed "Shelley Viareggio." Nor did the arrival in Leghorn bring him much time to relax, although by now even his superb strength must have felt the strain of all he had suffered both mentally and physically. Mary and Jane were waiting to hear from him. He had Shelley's ashes sent to Rome in charge of the English consul to await further instructions, and went on to Pisa.

He found the poor desolate women in their old quarters in the Tre Palazzi where he had spent so many happy evenings during the previous winter. They wanted to know everything. He told them—all that he could tell them! One may be sure he dwelt on the beauty of the scene rather than on what Hunt called its "distressing" features. He described the magnificent landscape, perfect background for a poet's last rites; he repeated the words he had used while pouring the libations: "I restore to nature, through fire, the elements of which this man was composed, earth, air, and water; everything is changed, but not annihilated; he is now a portion of that which he worshiped." And did not repeat Byron's comment—half jeering, half admiring: "Why, Trelawny, I knew you were a pagan, but not that you were a pagan priest! You do it very well!"

Although he contrived to give an air of majestic beauty to the scene most consoling to the sorrowing women, his appearance told them something of what he had gone through— Mary wrote later, "It was a fearful task; he stood before us at

* The account given above. It is condensed but not otherwise altered, and will be found at full length in Trelawny's *Letters*, edited by H. Buxton Forman. Trelawny wrote five accounts of the burning of the bodies. This one, being the first and the least polished in style, is probably the most reliable.

last, his hands scorched and blistered by the flames of the funeral pyre and by touching the burnt relics"—and he did not get away without making one bad mistake: he failed to allow for Mary's extreme fastidiousness.

He had brought with him the relic he had snatched from the flames, Shelley's heart, thinking Mary would wish to have it. But when he showed it to her—a little black shrivelled thing—she shrank away from it in horror. Hurt by her rejection and knowing that Hunt wanted the heart, he let him take it. (Later, Mary changed her mind; Hunt would not give it back; Jane Williams intervened. At last Shelley's heart found its way back to Mary and England.)

But Trelawny did not allow his momentary contempt for Mary's oversensitiveness to affect their relations. "During the whole of the proceedings," Leigh Hunt wrote later, "Mr. Shelley and Mr. Williams's friends were indebted to Mr. Trelawny for every kind of attention; the great burden of the inquiry fell upon him and he never ceased his good offices, either then or afterwards, until he had done everything that could have been expected to be done, either of the humblest or the highest friend."

One of these "good offices" was the wearisome dredging for the wreck of the *Ariel,* begun soon after the accident and continued in the face of long discouragement, chiefly because Mary wished to recover valuable books and papers known to have been on board; partly because both he and Roberts were anxious to find out whether she had capsized in the storm or been run down, as they suspected, by a felucca. The dredging was still going on without success when another errand for Mary took him to Rome. She wanted him to see that Shelley's ashes were properly interred in the place which she had chosen and Shelley had described as so suitable for the grave of Keats:

"The romantic and lonely cemetery of the Protestants in Rome, under the pyramid which is the tomb of Cestius, . . . an open space among the ruins, covered in winter with violets

and daisies. It might make one in love with death to think
that one should be buried in so sweet a place."

When Trelawny returned to Pisa he could tell Mary that
although it would be impossible to lay her husband beside
their little son as she had wished, he had found a spot worthy
of a poet's grave. There was a niche in the old moss-grown
Roman wall where a tomb could be built; he would buy the
plot of ground in front of it, and here later on, when the
masons had finished their work, he would plant flowers and
a row of the dark steeplelike Italian cypresses to stand like
guardians of the dead. Mary agreed to everything. His instinctive feeling for the beautiful in nature and in art had
helped him to choose and plan well; she was satisfied. She recalled Shelley's lines,

> "The One remains, the many change and pass;
>   Heaven's light forever shines, Earth's shadows fly;
>   Life, like a dome of many-coloured glass,
>   Stains the white radiance of Eternity,"

and found strength for difficulties she had never before faced
alone.

Mary needed strength: there was so much to be done. Pisa
had become impossible for the three women who loved Shelley, and they were going their separate ways: Jane and her
two babies to England, Clare to join her brother in Vienna,
Mary to share a flat with the Hunts at Albaro near Genoa.
By the end of September, Casa Magni had been dismantled,
Clare was gone, and Mary left to arrange for Jane's journey
to England, pack up, and make the many other fatiguing
preparations for settling in a new home.

Although in all this worrying work Trelawny was her chief
reliance—she wrote to him later, "We saw sorrow in other
faces, but we found help only from you"—for a while, Shelley's unselfish spirit seemed still to influence what was left of
the Pisa circle. Even Byron. Byron told Mary to call on him

if she needed funds. He did not, after all, withdraw his patronage from Hunt and the *Liberal*. When he found himself obliged to leave Pisa—the silly Gambas had got into another row with the government—he allowed Mary to rent a villa for him at Albaro very near the Hunts.

This was a real act of self-denial. Byron disliked children in general—he told his sister Augusta Leigh, "I have the greatest respect for the character of Herod"—and he had come to hate the young Hunts with peculiar animosity. Not unnaturally. The young Hunts were forever underfoot at the Palazzo Lanfranchi: crawling up and down the staircase, teasing the peacock, leaving bits of bread and butter on the steps, greeting Byron with awkward reminders of a friendlier past in London where he had enjoyed riding their rocking horse. His damning "Dirty and mischievous as Yahoos!" was probably justified. Hunt believed that "a child should never be corrected until old enough to be reasoned with," and Mrs. Hunt might have been sitting for Jane Austen when that acute spinster wrote: "A fond mother, though in pursuit of praise for her children, the most rapacious of human beings, is likewise the most credulous; her demands are exorbitant, but she will swallow anything." Moreover, there would be seven little olive branches in Genoa—a new twig must soon be added to Hunt's quiverful. But Byron did not, as might have been expected, cut them off and cast them from him. He refrained. He even made their flitting easy for the travellers. Trelawny was told to convey them to Genoa by sea; some would go in the *Bolivar,* others in feluccas. Trelawny was to see to everything.

Trelawny did. That autumn he was kept busy escorting and expediting various oddly assorted parties to Genoa. Mary and Jane with their children got off first; then the Hunts. Hunt, always sanguine and carefree, enjoyed the trip immensely. "It was a pretty sight," he wrote, "to see the boats with their white sails, gliding past the rocks, over the blue sea." Less pretty, one suspects, for Mary and Jane taking a last look at Pisa and the *pineta,* Lerici, Casa Magni and sad Viareggio, where the funeral pyres had burned and where the schooner *Ariel,* found at last, now rested on the shore.

A few days later Trelawny was back in Pisa again, for now Byron's two households were on the move. It needed a small flotilla to transport them. One boat took Madame Guiccioli and the Gambas; another, Byron's menservants and maidservants; still another was laden down with Byron's luggage and his vast assortment of beasts and birds—including a family of pet geese, though not Byron himself. He proposed to travel overland in his own carriage. As usual, however, he changed his mind at the last minute: Trelawny and the *Bolivar* were brought back to Leghorn and Byron went to Genoa by sea.

But this trip ended Trelawny's responsibilities. The four families—Byron and Gamba, Hunt and Shelley—settled down in their respective villas at Albaro; Jane began her long journey to England, and Trelawny himself found lodgings in the town.

He did not stay there long. He was too restless, too poignantly unhappy; for now he had time to think, and to realize his loneliness. Not since that sunrise on the bleak Jersey rock when he had just said goodbye to De Ruyter, had he felt so utterly alone in the world as now. Shelley was dead. Clare, the woman he so idealized that he imagined her love could console him for the loss of Shelley, had gone out of his life, leaving him frustrated, angry, and more than a little bewildered. He had asked Clare to marry him: Godwin had taught her a hearty contempt for matrimony. He had asked her to be his mistress: her experience with Byron had been too disillusioning. She had refused both offers—not, however, without sweetening her refusal with just enough hope to keep him on the anxious seat. All through the weeks since the wrecking of the *Ariel,* back of his grief for Shelley and his work for Mary, this hopeless passion for Clare had been gnawing at him and worrying him almost past endurance.

The affair had no good side. It not only embittered Trelawny and strengthened the distrust for women that Julia's betrayal had left him, it brought about a gradual change in his attitude towards Byron that was to have far-reaching and disastrous results. The somewhat naïve admiration tinged with awe for Byron's genius that had brought Trelawny to Pisa, as a pilgrim comes to a shrine, had faded with intimacy. But Byron could charm when he chose; he could be a delightful companion, and there had been pleasant days that summer on board the *Bolivar*. If Trelawny had not fallen in love with Clare, he would never have come to hate Byron— as he did come to hate him—and to give vent to those violent alternations of praise and blame, when he wrote of Byron, which were to shock his contemporaries, and which Byron's more recent biographers consider a proof of unreliability. These critics are willing to accept Trelawny's fine story of the *events* of 1822 and 1823, and repeat it without question (and even without "quotes"!), but they reject his criticisms of Byron's character with angry incredulity. The fellow is as inconsistent as Balaam, cursing and blessing in the same breath, and no more to be believed than Balaam's ass!

But as a matter of fact, whether Trelawny's estimate of Byron is accepted or rejected, a most important element in the controversy has never been sufficiently taken into account: Trelawny's passion for Clare Clairmont. A man struggling in the depths of a hopeless infatuation can scarcely be expected to take a dispassionate view of the lady's former lover. In the miserable drama of Clare, Byron, and Allegra— Trelawny, of course, knew every scene by heart; Clare never tired of rehearsing it—Trelawny saw Byron as the mean, cold-hearted villain of the piece. Even years later, whenever he attempted to revive Byron's image he saw it out of focus, distorted and blurred by intruding memories of Clare and the child Allegra.

Trelawny himself probably never realized this; he was not given to acknowledging his prejudices or analyzing his emotions. There is no smallest hint of an unhappy love affair in his *Recollections* of this time; Clare Clairmont does not appear as one of the Pisa circle. But when she left Italy—rejection seems to have increased his passion—he began writing to her. She preserved his letters, and after his death they were published: * some sixty-five in all, the first dating from this autumn of 1822, the last written in 1875; a correspondence even longer than his correspondence with Augusta White.

The first are, of course, love letters: passionate, incoherent, as usual badly written, badly spelled, and sprinkled with quotations from Shakespeare; signed "your Edward" and varying in tone as his mood varied in response to hers. Sometimes reproachful and imploring: "The bitter feelings of disappointment, after having tortured me almost into convulsions, have left me gelid, morbid and broken-hearted. Oh dearest, how less than nothing are words. . . . Write dear, relieve some portion of the weight which oppresses my bosom, for I am sick at heart. . . . Remember, we are to meet again in the Spring—this let nothing put aside."

Sometimes they are tenderly mournful, as in a letter written on board the *Bolivar* in the Bay of Spezia, on a stormy night:

"This place fills me with gloomy and desponding thoughts. . . . I induced Shelley to reside here, and I designed the treacherous bark which proved his Coffin— Well, it is selfish to regret that he has at last found peace—but it is sorrowful to think so noble and worthy a being, so deserving of all joy on earth, could only attain it under the blue wave of the sea he loved. Would we were with him! . . . The storm is augmenting; the blue and sparkling Mediterranean white with foam raining a very deluge and the torrents descending from the mountains—white and black clouds scudding rapidly over the Moon which is struggling as if in suffocation to put forth his white and silvery horns—the dusky olive and mountain

* *Letters of Edward John Trelawny*, edited by H. Buxton Forman, C.B. Henry Frowde, Oxford University Press, 1910.

pine laboring—lightning turning the sombreness of night to brilliant day—the sailors getting out cables and anchors— But we are close to the shore in the little bay of Lerici that you know so well. And I sleep, dearest friend, in security, with thoughts of our friendship and a feeling that on my part it is unalterable. Good night, dearest."

But often a letter of hers would drive him to a fury of protest: "You have done me wrong— Proud, peevish, sullen, domineering, self-willed, revengeful, unrelenting and ascetic, are all of them terms which some actions of my life would warrant and therefore I must be content to bear with them; but hypocrisy, deceit, baseness, cowardice, or want of generosity or *heart*—what action have you seen or heard of my committing that warrants your accusation that I am guilty of this baseness? How can you, Clare, that know me, accuse me of being a cold-blooded, selfish, heartless villain?" It ends humbly: "I should like to come to Vienna in the Spring."

A few days later anger again got the better of him. He wrote:

"You! you! *torture* me, Clare—your cold, cruel, heartless letter has driven me mad— It is ungenerous under the mask of Love to enact the part of a demon. . . . In the sincerity and honesty of my affection, I wrote *unhesitatingly, unreflectingly,* my *vaguest, wildest* thoughts. . . . By the power of what I considered mutual and fervent affection you bared my heart, and gathered, and gathered my crudest, idlest, most entangled surmises— You then sum them up together in a cold, unfeeling, arithmetical manner. . . . I am hurt to the very soul, I am shamed and sick to death. . . . I fearlessly opened my heart, confessed my weaknesses, entreated your counsel, aid, judgement, looked to you as my destiny. I tell you, Clare, you use me most unjustly. . . . You have used your unlimited sway over me with a remorseless and unfeeling hand. . . . You are right in withdrawing your fate from mine, my nature has been perverted by neglect and disappointment in those I loved. My disposition is unamiable;

I am sullen, savage, suspicious and discontented. I can't help it—you have sealed me so! . . . You have made me hopelessly wretched."

Letters such as these, dozens of them, followed Clare as she moved farther and farther away from him on her journey to Vienna; bombarded her, as if he hoped to take her by violence, batter down her resistance. But before the new year of 1823 came in he was beginning to long for a change of scene, and to know that he must leave Genoa.

He had stayed on there, anxious to keep in touch with the remnants of the Pisa circle. But the Hunts' flat in Villa Negreto was very unlike Jane's and Mary's pleasant rooms in the Tre Palazzi, or the sunny, sea-scented sala of Casa Magni. He liked Hunt well enough, and he did not much mind noisy children or bad housekeeping. But the atmosphere was unhappy; Mary too sad and fretful, Hunt and his wife too worried for companionship. Of this time, he wrote in his *Recollections:*

"The fine spirit that had animated us and held us together was gone! Left to our own devices, we degenerated apace."

It was true. Jane, back in England again, became plumper, pinker, sillier, more complacent. In the end she was able to forget Pisa and the *pineta,* Casa Magni and Viareggio, Edward and Percy, just enough to let her marry Shelley's old friend Hogg yet keep the past a romantic background for domesticity. Mary also became "more so"; more fretful and more exacting—the Hunt ménage was extraordinarily uncomfortable; the stove smoked, the food was horrible, the children not always kind to her darling Persino. In the end, she became more conventional, and subsided—"degenerated" is too harsh a term—into a perfect English lady, prim, well dressed, a doting mother and a tactful mother-in-law. She often spoke of her divine Shelley and, like Jane, derived satisfaction from a romantic past, but gradually her grief became stereotyped; she wrote a great deal, but nothing half so good as *Frankenstein*. Clare, after the excitement of keeping Trelawny guessing had lost its zest, also took to living in the past, where Byron figured as a devil and Shelley as an archangel. In the end, she drifted into a dull governess routine; she became both dowdy and *dévote*.

Leigh Hunt most certainly degenerated that winter in Genoa. An oversweet nature sours easily; he had no business sense; too close association with Byron—"the most capricious of allies and the most parsimonious of paymasters"—intensified his faults. The *Liberal* was badly received in England, and after four numbers Byron allowed it to expire. But Hunt's demands for money went right on. For a while Byron groaned and paid. But, in the end, the Hunt family—nine of them now—were left to shift for themselves in a foreign land; for Byron too was degenerating. After Shelley's death he seems, for a time, to have slipped back without resistance into the old mood of cynical indifference to life from which Shelley had so often rescued him.

In his first grief for Shelley, Byron had begged Mary to apply to him if at any time she were in need of money. But penuriousness soon got the better of him. When Mary asked him to pay for some translating he had ordered and he discovered that it was Clare who had done the work, he refused; and by the time Mary had brought herself to leaving Italy for England, relations between herself and Byron had become so strained that she would accept nothing from him. In the end, it was Trelawny, not Byron, who provided Mary Shelley with money for the journey home.

This must have been done at considerable personal sacrifice. Trelawny was hard up that winter. His income, never large, had been reduced to some five hundred pounds a year by Julia's extravagance and the high cost of divorce, and he was trying to persuade Clare to let him help her. She resisted for some time, but he knew she was desperately poor; when she fell ill, he wrote to her:

"Those I have once loved become a part of me, and I only know peace and comfort in administering to theirs. . . . Dear

Clare, do pray use me, give me proof of your belief in my entire friendship by freely using me in your service.

> " 'My purse, my person, my extremest means
> Lye all unlocked for your occasions.' "

In the end she yielded, and took him at his word. He borrowed money from Dunn, the English shopkeeper in Pisa,
and sent Clare fifty napoleons.

This left him too poor to carry out any of his vague plans
for finding consolation in a change of scene. He had often
dreamed of fitting out an American privateer and resuming
his old life of adventure: that dream must wait. He could not
even afford a bout of fighting in Greece or some long voyage
that might heal him as that long voyage home from the Isle
of France had once helped to heal over, though not to efface,
the scar left by Zela's death. He considered a visit to his old
friend Sir John St. Aubyn in Geneva; decided it was not
worth the trouble of packing up. Sunk in the same apathy
that had held him while the divorce was dragging on, he let
himself drift: too restless to stay in Genoa, yet too inert to
move.

Listlessness was foreign to Trelawny's nature. It came now
largely from reaction. During the past summer he had touched
heights of unselfish love such as he had never before reached
—and would never reach again! Shelley, the "most celestial
of poets," had given him glimpses of mountaintops more
beautiful than any he had known. They were too high and
cold and clear for ordinary mortals, but if Shelley had lived
Trelawny might have learned to breathe that rarefied air. It
was not to be. Shelley died, and Trelawny, "left to his own
devices, degenerated apace."

There had been a time when lack of money would not have
kept him from adventure. Now, when at last his desire to escape from Byron got the best of his inertia, he did the easiest
thing. In December of 1822 he resigned his command of the

Bolivar and went duck-shooting in the Maremma with Dan Roberts.

The parting between the captain and the owner of the *Bolivar* was probably cool enough on both sides, for Byron was too discerning not to have perceived Trelawny's latent dislike although he probably remained unaware of its chief cause: Trelawny's infatuation for Clare—neither Mary Shelley nor the Hunts would have been so tactless as to mention Clare's name in Byron's presence.

But before the winter ended Byron was to regret Trelawny's departure and to wish him back.

CHAPTER XVI

"When a man hath no freedom to fight for at home,
Let him combat for that of his neighbours;
Let him think of the glories of Greece and of Rome,
And get knocked on the head for his labours."
—BYRON.

As the winter wore away Byron too became weary of Genoa; each day seemed more boring than the last. Tired of writing, tired of his pink villa, tired of the Hunts, tired of the Gambas, mortally tired of Teresa Guiccioli with her pale ringlets and vapid smile, he began asking himself whether youth were over, whether he must now face "a long and snake-like life of dull decay," and came at last to a great decision. He would essay a new rôle, the man of action. He would strike a blow for liberty. Where? Why, in Greece of course! Byron loved Greece—his love for Greece was the one genuine emotion satiety had left him. The revolution had been going on there now for more than a year. Mavrocordato, already in the thick of the fight, must be in need of help. There was no time to lose. Byron told the Gambas, *père et fils,* that he had decided to free Greece from the Turkish yoke. They approved. Young Gamba, "Pierino," said he would go too. This was a good beginning. But for a time the Gambas were Byron's only adherents; nobody else seemed able to believe that he meant what he said. When Captain Roberts—returned to Genoa after a long shooting trip in the Maremma—was told the great news, he preserved an attitude of indifference and incredulity that must have been sufficiently annoying. Nor did Trelawny, although soon aware that the vague plans he and Byron had so often discussed were becoming less vague, offer himself as a recruit; he remained con-

269

vinced that Byron was constitutionally incapable of holding
to any idea long enough to translate it into action.

On the other hand, Byron had plenty of money and a great
name. It occurred to Trelawny that the Greek Committee in
London ought to be put into communication with Byron. He
happened to be writing to an acquaintance, Lieutenant Blaquiere, making inquiries on his own account—Greece was
beginning to seem a most promising theatre for adventure—
and added a suggestion: Lord Byron was undoubtedly interested; the Committee might get money out of him; in any
case, they could make good use of his name when they appealed for funds.

This casual suggestion was to have far-reaching results.
"Byron" and "Greece" were words that went inspiringly together in the public mind; Byron's poems had already
aroused the public conscience. England was discussing the
wrongs of Greece, and politicians were debating which way
to jump. Should England be told to mind her own business,
or be exhorted to champion the cause of a small oppressed
nation struggling to be free? Government remained apathetic. But the more advanced Whigs finally came out strong
for Greece and formed a Committee. Although already aware
of Byron's interest in Greece they had done nothing about it;
but when Trelawny's suggestion was passed on to them by
Blaquiere, Blaquiere was told to write to Byron. The reply
was favorable. In due time Byron was elected a member of
the Committee and when Blaquiere was sent to Greece to
look over the situation and report, he was told to stop in
Genoa, see Byron and inform him of his election.

This flattering news brought Byron to the sticking point.
From then on he ceased to hesitate. But his friends in England remained sceptical. So did Roberts; he wrote to Trelawny that he thought Byron was merely restless; "determined to go somewhere . . . tired of this place and everybody
in it," and Trelawny still believed that Byron would, as
usual, "exhaust himself in planning, projecting, beginning,

wishing, intending, postponing, regretting and doing nothing." For neither Roberts nor Trelawny was sufficiently acute or sufficiently unprejudiced to realize what had happened.

Byron had turned over a new leaf. He was in earnest—so in earnest that he soon forced himself to something he loathed and had never before undertaken: make arrangements. Shelley was dead; other friends, too far away. Fletcher, his valet, could not be asked to fit out a martial expedition. And there was so much to do! Find a ship, find men, buy supplies, guns, arms, ammunition, and God alone knew what else. Homes must be found for the peacocks and the monkeys and the four geese. Byron was at his wit's end. He turned to the Gambas, always so willing to oblige. Pierino assured him he would see to everything. *Mio caro* Byron need not give the outfitting another thought. All Byron had to do was to provide plenty of money and say goodbye to Teresa. Teresa was a good girl. Once make it plain where her duty lay and she would let him go.

This saying goodbye to Teresa Guiccioli was of course an essential part of the programme—from the first, escape from the "ignoble chains of love" had helped to stiffen Byron's determination; and Teresa was undoubtedly a very good girl— she had taught Byron to observe the Angelus with a prayer. But she was not so good as all that. She clung. There was a dreadful fuss. Unfortunately Byron could not rid himself of Teresa as easily as he had rid himself of Clare. Clare's feelings didn't matter one way or the other, for Clare was of plain extraction. Whereas Teresa, clothed in aristocracy, required the most delicate consideration. Of Teresa, Byron wrote sadly: "As neither her birth nor her rank nor her connexions by birth and marriage are inferior to my own, I am in honour bound to support her through."

In the end, of course, Teresa had to give in. Her husband— described by M. Maurois as "quite a pleasant old man, although reported to have poisoned his first wife and to have been the murderer of Manzoni"—thought she had been away from home long enough. So did the Pope—from the first, the Pope had taken a benevolent interest in the Byron-Guiccioli triangle. Pierino seemed to think she was selfish. Teresa wept and continued to weep, but she gave in. She not only told her lord he might go to the wars but, what was even more important, consented to stay at home herself.

Byron could now give his whole attention to that wearisome matter of arrangements. Things were not going any too well. He could not feel altogether safe in Pierino's hands— young Gamba, according to Harold Nicolson, "was a youth of infinite charm and enthusiasm, but of great ill fortune in the conduct of affairs"—and towards spring he became increasingly anxious for more expert assistance.

Unaccustomed work and worry were not, however, allowed to weaken his fixed determination to go to Greece. When in April the Blessingtons and Count d'Orsay arrived in Genoa (their visit was the one pleasant interlude in Byron's dreary life at Albaro; Lady Blessington came to understand Byron at least in part, and to like him), they found him absorbed in planning the expedition to Greece. His enthusiasm was contagious. Lord Blessington was persuaded to buy the *Bolivar*—after a good deal of bargaining—for four hundred guineas, and Lady Blessington sold him her favorite horse Mameluke to take to Greece though she was extremely fond of him and Byron refused to pay anything like what he had cost her. Then a fine vessel was secured for the expedition: the *Hercules,* a Genoese ship recommended by Pierino Gamba. Not perhaps as fast as a three-masted clipper Dan Roberts had shown Byron in Leghorn, but very cheap—and by this time Byron was getting pretty tired of Roberts. Roberts had taken the part of the sailors in a dispute over some old clothes left on the *Bolivar*—an affair, according to Mary Shelley, "quite in the auctioneering taste"; and although Roberts had been asked to join the expedition, he remained singularly indifferent to the wrongs of Greece. It might be just as well if he decided not to avail himself of the opportunity.

On the other hand, his defection would leave young Gamba as Byron's sole support. This was an alarming prospect. The expedition still lacked a surgeon; Pierino had been unable to find one. There were a thousand little matters to see to; Pierino never finished anything. At last, Byron was driven to a decision. One evening Lady Blessington made a note in the journal she was keeping to use in her *Conversations,* which M. Maurois considers "one of the truest and most living books ever written about Byron." It ran:

"Byron told us that he had written to Rome to request his friend Mr. Trelawny to join him in the expedition to Greece, and spoke of that gentleman in terms of highest eulogium. He said that since the death of Shelley he had become justly attached to Mr. Trelawny who, on that melancholy occasion, had evinced such devotion to the dead and kindness to the living, as could only spring from a fine nature."

Some weeks were to go by, however, before Trelawny heard directly from Byron, for Byron put off writing; and when he did so, Trelawny had left Rome. But recent reports of Byron's expedition were more encouraging, and Trelawny was already aware that he might join if he chose to do so. The idea tempted him, for he was becoming passionately eager for Greek independence—or rather, passionately eager to get into a fight somewhere or other, and Greece seemed to offer the best opportunity. He longed to join "the motley assortment," as Harold Nicolson puts it, "of Napoleonic veterans, of Jena students, of Russian mystics and of disappointed Carbonari that flocked to Greece under the generic title of Philhellenes." But he was too poor. If he went with Byron that difficulty would be solved. The trip would cost him nothing and, once in Greece, if he and Byron couldn't get on he would say goodbye and shift for himself. Such practical considerations never weighed heavily with Trelawny, and in all probability, if the suggestion had come during the winter, he would have dismissed it without hesitation. But as winter wore away and spring came, Trelawny's hatred of Byron began fading to tolerance, for Trelawny's passion for Clare was fading to friendship—a lifelong friendship: the most fickle of lovers, Trelawny was the most constant of friends.

A few weeks of disconsolate wandering in the fever-haunted swamps of the Maremma had been enough to cool his ardor. But he was still sending a love letter to Clare from almost every village along that melancholy coast when the fever got him. He came down with malaria of a peculiarly virulent type, Maremma fever. Here, as in Borneo, mosquitoes rose in clouds from the marshes, bringing malaria just as they brought it in Borneo; but Italian peasants, less intelligent than savages, never built smudges to drive away the "noxious exhalations." As Trelawny lay on a hard dirty palliasse in some *podere,* he merely cursed the mosquitoes as an added annoyance and continued to shiver with teeth-chattering ague or shudder and burn with fever, helpless as any Georgia cracker until, aided perhaps by doses of "Peruvian bark"—he may have known enough for that— the disease wore itself out. But he had had a narrow escape; had come near echoing the latter part of Pia's lament to Dante:

"Sienna made me, unmade me Maremma."

He was a pale languid ghost of himself when at last he felt strong enough to travel and could go to Rome to complete his plans for the proper interment of Shelley's ashes.

Malaria is a strange disease. It has been known to cure rheumatism; Trelawny, it seems to have cured of love. His letters to Clare from Rome were still affectionate; he went on begging her to leave "that gelid north" and return to Italy, and to worry over her poor health and her poverty—though she had finally consented to borrow from him. But he began to make excuses for not going to Vienna, as she suggested— characteristically, when he no longer wanted to come she became anxious to see him; family matters might take him elsewhere. His mother had been in Paris "pestering him with letters." "There is my old Cousin too," he wrote, "sick and miserable from the cold climate she is in and regret at our long absence. I have not heard a word from my little Eliza [Julia's youngest child] for eighteen months and that fills me with uneasiness. I have a variety of other vexations pressing upon me." He wrote at length of what was now absorbing his whole attention, Shelley's grave:

"I have placed his ashes in a beautiful and lonely spot apart from all base and worldly remains, for I would not have them mingled. He was alone in the world and so are his mortal remains. By his side I am fixing a grave and tomb for myself, and if possible there will I lie. Of all the human beings I have ever met I think him the most estimable and would be near him hereafter. People here smile at my idea, but I have none to do the office or execute my wishes when dead—so in this instance at least I am prudent and reasonable."

This preoccupation with his own last resting place seems strange in a man of only thirty. But he spoke of it more than once in his letters to Mary Shelley. That April, after expressing the indignation he had felt at finding "the ashes of my noble Shelley confusedly mingled in a heap with five or six common vagabonds," and describing the spot he had chosen as "the most interesting," he added: "I have ordered a granite to be prepared for myself to be placed in this same beautiful recess." A week later he wrote:

"The new Protestant burying ground is protected by a wall and gates, and the ashes are placed apart, and yet in the centre and most conspicuous spot. I have just planted six young cypresses and four laurels in front of the recess you see, by the enclosed drawing, is formed by two projecting slabs of the old ruin. My own stone is placed on the left hand. I have likewise dug my grave, so that when I die there is only to lift my coverlet and roll me into it. You may lie on the other side

if you like. It is a lovely spot. On Shelley's stone, besides the
cor cordium of Hunt, are the lines from Shakespeare:

> " 'Nothing of him that doth fade
> But doth suffer a sea-change
> Into something rich and strange.'

This quotation alludes both to the manner of his death and
to his genius, and I think the element on which his soul took
wing and the subtle essence of his being, mingled, may still
retain him in some other shape. The waters may keep the
dead, as the earth may, and fire and air. His passionate fondness might have been from some secret sympathy in their natures. Thence the fascination which attracted him without
fear to trust an element almost all others hold in superstitious
dread. . . . I shall assuredly see you in Genoa before you leave.
Do not go to England to encounter poverty and bitter
retrospections. Stay in Italy. I will most gladly share my
income with you, and if, under the same circumstances, you
would do the same by me, why then you will not hesitate to
accept it. I know of nothing would give me half so much
pleasure."

Mary wrote in answer: "You appear to have fulfilled my
entire wish in all you have done at Rome. Do you remember
the day you made that quotation from Shakespeare in our living room at Pisa? Mine own Shelley was delighted with it."

Trelawny's pious task was over now, and he could leave
Rome. His plans for the summer were still uncertain, but he
had promised Mary to see her in Genoa before she left for
England. He decided to make the journey on horseback. His
luggage was forwarded to Leghorn; he bought two excellent
Hungarian cavalry horses from an Austrian colonel; engaged
an American Negro manservant to care for them, and started
off. Riding only in the cool of early morning, resting at noonday, they would spend the night in a village, or make camp
in some wood that promised shade and water, feed the horses,

build a fire, boil coffee, sup off "the provender carried by the black in old-fashioned saddle-bags," smoke their pipes, and sleep. "If there is any healthier or pleasanter way of life than this," Trelawny remarked, "I have never enjoyed it."

He was rather sorry when in the middle of May he reached Florence. A letter from Roberts was waiting there; the latest reports of the Byron expedition were not encouraging. Roberts wrote: "Between you and me, I think there is small chance of Byron's going to Greece; this I think from the wavering manner in which he speaks of it." It was followed by a letter from Mary:

"Lord Byron says that as he has not heard from Greece, his going there is uncertain; but if he does go, he is extremely anxious that you should join him, and if you will continue to let him know where you may be found, he will inform you as soon as he comes to any decision."

This left Trelawny more undecided than ever: flattered that Byron felt the need of his assistance, but still sharing Roberts's fear that the expedition would come to nothing. He was merely flirting with the idea, when the long-delayed letter from Byron arrived. Now he was seriously tempted; and not only because the wrongs of Clare and Allegra had ceased to obsess him. The letter presented Byron in a new light, calm and sincere. It was dated June 15, 1823, and ran:

"Dear T. You may have heard that I am going to Greece. Why do you not come with me? I want your aid, and am exceedingly anxious to see you. Pray come, for I am at last determined to go to Greece; it is the only place I was ever contented in. I am serious, and did not write before, as I might have given you a journey for nothing; they all say I can be of use in Greece. I do not know how, nor do they; but at all events let us go. Yours, etc. truly, N. Byron."

It was a good letter. Trelawny still doubted, still hesitated, but his reply was favorable; and another letter soon came. Byron wrote that he had chartered a vessel—the *Hercules*, Captain Scott; asked Trelawny to try to find a surgeon for the trip; pressed him to come—"I need not say I shall like your company of all things"—and ended: "I expect you with impatience and am ever yours, N. B." This put an end to indecision. Trelawny at once flung himself into all the delightful preparations for adventure. He wrote to Dan Roberts:

"I am collecting together the things necessary for the expedition. I am going with as few things as possible, my little horse, and two very small saddle portmanteaus, a sword and pistol, but not my Manton gun, a military frock undress coat and one for superfluity, 18 shirts, etc. I have a Negro servant who speaks English, a smattering of French and Italian, understands horses and cooking, a willing though not a very bright fellow; he has been the afterguard of a man of war. . . . Tell me if you wish to have all three dogs. But perhaps you will accompany us. All I can say is, if you go, I will share what I have freely with you—I need not add with what pleasure! Lord B. has desired me to look after a surgeon. He has given the same directions to Dr. Vacca and Dunn. I could have induced a clever gentlemanly fellow to have gone with us, an Englishman, not for the salary but for the spirit of enterprise and love of travel. But I am afraid to act as Vacca will most likely have engaged some mercenary Italian."

But there still remained Clare to reckon with: she would be hurt at his going to Greece instead of visiting her in Vienna, angry when she heard he was going with Byron. A letter from Florence prepared her with a hint. He wrote:

"My head is full of plans for leading an active life—of buckling on the sword in the great struggle of Liberty, either in Spain or Greece. . . . I like Florence much, there have been some agreeable people here; but they are breaking up now for Leghorn and Lucca."

A week later, he wrote: "How shall I tell you, dearest, that —that—I am actually now on my road—to embark for Greece? And that I am to accompany a man whom you disesteem? Forgive me. . . . And remember that you have in some degree driven me into an active life to get rid of the pain and weariness of my lonely existence. How can I live, or rather exist, as I have been for some time? . . . When was there so glorious banner as that unfurled in Greece? Who would not fight under it? I have long contemplated this, but was deterred by the fear that an unknown stranger without money, etc., would be ill received. I now go under better auspices. Lord B. is one of the Greek committee; he takes out arms, ammunition, money and protection to them. When once there I can shift for myself, and shall see what can be done. . . . It is only within the last few days that I have engaged myself in this expedition, or I should have given you earlier notice. I am sure you will approve the principle I am acting on, though you may regret I am not accompanied by such a being as Shelley. Alas, that noble breed is extinct. All others are nearly alike indifferent to me. We are but drawn together to amuse, or serve ourselves—I expect nothing more."

There is a new note of cynicism in this letter, and in another written to Mary Shelley a few days later. After inquiring how much money she would need for her journey home, he went on: "You must from time to time let me know your wants that I may do my best to relieve them. You are sure of me, so let us use no more words about it," and ended: "I have been racking my memory to remember some person in England that would be of service to you for my sake, but my rich friends and relations are without hearts, and it is useless to introduce you to the unfortunate; it would but augment your repinings at the injustice of Fortune. My knight-errant heart has led me many a weary journey foolishly seeking the unfortunate, the miserable and the outcast; and when found, I have only made myself one of them without redressing their grievances; so I pray you avoid, as you value your peace of mind, the wretched."

His outfitting completed, he set out for Genoa; reached the coast and turned northward. Now everything he saw "was associated," he wrote "with memories of my lost friends. My horses stopped at the accustomed locandas, many familiar faces came out to welcome me." Arrived at Lerici, he decided to sleep there, and that evening he walked out alone to Casa Magni.

It was deserted. He entered the open lower story; Shelley's skiff still lay there on the mud floor, the mast and the oars broken. Trelawny thought of the happy days Shelley had spent in that little flat-bottomed boat "adventuring" on the rivers and canals of Pisa, of the lines,

> "Our boat is asleep on Serchio's stream,
> Its sails are folded like thoughts in a dream,"

and went sadly on upstairs and into the sala.

"As I surveyed the splotchy walls, broken floor, cracked ceiling and poverty-struck appearance," he wrote, "and noted the loneliness of the situation and remembered the fury of the storms, I did not marvel at Mrs. Shelley's and Mrs. Williams's groans on first entering it. We men had only looked at the sea and scenery, and would have been satisfied with a tent. But women look to a house as their empire. . . . They soon transformed it into a very pleasant abode."

The next evening found him in Genoa. He put up as usual at the Croix de Malte and walked out to Albaro. Byron's welcome was cordial; they discussed the expedition, and Trelawny was pressed to stay for a meal. But he declined; promised to look over the *Hercules* next day, and went on to Casa Negroto to see Mary Shelley and the Hunts.

He spent a pleasant evening there, though Mary was sad enough. The anniversary of Shelley's death had just come around; she was sorry to leave Italy, and uncertain of her future in England. But Trelawny's generosity would enable her to travel in comfort, and she was grateful.

Next day he went down to the water front to examine the *Hercules*. He found nothing to praise. "She was a collier-built tub, of 120 tons, round-bottomed and bluff-bowed, and of course a dull sailer, with the bulkheads, the horse-boxes and other fittings newly put up, ill contrived and scamped by the contractor. The captain, one of the rough old John Bull stamp, was well enough—the mate better and no fault to be found with the crew but that they were too few in number."

He made no secret of his dissatisfaction; he told Byron he should have let Roberts find him "a well-manned and fast-sailing, clipper-built craft, adapted to the light winds and summer seas prevailing in the Greek archipelago." In such a vessel they could have cruised along the coasts, "touching at ports not yet blockaded by the Turks, ascertained the exact state of the war, its wants, capabilities and, more especially, the character of those who were conducting it."

Byron agreed; but he insisted that the *Hercules* would get them to Greece, and that was all that was necessary. He remarked, with a smile, that he had bought her "on very easy terms," and reminded Trelawny that if he wished to choose a vessel himself, he should have come sooner. This was true. Trelawny said no more, but he remained dissatisfied.

Another feature of the expedition met with even less approval. Byron, intent on presenting a handsome appearance, had had special uniforms and helmets made for Gamba, Trelawny, and himself in Genoa, by Giovanni Aspe, after his own design. The uniforms were all of scarlet and gold, but Gamba's helmet was not quite so gorgeous as the other two. Pierino, according to Harold Nicolson, was to wear "a polygon of green cloth rising in the shape of a Uhlan's shako from a base of brass and black leather," but Byron and Trelawny would land on the shores of Hellas "in helmets of heroic proportions, such as, in the Sixth book of the Iliad, had so dismayed the infant Astyanax. Below the nodding plumes figured his own coat of arms, and the motto 'crede Biron,' while the whole was secured by a wide chin-strap of a very menacing aspect." Byron had been so pleased with the effect of his helmet that he had allowed a local artist to make a sketch of him thus arrayed; but Trelawny, when he saw them, "refused vehemently to put his on." Byron was disconcerted; in the end "the helmets were returned to their pink cardboard boxes, and the order for the uniforms was countermanded."

But this was merely a difference of taste. More serious matters were attended to. At last all was ready. On the 13th of July, 1823, Byron's dogs, Moretto and Lion, and five horses (Trelawny's and four of Byron's) were shipped, together with medical supplies, arms, ammunition, and two small cannon —but not the pet geese; through some oversight they had been left behind. That evening Byron, Trelawny, Gamba, and "an unfledged medical student" named Bruno, with eight servants—including Fletcher, Byron's valet, Tita his gondolier, and Trelawny's Negro boy, went on board and attempted to sail. There was no wind, they all came back to land and waited.

A few days later Mary wrote to Jane Williams: "Lord Byron, Trelawny and Pierino Gamba sailed for Greece on the 17th inst. I did not see the former. His unconquerable avarice prevented his supplying me with money, and a remnant of shame caused him to avoid me. . . . Trelawny more than balanced the moral account. His whole conduct during his last stay here has impressed us all with an affectionate regard, and a perfect faith in the unalterable goodness of his heart. They sailed together; Lord Byron with £10,000, Trelawny with £50. . . . The Guiccioli is gone to Bologna—*e poi cosa farà? Chi lo sa? Cosa vuoi che lo dico?*"

Mary's date was a day out. It was the 16th when the *Hercules* finally got off. But not easily. Her first attempt had been on the 13th, although Byron was extremely superstitious and Trelawny had never liked unlucky days since the memorable Friday sailing that had ended with a storm off Borneo. If they had forebodings, they were justified.

When at last wind came, the *Hercules* ran into rough water. "Constructed on the lines of a baby's cradle," she began "to play at pitch and toss." Gamba became violently seasick. The frightened horses demolished their flimsy stalls;

Trelawny and his Negro groom managed to secure them, but with difficulty. The *Hercules* was obliged to return to Genoa for the second time. They all went ashore and waited. Trelawny and three English carpenters repaired the damage. The weather improved. By afternoon of the 16th the expedition was really on its way.

But the poor old *Hercules* proved to be as wretched a sailer as Trelawny had predicted. It took her five days to get to Leghorn. Byron, naturally irritated by the delay, sank into melancholy. "The conviction of voluntary immolation," as Harold Nicolson puts it, "hung heavily upon his spirits." He had told Lady Blessington that he did not expect to return alive from Greece and only hoped that he might "die on the field of glory, rather than on the bed of disease." She had noted sadly: "There was a helplessness about Byron, a sort of abandonment of himself to his destiny, as he called it, that commonplace people can as little pity as understand."

And not only the commonplace. Trelawny neither pitied nor understood. He merely observed, as he wrote later, that "the Pilgrim sat about, solemn and sad,—he took no notice of anything, nor spoke a word." However, arrival at Leghorn made an agreeable break for everyone, including Byron. A friend of Trelawny's brought him some newspapers and books that Byron seized upon with avidity. More provisions were taken in, and three passengers came aboard—a young Scotchman, Hamilton Browne, and two Greeks, a relation of Mavrocordato named Schelizzi, and Captain Vitali—all bound for Greece and availing themselves of Byron's offer of a free passage. It was whispered that Schelizzi was a Russian spy and Vitali in the pay of the Turkish government, but Browne turned out to be an acquisition. He was an agreeable cultivated man, with a good knowledge of Romaic languages; and as he had been for some time connected with the British service in the Ionian Islands, and had lost his position only because of too pronounced Hellenic sympathies, what he had to say of Greece and her people was worth considering. It was by his advice that Byron decided to change his destination: to land first, not in Zante as he had intended, but in Cephalonia. All seven of the Ionian Islands, after belonging to Venice for some six hundred years, had rather recently come under the protection of Great Britain, and each had its Resident. Most of the Residents, according to Browne, were hostile to the Revolution, and of them all only Colonel Napier of Cephalonia could be considered a friend; Captain Scott was ordered to make for Argostoli in that island.

Leghorn once left behind, Byron gradually recovered his spirits. He remarked that "he felt better than he had for years," and Trelawny could write:

"I never was on shipboard with a better companion than Byron; he was generally cheerful, gave no trouble, assumed no authority, uttered no complaints, and did not interfere with the working of the ship; when appealed to, he always answered, 'Do as you like.' Every day at noon he and I jumped overboard, in defiance of sharks or weather; it was the only exercise he had for he could not walk the deck. His favorite toys—pistols—were not forgotten; empty bottles and live poultry served as targets." Byron even amused himself by teasing Captain Scott. The old fellow was very proud of a certain scarlet waistcoat worn only on great occasions. Byron had made fun of its size, insisting that Trelawny and himself could both get into it at the same time. One hot, windless day, with a sea like glass, Trelawny let the poultry out of their coops for an airing. The ducks and geese took to the water; Moretto and Lion jumped in after them. Byron had contrived to get hold of the famous waistcoat; standing on the gangplank, with an arm in one armhole, he called to Trelawny:

"Put your arm in, Tre; we will jump overboard and take the shine out of it."

Over they went—both buttoned into the waistcoat. There was a tremendous splash; fowls squawked, dogs barked; the

captain came on deck in a rage. But Trelawny called in the
dogs, went after the fowls in a boat; Byron soothed the captain, and all was well. Day after day the "baby's cradle"
rocked heavily but persistently on her way down the coast;
past the fever-haunted Maremma so familiar to Trelawny,
past the mouth of the Tiber, through the straits of Messina,
out into the Ionian Sea.

Never since their first meeting had Trelawny and Byron
been on such good terms. Both were always happiest at sea.
The absence of women made for peace. Teresa Guiccioli's
tears were a thing of the past. Trelawny had sent Clare a
handsome farewell letter from Leghorn; the ladies could
be permitted to retire gracefully into the background. What
was still more important, the two men so antagonistic by
nature found themselves for the time being in accord; united
by a common hatred of despotism and a common love for
liberty, "eternal spirit of the chainless mind." The mask of
cynical indifference that Byron usually affected seems to have
been allowed to slip now and then during this voyage. Passing the islet of Ponza, used as a prison by the Neapolitan
government, he had exclaimed: "What dolts the people are
to submit to despotism. I should like to see, from this our
ark, the world submerged and all the rascals in it drowning
like rats." Passing the glittering palaces of Messina, Trelawny's remark that, from a distance, the city seemed a
paradise brought an indignant "And the devil has converted
it into a Hell!" which Trelawny willingly accepted. For
neither of them had any illusions as to the true character
of the vile King and Queen of Naples that Nelson had sacri-
ficed his honor to preserve.

The two shared another sentiment: both were extraordinarily alive to the beauties of nature. Lady Blessington
had observed that "Byron had little taste for the fine arts."
Trelawny wrote: "He had an antipathy to everything scientific; maps and charts offended him; he would not look
through a spy glass and only knew the cardinal points of

the compass; buildings ancient or modern he was as indifferent to as he was to painting, sculpture and music. But all natural objects, and changes in the elements, he was the first to point out and the last to lose sight of. We lay-to all night off Stromboli, shrouded in smoke from its eternal volcanic fires, the waves rolling into its caverns, booming dismally. Byron sat up watching it. As he went down to his cabin at daylight, he said: "If I live another year, you will see this scene in a fifth canto of *Childe Harold.'* "

But why wait? Trelawny asked himself, and was disappointed when, having provided the poet with pencil and paper and kept intruders at a distance, he merely scribbled for a while and then tore the paper to bits with an angry "I must chew the cud before I write—I have thought over most of my subjects for years before writing a line," that left Trelawny puzzled and on the verge of reproof. He did not venture quite so far as that, but this easy intimacy with a man of whom he stood in awe was beginning to go to Trelawny's head.

The welcome he had received from Byron when he appeared in Genoa had already flattered him into a naïve self-confidence. From Leghorn, he had written to Dan Roberts to express his regret that Roberts was not joining the expedition as he had hoped up to the last moment, and, after devoting a page to the three hunting dogs left in Florence, had ended on a boastful note worthy of his Trelawny ancestry: "Lord B. and myself are extraordinarily thick, we are inseparable. But mind, this does not flatter me. He has known me long enough to know the sacrifices I make in devoting myself to serve him. This is new to him, who is surrounded by mercenaries. I am no expense to him, fight my own way, lay in my own stock, etc. . . . Lord B. indeed does everything so far as I wish him."

Byron must have been amused at this childish arrogance and put up with it only because he had no one else to talk to on board ship. Gamba, Browne, and the Greeks were too seasick; little Dr. Bruno, too frightened—mortally afraid of the sea, the dogs, and black-browed Tita; and Fletcher, too sulky. From the first, Fletcher had disapproved of the expedition; his remembrances of Greece were less agreeable than his master's. "A country of savages," he grumbled, "nothing to eat but tough billy goats, or to drink but spirits of turpentine; no knives or forks. There is nothing there but rocks, robbers and vermin."

Byron smiled at this outburst. Neither he nor Trelawny felt any admiration for the modern Greeks: a dishonest, treacherous, and cowardly race. Trelawny's flamboyant answer to Fletcher that day, "We shall have excitement, the greatest of all—fighting!" did not surprise Byron; he had realized all along that, with Trelawny, freeing Greece from the Turkish yoke was a minor consideration, would probably never become more than a by-product of adventure.

By now, however, he must have become aware of a change in his own point of view, to suspect that his first vague desire for applause was crystallizing to something finer, to nerve himself to face whatever the future might bring.

One dark night, as he and Trelawny sat alone on deck after a long silence, he murmured: "If Death comes in the shape of a cannon-ball and takes off my head, he is welcome. I have no wish to live, but I can't bear pain," with the bitter comment: "Mind you, Trelawny, don't repeat the ceremony you went through with Shelley—no one wants my ashes." Trelawny's suggestion of Westminster Abbey was brushed aside; he spoke of a certain rocky islet off Maina, the "Pirates' Isle," that had suggested *The Corsair*. "There is the spot I should like my bones to lie," he said, and added a plea (that Trelawny would recall later on—too late!): "If you are with me when I die, don't let the blundering blockhead doctors bleed me, or when I am dead maul my carcase."

But such gloomy premonitions were not of course aired in public. When his other guests, recovering from seasickness, began to crawl up on deck one by one, eager to discuss

the situation in Greece, Byron resumed his usual attitude
of bored indifference. But he listened, for Browne and the
two Greeks had much to say—or rather, to conjecture. What
had happened in Greece since the last vague—and most contradictory—reports received at Leghorn? How was the Revolution getting on? What government, if any, was functioning
now? Who were the leaders? Various names came up for
discussion. Mavrocordato, Marco Bozzaris, Colocotronis, and
Odysseus were those most often mentioned. It was agreed
that Prince Mavrocordato—Mary Shelley's Greek teacher,
whom Byron had known in Pisa—was likely to retain his
popularity in western Greece, and the brigand Colocotronis,
in the Morea. But eastern Greece might remain under the
domination of the mountain chieftains led by Odysseus, undoubtedly a very strong man. On the other hand, one turn
of the kaleidoscope—a decisive victory for either the Turks
or the Greeks—would change the pattern, bring a new ar-
rangement beyond the guessing of any prophet. It was all
very confusing. There was rather more unanimity when the
conversation turned to discussion of the seven Residents—
the English governors of the Ionian Islands. No one had a
good word for the Resident at Corfu, the largest island, who
was the most important. Sir Thomas Maitland—nicknamed
"King Tom" by friends and enemies alike—was a benevolent but irascible despot, given to drink, and so bent on preserving the strict neutrality of the Islands that he had made
it impossible for either side to use them as a base for military
operations. "King Tom" was of course hated by all Philhellenes. Colonel Napier of Cephalonia was reported to be a
very different type of ruler. He had travelled in Greece for
months in order to make himself personally familiar with
the country and its needs, and as Resident had set himself
to improving his island (years later, when he had conquered
Sind and become a national hero, Napier wrote, "I would
rather have finished the roads of Cephalonia than have
fought Austerlitz or Waterloo"); he was universally respected

and, what was still more important to Philhellenes, had come out as strongly on their side in the present conflict as neutrality would permit.

To all this Byron listened without pledging himself to any course of action. He was determined not to take sides until after hearing from Blaquiere—Trelawny's friend of the London Committee who had called on him at Albaro. Blaquiere was in Zante, but they would soon meet in Cephalonia. Until he knew in just what way the Committee felt he could be most useful to the Cause, planning, and even thinking, was a waste of time.

CHAPTER XVII

"And over the seas we were bidden
A country to take and to keep;
And far with the brave I have ridden,
And now with the brave I shall sleep."
—A. E. HOUSMAN.

The voyage of the *Hercules* was nearing its end—Corfu left behind, Cephalonia and Zante in sight. As Byron and his oddly assorted house party stood on deck watching the coast of the Morea begin to take shape, the premonitions that had so often oppressed him faded to nothing, blown away by a breath from the past. He murmured to Trelawny:

"I feel as if the eleven long years of bitterness I have passed through, since I was last here, were taken off my shoulders, and I was scudding through the Greek Archipelago with old Bathurst in his frigate."

That night they came to anchor in the roadstead off Argostoli, the chief port of Cephalonia, and next morning—the morning of August 2, 1823—they entered the harbor and anchored again close to the town. The little whitewashed houses gay with red and green shutters made a bright pattern against the bare, brown hillsides of the arid island; the air was warm and still; the village sounds, the smells of thyme and aromatic shrubs drifting from the shore, seemed pleasant after long days at sea; now and then a bugle from the English garrison would remind Byron of old days at Malta. Boats began coming out, bringing provisions, port officers, refugees clamoring for help, and the Resident's secretary, Captain Kennedy—Napier himself being away at the time. The news they brought was as varied as the craft. Civil war had been ravaging Greece for some time now, with incredible brutality on both sides; no one could guess which faction would emerge victorious. As for the Revolution, some said Greece would soon be free; others, that the Turkish fleet would soon put an end to hostilities; according to Kennedy, for the moment a strange apathy seemed to have overtaken both Greeks and Turks. All this was discouraging. Another bit of news aroused Byron's rage, and justly so. Blaquiere, on whom he was depending for instructions, had just sailed for England!

The letter of explanation which Kennedy handed him did little to soothe Byron's anger. Blaquiere wrote of "an unforeseen necessity" that had obliged him to return to England "in the interests of Greece." Byron knew better! Blaquiere's reason was purely selfish; he was hurrying home with a manuscript he wanted to get published before England lost interest in Greek affairs. Moreover, his defection made it plain that neither he nor the London Committee was taking Byron seriously. Now that they had his name to use in raising funds and had got him out to Greece, they could let him drift, sure that he would soon drift into the hands of whichever faction the local Philhellenes approved, give them all the money he had brought with him, and then drift home again.

"They are deceived," Byron told Trelawny. "I won't budge a step further until I see my way." That, he added, might mean a long stay in Greece. No matter. If British neutrality obliged him to leave Cephalonia he would buy an island from either the Greeks or the Turks—islands must be cheap at the moment—and live there while he studied the problem in all its intricacies. Until he saw every square of the chessboard in clear black and white, he could not take part in the game; not so much as a pawn would he advance.

This was a new Byron. Too new for his friends to understand; most of all, for Trelawny—he applauded Byron's sentiments, but that old doubt of Byron's stability would not down. However, no one felt any objection to staying on in Cephalonia for a week or so. If Colonel Napier's ideas of neutrality were sufficiently elastic to permit them to remain, they agreed it would be a good plan to stay until they got their bearings.

Colonel Napier's ideas turned out to be most elastic. He came to call next day. Everybody was delighted with Colonel Napier. Byron admired his executive ability; Trelawny, his fiery spirit. They all listened with respect to his account of conditions in Greece. He spoke of the stupidity and inertia of the Turks and of the dangerous optimism of the revolutionary leaders induced by their early successes; the Greek finances were in a very bad way; incessant quarrelling between the military and civil authorities prevented any unity of action. The Greeks were like that. But, with all their faults, he had become very fond of the Greeks: they were as good-natured as the Irish and much cleaner than the Italians. As for Byron's plans, he approved his staying on in Cephalonia, and not only gave permission for the *Hercules* to remain in the harbor but urged Byron to come ashore and make him a visit at the Residency. If properly handled, "King Tom of Corfu" could be induced to look the other way and not to inquire too closely into Byron's purpose in coming to Greece.

The invitation after so long a voyage must have been tempting; but Byron, anxious to avoid any clash with British authority, declined. Another invitation, however, was accepted. Byron and his guests, Trelawny, Gamba, Hamilton Browne, and Dr. Bruno—the two Greek gentlemen had gone their several, and no doubt devious, ways—were given a dinner by the officers of the English garrison. It went off very nicely. Byron attended with some trepidation, unsure of a welcome after his years of banishment from English society; but everyone was extremely polite. The young fellows drank his health, and quoted *Don Juan,* and told him what a great man he was, and Byron made a little speech; all together it was a most agreeable occasion.

A trip to Ithaca, arranged a few days later, also went off very well—on the whole. Ithaca was a charming island, green and flowery; the Resident, Colonel Knox, and his lady, most polite; the Fountain of Arethusa, well worth seeing. On the other hand, Byron was obliged to look at ruins, which he hated, and to talk to monks, which he disliked even more; and he came down with an odd sort of seizure, rather like a fit, extremely alarming both to himself and to his friends. But Dr. Bruno administered his *benedette pillule;* Byron recovered. They all returned to Cephalonia to wait, with as much patience as was in them, while Byron made up his mind what to do next.

It was not so pleasant on board now. For one thing, the vessel swarmed with greedy Suliot refugees in increasing numbers. Legà, the steward, mounted guard on his money chest, "coiled up like a viper"; Captain Scott advocated driving off these "Zodiacs" with hand-spikes; but Byron found their "savage aspect and wild attire" amusing and, "as was his wont," Trelawny wrote, "promised more than he should have done; day and night they clung to his heels, till he stood at bay like a hunted lion, and was glad to buy them off by shipping them to the Morea." Other beggars were less easily disposed of. As the glad tidings of Byron's arrival spread through the country—an English milord, rich, generous, gullible—every faction, civil or military, sent an emissary to plead its cause. "To nobody," Finlay writes, "did the Greeks ever unmask their selfishness and deceit so candidly."

Colocotronis invited him to Salamis; Mavrocordato, to Hydra; the Governor of Missolonghi thought he was badly needed there; Petro Bey insisted the best way to end the war was to lend him a thousand pounds.

Byron remained aloof, refusing to be taken in. His journal recorded: "I have received invitations from more than one of the contending parties, always under the pretext that *they*

are the real Simon Pure. . . . Whoever goes into Greece at
present should do it as Mrs. Fry went into Newgate—not
in the expectation of meeting with any especial indication
of existing probity, but in the hope that time and better
treatment will reclaim the present burglarious and larce-
nous tendencies, which have followed the General Gaol de-
livery. . . . The Saturnalia is still too recent to have converted the Slave into a sober Citizen. The worst of them is,
that they are such damned liars; there never was such an
incapacity for veracity shown since Eve lived in Paradise."

To add to these annoyances, the war news that came
trickling in from the mainland to Cephalonia was as bad
as bad could be. Of the various revolutionary leaders, Byron
had been relying most on the two to whom he had been
recommended by the London Committee, Prince Mavrocordato and Marco Bozzaris, the Suliot chief. He had communicated with them at once on his arrival and was expecting their answers when word came that Mavrocordato
was in flight, driven out of Greece and refuging in the island
of Hydra, and Marco Bozzaris was dead—killed in the attempt "at midnight in the guarded tent" of Omar Pasha at
Carpensini.

There was, however, one pleasant feature of this time of
waiting. Every afternoon Byron and Trelawny would row
across the harbor and land on a rock for a bathe as in the
old days on board the *Bolivar*. Byron was still happiest while
swimming, still morbid when, emerging from the water, he
remembered his bad foot.

One day he thrust it out, muttering, "I hope this cursed
leg will be knocked off in the war," and refused to be consoled by Trelawny's offer to exchange his legs for Byron's
brains. "You would repent your bargain," he said. "At times
I feel my brains boiling as Shelley's did, whilst you were
grilling him."

A lunch of fruit and cheese, suited to what Gamba called
Byron's "Pythagorean" habits, in the shade of an olive grove

would end the day and send Byron back to his ship sufficiently refreshed to resume the wearisome burden of recon-
ciling conflicting claims and distributing largesse wherever
Colonel Napier, a wise and trustworthy adviser, thought it
would do the most good.

But to Trelawny's mind these negotiations were not only
wearisome but futile. For although he and Byron were still
animated by a common aim, the freedom of Greece, they
were by nature incapable of agreeing as to the best methods
of attaining it; they were centuries apart in their conception
of warfare. Byron, a modern, saw it as an intricate game to
be won by brains and cash. Trelawny belonged to a bygone
age; he saw it as his ancestor, old John Hawkins, had seen
it: a physical struggle won by daring and personal courage.
He began to urge Byron to action. All this talk, all this trying to make silk purses out of the ears of wild boars, was a
waste of time and must end in disaster. The Greeks were
savages and should be treated as such. You took Athens or
Corinth as you would take a pirate town in Madagascar;
you captured the Turkish squadron as you would capture
a Chinese junk. Byron must act; leave this dull island; get
to Greece. Fire and sword, he insisted, not money, would
win the war.

These arguments were of course too crude to appeal to
Byron—and yet, in a sense, Trelawny was right; Byron's money
was spent in vain; the Revolution would undoubtedly have
been won or lost on savage lines if the civilized nations had
not finally taken a hand and ended it in their own interests.
So although Byron listened, and even went so far as to talk
seriously of leaving Cephalonia for the mainland, he soon
changed his mind. Captain Scott refused to risk the *Hercules* in dangerous waters. Byron thought it might be a good
idea to pay off the *Hercules*—life on board ship was becoming monotonous—and take a house on the island; not at Argostoli, for that might embarrass Colonel Napier, but in
some other town. Metaxata, perhaps.

This proposal brought an end to Trelawny's patience. "I well knew," he wrote later, "that, once on shore, Byron would return to his old routine of dawdling habits—plotting, planning, shillyshallying, and doing nothing," or, rather, doing nothing but hand out money. It was all very well for Byron to turn lavish all of a sudden and dedicate the whole thirty-four thousand pounds he had just received from the sale of his estate of Rochdale to the Greek cause, and to toy with the idea of being tendered a handsome reward—a gold crown in exchange for his silver one. He, Trelawny, had not come out here to engage in the banking business, to sit cooling his heels either on the deck of a "baby's cradle" or on the balcony of a squalid little island cottage, while glorious fighting was going on a few miles away across the water.

He waited a few days longer, as much on Byron's account as on his own, still hoping to spur Byron to action, still convinced that one bold step might take Byron straight through the cobwebs of inertia that had always muffled his spirit and might set him free. (A belief Trelawny was to retain. Long after, he wrote of Byron: "I never doubted, for he was indifferent to life and prouder than Lucifer, that if he had drawn his sword in Greece or elsewhere, he would have thrown away the scabbard.")

Vain hope. Byron rented an ivy-covered cottage at Metaxata, a village near Argostoli; Fletcher began packing up; Trelawny told Byron he had other plans, and offered a suggestion: The news from the Morea was most contradictory —might it not be a good idea for Hamilton Browne and himself to go there, find out just how the Revolution was getting on, and report? At first Byron protested: It was a pity to break up the party—why not wait a little longer and all go to Greece together? But Trelawny held to his resolution and Byron, probably willing enough to let him go—in his present restless fault-finding mood, Trelawny must have been an unsatisfactory companion—ended by approving the plan. Trelawny could act as his emissary: take letters from him to the heads of whatever governments were found to be functioning in Greece, "expressing his readiness to serve them when they had satisfied him how he could best do so." This matter settled, all hands on the *Hercules* began preparing for departure.

As usual with Byron, moving was a terrible business. Trelawny and Browne decided to stay on board a day or two, and defer their much simpler packing-up until the confusion of the great man's disembarkation was over. At last, the horses, the dogs and the servants—all eight of them, for Byron had taken a fancy to Trelawny's Negro boy and Trelawny had let him go (to regret it: the Suliot engaged as a substitute turned out to be both sulky and lazy)—were safe ashore. Byron's vast amount of paraphernalia—his bed, his linen, his silver, his books, his weapons, and his clothes (including a green embroidered military jacket discarded by Trelawny as too tight, which Byron had also taken a fancy to)—had been transported to his new quarters. Byron and Gamba and Dr. Bruno were gathered on deck ready to be rowed to Metaxata. The moment of parting had arrived.

The parting was entirely amicable. Byron shook hands with Trelawny—with no premonition that it was for the last time, only a cheerful: "Let me hear from you often, come back soon. If things are farcical, they will do for *Don Juan;* if heroical you shall have another canto of *Childe Harold.*" Next day Trelawny sent a last farewell note to Metaxata, ending: "We missed you sadly last night at grog-time."

The following day, the 4th of September, 1823, Trelawny and Hamilton Browne said goodbye to Captain Scott, wished him a good voyage to England, and set sail for the Morea in a small vessel, a caïque (too small to carry a horse, so Trelawny's fine Hungarian cavalry horse must also have gone to Byron), and a fair wind landed them early next morning on the beach below a ruined tower near Pyrgos.

And now Trelawny was at last in Greece! The first glimpse
was disillusioning. A squad of Moorish mercenaries, quartered in the tower, came out to meet them and escorted
them to the village. They were friendly enough, but dirty
and undisciplined; Pyrgos was a wretched little place. No
horses were to be had there. But next day, a little farther on,
they were able to buy horses and could begin their journey
eastward across the Morea to Tripolitza, the capital of the
Peloponnesus, visiting military stations and sleeping as best
they could in the filthy hovels of ruined villages.

Trelawny's description in his *Recollections* of the devas-
tated regions they passed through deserves to be given very
nearly in full as a sample of his admirable style. Its vividness suggests a bond between himself and Byron too often
forgotten; Trelawny was not only extraordinarily sensitive
to artistic impressions, he was able to translate his feeling
into words. Since Shelley, he was probably the only person
with whom Byron could discuss literature with any hope
of being understood.

"The country is so poor and barren," he wrote, "that in
the best of times, there would not be plenty; now that war
had passed over the land with fire and slaughter there was
scarcely a vestige of habitation or cultivation. The only people we met, besides soldiers, looked like tribes of half-starved
gipsies. Over our heads on some towering rock, occasionally
we saw a shepherd with his long gun, watching us and keeping guard over small flocks of goats and sheep while they
fed on the scanty shrubs that grew in the crevices above
them; they were attended by packs of the most savage dogs
I ever saw. Except in considerable force, the Greek soldiers
dare not meddle with these warlike shepherds and their
flocks. Many of the most distinguished leaders in the war,
and the bravest of their followers, had been shepherds. . . .
Every step of our way to Tripolitza and on to Argos was
marked by the ravages of the war. Our road to Corinth took
us through the defiles of Dorvenskia; it was a mere mule

path for about two leagues, winding along in the bed of a brook, flanked by rugged precipices. In this gorge, and a more rugged path above it, a large Ottoman force, principally cavalry, had been stopped in the previous autumn by barricades of rocks and trees, and slaughtered like droves of cattle by the wild and exasperated Greeks. It was a perfect picture of the war, and told its own story of the sagacity of the nimble-footed Greeks, and the hopeless stupidity of the Turkish commanders. . . . The Turks might have been a herd of bisons trapped and butchered in the gorges of the Rocky Mountains. . . . There, grouped in a narrow space, we saw five thousand or more skeletons of men, horses, mules and camels; vultures had eaten the flesh and the sun had bleached their bones. Detached from the heaps of dead, we saw the skeletons of some bold riders who had attempted to scale the acclivities, still astride the skeletons of their horses, and in the rear, as if in the attempt to back out of the fray, the bleached bones of the Negroes' hands still holding the hair ropes attached to the skulls of their camels—death like sleep is a strange posture-maker."

Even in peace times the trip would have been exhausting, and the fare scanty. "But there were compensations," Trelawny wrote, "ample food for the mind for those who love the haunts of genius. Every object we saw was associated with some great name, or deed of arts or arms, that still live in the memory of mankind." And as he thought of the years of slavery the Greeks had undergone since their Golden Age, he marvelled they still had spirit enough to revolt. "No people," he reflected, "who retain their nation and language, need despair. 'There is nothing constant but mutability.' "

In Corinth they came face to face with revolutionary leaders known hitherto only in name. Colocotronis was there, and others of the "same predatory type." They found Corinth as inclined to split up into senseless factions as St. Paul had found her in his day; they saw nothing to admire and much to distrust in all the leaders, including Colocotronis. However, he was undoubtedly in control of the Morea, which meant that the civil authorities were at the mercy of the military. A report of this most unsatisfactory state of affairs was sent off at once to Byron, who was still at Metaxata, still busy with conflicting claims on his purse and waiting anxiously for news. He received the despatches in October. After informing him of the dangerous supremacy of Colocotronis, Trelawny and Browne went on to offer Byron some advice: he would do well to help Mavrocordato get the Greek fleet away from Hydra as soon as possible, to break the Turkish blockade; and the two representatives Greece was sending to London, to negotiate a loan, should be expedited on their way, for there was no time to lose. The advice was good. "They foresaw," Harold Nicolson says, "that if such a loan could be given to the constitutional government, the usurped authority of the military chieftains would from that moment diminish. And the event proved they were correct in this assumption. Byron was gratified by this intelligence; it gave him something definite to do; it gave him an added excuse for remaining in Metaxata."

Meanwhile Trelawny and Browne had left Corinth for Salamis, and had found the chiefs there even less to their liking; of many different tribes but "each and all intent on their own individual interests." The most dangerous in Trelawny's opinion were the Phanariots. "These dextrous intriguers," he wrote, "glided stealthily from tent to tent and from chief to chief, envenoming their feuds, and causing universal anarchy." The outlook was depressing; when word came from Byron, that he had received a pressing invitation from Mavrocordato to visit him in Hydra, and wanted them to go there in his place, they were more than willing to obey.

Prince Mavrocordato proved to be a very different type from Colocotronis; he was a good-looking, well mannered, cultivated gentleman, and apparently Trelawny liked him—

everyone liked Mavrocordato on first acquaintance. He remembered Shelley's admiration for the prince and forgot—
until later—that he was a Phanariot. The report that went
from Hydra to Byron was favorable; Colonel Napier gave
his approval. Before very long Mavrocordato became the
happy possessor of four thousand pounds lent him by Byron,
and could at last prepare to launch the Greek fleet.

Their mission in the Morea having been accomplished,
Trelawny and Browne, to their regret, found they must
part company. Browne thought he ought to see Byron in
Metaxata, and was expecting to go on from there to England
with the two Greek representatives in order to introduce
them to the Committee. Trelawny was sorry to say goodbye—he wrote later he had found Browne "a most valuable
ally." But if he considered accompanying his friend as far
as Cephalonia he soon decided against it. He felt no smallest
desire to see Metaxata or Byron, and he did very much wish
to see Athens.

The decision was to have far-reaching results. For by now
Byron was getting tired of Metaxata and trying to make up
his mind where else to go. If Trelawny had rejoined him at
this crucial moment Byron might have been persuaded to
seek some healthier and less repulsive spot than fever-
haunted, mud-soaked Missolonghi, and have lived to wear
the Greek crown. If Trelawny had not chosen to visit Athens at this time he might never have come under the influence of Odysseus, the klepht chieftain, the strongest leader
of the party opposed to Mavrocordato, who was in control
of Athens and eastern Greece.

But he did go to Athens. He met Odysseus, and Odysseus—
unfortunately for Trelawny—possessed all, or almost all, the
characteristics necessary for a romantic friendship. Trelawny, a hero-worshipper, must have been unconsciously on
the lookout for a hero ever since he had lost Shelley. It may
well be that Odysseus was, in a way, an inheritance from
Shelley; that Trelawny was drawn to Athens because of a

desire to see the leader (like his namesake of the Iliad, often called Ulysses) of whom Shelley had written in *Hellas,* his glorification of the Greek *risorgimento:*

"A brighter Hellas rears its mountains
   From waves serener far;
A new Peneus rolls his fountains
   Against the morning star.

  .   .   .   .

A new Ulysses leaves once more
 Calypso for his native shore."

His people were famous in Greek legend; he was descended from a long line of klephts, the robber barons who had taken over the mountains once dedicated to Apollo and the Muses and there maintained a precarious but glorious existence by terrorizing their weaker neighbors; alternately raiding and protecting, with a total disregard for the rights of whatever tyrant happened to consider them his subjects, and as little sense of loyalty as the Scottish border clans, who were wont to skip from a Scottish to an English king as seemed best to themselves at the moment. Odysseus himself was a fine figure of a man. He is described by a Greek writer as "of lofty stature and the greatest symmetry, thick hair, not only on his head—heavy eyebrows and bushy moustache —but on his breast. He had a stern and frowning look that showed confidence and daring. . . . Like the hero of the popular song:

" 'A sturdy rock his shoulders broad, his locks are chestnut
    brown,
  His breast is like a brazen wall—no force can break it
    down.'

Moreover he was very strong-handed, fleet-footed and able to make long marches; they even say he outran some of the swiftest horses. Certainly he had few equals in strength, courage, sagacity and manly beauty." Captain Humphries, an English Philhellene who knew him well, speaks of his "bent brow to be matched only by a Redgauntlet," and adds, "He had the tastes of a gentleman, and was fond of shooting, of horses and dogs, as so few Greeks are." Except for a few words of Italian, he spoke only Greek, but "his language in his own tongue was very elegant. He possessed the perfect military eye—observable in the spots he fixed on for halting at night, and in his pointing out as we passed the advantageous positions which the country afforded."

Such a combination of knightly qualities could scarcely fail to win Trelawny. He wrote to a friend, George Finlay, that Odysseus was "a Bolívar who might become a Washington"; to Mary Shelley, "he is a glorious being"; to Clare, "he is brave, clever and noble." In short, during the first few months of their friendship, Trelawny found Odysseus the bandit almost as fine a man as De Ruyter the privateer. Almost, but not quite. A superficial resemblance has convinced some writers that, to Trelawny, Odysseus was merely a reincarnation of De Ruyter; but, fundamentally, they were very different. Odysseus had none of De Ruyter's chivalric pity for the weak and oppressed, and although his "language was elegant" he must have been entirely lacking in De Ruyter's taste and feeling for good literature. Nor would Trelawny ever have written of De Ruyter, as he wrote of Odysseus, in his *Recollections:* "He was a thorough Greek in cunning."

But that suspicion would come later on. Here in Athens, Trelawny accepted Odysseus as the perfect leader and without hesitation plunged headlong into guerrilla warfare. "I bought horses," he wrote, "hired soldiers, and accompanied him on an expedition to Eubea, then in the hands of the Turks. . . . Our headquarters were on Parnassus. Our ambuscades, onslaughts, rock fighting, forays, stalking Turkish cavalry, successes and failures, intermingled with conferences, treaties, squabbles, intrigues and constant change, were exciting at the time; so is deer-stalking."

The last words suggest a change for the worse. War was now merely an exciting sport. Trelawny had reverted; the peaceful days with Shelley in Pisa forgotten as if they had never been. He was a boy again; boarding a pirate craft, killing for the pleasure of killing. Or the young captain who had pillaged a Chinese junk and put a bullet through her Tartar captain without a flicker of remorse. Guerrilla warfare—crouching behind rocks, taking pot shots at figures glimpsed on the sky line, dashing to cover—is probably the least brutalizing form of warfare. But Trelawny was a grown man now—thirty-one. Beyond a doubt, that "deer-stalking" with Odysseus coarsened his nature; left him harder, more reckless, more intolerant of control, readier to take offence and to return violence with violence.

Meanwhile a less romantic leader than Odysseus had arrived in Greece to take part in her struggle—Colonel Leicester Stanhope, C.B., a son of the Earl of Harrington, sent out by the London Committee in place of Blaquiere—now very busy with a second book. Stanhope had come by a devious route in order to visit various groups of Philhellenes in Germany, Switzerland, and Italy, to study the Swiss military system and the cultivation of silkworms, and call on the Greek Primate in Pisa. This last interview was disappointing: the Primate thought Greece needed a king—the Prince of Coburg, or a son of the deposed King of Sweden, might do—and Stanhope had to inform the London Committee that many Greeks appeared to hold these reactionary sentiments. "They consider democracies not suited to large states," he wrote, "because democracies possess less vigor and promptness, and forget," he added warmly, "the grandeur and stability of America." But with this interview Stanhope's preliminary investigations were at an end. From Pisa, he could hurry across Italy to Ancona, embark, and find himself at last headed for Greece.

One November evening of 1823, a note went from Pierino Gamba in Argostoli to "Mio Caro Byron" in Metaxata, marked "Urgente."

"Questa notte," it ran, "é arrivato da Ancona un bastimento papale con a bordo 20 passageri e due colonelli, uno inglese e l'altro prussiano. Il primo si chiami *Canop,* il secondo *Dylon.*"

Byron, being familiar with Pierino's odd spelling of proper names—even more peculiar than Trelawny's—realized at once that the *due colonelli* must be Stanhope and Delaunay, and prepared to welcome Stanhope with as much enthusiasm as he could feel for any disciple of Jeremy Bentham, that tiresome "utilitarian," known to brand poetry as mere "misrepresentation," yet entertain a crazy notion that canals ought to be cut through the isthmuses of Suez and Panama. But although Byron found Leicester Stanhope a bore, and would undoubtedly have preferred the company of the older brother —Charles Stanhope was "famous for many eccentricities, such as dressing like Henry IV of France"—and Stanhope disliked Byron's frivolous comments on serious subjects, they were united in a sincere desire to help Greece, and differed only as to the best methods. Stanhope expected to save her by education and the press, post offices and model prisons, while Byron had come to agree with Trelawny that she must be saved by force of arms. "It is odd enough," Byron wrote, "that Stanhope, the soldier, is all for writing down the Turks; and I, the writer, am all for fighting them down." So Byron labelled Stanhope "a typographical colonel," and was probably not too sorry when the latter left Argostoli for Missolonghi.

That unpleasant town was now the centre of many activities both civil and military. Before long Prince Mavrocordato arrived there. He succeeded in assembling the important chiefs and primates in western Greece for a conference, and was chosen Governor-General. The meeting with Stanhope went off well enough. Mavrocordato was cordial, and Stanhope recognized the Prince's ability—though he felt, and continued to feel, grave doubts of the latter's sincerity. He wrote later: "Mavrocordato is a clever, shrewd, insinuating and amiable man. He wins men, at first, by his yes's and his smiles." However, the two were agreed on one point: Lord Byron must be induced to abandon the idle seclusion of Metaxata, come to Missolonghi and take his rightful place there as wise counsellor, heroic leader, and head almoner of the London Committee. Urgent messages to this effect soon went off to Byron. The invitation found him in a receptive mood. Colonel Napier, Byron's best friend among the Philhellenes, had given up his post in order to devote himself to the Greek cause unhampered by neutrality, and was leaving Cephalonia for good. There was a lot in what Mavrocordato and Stanhope said. Reluctantly, by slow degrees, he overcame his repugnance to making a move. Fletcher was told to begin packing up; they were all to leave the island as soon as transportation could be secured.

At last two suitable vessels, a bomba and a mistico, were hired. Byron and his retinue betook themselves to Argostoli to wait for a favorable wind. It came. One December afternoon, Pierino Gamba, carrying a telescope and a Bible—parting present from the English chaplain—summoned Byron to the shore. He laid down his *Quentin Durward,* gave the chaplain "a small donation for the school for Greek females," strolled to the quay, was rowed out to the mistico; and after many mishaps (such as losing Pierino and the bomba for several days while the poor fellow got captured and released by the Turks, and Fletcher came down with a bad cold) the "Pilgrim of Eternity" arrived at the end of his last journey on earth.

CHAPTER XVIII

"Placed in the Arab's clime, he would have been
As bold a rover as the sands have seen;
And braved their thirst with as enduring lip
As Ishmael wafted on his Desert-Ship;
Fixed upon Chili's shore, a proud cacique;
On Hellas' mountains, a rebellious Greek."
                                        —BYRON.

On Monday the 5th of January, 1824, Byron landed at
Missolonghi, dressed in a scarlet uniform borrowed from an
obliging colonel, and was greeted, according to Mr. Nicolson, with "salvos of artillery, the discharge of guns and the
wild yells of the populace. The occasion was stupendous."
Everyone agreed that Byron appeared to be in excellent
health and spirits. "Hope and content were pictured on his
countenance," Pierino noted with satisfaction; but added—
still slightly hysterical, no doubt, after his escape from those
horrid Turks: "I cannot easily express the emotion which
the scene excited. I could scarcely restrain my tears."

Byron thus safely settled in Missolonghi, Stanhope felt he
could leave him for a while and departed for Athens. The
news of his arrival there, and also the more exciting news
of Byron's arrival in Missolonghi, reached Trelawny while
he was still happily engaged in "deer-stalking" with Odysseus.
Realizing its importance, he told the chief he should see
Stanhope before the latter became too intimate with any
of the other leaders, and they must return to Athens at
once. They did so. Stanhope seems to have found both to
his liking. He became Trelawny's friend. Of the chieftain,

he wrote later on to Byron: "I have been constantly with Odysseus. He has a very strong mind, a good heart, and is as brave as his sword. He is a doing man; he governs with a strong arm, and is the only man in Greece who can preserve order."

Odysseus may not have felt the same enthusiasm for a "typographical colonel," but he had the good sense to affect interest in Stanhope's theories, and agree that whatever money could be coaxed from the London Committee and the Quakers would be well spent on Bibles, newspapers, medical supplies, useful pamphlets, and the salaries of two schoolmasters trained in the Lancastrian system. But another plan of Stanhope's met with much sincerer approval; Stanhope, realizing that no improvements could thrive in a country ravaged by civil war, suggested a conference. Get the rival leaders face to face around a table to talk things over in a friendly spirit, and harmony would result in no time at all. Mavrocordato and his followers must be invited to represent western Greece; Colocotronis might be induced to come from the Morea; Odysseus would bring the chiefs of eastern Greece. Odysseus agreed; he thought Salona, near his headquarters on Parnassus, would be a convenient meeting place. This decided, the name of another guest came up—Byron! Byron's presence at the conference was essential to success: a large loan had been floated in London, and Byron and Stanhope held the purse strings. But would he come? Stanhope, recalling the mud and filth of Missolonghi, was hopeful. So was Trelawny. Parnassus! Why, the name in itself was a magnet to draw Byron away from his poisonous swamps up to the high clear air of Parnassus, home of Apollo and the Muses. Of course Byron would come! In March letters went to Byron from both Stanhope and Trelawny, explaining the importance of the congress. Stanhope wrote imploring Byron and Mavrocordato to attend, "as you love Greece and her sacred cause"; Trelawny, with the same urgency, and at great length. He ended: "I rejoin the

army with Ulysses [Odysseus] today. Corinth and Negro-
ponto are in close blockade. Ulysses defends the Pass of
Thermophilly [*sic*] with 3000. He is the most energetic, active and enterprising soldier I have ever met."

Byron's answer was favorable. But he had had another
attack of epilepsy; the turmoil and quarrelling among the
chiefs, the shocking discomfort of his life, gave no room
for any consideration beyond the anxieties of the moment.
Weeks went by. He stayed on in Missolonghi. Trelawny
came to a decision: he would fetch Byron himself.

So one April morning of 1824 a gallant company set out
from Athens with Trelawny at its head. Behind him came
a string of husky young bandits on good horses, and a couple
of pack mules. They made their way westward—cautiously,
for fear of enemies, Turks or Greeks—winding in single file
up and up through high mountain passes, down rocky defiles, along the beds of ice-cold brooks; all of them, from
the smallest donkey boy to Trelawny himself, in the best
of spirits. He had not felt such exhilaration since boyhood.
Nor such entire confidence in the future. He was in charge
of an important mission and sure of success. The War of
Independence had taken a turn for the better; no more
"deer-stalking." After the congress at Salona everything
would be different. Greece would be united, become at
last the Hellas of Shelley's dreams, and assume her place
among the nations—as a democracy, of course. God forbid
that Greece should ever submit to a king! But whatever form
it took, the new government would give Byron a high place
because of his name and his money, and Stanhope was in
line for some very important position. Odysseus would be
made commander-in-chief of a large, well organized, well
disciplined army. As for himself—time enough to think of
that. All three of them—Byron, Stanhope, Odysseus—were his
friends: they would see that he got a post where he could
make use of the energy he felt seething within him, energy
hitherto wasted on purposeless adventure. Now adventure

had an aim. He was moving towards a goal, a glorious goal. Riding with his Rumeliots through the mountains in the April weather—cool air, bright sun, his young robbers singing as they rode—Trelawny felt that life was worth living. Life was good—and would soon be better.

They had reached the river Evvenus and were starting to ford it; the horses stepped reluctantly into the angry stream, splashing, stumbling, feeling for a foothold among the stones —and stopped. A horse and rider came hurrying down the opposite bank, a messenger from Missolonghi to Salona. Disordered, riding fast, out of breath—obviously a bearer of bad tidings. He halted only long enough to fling Trelawny his news, to shout, "Byron is dead!" and disappeared at a gallop.

Byron dead! Trelawny looked after the man in incredulous dismay, hoping against hope that it was a mistake. But other men from Missolonghi came straggling by. He called to them. It was true—Byron was dead. That was all they knew. It was enough. As he wrote later, "By a stroke of fate, all my hopes of being of use in Greece were extinguished." They reached Missolonghi next day. Byron had been dead for nearly a week. He had died on the 19th of April, 1824.

"With despondent thoughts," Trelawny wrote, "I entered the town. It is situated on the verge of the most dismal swamp I ever saw. I marvelled that Byron, so prone to fevers, should have been induced to land on this mudbank and stick there for three months shut in by a circle of stagnant pools, a 'belt of death.' . . . I waded through the streets, between wind and water, to the house he had lived in; it was detached and on the margin of the shallow slimy sea-waters. For three months this house had been besieged, day and night, like a bank that has a run upon it. Now that death had closed the door, it was as silent as a cemetery. No one was within but Fletcher, of which I was glad. As if he knew my wishes, he led me up a narrow stair into a small room, with nothing in it but a coffin standing on trestles. No word was spoken by either of us; he withdrew the black pall and the white shroud, and there lay the embalmed body of the Pilgrim— more beautiful in death than in life. . . . Few marble busts could have matched its stainless white, the harmony of its proportions and perfect finish; yet he had been dissatisfied with that body, and longed to cast its slough. How often I had heard him curse it!"

Fletcher, realizing the trend of Trelawny's thoughts, sighed and drew the shroud higher over the body, murmuring: "That was the cause of all my lord's misfortunes."

Trelawny nodded, and, as he stood there looking down at the man for whom he had felt such a strange mingling of awe, admiration, and contempt, pity wiped out contempt; for Byron's fear that the doctors would "maul" him about was justified. They had done it—five of them, and very thoroughly. An autopsy had been performed—the brain opened, the intestines removed; the feet that had given Byron such agony of body and mind, handled and examined. What had they found to be the cause of the deformity? The tendon Achilles too tightly drawn? He sent Fletcher for a glass of water, then folded the shroud farther down. Yes; it was as he had thought. The legs were shrunken; the feet he had so often seen, of which Byron had so often complained, were both twisted to one side by the tendon. The right was the worse—the toes could not touch the ground; that accounted for Byron's odd tiptoeing gait, his inability to mount a horse without help.

"Poor fellow!" Trelawny sighed, and Fletcher, coming back, heard him.

"You may well say so, sir," Fletcher groaned. "These savages have robbed my Lord of all his money, and his life, too," and with trembling hands he replaced the shroud.

Trelawny turned away and went into the next room, where Byron had died, still in great confusion. Papers were scattered about on the desk and on the floor—a half-finished letter to Byron's sister Augusta Leigh, a drawing of his little daughter Ada, a woman's handkerchief, a ringlet, a ribbon, a small glove. Trelawny gathered these relics together and put them carefully aside. He found the verses Byron had written on his thirty-sixth birthday, such a short time ago, and read them. Two stanzas were prophetic:

> "My days are in the yellow leaf;
>   The flowers and fruits of Love are gone;
> The worm, the canker, and the grief
>   Are mine alone!
>
> .   .   .   .
>
> Seek out—less often sought than found—
>   A soldier's grave, for thee the best;
> Then look around, and choose thy ground,
>   And take thy Rest."

Next day, he and Gamba went through Byron's effects— destroying what was worthless, collecting his notebooks and fragments of poetry, assorting and docketing the papers— and arranged for the disposition of the body. (Trelawny, recalling Byron's wish, favored Athens; but, in the end, it was decided to send the body to England.) That same evening a long letter went off to Stanhope, giving a detailed account of Byron's illness, and expressed in the slightly pompous language that Stanhope would expect and approve at such a time. "With all his faults," Trelawny wrote, "I loved him truly; he is connected with every event of the most interesting years of my life. . . . I shall ever regret I was not with him when he gave up his mortality. . . . The world has lost its greatest man, I my best friend."

But a few hours later he wrote to Stanhope in a different vein. He had come to realize the persecution Byron had suffered from the rival factions, to see Mavrocordato without the mask he had worn in Hydra, and recognize this "wily Phanariot" as a formidable rival of Odysseus to be distrusted and feared. "The pestilential fever of these torpid waters," he wrote, "seems to have affected everything. The atmosphere is as dense as November in London, and it is infected by reptiles—everything is transacted, not under the rose but under the mud; imbecile councils, intriguing people, greedy soldiers and factious captains, are the beings I have to deal with. . . . There have been meetings and orations enough to settle all the affairs of Greece, if talking would do it. . . . I have so clearly pointed out to Mavrocordato the advantage of his attending the Congress in person, and through your good offices to effect a reconciliation with Odysseus, that he has pledged himself to accompany me to Salona. . . . The English artificers here and the brigade now wish to join Odysseus, or, at least, leave this hole. I know you will say I have seduced them. I like the brigade corps. . . . Letters from Zante inform us of the arrival there of Mr. Blaquiere, in the ship Florida. He has brought out in specie four hundred thousand pounds sterling consigned to the house of Barff. . . . I think Byron's name was the great means of getting the loan. . . . They talk here openly of a king; Mavrocordato says that all the primates of the Morea are for it. This is the worst news I have heard." By the following day, distrust of Mavrocordato had become enmity. "Everyone here says," he wrote, "Gamba and all, that neither Byron, nor anyone else has given the Committee's stores to Mavrocordato. You know the wants of Eastern Greece; could not you consign some portion of these stores to that part, on condition of the Greek government's approval? Divide the artillery brigade in two; for it is, in force, two brigades. I speak my sentiments fearlessly to all, so you will not object to my frankness."

Notwithstanding his increasing distrust of the chiefs, Trelawny could still think of Byron as a friend, for pity still held him; and as he pieced together the varying accounts of Byron's illness pity became remorse. If he had come sooner —persuaded Byron to leave this "belt of death"—Byron would have been alive now! Interviews with the two doctors—Bruno and Millingen—who had been with Byron at the end, increased his dismay. Bruno stammered out a story of shocking incompetence and blamed Millingen. Millingen was ill; Trelawny went to see him. He found him "a delicately complexioned, rosy-cheeked, dandy boy; of simpering and affected manners," and understood why Mavrocordato spoke of him as *mio caro ragazzino*. But the little fellow was ill, "whining and crying like a sick girl," convinced he was at the point of death, afraid of being robbed; thanking Trelawny for coming, begging not to be left alone. Trelawny concealed his dislike and reassured him; told him no one ever died of malaria, told him he would be taken care of, promised to come again, and left him.

But Trelawny was in a rage now. Furious with the two conceited puppies whose ignorance had killed Byron. Furious with Byron for letting himself be killed. It was all Byron's fault! He had hired Bruno because Bruno "came cheap"; he had stayed on here in this pestilential spot because he was too lazy to move. Miserliness and sloth had brought the poor fool to his death, and he, Trelawny, was to suffer for it! Pity was gone. He saw no heroism in Byron's having stuck to his post (as a matter of fact, no one did at the time—that was a discovery of Byron's later admirers); his old contempt for Byron's faults revived; his own self-confidence returned—he would show the world that he could rise without help from Byron! He glowed with a sense of superiority. That same week a long letter went off to Mary Shelley:

"I am transformed," he wrote, "from the listless being you knew me to one of energy and fire. Not content with the camp, I must be a great diplomatist. I am again, dear Mary, in my element, and playing no *second* part in Greece. If I live, the outcast Reginald will cut his name out on the Grecian hills, or set on its plains. I have had the merit of discovering and bringing out a noble fellow [Odysseus], a gallant soldier, and a man of most wonderful mind with as little bigotry as Shelley and nearly as much imagination; he

is a glorious being. He calls me brother—wants to connect me
with his family. . . . But I am sick at heart at losing Byron,
my friend, for still I call him so. With all his weakness, you
know I loved him. I cannot live with men for years without
feeling—it is want of judgment, of philosophy—but this is my
weakness. Dear Mary, if you love me, write—write—write.
. . . I am certain of our good cause triumphing. . . . A word
as to your wooden god Mavrocordato. . . . He is a mere shuffling soldier, an aristocratic brute—wants Kings and Con-
gresses; a poor, weak, shuffling, intriguing, cowardly fellow;
so no more about him. Dear Mary, dear Jane, I am serious,
turn your thoughts this way. I am now a Greek chieftain,
willing and able to shelter and protect you; and thus I will
continue, or follow my friends to wander over some other
planet, for I have nearly exhausted this. . . . Tell me of
Clare. Do write me of her."

This cock-o'-the-walk self-confidence did not make for
peace. The disagreement with Mavrocordato soon heightened to an open quarrel, for it became only too clear that
it was the prince's machinations—encouraging Byron's lazi-
ness, intercepting letters—that had prevented the meeting
with Odysseus at Salona from which Trelawny had hoped
such great things; and as he told the prince with extreme
frankness exactly what he thought of such conduct, his career
might well have ended then and there, like Byron's, in the
mud and filth of Missolonghi. For his position was one of
extreme danger, without a single friend, and surrounded by
enemies. But sheer audacity carried him through. He was bent
on downing the prince, and helping Odysseus. He succeeded.
Mavrocordato put in a claim for the cash Byron had left—
six or seven thousand pounds: Trelawny had it sent to Zante.
The soldiers of Byron's brigade were discontented—they had
not been paid; he persuaded a number to enlist under his
command for service with Odysseus. He even managed to
secure a quantity of the London Committee's stores, for
Stanhope's authority was back of him—Stanhope wrote, "You

appear to have conducted your mission in the most satisfactory manner," suggested his going to Zante "to give Napier
an honest and true account of the actual state of Greece,"
and sent an order to the man in charge of the stores: "Deliver to Captain Trelawny . . . a spy-glass and map of Greece
for General Odysseus," ammunition, five brass guns, other
useful articles, and—a most important item, for Trelawny
was as usual hard up—ten pounds for incidental expenses.

All this was most satisfactory. Meanwhile, the arrangements for shipping Byron's body to England had been completed. A day came when Trelawny could ride triumphantly
away from Missolonghi, accompanied by an agreeable acquaintance he had picked up—a Scottish artillery officer
named Fenton, at the head of a fine cavalcade of some fifty
horses and mules and a hundred men, including his own
Rumeliots, in the happy belief that the prince had been
left lamenting.

But Mavrocordato was only biding his time. He must have
watched that triumphant exit with a smile. For Fenton was
in his pay; he could trust Fenton. Fenton was a clever fellow
who knew his business. Some fine day that braggart Englishman would get a bullet through his head and cease to brag.

But if Trelawny saw that smile, he failed to interpret it;
he rode on, pleased with himself, despising the prince, proud
of his soldiers, liking his new friend Fenton, and reached
Salona in a mood of elation such as he had not felt since
Byron's death.

But all elation soon vanished. The Congress had expected
to be unified by Byron's presence. The news of his death
had thrown everything into confusion; nothing had been
accomplished. Colonel Stanhope was gone, having left for
Zante to escort Byron's coffin, servants, and dogs to England. Colonel Napier had not returned. Without an Englishman at the helm, Greece's ship of state was drifting perilously close to the rocks.

Trelawny was in two minds what to do. He knew it was

high time he left Greece. He had spent every penny of his income on the Cause. He was needed at home: his divorced wife Julia had died, it was his duty to see how his two little girls were getting on. He was heartily sick of the Greeks, their treacheries and squabbles. But he could not bear to leave Odysseus. Such a glorious being! So grateful for all that had been snatched from Mavrocordato in Missolonghi. In the end, he stayed.

He stayed, but in a black mood now. The future, without Byron, promised little glory. His anger with Byron grew and grew. In June, a bitter letter went to Jane Williams. After a tender allusion to the old days in Pisa, he went on: "I am engaged heart, soul and hand in the cause which drew me from Europe; no half measures with me. I separated, as you know, from Byron at Cephalonia—he was past hope—nothing could move or excite him. . . . He lived at Missolonghi as at Genoa—pursued the same habits—saw no one—did nothing. Could I longer waste my life in union with such imbecility?" By August, Mavrocordato was giving unmistakable evidence that he had been scotched, not killed, and Trelawny had worked himself up into a fury of indignation with Byron. He wrote to Mary Shelley: "Byron became the paltry tool of Mavrocordato—five months he dozed away. . . . With the aid of his name, his fame, his talents and his fortune he might have been a tower of strength in Greece. . . . The little he did was in favor of the aristocrats, to destroy the republic and smooth the way for a foreign king. I feel my face burn with shame that so weak and ignoble a soul could so long have influenced me. I wish he might have witnessed how I would have soared above him here, how I could have triumphed over his mean spirit."

But this arrogant self-confidence—the illusion that he could get on without Byron, that Byron was in fact his inferior—was too childish to uphold him long. He found that "deer-stalking" with Odysseus had lost its charm. He wrote drearily: "We carried on the war in the same inefficient

and desultory way as before, unaided by the government
and abandoned to our own resources. . . . The government
was a mere farce." He was glad whenever a pause came in
the fighting, and he could retire with Odysseus to the cavern
on Mount Parnassus, forget the war, and relax.

For he was happy there in the cavern. It was a wildly
romantic place, this stronghold on the west side of Mount
Parnassus above Valitza, where Odysseus was hiding his family and his treasures during the war. A cluster of little houses
had been built on a ledge—a terrace sixty feet long and high,
high up on the mountain side—under an enormous overhanging arch of rock, making a stronghold very much like
an Indian cliff dwelling in Arizona, inaccessible as an eagle's
nest. It was reached only by ladders bolted to the rock that
came zigzagging up from lower ledges to a trapdoor in the
floor that could be closed at a moment's notice; the terrace
overlooked the plain a thousand feet below from end to end
and was protected by a massive wall mounted with guns
running along the front and a guardhouse, and other guard-
houses halfway down and at the foot of the mountain. Odysseus could leave his family there, knowing they were far
safer than in Athens.

And the cavern was not only safe; it was comfortable and
it was beautiful. Odysseus had wanted to make a dwelling
worthy of the beautiful women who lived there, and he had
succeeded. Handsome furniture and curtains and chests of
clothes had been brought from his old home for their apartments, brass pots and pans for the kitchens; icons and jewelled altar vessels and embroidered hangings for the chapel
built in a grotto had been gathered from ruined churches in
the neighborhood. A spring of clear cold water fell tinkling
into a cistern at the back of the cavern; wine and oil and
firewood had been laid in; fresh food was brought by farmers
and shepherds below and hauled up in baskets; there were
plenty of servants to wait on the ladies and soldiers to do
the rough work. In short, the life that went on in that strange

place must have been much like that of a camp in the Adirondacks—a mingling of savagery and civilization, simplicity and luxury—and it satisfied Trelawny's nature to the full. No wonder he liked the cavern.

The ladies of the family may have pined now and then for the society of Athens and the islands; but years of war had taught them to value safety, they had children to look after, and they were all young. There were three of them: Acrive, stepmother of Odysseus; her little daughter Tarsitsa Kamenou, his half-sister; and Helen Kareli his wife, whose youngest child had been born in the cavern that spring of 1824. So there had been a christening for the old priest to perform in his small, dim, richly furnished chapel, and before very long there was a wedding.

The alliance with the family of Odysseus that Trelawny had hinted at in a letter to Mary Shelley became a fact. In that same year of 1824 he and Tarsitsa were married. She was a mere child; but her family seemed to think she was old enough, and she was pretty—had a look of the Orient in her eyes, though her hair was reddish gold, that reminded him of Zela. He admired her clothes for the same reason: graceful, flowing robes, embroidered veils, strings of jewels, such as Zela had worn, agreeably unlike the fashionable dress of the Englishwomen in the islands. It was pleasant when a man came home from fighting to find a nice little wife ready to welcome and listen and applaud.

So pleasant indeed that Trelawny was willing to stay at home now whenever Odysseus went off on an expedition and left him in charge of the cavern. The responsibility was not very great; he had six trustworthy men of his own, well armed, and a ferocious Thessalian watchdog to protect the cavern itself, and there were soldiers in the guardhouse in the foot of the mountain in charge of Captain Fenton, the Scotchman Trelawny had picked up in Missolonghi, who had a hut of his own. Fenton was so hard up that he was glad to get free board and lodging, and Trelawny had come to value his society and to trust him. "I sent him on many missions," Trelawny wrote later, "to the Ionian islands, to the seat of government to see what they were doing, and with letters to friendly chiefs. . . . My purse was his. [Trelawny's purse was always somebody else's!] No querulous word ever ruffled our friendly intercourse. I thought him honest and his staying with me a proof of his good will."

With home life going so easily in the intervals of fighting, Trelawny found leisure for a brisk correspondence. He wrote to Mary Shelley; he even got off a letter to Clare: a sentimental reminder of old days with a vague allusion to his affection for the family of Odysseus that Clare could interpret as she chose, and a glowing tribute to his hero, ending, "I am playing a first part here, and have work for all my energies, which have now awakened from their long torpor —Byron, who was mine as well as your evil genius, has ceased to be so."

He wrote to his friend George Finlay soon after arriving at Parnassus from Missolonghi, asking to have a white litter and other supplies sent from Athens, in order to make the cave "the most beautiful as well as strongest fortress in the world"; accounted for money Finlay had sent him to spend, and ended: "Give a few dollars to Tindale for my women at Athens; if you think it necessary, pay their removal to Calauria or Egina."

This last sentence doubtless refers to slaves Trelawny had bought and set free. As Mr. Massingham points out, freeing slaves seems to have been a habit with Trelawny. Colonel Napier wrote to him later on of three "poor females" at Patras, captured at Missolonghi and in need of ransom, who could be bought for ten or twenty dollars apiece. Napier offered to contribute part of this sum, and asked Trelawny to see the consul at Patras and arrange the whole thing, evidently taking for granted that he would be interested and do his best for the poor creatures. Still later, in South Carolina, Trelawny bought a Negro and set him free.

But "my women at Athens" were to start a scandal. Pierino Gamba told Mary Shelley, in his artless prattling way, that Mr. Trelawny had set up a harem in Athens; a fine large harem; twelve or fifteen *brutti mostri,* one of them black. Millingen, the "pink-cheeked, simpering" medical student whom Trelawny had befriended in Missolonghi, took care not to let the scandal die. The gossip mongers were not in agreement as to their dates; Gamba said the odalisks had been acquired after, and Millingen, before, Trelawny's first campaign with Odysseus. But, either way, Trelawny would have dismissed their fairy story with bitter amusement: there had been mighty little time for idle pleasure during those few months with Odysseus—cold, hunger, danger, excitement, incessant fighting, but no lolling about in harems—and he had been practically penniless, too poor to buy himself one houri, let alone fifteen! The tale was as silly as the tellers; no one who knew him would believe it for a moment. In this he was mistaken; Mary Shelley had not only lapped up Pierino's story with delighted horror but passed it on as true, and she must have made some allusion that let Trelawny guess her attitude, for he wrote sadly to her later on: "You err most egregiously if you think I am occupied with women or intrigues."

This credulity of Mary's must have surprised him considerably; she should have known that he was not like that. He was a most fickle lover and never what is called a "moral" man, but there is no hint anywhere in his life that he could be promiscuous; and Mary's readiness to believe the harem story may well have cast a first shadow on their friendship. On the other hand, a small shadow may have come before that. In his early glow of enthusiasm for the beauty and strangeness of his life on Parnassus he had sent Mary a long description of the cavern which he thought might do for a magazine article; but she didn't think much of it, and it never got published.

That trifling disappointment would come later. Meanwhile, life on the mountaintop went on to the same peaceful tune. Its monotony was broken now and then by the arrival of some friend who came climbing up from below. Finlay came and made notes for the history of Greece he was writing, and Captain Humphries came (and was pleased to find Trelawny reading the last Waverley novel and rearing two tiny native deer that he hoped to send to Sir Walter when the war was over), and several other Philhellenes found their way to the cavern and were impressed by its beauty and its strength. They all brought news of the outside world, most of it very bad. The Turks were getting stronger, the civil war still continued; Mavrocordato's party was in the ascendent, Odysseus losing ground. It was rumored that Gouras, his chief officer, was plotting against him and that he might lose the leadership of eastern Greece. That would mean the end of everything for Trelawny. But it was a most disheartening time for all Philhellenes; no one was so farsighted as to realize that Byron's death would save Greece.

The sad year ended. It was 1825 now, and the outlook darker than ever. Odysseus came and went, Trelawny usually stayed in charge of the fortress. Whenever they met, Trelawny saw that Odysseus was increasingly anxious and perplexed; weary of the war, appalled by the slaughter, in fear of treachery. He was not altogether surprised when Odysseus finally agreed to an armistice of three months with Omar Pasha. He knew the chief had made a fatal error, for the Turks were as treacherous as the Greeks, and he did his best to induce Odysseus to withdraw, stay in the fortress, and wait for better times. But Odysseus was too restless for inaction. He told the garrison they were to obey Captain Trelawny in every smallest particular; warned the latter to beware of accepting orders sent in his name—they might not be genuine—and departed.

Spring came. There had been messages from Odysseus; one was an order to surrender the fortress, which Trelawny of course disregarded. In May a pleasant young Englishman named Whitcombe arrived; Fenton liked him and took him into his hut. The two spent most of their time in the cavern, for it was very hot now down below. One afternoon as they sat smoking and drinking on the terrace in front of Trelawny's house, Fenton suggested shooting at a mark. Trelawny's Italian servant set up a board at the end of the terrace. Fenton and Whitcombe each took a shot with a carbine and stepped back. Trelawny drew a pistol from his belt, and as he turned towards the target, both Fenton and Whitcombe fired. Fenton's weapon missed fire; but Whitcombe sent two balls into Trelawny's back; one shattered his right arm and went on into his chest; the other pierced his neck and fractured his jaw.

Fenton sprang forward, shouting that it had been an accident; a soldier shot him dead. Whitcombe tried to reach the ladder; the Thessalian hound jumped on him and pinned him down. He was bound and dragged to the edge of the precipice, screaming for mercy.

Trelawny dropped on the ground and sat crouching. His mouth was full of blood; he spat out the bullet and a few teeth, and managed to mumble an order: Whitcombe was not to be killed—he still thought the whole thing might have been an accident. Whitcombe was to be imprisoned till he could see to him; he was not to be tortured.

Trelawny got himself into his house. He sat down in a corner propped against the wall. He sat there for nearly three weeks! Refusing treatment, refusing all nourishment except raw eggs and water, bent on letting Nature cure him with sun and cold fresh air. Nature justified his belief: on the twentieth day he was able to relish a shred of ham, although it was agony to move his jaw. Three months went by. They were months of mental as well as bodily suffering. Hysterical appeals came from Whitcombe; the poor wretch sent letter after letter from his cell, confessing guilt but vowing that the plot—a scheme to seize the cavern, its treasures, and its women—had originated with Fenton. Trelawny was puzzled. "I could not conceive it possible," he wrote later, "that an English gentleman, my guest, should have conspired to assassinate me. I ordered the execution to be postponed. . . . Everyone in the cave clamored for vengeance. They all swore if I died they would roast him over a slow fire." At last, pity got the better of justice. As soon as he was strong enough to exert his authority, he ordered Whitcombe to be set free.

There remained the thought of Fenton's duplicity to plague him; he realized he "had been a blind man led by a fiendish cur." Papers in Fenton's hut made it plain the Scotchman was a spy, had been foisted on him at Missolonghi. Trelawny—infallible judge of character, able to see through men at a glance—had been fooled for a whole year!

It was a bitter thought; but news from Athens soon wiped out all lesser feelings of sorrow. Word came to the cavern that Helen Kareli was a widow. Odysseus had been captured by Gouras, imprisoned in a tower of the Acropolis, tortured, then allowed to attempt escape by a rope left dangling over the wall. Some said he had been caught and strangled, others that he had let himself down halfway when the rope broke. Next morning his body was found at the foot of the precipice.

Contemporary writers usually see Gouras as a tool of Mavrocordato, and Fenton as a spy. Trelawny's friend Humphries wrote that summer to Captain Hamilton of the *Cambria*: "The villain Fenton was some months ago engaged by Mavrocordato to murder both Odysseus and Trelawny." They disagree in their estimate of Odysseus. He has been called a great leader; he has been called a traitor—the armistice was a subterfuge, he had been bought by the Turks. Trelawny himself emphatically denied this accusation; to the end of his life, Odysseus remained "a glorious being"—less respected than De Ruyter, never worshipped as Shelley had been worshipped, but a hero.

And a hero not only to Trelawny. Greece remembers Odysseus with gratitude, ranking him only next to Marco

Bozzaris as an apostle of freedom. The common people find
no fault with the inscription on the tomb at Athens, erected
by Helen Kareli, that praises the chieftain as "eager among
the first to proclaim his country's uprising," with its Christian ending:

"Under the Parthenon wall, strangled they left him dying;
Now from his grave he implores on them the grace of our
Lord."

Perhaps Trelawny and the common people are right.

However that may be, the news of Odysseus's death must
have added immeasurably to Trelawny's suffering and re-
tarded recovery. The summer was half over before his
wounds healed, and his right arm still dangled paralyzed.
He knew that he must see a surgeon. A klepht came; slashed
into his chest with a razor and explored it with long dirty
fingers, but could not find the ball. The situation was beginning to seem hopeless, when help came from outside. In
August an English friend, Major Bacon, with a message
from Captain Hamilton, succeeded in reaching the cavern,
prepared to escort Trelawny and his wife to safety in the
Islands.

Trelawny could not bear to leave the fortress. But he was
a cripple, useless as a defender. Acrive and Helen urged him
to go. Their men were trustworthy, the cave rich in treasure.
If enemies came they would bribe them and get a safe passage to Athens. (In the end this happened; Helen and Acrive
returned safely to their old homes.) At last, very reluctantly,
Trelawny decided to accept Hamilton's offer. He and Tarsitsa climbed down the ladders for the last time. British vessels took them first to Smyrna and then to Cephalonia.

The Grecian adventure was over, and Trelawny back at
his starting point. But in a very different mood. When he
and Byron had first glimpsed that arid island, both had been
looking forward to a glorious campaign and high with hope.

Now, he was utterly disillusioned. A letter he sent from Cephalonia to Dan Roberts, describing his narrow escape, ends: "I have lost *all* my traps, papers, and spent 12 hundred pd. to serve the Greeks, and yet the English papers call me Turk."

Spring found him weary of the raw red hills of Cephalonia. He took Tarsitsa to Zante, and they settled down there in "Straney Hill" near his friend Colonel Gordon. It was the prettiest villa in that green and lovely island; Tersitsa should have been happy, for her baby was born that spring of 1826—a little girl. But she was a mere child herself, too immature for a husband of thirty-two. They quarrelled. Family tradition says it was her liking for European fashions that brought about the final break. Having relinquished his own comfortable and beautiful Albanian dress with reluctance he hated to see her in the full skirt and tight-laced bodices of the Englishwomen in the Islands. He warned her that, if she persisted in making herself ridiculous, he would cut off her hair. She disobeyed him; he carried out his threat. She returned to her family.

They were rich and powerful. The Church gave her a divorce, and after months of litigation—probably connected with alimony and the custody of the child—Trelawny was a bachelor again, with nothing to show for his last matrimonial experiment, except the child. He must have loved the child, for he kept her, and went back to the happiest time of his life for her name. He called her *Zella* (English for Zela).

He could have left Zante now, but he stayed on, although after the sickening finish of the siege of Missolonghi all friends of Greece began to lose hope. Trelawny wrote despairingly to Mary Shelley that the revolution had been "begun by slaves, and that the survivors would be slaves of slaves, sunk into abject and eternal slavery," though he was doing what he could for the refugees: "I have still a deep interest in saving some of these miserable Greeks by getting them to the Islands."

But the end was nearer than anyone expected. Sympathy in England had been aroused by Byron's tragic death; pressure was brought to bear on the Government. The three Powers—England, France, and Russia—were getting tired of the turmoil in Greece and decided to stop it in their own interests. In the autumn of 1827, the naval victory of Navarino freed Greece from Turkish rule, and she became a republic. But she was forced to accept a Russian as president, and, before long, Trelawny's fears were realized; she found herself saddled with a king—another foreigner, Otto of Bavaria—and Mavrocordato was made prime minister. No wonder Trelawny felt that Byron had died, and he had fought for Greece, in vain!

After Navarino, there was nothing to keep him in Greece, and he soon left Zante. Except for an occasional bout of malaria, he was a well man now, as strong and as handsome as ever. Whitcombe's bullet had not been extracted, but it no longer troubled him—physically. There remained, however, an inner wound—a wound of the spirit, that was never to heal. He would still feel pity for the oppressed, still enjoy travelling, still respond to all that was beautiful in nature and art; but the desire for adventure was dead. He would never go "deer-stalking" again. Odysseus was his last hero.

CHAPTER XIX

"It isn't often that a rolling stone sets down, quite so plainly, the ways in which he has avoided moss."
—LAWRENCE OF ARABIA.

The spring of 1829 found Trelawny in Florence, still inclined to brood over his failure as a liberator, but reviving, and ready to enjoy civilized society to the full. Its intelligentsia were less glorious than the Pisa circle: Landor could not quite take the place of Shelley or Byron, Charles Armitage Brown shone only as a friend of Keats, and Seymour Kirkup was a mediocre painter. But there were agreeable people in the English colony, he had always liked Florence, and before long he decided to rent a house.

The main reason for tying himself down seems to have been a desire to make a home for two of his three children: Zella, Tarsitsa's daughter, and Eliza—the "dear baby," now about thirteen. He found a charming villa, called "Paradise," near the Tower of Galileo; engaged servants, and was ready to welcome Eliza when he heard that she was dead.

"She was the only creature," he wrote to Clare, "from whom I expected nothing but sweet remembrances, perfect love. . . . By her death Fortune has expended her utmost malice on me—Fortune never gave me anything—and those few good things I wrested from her by desperate adventuring she has most revengefully taken from me."

Meanwhile, little Zella was on her way from the Ionian Islands. He went to Ancona to meet her. Ship after ship arrived from Greece; still the child did not come. His patience was wearing thin, when he received an annoying explanation. "An officious reptile," he wrote to a friend, "had taken it into her head that 'for the honour of an English gentleman' the child should be clothed in the English fashion before it could be sent to Ancona; consequently it had been landed at Corfu and the graceful robes of the Greek girl were exchanged for the unseemly doll-like shreds and patches of the European. . . . I have written to the lady that I cannot comprehend what the devil honour has to do with the cut of a child's frock, and I shall most assuredly commit the English rags to the flames, and as the lady, though loose in her morals, is tight-laced in her religion, I added that even if the Virgin Mary herself made the dresses, it should not avert my profane purpose."

But this delay was the last. Zella arrived, and before long he could write to Clare that the child, nearly four now, was his "great consolation for Eliza's death," and that the pure air had cured her of malaria. "She is growing a strong handsome girl," he went on; "I have an excellent nurse for her and a contadino and his wife as servants. My occupation is writing—the second volume of my life is nearly finished."

Writing. He had discovered a new interest, a new way of quieting his restlessness, a new outlet for energy. Leisure, stimulating conversation, the flattering attention that his tales of adventure in the Orient drew from every listener, and the hearty encouragement of Armitage Brown had suggested that he too might become a literary light. It was an exciting idea. The intelligentsia urged him on; even Landor approved.

All poets seem to have found Trelawny stimulating. Landor not only listened to his tales with interest, but made them grist for his own mill. The scene of one of his celebrated *Imaginary Conversations* is the famous cave on Mount Parnassus; the protagonists being Odysseus and Acrive, Trelawny and Tarsitsa—all chatting together, rather dully, about the Rights of Man. But in any case Trelawny and Landor would have become intimate, for they had much in common—in fact, if Emerson's description of the poet a few years later is to be trusted, they must have been a good deal alike.

"I found Mr. Landor noble and courteous," Emerson wrote, "living in a cloud of pictures at his Villa Gherardesca. . . . He has a wonderful brain, despotic, violent, and inexhaustible, meant for a soldier, by what chance converted to letters . . . with an English appetite for action and heroes. The thing done avails, and not what is said about it."

Landor's "conversion" to letters had come in youth, and Trelawny might well have paused to wonder if he had waited too long, if the Muses, so ignored on Mount Parnassus, could be expected to help him now. But he seems to have rushed into literature with as little hesitation as if he had been proposing to take a pirate town; and the more he wrote, the more excited he became. There was, he discovered, an extraordinary exhilaration in the mere putting pen to paper, if a book might result from the effort. Letter after letter went off to Mary Shelley in London, outlining his plan, demanding her approval, asking advice.

He was calling his book, *A Man's Life*. Did she like that title? The author's real name must not appear—for obvious reasons. Should it be anonymous, or would it be a good idea to use the old form of the family name, Treloen? He could not go to London himself, for he had Zella on his hands. Would Mary find him a publisher? How much did she think he could get for the book? He needed money; Zella made housekeeping expensive, and the Johnsons, who had been so kind to little Eliza, were ruined, and he wanted to help them. Did Mary think he could get as much as five hundred pounds?

Mary was kind—though a trifle condescending, being the author of a best seller, *Frankenstein*. She answered all his questions and gave him a vast amount of advice. In due course, the manuscript was despatched to her in charge of Mr. George Baring. Her report was not quite so enthusiastic as he had expected—no embryo author ever gets what he expects in the way of praise. She reminded him that it was a very poor time to publish a book—she herself had been obliged to come down in her prices. What with the Reform Bill and the depression, no one seemed to care for reading any more. Mary knew the publishing business well; Trelawny was obliged to moderate his hopes of a large sale.

But in another respect he faced her down. She objected to certain passages as being improper! The scene in Portsmouth, with the mate showing the boys about the town before taking them to school, was too broad; so was the description of the burning of Muckery's house at Dungaree, and there were also a few words here and there that should be omitted, or he "would not obtain feminine readers." She ended: "I beseech you to let me deal with them. . . . I strongly object to coarseness, now wholly out of date. . . . Amidst so much that is beautiful and imaginative and exalting why leave spots which, believe me, are blemishes?"

His answer was characteristically hot: "It has been a painful and arduous undertaking narrating my life, I have omitted a great deal, and avoided being a pander to the public for the sake of novelty or effect. Landor, a man of superior literary acquirements; Kirkup, an artist of superior taste; Baring, a man of the world and very religious; Mrs. Baring, moral and squeamish; Lady Burghersh, aristocratic and proud as a queen, and Charles Brown, a plain, downright cockney critic, all have read and passed on my narrative. My life—though I have sent it to you as the dearest friend I have, is not written for the amusement of women; it is not a novel. If you begin clipping the wings of my true story, if you begin erasing words, you must then omit sentences, then chapters; it will be pruning an Indian jungle down to a clipped French garden. Dear Mary, I love women, and you know it; but my life is not dedicated to them; it is to men I write. . . . I predict it will be popular with sailors."

He could afford to dismiss such criticisms as mere prudery,

but in another matter she hurt him more than a little. Encouraged by finding he could write, he became ambitious, decided to try his hand on a life of Shelley and, taking Mary's approval for granted, asked her to help him.

She refused, for reasons he rightly considered "mawkish cant." A life of Shelley would have to include hers—"I should be terrified at arousing the slumbering voice of the public. . . . No woman can emerge from privacy without regret. . . . It would destroy me to be brought forward in print. . . . Shelley's life must be written. I hope one day to do it myself, but it must not be published now. . . . It is still too sore a subject."

He was bitterly disappointed. Mary's lack of confidence hurt him; he guessed that she was preparing to create a false image of her husband for the benefit of future generations, and was shocked by her lack of integrity. He sent her a "cross letter" in answer. But he could not continue to reproach her. She had been too kind. He knew how hard she had worked for him, and he was grateful.

In the summer of 1831 *Adventures of a Younger Son* was brought out by Colburn and Bentley. He did not like the too romantic title—which the publishers had substituted for the original name, *A Man's Life,** and Mary had accepted without consulting him; he was annoyed to find a few changes (what they were is not clear) intended to placate Mrs. Grundy, and he was to get only three hundred pounds for the first edition. But the three small volumes were neatly bound; he was pleased with the quotations for the chapter headings that Armitage Brown had helped him choose from Byron, Shelley, and Keats—those "three, staunch advocates of freedom"; and he found the reviews most entertaining, for he had always delighted in shocking the prudish. The *Athenæum* deprecated the book's "grossness." "What," it demanded, "is the utility of drawing a character in which there is not a single redeeming point?" And it declared that

---

* Hence, the subtitle of this book.

the author must have been "a kind of ruffian from birth." The *Military Review* came nearer the truth; it called the *Adventures* "wild, libertine and eccentric; savage, yet sentimental . . . as if its pictures had been alternately drawn by a fiend and a fairy."

That sort of review of course helped rather than hindered, and the book "sold like wild-fire." For some time, however, he denied the authorship—no doubt because of the harsh description of his parents. But a secret open in Florence could not remain unguessed in London, and even before his book appeared Mary had written to him: "Your mother speaks openly in society of your forthcoming memoirs." He probably came to realize that his mother—always an incalculable person—might be so amused at having an author in the family she would not much care what he said about her. Within a year he was not only acknowledging he had written the much talked-of *Adventures,* but insisting that the story was *true,* and regretting more than ever that the original title, *A Man's Life,* had not been used.

His name, already well known because of its association with Byron and Greece, naturally added to the public interest. But without that, the book would have been popular (*Adventures of a Younger Son* has gone into many editions and is still widely read today after more than a hundred years); for it is one of the best stories of adventure ever written, shot through and through with his own inexhaustible vitality and zest for life. As he said himself: "Who that lives and has a heart not grown sabre-proof does not glow with pleasure at the remembrance of what he did and felt from seventeen to twenty!" He glowed and made his readers glow.

And the book came near changing his future. If the times had been propitious, its success would have continued long enough to satisfy him—or if Mary had let him write Shelley's life, he might have taken up writing as a profession, "sublimated" his desire for adventure, lived and died a contented, if not a happy, man.

That was not to be. The year 1832 turned out to be the most utterly wretched of the nineteenth century. All the world was in turmoil: "We fall asleep," Chateaubriand wrote, "to the sound of kingdoms crashing in the night, and every morning they are swept up before our doors." Even England lived in fear of revolution: there was rioting in London; bands of miners out of work terrorized the country-side, and night skies blazed with burning ricks. To cap the climax, Asiatic cholera at last crossed the Channel. England had hoped against hope that the new disease was not con-tagious and, like Lord Macaulay, "reposed great confidence in the good food and cleanliness of the English." But they were wrong. The plague came and stayed, and would not go.

In an atmosphere of such anxious misery no book could thrive; the hint of revolution in the air increased Trelawny's habitual restlessness. He began planning a trip to some wild, far distant land, he didn't much care where—any country that promised escape from civilization; and he could plan now with a clear conscience, for he was no longer tied to Florence. An old Devonshire friend of his, Jane Bocella, wife of an Italian marchese, had become very fond of Zella—a most engaging child—and asked to be allowed to have her for a while. He wrote to Clare that, as Jane was "frank, honest and generous; warm-hearted and single-minded," he had been thankful to accept her offer; Jane was far better fitted to bring up a little girl than he was himself.

Meantime another matter had been attended to—a matter of punishment, but with a new weapon, the pen, not the sword. His book had started people talking about the author. Writers on the Greek revolution all mentioned Trelawny: historians, such as Finlay and Gordon, with respect. But any adventurer who had spent a month in Greece could rush successfully into print, and these small fry, finding their sales increased by a whiff of gossip, let their imaginations run riot. Trelawny usually considered them beneath his notice. But a review in the *Literary Gazette* of a book of memoirs by Julius Millingen—the pink-cheeked medical student who had helped to kill Byron at Missolonghi—could not be ignored. It was a farrago of lies, ranging from a description of Byron as "wrapped in a cloak of *Stewart* tartan," and Trelawny as "somewhat below the full-grown stature," to his calling Byron a sot, a *petit-maître*, a vilifier of the Greek nation, and Trelawny a coward and a traitor, a sensualist who had gone to Italy merely to "indulge his oriental habits," and in Athens had found relaxation in "the enjoyment of a numerous harem" (the story passed on by Gamba), and a notorious liar—Byron had often observed that you couldn't believe anything Trelawny said.

As a matter of fact, these remarks might all have been applied to the writer himself. (Harold Nicolson describes Millingen as "not in any way a desirable person," who had "entered the Turkish service, resided at Constantinople for over fifty years as physician to five successive Sultans, and married four wives, the first of whom he treated abominably," and adds that Millingen, in his record, often "bears false witness.") But the public could not be expected to know this; Trelawny decided that Millingen must be answered, and a dozen pages of enraged contradiction went off to the *Gazette.*

They printed his article—though with a liberal sprinkling of asterisks substituted for "epithets which we would not ourselves sanction, or apply to the worst of human beings." It began moderately enough with a review of what had gone on in Missolonghi before and after Byron's death, fairly dispassionate except for calling Mavrocordato a thief and a coward, "who had ground down the sword of justice to an assassin's dagger that had finally reached both himself and Odysseus." His story of Byron's tragic last hours was merely a sympathetic and careful summary of what Fletcher had told him. But when he came to describing the visit to Millingen's sickroom at Missolonghi, he grew sarcastic, and at the end reached heights of fury—needing many asterisks—that even thick-skinned Dr. Millingen must have found pretty unpleasant.

"Now the Greeks love money," he wrote. "Gold is their idol—gold is dearer to them than the bright eyes of their mistresses; but out of three thousand adventurers of all sorts and conditions, all serving for pay and plunder, one man alone was base enough to abandon the cause in which he was engaged, and for which he received pay, even to be a deserter to the enemy—and that was Millingen. . . . His name was never mentioned after his treachery except with universal execrations. Yet this * * * * comments, criticizes and runs amuck with his scalpel, stabbing at honorable man. . . . It is probable that I should not thus have troubled you, by replying to Dr. Millingen with my pen, had it been possible to reach him with my hand; but the renegade is settled at Constantinople, protected by the firman of the Porte."

Throughout the article the various slurs on his own character were ignored—it was enough to show up Millingen as the treacherous cur he really was, and as other gossip writers were treated with the same disdain, their stories usually died a natural death. But one tale—so fantastic that it should never have been born—was to be revived fifty years later. Sharp's *Life of Severn*, 1878, gives a letter from Lieutenant Cook telling the story but merely as current among "the midshipmen of the Mediterranean in 1835"; and it would not be mentioned here if it had not been repeated by recent biographers of Byron willing to "sacrifice the lamb of truth" for the sake of a good story. There are two versions. As Harold Nicolson tells it in his *Byron*, a daughter was born to Tarsitsa "in June of 1826, and died a few months later. Meanwhile Trelawny had quarreled with Tarsitsa, whom he had relegated to a convent. As a final revenge he sent her in a little box the dead body of their infant daughter." The other version exonerates Trelawny. He was the recipient of the little box with its grewsome contents; it had been sent to him from the convent by the abbess—for some reason left entirely unexplained.

Either way the story is incredibly silly, for there was no dead baby to send or to receive. The child born to Tarsitsa in the spring of 1826 was Zella, and she was very much alive— a healthy, handsome, quick-tempered child much like her father in temperament; Trelawny told Mary Shelley that little Zella was "a soul of fire." When "the midshipmen of the Mediterranean" started their scandal on its long career, she was living in Lucca with the Marchesa Bocella, treated as a daughter of the house.

Zella thus happily disposed of in Lucca, Trelawny was free to roam. April, 1832, found him in Paris. The cholera epidemic was at its height—ten thousand persons died there that year; he wrote to Clare that "all foreigners who could go have fled on the wings of fear," and that he was staying on from mere contrariness. "Since my arms had seven years pith," he explained, "I have always struggled against the stream. I know not how it is, but if I see a crowd all marching one way, I feel myself impelled to jostle through them in a contrary direction. So many people advised me not to come that I began thinking of buying a house."

But he had no real intention of staying in Paris. He was considering a trip to North America. It was the only continent he had left entirely unexplored; Augusta White was living in Canada, he rather liked the idea of seeing Augusta again. In May he went to England; saw his solicitor, John Burley, of the Temple, and arranged his affairs; saw his daughter Maria Julia, grown up now, who had been living with a friend, referred to as "Mrs. B." (probably John Burley's mother, for later on Julia married John Burley), and took her to Sandgate to make Mary Shelley a visit.

Julia stayed with Mary three months, but a few days were enough for her father. Trelawny and Mary had been growing apart through the years. Her innate conventionality was

more apparent now, and she had developed a coquettish
streak that did not suit her. A carelessly affectionate remark
of his in a letter from Florence, "fate might yet unite them,"
had been taken as an offer of marriage and was answered with
an airy refusal, "My name will never be Trelawny!" that he
must have found disconcerting. So it is scarcely surprising
that Mary's journal at Sandgate—though referring pleasantly
to Julia, "Julia and I went to Ascot and were a good deal
amused"—should describe Trelawny as "so gloomy he
destroyed me," or that, after this visit, their relation was
never the same. The correspondence continued after a
fashion, they met now and then; but the ten years' firm
friendship was at an end.

Early in 1833 Trelawny was in Canada. The visit to
Augusta White (Mrs. William Draper now) at Little York
went off well. He liked her husband; he was charmed with
her little girl Mary. He saw Niagara, and wandered southward to New York. It was a shabby town, half deserted
because of the cholera; few carriages were to be seen in
Broadway, very few fashionably dressed persons anywhere.
On the other hand, there were no poor to be seen either;
nobody in rags, nobody who looked hungry, no signs whatever of the unemployment that was making London a misery.
He admired the harbor, as fine as Naples or Bombay, and
crowded with sails—many, many replicas of the little American schooner that had played such a tragic part in his life.
He liked the climate, hot, dry, and sunny. He was introduced to several agreeable people; he found New York well
enough. But he might not have stayed on if summer had not
brought him another of the long warm friendships which,
with Trelawny, were always so much more enduring than
love. He met Fanny Kemble.

She was a very famous, very young, English actress who
had left home because of the depression and was touring the
States and Canada with her father, Charles Kemble. Trelawny
had known her family in London, and had probably seen her

on the stage, but they had never spoken to each other until now. They liked each other at first sight. She had read *Adventures of a Younger Son* on the voyage over and was eager to meet the author, a man who had actually been intimate with Byron and Shelley! She was the sort of woman Trelawny most admired—like Jane Bocella, frank, generous, warm-hearted, single-minded. The Kembles were about to leave New York for Canada; when Charles invited him to join their party he was only too delighted to accept.

The weeks that followed were among the happiest of Trelawny's life. The country of mountains, lakes, and rivers they traversed, was beautiful and often wild. The party was agreeable, and would have been perfect except for the presence of another young man, a Philadelphian named Pierce Butler, good-looking and extremely well dressed, but supercilious, provincial, and self-satisfied, inclined to talk of his money and his ancestors—in short, the sort of man Trelawny particularly disliked! He couldn't for the life of him understand why Pierce Butler had been invited (Mr. Kemble was barely civil to the young man), nor why Miss Kemble tolerated his advances—Butler was obviously very much in love.

However, as a rule, the other guest could be ignored, for Miss Fanny showed a marked preference for his, Trelawny's, society. On the way to Albany in the Hudson River steamboat, she let him sit beside her on the deck while she sewed and he talked, leaving young Butler to stroll about by himself. When a sudden shower soaked her frock and Trelawny took her to the engine room, they stood there together for a long time, the firelight shining on her vivid face as she listened and he talked—talked of the East, of Byron and Shelley; of Mary and Clare; he showed her a letter from Clare, Byron's Clare! It was all very exciting: the talk, Trelawny himself. "A strange being," she decided, "half a savage." She wasn't sure whether she liked him or not.

But this uncertainty was not lasting. A cleverer woman than either Mary Shelley or Clare Clairmont, less conventional than Mary, with far more heart than Clare, Fanny Kemble soon came to understand Trelawny better than those two had ever done—better, perhaps, than any other of his many friends.

As their canal boat went slipping lazily along through the Mohawk valley, Trelawny seems to have become the life of the party. He took to reading aloud, and Fanny's journal would note later: "He read Don Quixote to us. He reads very peculiarly; slowly and with marked emphasis. He has a strong feeling of humour as well as poetry. When he gave us some of Byron's sayings and doings—whimsical, eccentric and unamiable, he nearly killed us with laughter. . . . Talking about Greece, he became so excited that he suddenly burst forth into 'The isles of Greece, the isles of Greece,' and reminded me of Kean; while he was declaiming he looked like a tiger. . . . 'Tis strange, how, in spite of the contempt, and even hatred, which he often expresses for England, all his plans, all the energies of his mind seem forever bent upon changes to be wrought in England—freer government—purer laws—more equal rights. Occasionally, in his horror of one class of prejudices, he embraces the opposite ones." The various notes she made of his appearance give a more lifelike picture of him than any portrait he ever had painted. "He is strikingly handsome," she wrote, "with a countenance habitually serene and occasionally sweet in expression; a giant for strength and agility, taller, straighter, and broader than most men, yet with the most listless indolent carelessness of gait, as if he didn't know where he was going, and didn't much wish to go anywhere. His face is as dark as a Moor's, with a wild strange look about the eyes and forehead, and a mark like a scar upon his cheek; his whole appearance giving one an idea of toil, hardship, peril and wild adventure. His voice is low and gentle. His hands are brown as a laborer's; he never profanes them with gloves, but wears two strange, magical-looking rings, which he showed me; one is made of elephants' hair."

Those last words are a proof, if any proof were needed, that Trelawny still treasured the memory of his "Arab maid." One ring must have been the Sheik's signet that had married him to Zela; the other was the circle he had woven for Zela in Borneo from the tuft of hair she had clipped from the ear of her little elephant after kissing it goodbye.

He seems not to have told Fanny the story of the rings. Perhaps the memory was too painful to revive. But it is more likely that her sympathetic tact forbade any expression of curiosity. For it was her good breeding that he dwelt on when he wrote of her to Augusta Draper:

"I particularly wish you and William to know Miss Kemble. She is an admirable musician, a poetess and altogether a lady—in circumnavigating the globe one finds but few, how few."

Nevertheless, it was not Fanny's ladylikeness, but her vitality, her adoration for the wilder beauties of nature, her mystical passion for waterfalls that Trelawny was counting on when he looked forward to showing her "the only marvel he cared to see twice," Niagara. She did not disappoint him. Of that never-to-be-forgotten moment, she wrote:

"A frenzy of impatience seized upon me. I rushed down the foot path cut in the rocks; Trelawny followed me. Down, down I sprang; I saw through the boughs the white glimmer of that sea of foam. 'Go on, go on!' shouted Trelawny, and in another moment the thicket was passed. I stood upon Table Rock. Trelawny seized me by the arm, and, without a word, dragged me to the edge of the rapids, to the brink of the abyss. I saw Niagara— Oh God! who can describe that sight!"

Meanwhile, through all this story-telling and reading aloud and viewing the beauties of Nature, where was Fanny's other travelling companion, Mr. Pierce Butler? Mr. Butler seems to have remained discreetly in the background, biding his time. A conceited young man, and remarkably obstinate, having once decided to marry Miss Kemble—to risk introducing an actress to Philadelphia society—he held to his purpose;

and being also shrewd, made no attempt to outshine this very
peculiar Mr. Trelawny the Kembles had taken a fancy to.
Mr. Butler merely made himself useful in small ways; looked
after the luggage, brought Fanny glasses of milk, provided
the party with silver forks brought from home. Nevertheless,
as the days went by it became plain that Mr. Butler was
getting on; he had most certainly touched Fanny's heart and
might, in the end, win her hand.

Nobody approved. But there was nothing to be done.
Trelawny found himself playing second fiddle. As that was
an instrument he never played with any enthusiasm, it may
have been his reason for leaving the party when they went
on to Quebec. Anyway, he let them go without him, and
returned to Niagara for another look at the Falls.

It came near being his last look at anything in this world.
He tried to swim across the Niagara River—too close to the
Falls! That same evening he wrote an account—eight brilliant
pages—of his narrow escape, and exactly what it felt like to
meet death by drowning. It begins: "Today I have been
mortified, bitterly." For it was chance, not his own strength,
that had saved him. If he had not been caught, just in time,
by a cross current that happened to be sweeping towards
shore he would have gone on, over the edge, been dashed to
pieces. He ended: "The motto which has so long borne me
to my desires, 'Go on till you are stopped,' has failed me.
I have been stopped—there is no denying it; death would
have pained me less than this conviction. I must change my
vaunting crest. My youth and strength have fled."

It was in this dreary mood that he turned westward and
began a haphazard, purposeless wandering across the continent. He may have intended to make notes of his travels
for another volume of autobiography—the long careful
account of his Niagara escape suggests that he was making a
beginning. But he did not do so. Perhaps restlessness prevented any sustained effort—he had written to Augusta

Draper: "My body is perpetual motion. I want rest and cannot find it." But before long he must have found some measure of peace. For he wrote to Clare: "These endless and eternal forests are my delight—so are the rivers. I go two thousand miles up the Mississippi—fifteen hundred up the Ohio, a thousand miles through the woods or along the mountains. . . . In the wilderness, where the boundless horizon is unbroken by the trumpery works of man, I feel so elated that life is of itself a pleasure—when I enter a town it is a pain." But this did not imply aversion to American towns in particular. The squalid frontier settlements, that Dickens and other travellers found so shocking they could see nothing else, appear to have made little impression upon Trelawny. It was the people of America that interested him. "The wealthier classes," he told Clare, "attempt to imitate the English, but they are a small sect, with small means and little influence. . . . Democratic institutions are using up their goose quills to the hilt. . . . The Sovereign people are working out this grand experiment—that all men are born free and equal! The only blot on their charter, slavery, will gradually disappear—it must be spunged out—or cut out, soon."

This letter was written from Charleston, South Carolina, so the allusion to slavery is natural enough. But he did not tell Clare—he seems never to have told anyone—that he was intending to give practical expression to the pity he had felt for slaves ever since that hot afternoon, so long ago now, when he had watched the slaves beaten and tortured by their drivers on the water front of Port Louis. A week after this letter went to Clare he repeated the experiment made in Greece; he bought a slave and set him free. The receipt, found among Trelawny's papers after his death, is for a thousand dollars paid for "a black boy John." Why this particular slave was chosen is not clear. But as that sum would have bought a young, healthy carpenter or mechanic, John must have been a prime buck nigger, neither sick nor old, and, more than likely, had a trade and gave promise of being able to support himself as a free man.

No doubt the transaction left Trelawny with an agreeable sense of duty done, but it also left him poor—a thousand dollars was more than he could afford to waste on sentiment. It may have been lack of funds that prevented any further exploration of the West; 1834 seems to have been spent in a leisurely survey of the Atlantic seaboard. Autumn found him in Philadelphia. Fanny Kemble was Mrs. Pierce Butler now— after much backing and filling she had married her persistent suitor; but she was as charming as ever and, having already perceived a few flaws in the holy estate of matrimony and in Philadelphia society, was only too pleased when this amusing compatriot turned up again. That October she wrote to a friend: "I am just now seeing a great deal of Edward Trelawny." She must have been sorry when at last, for no particular reason, he took his departure. In 1835, as aimlessly as he had come to America, he went wandering home again.

England was pleasant enough. His old friends seemed glad to have him back; on the other hand, he was obliged to remember that he was a father. Julia was probably married by now—no doubt with his approval, for John Burley had been at Eton with Shelley; but Zella had been giving him some anxiety. From London he wrote to Clare in Florence: "Jane Bocella's account of Zella's temper vexes me." He feared she had "inherited her father's waywardness." As she had also inherited "the family virtues—an affectionate disposition and strong passions," temper might be "only the boiling over of feelings"; but he added, despondently, "the women of our family are all devils," and begged Clare to give him her very best advice.

This rather pathetic dwelling on the child's resemblance to himself was justified. Family tradition pictures Zella as a chip of the old block, a true Trelawny. She remembered sitting on the Duke of Lucca's knee and pulling his nose; she was so fond of fruit—forbidden fruit—that the gardener tied her hands; but she managed to reach the peaches with her mouth, and she bit them off the branches. It was the raven story over again! Some such anecdote must have convinced Trelawny that the child needed discipline, for when Clare suggested boarding school he consented, unwillingly— "I detest everything that has any resemblance to a school," he told her. But Zella soon "developed an antipathy to school," her health suffered. He sent for her, and from then on she lived either with him or with her grandmother, old Mrs. Trelawny. He wrote to Augusta Draper of Zella: "We are as fond as Lyons and their cubs can be; sometimes interrupted by growls and snarls—no further, we don't bite."

Through all these parental anxieties his friends were kind. Seymour Kirkup had watched over Zella in Florence; in England, Mary Shelley bought her pretty frocks and a Leghorn hat. But it was to Clare that Trelawny turned for advice. She often annoyed him; he would write indignantly: "Kirkup tells me that you and Grandmama bore Zella about going to church—it's all very well for an old crone in her dotage to mumble such stuff!" He would laugh at her, try to lighten her sombre view of life; would protest: "You are becoming so horribly prudish. I consider you very fishlike, bloodless and insensible—a counterpart of Werther's Charlotte, all bread, butter and worsted stockings." And he would end, "Adieu old Aunt." Or again, "Clare hollo—do you hear? Are you alive, or transformed into a tree, girdled round by the axe—leafless, lifeless?" A letter from Cornwall takes a gentler tone: "I prowl in narrower circles. This summer I have passed dreamily in an old Cornish mansion, very much to my satisfaction. I must be strangely changed. Or is it that I look upon this house standing in its wide green domain as a ship on a wide sea? I have been at anchor here three months."

Those months went pleasantly. The green domain, Pencarrow, was "an Eden even among the gardens of Cornwall," and Trelawny's host, Sir William Molesworth, was known as "a radical in politics and an infidel in religion"—terms which Trelawny would cheerfully have applied to himself, although as a matter of fact neither word meant quite what it would today. Advocates of the Reform Bill, or prison reform, or any other reform, were considered dangerous meddlers, and denying the Doctrine of the Trinity was still a crime that brought death for a third offence. So the Pencarrow guests were neither very red nor very black; merely modern. Most of the intelligentsia of that day seem to have found their way to Pencarrow. Thackeray's souvenir of his visit was a caricature, "Pencarrow Academy": Molesworth as schoolmaster, birch in hand, threatening a group of boys. Among them Trelawny himself—labelled "Greek Trelawny"—Charles Buller, and John Temple Leader. These two must already have been acquaintances—Trelawny would have met Leader in Florence, for he was often there, and Buller had just been elected member for West Looe, the Trelawny village—but Leader was to become a friend, the most important figure in Trelawny's life for the next few years. At about the time of this Pencarrow visit, he was invited to make the Leaders' London house his home.

The two were drawn to each other for the same old reasons. Temple Leader was a "radical," out for reform; he longed to purge the House of Lords of its bishops, abolish military flogging and the "taxes on knowledge," and modify the laws of primogeniture—this last would have appealed to Trelawny, a younger son. They shared the same tastes; Leader was a patron of the arts. "Upper House," on Putney Hill, was a beautiful house, beautifully set in green lawns, terraces, and Italian gardens, shaded by magnificent trees; later on, his Castello di Vincigliata was to become one of the sights of Florence. There must also have been a certain similarity of character. They trusted each other. Leader, writing in his memoirs of this old friend who had lived with him "for many years at Upper House," added gratefully: "He used to say

I was the most sincere man he had ever known." It was for
Leader that Seymour Kirkup painted the well-known portrait of Trelawny in Albanian dress.

Present-day writers seem to grudge Trelawny these years
at Upper House. They condemn them as empty years, given
over to frivolous society. It is true that he became a conspicuous figure in many fashionable drawing rooms—partly,
no doubt, because of his association with Byron and Greece—
but he himself remained singularly untouched by fashion.
The old flavor of the privateer, the sailor, and the soldier
still hung about him; he was still too flamboyant, too large,
too breezy for drawing rooms, too exaggerated in conversation, too careless in dress—when his friends remarked that
Hyde Park was not the place for bare ankles they would get
merely a growling: "Why wear stockings?" But a touch of
eccentricity was considered attractive rather than otherwise
by the most popular hostesses of the day. All that Lady
Blessington and Mrs. Norton and Mrs. Basil Montague asked
of a guest was entertainment—Mrs. Montague "never let a
bore get in twice"—and in consequence the cleverest people
in London were to be found at their parties. Gore House is
remembered for "its atmosphere of rapid and amusing nonsense"; but Trelawny met Bulwer-Lytton and Disraeli there,
both of them at the height of their popularity as novelists
and the latter, "the gentleman in the green velvet trousers,"
already on the upgrade politically; he became intimate with
Chorley, the musical critic of the *Athenæum,* and with that
charmingly ornamental person, Lady Blessington's D'Orsay,
who was so fascinated by the piratical profile that Trelawny
had to sit to him for a portrait. On the other hand, because
of this same D'Orsay ladies could not go to Gore House—
except such ladies as Byron's Countess Guiccioli, described
by Chorley as "sweet, artless, earnest, untidy and very guilt-
less of mind"—while Mrs. Norton's less pretentious house on
Birdcage Walk could be visited by all except the absurdly
strait-laced. Caroline Norton drew clever women to her salon

as well as clever men, and with both she herself was the magnet. Trelawny became not only an admirer but a friend. When all London rang with the Norton divorce case— Caroline's unpleasant husband tried, without success, to divorce her naming Lord Melbourne as co-respondent— Trelawny took her side so hotly and loudly that he was included in the list of other possible lovers that Mr. Norton drew up for the lawyers. He would have considered the enthusiasm of his old friend Fanny Kemble entirely justified when she wrote of the Divine Lady: "She looks as if she were made of precious stones; diamonds, emeralds, rubies; she is radiant with beauty. So is her sister, the Duchess of Somerset. To look at such creatures for an hour is enough to make the world brighter for several hours."

But Fanny Kemble herself was an excellent brightener of hours. In becoming Mrs. Pierce Butler she had not lost her happy talent for enlivening whatever society she happened to be in, and the days Trelawny spent with her and her sister —Adelaide Kemble of the beautiful face and golden voice— when Fanny came from America for a visit, gave him the pleasantest memories of this time. They talked and laughed and sang—all of them in the highest spirits, and discussed a scheme the girls had devised to raise money for charity: a street-singing expedition that Fanny recalled later on with amusement. Disguised in "large battered poke bonnets," they would sing from door to door and make lots of money— well guarded, however, from across the street by their father and their "formidable pirate friend, Trelawny."

Another drawing room much more important than Fanny Butler's—though less gay—was that of Mrs. Grote, wife of the historian of Greece. The atmosphere there was far from frivolous, for the Grotes were "philosophical radicals" and Mrs. Grote herself "a not-young-nor-handsome female oracle," Fanny wrote, "among a set of very clever half heathenish men, in whose drawing-room Sydney Smith used to say he always expected to find an altar to Zeus. The persons one most frequently met at her house in Eccleston Street were Roebuck [a well-known radical], Leader, Trelawny and Sir William Molesworth." But fortunately Mrs. Grote was musical as well as political; all the great musicians found their way to her parties and enlivened them with superlatively good music. Among them Fanny remembered meeting "Liszt, Madame Viardot, Dessauer, Thalberg, Mademoiselle Lind and Mendelssohn."

Add all the wits that frequented these London drawing rooms—Sydney Smith, Theodore Hook, Luttrell, Mrs. Norton herself, and a dozen others—and you have a society that was probably the most agreeable the world has ever known. But it was more than that; according to Trevelyan, "in the breed of men and in the noblest trophies of arts and letters, the earlier years of the nineteenth century were the greatest in England's history." So perhaps Trelawny's time was not entirely wasted; he may, indeed, have been better employed than in boarding pirate ships or killing Turks.

However, it must be acknowledged that he should have been more than a looker-on and a listener. This stimulating environment might have started him writing another book. He seems to have contributed in a vague sort of way to the *Metropolitan Magazine,* edited by his friend Captain Marryat, and then relapsed into silence. He might have gone in for politics. The atmosphere of Upper House was fiercely political; Leader was always either just in or just out of Parliament. The election of 1837, when he contested the Westminster seat with Sir Francis Burdett, is remembered as the most exciting of its time. A fight between "St. George and the dragon of Toryism." The radical newspapers did their best. Burdett was old now. Byron's jeering, "as sweet and silvery as Belial," no longer applied; they called him a renegade, "a poor misguided old man," and "a faded fox hunter." But he spoke so wisely of the danger of making any change in anything, of the horrible results that would inevitably follow if the House of Lords, the Church, and the

Constitution were not preserved intact, and his friends spoke so tenderly of his age and reminded the electors that a statesman should be treated "as the Duke of Wellington had treated his charger Copenhagen; given the run of the paddock till death as reward for faithful service," that Leader was beaten—temporarily—by a large majority. He was victorious three months later.

No doubt Trelawny worked hard for Leader during those elections, and if another interest had not just then come into his life, an idea he had once confided to Mary Shelley might have come to something. He had told her that if reform ever made sufficient headway in England he would try for Parliament himself—knowing, of course, that he could rely on the family influence, still strong in a Cornwall still plentifully supplied with rotten boroughs.

CHAPTER XX

"Englishmen, who are restricted to one wife, cannot be too careful."
　　　　　　　　　　　　　　　　　　—SIR RICHARD BURTON.

W hether or not ambition, political or literary, had come near spurring Trelawny to action during these London years, it was to evaporate in the warmth of a more absorbing emotion. He fell in love. That, in itself, would not have been important—love was seldom more than a brief excitement with Trelawny. He had often found himself caught into the current of another life, in danger of being swept off his feet, and been able to escape—swim away, or get rescued by chance as in the Niagara River. This time he was to venture too near the rapids—as he had ventured in the old days, drawn on by Julia Addison—and go over, plunge headlong into the whirlpool he most dreaded: matrimony.

The marriage with Julia, however, had come about in his youth. Fresh from the sea, vain, naïve, amazed at finding himself a romantic figure, he had been as vulnerable as a soft-shell crab. He was forty-five now and imagined himself a tough old sea dog, a reckless soldier, a cynical man of the world. In reality, the years had left as little impression on his spirit as on his body. He was never to become a man of the world; to the end he would remain a *fauve,* vulnerable in all the old ways. Still proud of following instinct rather than reason, still arrogantly self-confident, easily flattered, too easily moved by pity and, if a remark in a letter of this time to Mary Shelley is taken as sincere, the old hankering for forbidden fruit was as strong in the man as it had been in the child of five.

"Six days I rest," he wrote, "and do all that I have to do on the seventh, because it is forbidden. If they would make it felony to obey the Commandments (without benefit of clergy) don't you think the pleasures of breaking the law would make me keep them?"

Of all these dangerous characteristics, the two last—pity and the desire for what seemed out of reach—were probably the most disarming. For, as luck would have it, the woman he fell in love with was unhappy, and she was married to another man.

The affair seems to have begun not very long after Trelawny's return from America. Augusta Goring had been badly treated by her husband, Sir Harry Dent Goring, of Highden, Sussex; she was handsome, cultivated, well bred, modern in her way of thinking. They fell in love. They eloped. In due time Trelawny found himself involved in a third divorce case. It was more unpleasant than the other two. Tarsitsa's had passed off almost unnoticed—Greece was so far away, marriage to the sister of a robber chief seemed so unreal. It must have been far more disagreeable for him than Julia's, for the parts were reversed. Now it was Trelawny who was the "wretch" obliged to pay damages for trespass and then figure as co-respondent. Anyway, in 1841 Sir Harry won the suit, without the slightest difficulty, and Trelawny was able to marry his Augusta.

Whether or not the marriage was happy at first is impossible to decide at this late date. Domesticity after long intrigue must always be something of an anticlimax, and Trelawny could never have been easy to live with. In youth, Julia had found him difficult; by now he had probably become too difficult for any woman to endure; except, perhaps, a very clinging, very flowery vine. And Augusta was not that. Her letters to Mary Shelley—they were intimate friends—suggest a strong character, rather lacking in tenderness, reckless or she would not have trusted herself to Trelawny, passionate but able to see where she was going. A letter written just before marriage, affectionate in tone, describes the arrangements that have been made for her by her brother and Lord Monmouth, tells Mary they are keeping the London house and may go there for the wedding in April, and assures her that "Edward behaved very well today. . . . He gives up his point *entirely,* and wishes to do all things to please me." But she goes on: "My first object will be to estrange him from my enemies in his own family—then to gain power, as I may— over self first, then over him."

That sentence has an ominous ring. Trelawny's intimacy with Lady Goring had probably already begun when he wrote to Clare: "At the very sight of harness (particularly double) I plunge with fury and scream with horror." A wife who thought she could use a tight rein on that sort of husband must soon have discovered her mistake. Another cause for dissension is suggested by a family anecdote of the time: It seems Augusta was extravagant and ran up bills. Now Trelawny was careless in money matters, but hated getting into debt. So one day she came home to find the house bare of furniture; it had all been sold to pay her bills.

Mutual extravagance is not easy to cure, it may have necessitated a move. About 1847 Trelawny, like his father before him, decided to try a country life—perhaps for the same reason, economy; perhaps because he was tired of the noise and bad air and formality of town. Perhaps, subconsciously, he was afraid of being drawn into the rising tide of revolution that was threatening Europe. For 1848 was the Year of Trouble. The crowned heads took to "running about," Carlyle noted with satisfaction, "like coiners when the police are come among them"; and although Victoria still sat tight the royal children were "evacuated" from Buckingham Palace to the Isle of Wight, and Chartist riots set London shivering in its shoes.

Whatever the reason for the move may have been, it seems unlikely that Mrs. Trelawny had anything to say about it, for tradition remembers him at this time as always "doing

exactly what he chose." Unless Augusta disliked the country
in itself, however, she must have approved the place that,
after a little wandering, became her home. For Trelawny had
selected it with his usual eye for beauty and picturesqueness.

Usk, in Monmouthshire, was as charming a village as one
could find in a month of Sundays: a very ancient market
town, with narrow crooked cobblestoned streets, a ruined
castle, an old church, old bridges crossing clear streams—a
guide book of Trelawny's time remarks, "Anglers will find
this a peculiarly eligible station"—brightened by little flower
gardens, backed by orchards sloping up to green hillsides.

For a while the Trelawnys lived in a cottage in the village.
Then he bought a small place called Twyn Bell, and finally
treated himself to the largest estate in the parish, Cefn Ila;
built a house and settled down to a brand-new life, the life
of a country gentleman. It was a good life. It suited him. It
suited the children—there were three of them now: Edgar,
Frank, and Letitia. For a time all the family seem to have
enjoyed themselves at Cefn Ila. He planted trees and lawns
and flower gardens, and found satisfaction in these mild occupations as De Ruyter had found in the Isle of France, Sir
William Molesworth in Cornwall, and Temple Leader in
Putney.

The village liked him, in an awestruck sort of way, admired his handsomeness and strength and indomitable
energy. He paid good wages; he was friendly with all classes
alike. Children feared him at first sight—he was too big, too
overpowering; but they soon discovered he could be played
with in safety. The village approved of Mrs. Trelawny, too:
she was a kind neighbor. Every Sunday afternoon the local
intelligentsia gathered at Cefn Ila. Trelawny made tea for
them "after an Oriental fashion peculiar to himself and the
cronies drank it out of large basins." The doctor came and
the lawyer and even the vicar—the latter must have been a
tolerant person, for Trelawny still enjoyed shocking the pious
and would be seen planting trees on Llanbadoc Rock of a

Sunday when the congregation was coming home from church!

But Sabbath-breaking was not the only shock the village had to suffer, according to a Mrs. M. B. Byrde who, long after, pieced together what she could learn of the Trelawnys' life at Cefn Ila. In summer they all went swimming in the river! A tent would be set up on the shore, and not only Mr. Trelawny himself but Mrs. Trelawny and the children were to be seen splashing about in the water with any guests who might happen to be visiting them.

One of these aquatic guests was young Zella, escaped from London and her grandmother. To her Cefn Ila seemed like heaven after the long dull afternoons driving round and round the Serpentine in a yellow chariot with two fat horses, a fat coachman in front and two footmen hanging on behind. But dullness had made no change in Zella; as wild as ever, a true Trelawny, she would go running down to the river— Mrs. Byrde again—leaving yards of lace from her petticoats on the bramble bushes as she ran.

A pleasant, easy, healthy life. But not stimulating. Why was it that in the midst of his farming and gardening, shooting and riding and fishing, his swimming with the children and chatting with the vicar, Trelawny suddenly wrote another book? A very good book. *Recollections of the Last Days of Shelley and Byron* is one of the best books of its kind ever written. But why had he waited so long? To judge from a letter to Clare asking for details of Shelley's early life, it was not begun until 1857. Why was it written now, after thirty years of silence? He could not have been held back by regard for Mary Shelley's feelings, for Mary had died six years before. Was he getting restless again? In this letter to Clare he complained: "I am tired of doing the same thing day by day." Perhaps. Or it may have been the unexpected revival of an old friendship at this time that, by turning his thoughts back to the past, gave him a desire to record his memories.

In that same year, 1857, the Drapers came from Canada to

spend a few months in England, and such an affectionate letter went from Trelawny to "My oldest and most attached friend" that Mrs. Draper came to Cefn Ila for a visit. It would be interesting—and illuminating—to know what the two Augustas—Augusta White and Augusta Goring—thought of each other. Unfortunately, Trelawny's letters of this time leave the visit a blank; his family are not mentioned—except for an allusion to a French doll Mrs. Draper is sending to Baby— and as he does not speak of having started a book, in all probability Augusta Draper's visit had little or nothing to do with this second literary venture.

There was another, and more definite, reason: Trelawny was unhappy. He wrote of the past in order to distract his thoughts from the present. In the letter of inquiry to Clare he says, "We blunder and brag, die and are forgot, and some other fool takes our place." Letters to Augusta Draper show increasing anxiety about his boys: Edgar, because of a weak character; Frank—"who is all I could wish"—because of delicate health (he died young of consumption). But both discouragement and anxiety could have been borne if the Trelawnys' married life had been happy. By now the first fine careless rapture of elopement was forgotten as though it had never been. The remark, to Mrs. Byrde, of an old Cefn Ila servant, "Mrs. Trelawny never sat in the room with him except for business," suggests that what Mrs. Byrde calls "the drama of disillusionment, bitterness and alienation" would have come to a dusty death even without the exciting reason given by the village for the final break.

Village gossip is open to suspicion, and Mrs. Byrde's record is not flawless (the seedlings planted at Cefn Ila "with loving care" were from Shelley's grave, not Byron's, and the girl sitting at Trelawny's feet in Millais's picture, the *Northwest Passage,* was drawn from a model, not from Letitia); but the village could sum up Trelawny's character to perfection: "Big in every way he must have been," Mrs. Byrde concluded, "but not great. . . . Selfish, yet capable of unselfish deeds; brave always, noble sometimes, commonplace never." And the village story of a new figure making its appearance in the family "conversation piece" with disastrous results certainly bears the earmarks of truth.

A vague little figure, drifting in and drifting out again, nameless except for an initial (she comes down to us as "Miss B."); small, not very pretty according to the village; but weak —that damnable pity again! So weak that when she came to Cefn Ila Mr. Trelawny had to carry her up the slope to the door in his arms. The sight would have revolted *any* wife; it was enough for Augusta Goring Trelawny. She left Cefn Ila and took the children with her.

Mrs. Byrde winds it all up in fine style. "Cefn Ila was sold," she writes, "with all its furniture and most of the books. It was a three days' auction and is still talked of by the old people, because of Trelawny's unexampled hospitality during the proceedings. Open house was kept, and no embargo placed on any supplies except whiskey for which he had a great dislike. And so he departed from Monmouthshire and was seen no more."

The break seems, at first, to have given Trelawny a sense of release. Writing to his old friend Dan Roberts in the spring of 1858, he speaks of having sold Cefn Ila, and adds airily, "I shall ride at single anchor for a while," as if he rather liked the prospect. But he was whistling to keep his courage up. It was too late for him to resume a vagabond existence. He was sixty-six; he had had a home for eleven years; he was devoted to Frank and Letitia, his youngest children; he respected his wife—according to the village, Mrs. Trelawny behaved throughout her trying experience "with dignity and did not make a scene." He could not have looked back on the squalid *finale* he had himself provided for the domestic drama—whether or not the village was right in believing "Miss B." his mistress—without intense mortification. He had behaved abominably, and he knew it. His regret for this last matrimonial failure must have been lasting, for—

long after—he wrote to Clare: "Marriage is a most unnatural state of things. . . . Custom and the way we are reared makes men the Calibans we are; grossly selfish and capable of all ill—no good. . . . We are all fools. Nothing amazes me so much as the labyrinth of follies I have wandered in all my life."

So the months that followed Trelawny's departure from Usk must have been dreary enough. Fortunately, his new book—the one thing that had made the last year bearable—still provided some distraction for his thoughts. *Recollections of the Last Days of Shelley and Byron* had just been published by Moxon. There were reviews to be read, copies must be sent to old friends. He had taken great pains with the looks of his "bantling" and was satisfied. The paper was good. The illustrations—Clint's lovely portrait of Shelley, Casa Magni from a sketch Roberts had made long ago and he himself had redrawn, the cave on Mount Parnassus drawn from memory, a profile of his own head by Seymour Kirkup—had come out well. He could write to Roberts: "The book is by all votes amusing and the style vigorous and clear."

It was a modest summing up. The style is startlingly original, spirited, and daring as well as clear. He never loses sight of his chief object: to make the world see Byron and Shelley *plain,* as he had seen them. He succeeded. His portraits are as lifelike as any ever drawn in words. A biographer who tried to write of either Byron or Shelley without consulting Trelawny—and who depended on dull Medwin, or silly Gamba, or lying Millingen for the record of those last years—would be hard put to it! But the book made him enemies. He had never considered Mary Shelley worthy of her husband, and said so. He had always heartily disliked Byron, and said so. That he spoke of Mary as pretty and kind, insisted that Byron was not a sot and that "if he had drawn the sword in Greece he would have thrown away the scabbard," and branded the scandal about Byron and Mrs. Leigh a falsehood, was not enough. Admirers of Shelley believe every word. Admirers of Byron and Mary Shelley pick and choose.

Trelawny, in both his books, was trying to tell the truth,* *as he saw it.* His memory for facts was bad. In *Adventures of a Younger Son,* incidents often come in the wrong order. He exaggerated—Gilbert Murray says, "The romanticist is never happy unless he exaggerates." His contempt for dates was ludicrous. Writing to Ned Williams before Christmas and dating the letter January 1st was one of a dozen such mistakes. He made hash of proper names. But as Trollope says, "A man who writes with a rapidity that will not admit of accuracy may be, in one sense, as trustworthy as he who bases every word upon a rock of fact," and the book, both for its subject and for its style, deserved more success than it met with.

But he had waited too long. The "age of Byron" was over. Shelley had been dead for thirty years now—a generation— and no generation ever regards the one just past with any enthusiasm. Worse yet, like *Adventures of a Younger Son,* it came at a bad time. The Indian Mutiny was at its height! Who wanted to read about some half-forgotten revolution in Greece when the Siege of Lucknow was keeping every heart in sickening suspense? So the sales soon fell off, and as the book had been published at his own expense and Moxon, his publisher, died that same year, Trelawny made less from his second "bantling" than from the first.

Not that he cared. Money was never important to him, and his spirits were on the mend. The autumn of 1858 found him writing to Dan Roberts (raising grapes in a Sardinian island): "I have been for some months driving about in a light trap along the southern and eastern coast of England, as

* Richard Edgcumbe wrote of Trelawny, whom he knew personally: "He may have embroidered his stories, but he never told a lie to shield a fault, or gain a prize."

you and I did years agone; and I enjoy it much after having stuck so long in the mud of Monmouthshire." He was reviving! The sea had worked its familiar spell and, as the idle summer days drifted by, family affairs ceased to absorb him; lawful wife, unlawful Miss B., faded into the background.

For a while life went pleasantly enough. He felt himself untouched by age and was proud of it. That same summer he wrote to Roberts: "I am still hard and strong, can swim a mile and walk ten without effort, and live on fruit and trash as of old. No wine, or very rarely; beer occasionally; tobacco regularly, but no excess; a cold bath every day summer and winter." Ten years later he could tell Clare with immense satisfaction that he still tipped the scales in the Burlington Arcade at thirteen stone (182 pounds), hadn't gained an ounce since he had weighed in the same place in 1831; sight, hearing, and feeling were all perfect; he still enjoyed riding and walking and bathing in the sea, and ended, characteristically, with a misspelled word: "Warm clothing and *caudling* I abhor."

This ascetic way of living once adopted, he found it could best be pursued in the country. So he bought a cottage and a few acres of land in the village of Sompting, near Worthing in Sussex, and before long it became his headquarters.

He went abroad now and then—in Baden-Baden one autumn he saw the Prince of Wales (Albert Edward) at a race meeting, young, but already "fat, yellow and bald." If he went to Florence he would have stayed with the Temple Leaders at Vincigliata, and found it interesting not only because of its association with Sir John Hawkwood and the White Company, but because Hawkwood could number Shelley as a descendant. The season often found him in town; here he kept a *pied-à-terre*, 7 Pelham Crescent, Brompton— for of all cities he liked London best. He saw his children now and then, especially Letitia, the youngest (later on, she married Lieutenant Colonel Charles Call of the British Army); but both his sons died before he did, and Zella be-

came Mrs. Olguin and lived mostly in the Argentine. He
often dropped in at the Savage Club where he would be
pointed out to awestruck strangers as "Old Tre," and was
regarded with pride as a sort of museum piece. He made new
friends: Swinburne, William Rossetti, Boehm the sculptor,
Richard Edgcumbe. Millais persuaded him, with the greatest
difficulty, to sit for the old sea captain in *Northwest Passage*
(not very like—a photograph of the time shows him as one
of the handsomest old gentlemen it is possible to imagine,
with a head like that on a Greek coin). Meredith drew a better portrait; his long description of the Old Buccaneer in
The Amazing Marriage is Trelawny to the life, from the first
line, "Kirby was a magnificent figure of a man and used to
be compared to a three-decker entering harbour after a victory," to the summing up: "But his heart was on salt water.
He was never so much at home as in a ship foundering or
splitting into the clouds. . . . A truly terrible man."

That "his heart was on salt water" probably accounts for
the intimacy with Swinburne—at his best when he wrote of
the sea—who found Trelawny exciting, as other and greater
poets had found him in the past. But of all his new friends,
William Michael Rossetti was to become the most welcome.
Their acquaintance went back to two meetings in William's
boyhood when Trelawny had come to the Rossettis' house in
Charlotte Street with invitations from Temple Leader, and
had been well remembered for his striking personality.

Now in these later years intimacy ripened to friendship;
chiefly, no doubt, because Rossetti happened to be busy with
a new edition of Shelley's poems and was eager to listen as
long as Trelawny cared to talk—and that was unceasingly—
of anything connected with the Pisa circle. It must have been
Rossetti's influence that spurred Trelawny on to a last, very
slight literary undertaking, getting out a revised version of
the *Recollections,* to be called *Records of Shelley, Byron and
the Author,* with a few more memories and a few correc-
tions. One page was entirely rewritten; in discussing the

cause of Byron's deformity such exaggerated phrases as "the form of an Apollo with the feet and legs of a sylvan satyr" were replaced by a technical summing-up of the effect of a *tendo Achillis* too tightly drawn. But accuracy was never important to Trelawny; it is unlikely he would have been persuaded to any literary undertaking if he had not hoped to revive interest in Shelley. His visual memory of all that bygone time was extraordinarily keen. Discussing the illustrations with Rossetti, he criticized an engraving done from a sketch his daughter Letitia had made of the Gulf of Spezia as if he had been standing on the beach!

"The scenery," he wrote, "is correct. Sand, sea and tall branchless pines; their dark blue tops packed so close together that no ray of sun could penetrate. The white sandy beach, the air tremulous with noonday heat—not a weed or green tuft—everything brown and scorched and desolation all round. . . . But the artist is thinking of a gipsy fire in our wet climate. There was no smoke, only a light transparent vapoury exhalation; the thinnest white gauze would represent it; it was trembling under the noonday heat."

But there was a good reason for his seeing that landscape so clearly: by now it was more real to him than any other.

CHAPTER XXI

"There is no perfect happiness.
A quick death swept away glorious Achilles,
A long old age wore down Tithonus."
—HORACE.

An Arab sibyl had warned Trelawny long ago in his youth that he was marked for sudden death; he would "die and be buried in the same instant like a drop of rain falling on the sand."

He had recalled that saying at the worst moment of his agonizing struggle with Niagara and when at last, rescued by chance, he lay exhausted on the river's edge, relief had been darkened by regret; he knew that the final curtain should have come down then and there. "It had always been my prayer," he wrote that night, "to die in the pride of my strength, to perish before age had touched me with his withering fingers. To die in that wild place, on a foreign shore, Niagara 'chanting a thunder-psalm' as a requiem would have been a fitting end for my wild meteorlike life."

Whether that prayer was addressed to Pan or Apollo, to Zela's Allah or Shelley's Mighty Mother, "there was no voice, nor any that answered." He must have wondered now and then, as the slow years went by, why he had been so ignored by the gods. Were they all, like Baal, talking, pursuing, asleep, or on a journey? He had always treated death with supreme indifference: was death now become indifferent to him? It began to seem so. Anyway, whatever time death did choose to come, it would be too late to give his "meteor life" a glittering finish. He knew that he would die here in this Sussex village as unresistingly, as ingloriously, as if, like

363

his neighbors, he had never set foot outside the Weald.

Not that this thought gave him the smallest regret. He had wanted to find a backwater for old age where he could live and die remote from the world. He had found it here in Sompting. Just why he had chosen this particular village can only be guessed at. He may have taken a fancy to it while he was driving along the coast in 1858; perhaps earlier still, during his illicit courtship of Augusta Goring, for Highden, her husband's estate, was in the immediate neighborhood. At any time the Sussex landscape must have seemed tame after the wildness of Cornwall and the picturesque beauty of Monmouthshire; but it gave him what he wanted now. The ample, suave, swelling contours of the South Downs, the wide horizon, the sight and sound of the sea, were enough.

The Weald suited him; so did his cottage: a red cottage, old-fashioned, standing a little back from the street, it was neither too large nor too small; from his bedroom windows he could see the ocean two miles away. The sitting room was papered with small brightly colored scenes of "different nations engaged in characteristic occupations," but there were no curtains at the windows; it was sparsely furnished, and the air blew in so freshly from the sea that, to visitors coming from the dark stuffiness of Victorian parlors crowded with upholstery, the room had the look of a ship's cabin.

There were books, of course: plenty of books, new as well as old. Visitors would be astonished to find an octogenarian ready to discuss the *Origin of Species* and the latest philosophic works, to advocate the emancipation of women and exult over John Brown's magnificent gesture at Harpers Ferry. Age had not narrowed him. When he declaimed, in that great impassioned voice of his, such lines as Blake's,

"In every cry of every man,
In every infant's cry of fear,
In every voice, in every ban
The mind-forged manacles I hear,"

he was the Trelawny who had fought for Greece, pitied slaves, struggled with a tyrant raven to protect a little favorite sister.

But it was not books nor talk, it was outdoor life that meant most to him in Sompting. He had brought one precious thing away from the ruin at Usk: a love of agriculture. It could not take so wide a sweep, of course. There, he had busied himself with a large estate. Here, his energies were confined to a garden within four walls. That did not matter: it was as exciting to plant a rosebush as to plant an oak, to watch a dozen figs swell to purple as to see a wheat field wave with gold.

As his garden grew to sweet perfection—flower-scented, bird-haunted—he found peace, which by now was all he asked of life. For gradually, and without deliberate intention, here in Sompting he began to withdraw from the world. The loss of his home must have cut deeper than either he or anyone else suspected at the time. Life at Usk had been crowded with activity, both of body and of mind. Now it was as if some mainspring of the spirit had given way and left him slack, too discouraged ever again to rouse himself to any important action. After that last worst failure he turned the clock back to 1822.

The retreat into the past must have begun during his drive along the coast in 1858, for he had given himself then to memories of that other trip so "long agone," the drive from Geneva to Pisa in his little Swiss carriage; reaching the ancient town at night, putting up his horse at the inn, making his way through the dim silent streets to the Williamses' flat in the Tre Palazzi, coming at last to that unforgettable moment when, "swiftly gliding in, blushing like a girl, a tall thin stripling held out both his hands."

Of all the strange contradictions in Trelawny's character, this retreat into the past of an adventurous nature, still open to new ideas, still aware of all that was going on in the world, is the most difficult to account for. One suspects that he put the clock back after failure in order to save his self-respect: he would live in the past with Shelley, for only then had he risen to the best that was in him. Anyway, having once moved the clock's hands to 1822, he never changed the time again!

Yet his integrity of body and mind was very nearly as perfect at eighty as at forty. He made no concessions to weather; scorned underclothes, never wore an overcoat. He drank only water now—Shelley had not cared for wine; ate no meat—Shelley had been a vegetarian. But there is a flavor of the East in this asceticism that hints of an even earlier influence. T. E. Lawrence was to discover that a man who lets himself sink too deep into the East will never be the same again, and this may account for a curious similarity in the behavior of these two, otherwise so dissimilar. After what he considered his failure in Arabia, Lawrence too retired from the world. "I have no dependents," he wrote, "no sense of public spirit, or of duty to my neighbor. . . . The golden rule seems to direct me to live peaceably in my cottage."

But whether or not Trelawny did feel the pull of the East here in Sussex, his ascetic way of life gave him more satisfaction than it seems to have given Lawrence. For one thing, it kept him in the pink of condition, and he was still vastly proud of his physique; for another, his régime made him independent of servants (it seems to have been only in extreme old age that he condescended to engage a housekeeper, Miss Taylor, to look after him), and he liked chopping wood and drawing water, any outdoor work—even in winter. It was December when he wrote to Clare: "I have an icy cold bath every morning and then go out with my shirtsleeves tucked up and work in the garden. My gardener is eighty-seven and has nothing the matter with him and works hard. I ride and drive and in the summer bathe off the beach and can't believe in my age." He was eighty-two. But though he would ask after Clare's health and offer to lend her money, as he had been doing ever since her girlhood, and tease her a little at having become *dévote,* there was always some allusion to

1822: "Life is not much good after thirty—we were all under thirty in Pisa, except Byron. . . . I live within sight of the sea—I have Shelley's mania for water. . . . I gave Mrs. Shelley the poet's heart; she foolishly gave it to Leigh Hunt—the family have it now." And it was on this last nostalgic note that the correspondence of more than fifty years came to an end. In 1879 Clare died in Florence.

Old Dan Roberts was dead too. The last links with the Pisa circle were broken; there was no one left worth writing to now. His letters dwindled to messages, often dictated. When Clare's death made him think of his own, and instructions had to be sent to the custodian of the Protestant cemetery in Rome, he asked William Rossetti to translate and despatch them. The first ran:

"In the year 1822 I purchased a piece of land of the then Custodian—I believe your father—under the Pyramid of Caius Cestius. I deposited the ashes of my Friend Shelley in the one tomb and the other I left for my own ashes. I planted seven upright cedars round it. I now desire at my decease, which cannot be far distant, that my ashes may be placed there. . . ."

John Trucchi's reply was satisfactory. William Rossetti and Miss Taylor promised to see to everything. His body was to be cremated; Miss Taylor would take the ashes to Rome herself. With this off his mind, he could resume his quiet village life.

In Sompting as in Usk, the neighbors gave him a reluctant and awestruck admiration. They were proud of his great age, of course; they approved his reckless charity—Mr. Trelawny would give the coat off his back to a beggar and come home in his shirtsleeves. Children were afraid of him until he had coaxed them to friendliness with bits of his favorite sweet, Turkish Delight. Sportsmen, however—any man or boy who dared to set foot on his land with a gun—would be driven away with loud curses. In old age Trelawny would neither shoot nor fish; he had made his garden a bird sanctuary; his best friends were his two black-and-tan terriers. Every day he took them for a run on the Downs; every day he went to the village pond to feed the ducks. For he had grown very tender towards animals as he grew less tolerant of mankind.

No doubt one of Miss Taylor's duties was to ward off inquisitive strangers, for a good many strangers came now: he had become a legend. If they peered at him through the garden gate—that old gentleman raking the path had known Byron!—he turned his back and let them stare. Even when people worth talking to found their way to his cottage he could not be roused to conversation until they spoke of Shelley. For Shelley, a friend of this time observed, "seems to have been the only one who ever touched that proud rebel spirit."

But at eighty-nine even a rebel spirit, even an Old Buccaneer, has the right to a little idleness, to let a summer drift by in lazy enjoyment of a garden rather than work. It was pleasant there in his garden that last summer: warm and sunny; drowsy with the hum of bees, but gay with birds; the air sweet with the good rich smell of fruit—grapes, peaches, figs; the lighter scent of flowers—roses, carnations, mignonette. He could relax and give himself to memories of 1822.

And, perhaps, as he sat there in the sun against the garden wall, the exotic smell of the figs—he was very proud of his figs—ripening overhead mingled with a salty whiff from the sea, his thoughts would wander to a more remote past. He was sailing farther and farther east; east of the Adriatic; east of the Aegean, to the Indian Ocean. He was in another warm sunny garden, De Ruyter's garden in the Isle of France; not alone, with Zela under the yakoonoo tree, watching her make little pictures in the sand and spell his name with scarlet pomegranate seeds.

But whether he was thinking of Zela or of Shelley at the end, death came quick and kind—he simply ceased to live. One midsummer day found him up and about as usual though "feeling a little tired." The next—the 13th of August, 1881—a telegram went from Miss Taylor to William Rossetti: "All is over."

Rossetti saw to everything; Miss Taylor carried out his final instructions to the letter. Swinburne, writing him a long lament, could end with lines addressed to the "Heart of hearts," ending:

"Shelley, Trelawny rejoins thee here."

Trelawny's cottage is still there in Sompting. He is still dimly remembered. This summer one ancient inhabitant said of him, "He was a funny old fellow—he used to ring a bell to call the birds"; and another, still more ancient:
"I believe I almost remember he was buried in Rome."

August, 1938—January, 1940

PRINCIPAL AUTHORITIES

The Adventures of a Younger Son, by E. J. Trelawny, 1831.
Recollections of the Last Days of Shelley and Byron, by E. J. Trelawny, 1858.
Records of Shelley, Byron, and the Author, by E. J. Trelawny, 1878.
Letters of Edward John Trelawny, edited by H. Buxton Forman, 1910.
Twenty-one letters from E. J. Trelawny to Augusta White, 1817 to 1873, unpublished, lent by the Misses Draper of Montreal.
The Friend of Shelley: A Memoir of Edward John Trelawny, by H. J. Massingham, 1930.

FAMILY BACKGROUND

A Book of the West, by S. Baring-Gould, 1899. *Cornwall and the Cornish,* by A. K. Hamilton Jenkin, 1933. *Trelawny of Trelawne,* by Anna Eliza Bray, 1845. *History of the County of Cheshire,* by George Ormerod, 1819. *History, Gazetteer, and Directory of Cheshire:* Francis White and Co., 1860. *Voyages* (1598–1600), by Richard Hakluyt, 1809–1812. *Seven Bishops of the Tower,* by Agnes Strickland, 1866. *Burke's Peerage, Baronetage and Landed Gentry.* College of Arms, London, 1939.

THE NAVY

Naval Chronicle (1805, 1806, 1808), 1799–1818. *Royal Navy Biography,* by John Marshall, 1823–1835. *Sea Life in Nelson's Time,* by John Masefield, 1905. *Captain Marryat and the Old Navy,* by Christopher Lloyd, 1939. *Life and Letters of Captain Marryat,* Florence Marryat, 1872. *Mr. Midshipman Easy,* by Frederick Marryat, 1836. *Mutiny at Spithead and the Nore,* by W. J. Neale, 1842.

THE ORIENT

British India, by Hugh Murray, 1855. *Life and Letters of the 1st Earl of Minto* (1807–1814), ed. by the Countess of Minto, 1874. *Corsairs of France,* by C. B. Norman, 1929. *Madagascar,* by Chase Salmon Osborn, 1924. *Mauritius,* by Charles Grant, Vi-

comte de Vaux, 1801. *Voyage Pittoresque de l'Isle de France,* by
J. Milbert, 1812. *Paul and Virginia,* by Bernardin de Saint-Pierre,
1788. *Java,* by Peyfer de Neueck, 1837. *In Java,* by John C. Van
Dyke, 1929. *The Malay Archipelago,* by Alfred Russel Wallace,
1869. *The Arabian Nights Entertainments,* transl. by A. Galland,
1704. *Seven Pillars of Wisdom,* by T. E. Lawrence, 1935. *Animal
Treasure,* by Ivan Sanderson, 1937.

SHELLEY AND BYRON

Life of Shelley, by Edward Dowden, 1886. *Ariel,* by André
Maurois, 1924. *Shelley,* by Walter Edwin Peck, 1927. *Angler in
Wales,* by Thomas Medwin, 1834. *Shelley's Letters,* ed. by Roger
Ingpen, 1915. *Mary Shelley,* by Mrs. Julian Marshall, 1889. *Mary
Shelley,* by R. Glynn Grylls, 1938. *Claire Clairmont,* by R. Glynn
Grylls, 1939. *Letters About Shelley,* ed. by Robert S. Garnett,
1917. *Autobiography of Leigh Hunt,* 1850. *Letters and Journals
of Lord Byron,* ed. by Thomas Moore, 1830. *Byron: The Last
Phase,* by Richard Edgcumbe, 1909. *Byron: The Last Journey,* by
Harold Nicolson, 1924. *Byron,* by André Maurois, 1930. *Correspondence of Lord Byron,* ed. by John Murray, 1922. *Confes-
sions of Lord Byron,* by W. A. Lewis Bettany, 1905. *Idler in Italy,*
by Lady Blessington, 1839.

GREECE

Greece in 1823–1824, by Col. Leicester Stanhope, 1824. *Greek
Revolution,* by Samuel Gridley Howe, 1828. *Affairs of Greece,*
by Julius Millingen, 1831. "Odysseus and Trelawny," by F. B.
Sanborn, *Scribner's Magazine,* 1897. *Imaginary Conversations*
(early editions), by Walter Savage Landor, 1824–1829. *Life and
Letters of Joseph Severn,* by William Sharp, 1892.

MIDDLE DISTANCE

Journal, 1835, *Records of a Girlhood,* 1878, *Records of Later
Life,* 1882, *Further Records,* 1891, by Frances Ann Kemble. *Life
of Sir William Molesworth,* by Mrs. Fawcett, 1903. *Some Aspects
of Thackeray,* by L. S. Benjamin, 1911. *Rough and Rambling
Notes,* by John Temple Leader, 1899. *Recent Art and Society,*
H. F. Chorley, 1874. *The Diary, Reminiscences, and Correspondence of Henry Crabbe Robinson* (1837), ed. by Thomas Sadler,
1869. "Trelawny at Usk," by M. B. Byrde, *Athenæum,* Aug., 1897.
Monmouthshire—Black's Picturesque Guide, 1856. *Monmouthshire,* by J. A. Bradney, 1904.

LAST YEARS

The County of Sussex, by Hilaire Belloc, 1936. *Sussex,* ed. by Arthur Mee, 1937. *Some Reminiscences,* by William Michael Rossetti, 1906. *The Amazing Marriage,* by George Meredith, 1895. *The Powder of Sympathy,* by Christopher Morley, 1923. "Mr. Trelawny on Byron and Shelley," by Mathilde Blind, *Whitehall Review,* Jan., 1880. "Talks with Trelawny," by Richard Edgcumbe, *Living Age,* May, 1890. "Edward John Trelawny," by Richard Edgcumbe, *Athenæum,* Dec., 1901. *Memories and Notes,* by Sir Sidney Colvin, 1921.

INDEX